WOMEN'S RIGHTS

**Recent Titles in
Major Issues in American History**

WOMEN'S RIGHTS

Sharon Hartman Strom

Major Issues in American History
Randall M. Miller, Series Editor

GREENWOOD PRESS
Westport, Connecticut • London

Library of Congress Cataloging-in-Publication Data

Strom, Sharon Hartman.
   Women's rights / Sharon Hartman Strom.
      p.   cm.—(Major issues in American history, ISSN 1535–3192)
   Includes bibliographical references and index.
   ISBN 0–313–31135–8 (alk. paper)
      1. Women's rights—United States—History.   2. Women's rights—United States—
   History—Sources.   I. Title.   II. Series.
   HQ1236.5.U6 S77 2003
   305.42'0973—dc21   2002075337

British Library Cataloguing in Publication Data is available.

Library of Congress Catalog Card Number: 2002075337
ISBN: 0–313–31135–8
ISSN: 1535–3192

First published in 2003

Greenwood Press, 88 Post Road West, Westport, CT 06881
An imprint of Greenwood Publishing Group, Inc.
www.greenwood.com

Printed in the United States of America

The paper used in this book complies with the
Permanent Paper Standard issued by the National
Information Standards Organization (Z39.48–1984).

10 9 8 7 6 5 4 3 2 1

Copyright Acknowledgments

The author and publisher gratefully acknowledge permission for use of the following material:

Excerpts from Elizabeth Faulkner Baker, "At the Crossroads of Women in Industry," *The ANNALS of the American Academy of Political and Social Science*, 143 (May 1929): 265–79, reprinted with permission.

Excerpts from Joan Morrison and Charlotte Fox Zabusky, *American Mosaic: The Immigrant Experience in the Words of Those Who Lived It*. New York: Dutton, 1980. Copyright © 1980 by Joan Morrison and Charlotte Fox Zabusky. (Currently available in paperback from the University of Pittsburgh Press.)

Excerpts from Phyllis Schlafly, *The Power of the Positive Woman*. New Rochelle, NY: Arlington House, 1977. Reprinted with permission.

Excerpts from John T. Noonan, Jr., *A Private Choice: Abortion in America in the Seventies*. New York: The Free Press. Reprinted with permission of The Free Press, a Division of Simon & Schuster, Inc. Copyright © 1979 by The Free Press.

Excerpts from George Gilder, *Sexual Suicide*. Copyright © 1973 by George Gilder. Reprinted with permission of Georges Borchardt, Inc.

Excerpts from Karen Kahn, ed., *Frontline Feminism, 1975–1995: Essays From Sojourner's First 20 Years* © 1995 by Sojourner, Incorporated. Reprinted by permission of Aunt Lute Books.

Excerpts from Margaret Cerullo, "Hidden History: An Illegal Abortion in 1968," in *From Abortion to Reproductive Freedom*, ed. Marlene Gerber Fried. Boston, MA: South End Press, 1990. Reprinted with permission.

Excerpts from papers from the Simon Greenleaf Collection, Harvard Law School reprinted with permission.

Excerpts from pamphlets held by the Sophia Smith Collection reprinted with permission. These include: Jennie Loitman Baron, *Jury Service for Women* (League of Women Voters, 1924); Florence Kelley, *Twenty Questions* [about the ERA] (National Consumers' League, 1924); Margaret Sanger, *Family Limitation* (1914); Margaret Sanger, "The Importance of Voluntary Motherhood" (National Birth Control League, 1914); Lyman Abbott, *Why Women Do Not Wish the Suffrage* (Massachusetts Association Opposed to the Further Extension of Suffrage, 1898); *Letters and Addresses on Woman Suffrage by Catholic Ecclesiastics* (1914); *The Case Against Woman Suffrage* (National Anti-Suffrage Association, 1914).

Excerpts from Linda Wood, *"What Did You Do in the War, Grandma?"* Reprinted with permission from the Rhode Island Historical Society.

Excerpts from Kristin Luker, *Abortion and the Politics of Motherhood*. Berkeley: University of California Press. Copyright © 1984 The Regents of the University of California.

Excerpts from Donna Lopiano, "The Real Culprit in the Cutting of Men's Olympic Sports." Available online at http://www.womenssportsfoundation.org. Reprinted with permission of Women's Sports Foundation, East Meadow, New York.

The "NOW Statement of Purpose" is reprinted by permission of the National Organization for Women. This is a historic document (1966) and does not reflect the current language or priorities of the organization.

Every reasonable effort has been made to trace the owners of copyright materials in this book, but in some instances this has proven impossible. The author and publisher will be glad to receive information leading to more complete acknowledgments in subsequent printings of the book and in the meantime extend their apologies for any omissions.

ADVISORY BOARD

For Kathy, Erin, Kevin, Adam and Caitlin

Contents

Series Foreword

This series of books presents major issues in American history as they have developed since the republic's inception to their present incarnation. The issues range across the spectrum of American experience and encompass political, economic, social, and cultural concerns. By focusing on the "major issues" in American history, the series emphasizes the importance of an issues-centered approach to teaching and thinking about America's past. *Major Issues in American History* thus reframes historical inquiry in terms of themes and problems rather than as mere chronology. In so doing, the series addresses the current, pressing need among educators and policymakers for case studies charting the development of major issues over time, so as to make it possible to approach such issues intelligently in our time.

The series is premised on the belief that understanding America demands grasping the contentious nature of its past and applying that understanding to current issues in politics, law, government, society, and culture. If "America" was born, and remains, as an idea and an experiment, as so many thinkers and observers have argued, issues inevitably have shaped whatever that America was and is. In 1801, in his presidential inaugural, Thomas Jefferson reminded Americans that the great strength of the new nation resided in the broad consensus citizens shared as to the rightness and necessity of republican government and the Constitution. That consensus, Jefferson continued, made dissent possible and tolerable, and, we might add, encouraged dissent and debate about critical issues thereafter. Every generation of Americans has wrestled with such issues as defining and defending freedom(s), determining America's place in the world, waging war and making peace, receiving and assimilating new peoples, balancing church and state, forming a "more perfect union," and pursuing "happiness." American identity(ies) and interest(s) are not fixed. A nation of many peoples on the move across space and up and down the socioeconomic ladder cannot have it so. A nation charged with ensuring that, in Lincoln's words, "government of the people, by the people, and for the people shall not perish from the earth" cannot have it so. A nation whose heroes are not only soldiers and statesmen but also ex-slaves, women reformers, inventors, thinkers, and cowboys and Indians cannot have it so. Americans have never rested content locked into set molds in thinking and doing—not so long as dissent and difference are built into the character of a people that dates its birth to an American Revolution and annually celebrates that lineage. As such, Americans have been, and are, by heritage and habit an issues-oriented people.

We are also a political people. Issues as varied as race relations, labor organizing, women's place in the work force, the practice of religious beliefs, immigration, westward movement, and environmental protection have been, and remain, matters of public concern and debate and readily intrude into politics. A people committed to "rights" invariably argues for them, low voter turnout in recent elections notwithstanding. All the major issues in American history have involved political controversies as to their meaning and application. But the extent to which issues assume a political cast varies.

As the public interest spread to virtually every aspect of life during the twentieth century—into boardrooms, ballparks, and even bedrooms—the political compass enlarged with it. In time, every economic, social, and cultural issue of consequence in the United States has entered the public realm of debate and political engagement. Questions of rights—for example, to free speech, to freedom of religion, to equality before the law—and authority are political by nature. So, too, are questions about war and society, foreign policy, law and order, the delivery of public services, the control of the nation's borders, and access to and the uses of public land and resources. The books in *Major Issues in American History* take up just those issues. Thus, all the books in this series build political and public policy concerns into their basic framework.

The format for the series speaks directly to the issues-oriented character of the American people and the democratic polity and to the teaching of issues-centered history. The issues-centered approach to history views the past thematically. Such a history respects chronology but does not attempt to recite a single narrative or simple historical chronology of "facts." Rather, issues-centered history is problem-solving history. It organizes historical inquiry around a series of questions central to understanding the character and functions of American life, culture, ideas, politics, and institutions. Such questions invariably derive from current concerns that demand historical perspective. Whatever determining the role of women and minorities and shaping public policy, or considering the "proper" relationship between church and state, or thinking about U.S. military obligations in the global context, to name several persistent issues, the teacher and student—indeed, responsible citizens every-where—must ask such questions as "how and why did the present cir-cumstance and interests come to be as they are" and "what other choices as to a policy and practice have there been" so as to measure the di-mensions and point the direction of the issue. History matters in that regard.

Each book in the series focuses on a particular issue, with an eye to encouraging readers and users to consider how Americans at different times engaged the issue based on the particular values, interests, and political and social structures of the day. As such, each book is also necessarily events-based in that the key event that triggered public con-cern and debate about a major issue at a particular moment serves as the case study for the issue as it was understood and presented during that historical period. Each book offers a historical narrative overview of a major issue as it evolved; the narrative provides both the context for understanding the issue's place in the larger American experience and the touchstone for considering the ways Americans encountered and en-gaged the issue at different times. A timeline further establishes the chro-nology and place of the issue in American history. The core of each book is the series of between ten to fifteen case studies of watershed events that defined the issue, arranged chronologically to make it possible to track the development of the issue closely over time. Each case study stands as a separate chapter. Each case study opens with a historical overview of the event and a discussion of the significant contemporary opposing views of the issue as occasioned by the event. A selection of four to nine critical primary documents (printed whole or in excerpts and introduced with brief headnotes) from the period under review pres-ents differing points of view on the issue. In some volumes, each chapter also includes an annotated research guide of print and non-print sources to guide further research and reflection on the event and the issue. Each volume in the series concludes with a general bibliography that provides ready reference to the key works on the subject at issue.

Such an arrangement ensures that readers and users—students and teachers alike—will approach the major issues within a problem-solving framework. Indeed, the design of the series and each book in it demands that students and teachers understand that the crucial issues of American history have histories and that the significance of those issues might best be discovered and recovered by understanding how Americans at different times addressed them, shaped them, and bequeathed them to the next generation. Such a dialectic for each issue encourages a comparative perspective not only in seeing America's past but also, and perhaps even more so, in thinking about its present. Individually and collectively, the books in *Major Issues in American History* thereby demonstrate anew William Faulkner's dictum that the past is never past.

Randall M. Miller
Series Editor

Preface and Acknowledgments

I have taught U.S. women's history and women's studies courses at the University of Rhode Island for three decades, and that experience has shaped the contours of this volume. Inspired by the political movements of the 1970s, I began my early teaching of women's history with a determination to bring race and class into any discussion of women's rights. In those early days there tended to be a bifurcation between the formal women's rights movement, often dismissed as *bourgeois*, even reactionary, and what seemed to be the more stirring rebellions of the labor, women's liberation, and civil rights movements. Women who were participants in the second wave of feminism were often dismissive of the suffrage movement and of reformists' attempts to end prostitution and promote temperance. At the same time, many modern feminists were blind to the way in which their own struggle for women's freedom carried some of the class and race prejudices of the first women's rights movement. They were also remarkably over-optimistic about the possibility of convincing all women that the constraints of traditional gender norms, sexual conventions, and conservative values should be overthrown.

Women's history scholars like myself have been forced to adopt a less self-centered analysis of women's rights. In teaching the evolution of women's rights I have developed a number of guiding principles, principles that have also characterized much of the new women's history scholarship. First and foremost, I have tried to expand the notion of women's rights beyond the realm of liberal feminism where it has, in classic treatments, been lodged. Instead, I have pointed to the complex interweaving of women's varied experiences in historical situations affected as much by class and ethnicity as by gender. I have also stressed the ways in which more radical women's movements often grew out of earlier, more tentative challenges to male authority, and how critical the drive for suffrage was to the contemporary political position of women. There is, in other words, a foregrounding of modern feminism in earlier social movements, ranging from left to conservative. Second, I have emphasized the extent to which, as women gain equal rights under the law, questions arise about their sexual and biological vulnerability in a world that still sees women through the lenses of potential motherhood and sexual objectification. Thus, the difference-equality debate usually runs alongside any discussion of expanding women's equality under the law. Third, I have outlined the considerable force that conservative arguments have always had for many Americans, including women, and that these arguments have been given a new potency in light of the Ronald Reagan revolution. Finally, I have suggested that the rights of women are hardly settled matters in American cultural and political life. The twenty-first century, with its dramatic changes in world stability, crises in the delivery of health care, rise in immigration to the United States, and the issues of women's rights in other parts of the world, to name only a few dynamics of historical change, will continue to foster vigorous debates among Americans about the rights of women.

Thirty years ago there were only a few texts on women's rights to use in the classroom; today there are dozens, but few present the issue of women's rights in a format that covers the history of the nation up to the present. I believe the issues studied here are central to the debate over women's rights and should provoke and inform discussions among students and their teachers at both the high school and college levels across the political spectrum. Documents have been reproduced with original spelling and capitalization; archaic forms of "negro," for example, will rankle modern readers but are a reminder of how slowly current racial terminology crept into the language.

Those in search of reference materials on the debate over women's rights should also find this volume of use. In addition to reading guides describing critical works, there is a supplemental bibliography that includes books, documentary films, and Web sites. Biographies of important women now number in the dozens, and in the interests of space for other things I have omitted most of them. I urge readers in search of biography to use the names mentioned in *Women's Rights in the United States* as a guide to further research on individuals.

My first debt of gratitude goes to the hundreds of students who have studied U.S. women's history and women's studies in my courses at the University of Rhode Island. My second is to my colleagues in women's studies and to the many women's historians I have collaborated with over the years. More specifically, Greta Cohen and Penny Hastings gave me invaluable advice on how to approach the topic of Title IX. Susan Porter Benson shared resources about women's labor history. The staff of the Sophia Smith Collection of Smith College was especially helpful in providing access to critical documents. Donald Sockol alerted me to *Are Women People?* Kimberly Nusco helped me with research in the library and the processing of documents. Louise Hilliard handled numerous faxes for permissions with aplomb and rescued some chapters after a computer crash left me in a panic. Series editor Randall M. Miller has been a model of patience, providing constructive criticism, careful readings, and the intellectual pleasure of dissent and debate. Barbara Rader solicited the manuscript and kept me working at as fast a pace as I could, and Kevin Ohe and Susan Baker brought the book to publication with patience and courtesy.

My husband Frederick Stirton Weaver has been an invaluable reader, critic, and editor, despite the pressures of his own work. I hope this book will be of use to all our children and our grandchildren in years to come.

Chronology of Events

1776 Declaration of Independence.
Abigail Adams exhorts her husband John to "Remember the Ladies" in any "new code of laws" for the United States.

1789 U.S. Constitution goes into effect.

1789 Judith Sargent Murray publishes *On the Equality of the Sexes*.

1791 Bill of Rights (first ten amendments) added to the Constitution.

1792 Mary Wollstonecraft publishes *Vindication of the Rights of Women*.

1807 State of New Jersey nullifies votes for women.

1836 Factory women "turnout" in Lowell, Massachusetts.

1837 Grimké sisters speak to "promiscuous audiences" in their anti-slavery lecture tour.
Catharine Beecher publishes *An Essay . . . with Reference to the Duty of American Females*.
Sarah Grimké publishes "Letters on the Equality of the Sexes."

1844 Lowell Female Reform Association agitates for a ten-hour day.

1847 Elizabeth Blackwell enters Geneva Medical School.

1848 New York State passes Married Women's Property Act.
Declaration of Sentiments issued at Seneca Falls, New York.

1853 Antionette Brown Blackwell becomes first ordained woman minister.

1861 Harriet Jacobs publishes *Incidents in the Life of a Slave Girl.*
      Civil War begins.

1863 Women's National Loyal League collects petitions asking Congress to end slavery.
      Emancipation Proclamation.

1865 Civil War ends.
      Thirteenth Amendment abolishes slavery.

1866 Equal Rights Association established.

1868 Fourteenth Amendment ratified but puts the word "male" into the Constitution.

1869 Elizabeth Cady Stanton and Susan B. Anthony found National Woman Suffrage Association.
      Arabella Mansfield licensed by state of Iowa to practice law.

1870 Lucy Stone and Henry Blackwell found American Woman Suffrage Association.
      Fifteenth Amendment ratified.

1872 Women attempt to vote in the "New Departure."
      Susan B. Anthony arrested by federal marshals for "the crime of voting."

1873 Comstock Act passed by Congress.

1874 Founding of Woman's Christian Temperance Union.

1875 *Minor v. Happersett* says Fourteenth and Fifteenth Amendments do not give women voting rights, state or federal constitutions must be amended to do so.

1877 End of federal Reconstruction in the South.

1881 Atlanta laundresses' strike.

1890 National American Woman Suffrage Association formed.

1893 State of Colorado gives women voting rights.

1896 Founding of National Association of Colored Women's Clubs.
      Plessy v. Ferguson sanctions "separate but equal" public facilities.

1903 Founding of Women's Trade Union League.

1909 *Muller v. Oregon* establishes constitutionality of maximum hours for women.

1909   Shirtwaist Strike in New York City ("Uprising of the Twenty Thousand").

1911   Triangle Shirtwaist Factory fire.

1915   Margaret Sanger is arrested for distributing *Family Limitation*.

1916   National Woman's Party founded by Alice Paul.

1920   Nineteenth Amendment ratified giving women full voting rights.

1923   Equal Rights Amendment introduced into Congress.

1924   *Adkins v. Children's Hospital* declares minimum wages for women unconstitutional.

1935   Fair Labor Standards Act creates minimum wage and maximum hour standards for all workers.

1954   *Brown v. Board of Education* overturns *Plessy v. Ferguson*.

1963   Equal Pay Act passed by Congress.
        President Kennedy's Commission on the Status of Women issues its report.
        Betty Friedan publishes *The Feminist Mystique*.

1964   Freedom Summer in Missisippi; Cassie Hayden and Mary King write a "memo" regarding women's position in the civil rights movement.
        Civil Rights Act, which includes Title VII, passed by Congress.

1965   *Griswold v. Connecticut* finds that married couples have a right to birth control information based on a constitutional "right to privacy."

1966   National Organization for Women is founded.

1967   National Welfare Rights Organization is founded.

1968   Carol Hanisch, a women's liberation activist, says "the personal is political."
        Women's liberationists protest the Miss America pageant in Atlantic City.

1972   Congress passes Title IX of the Educational Amendments to the Civil Rights Act.
        Congress sends the Equal Rights Amendment to the states for ratification.
        Phyllis Schlafly founds STOP ERA.

1973   *Roe v. Wade* establishes a woman's right to abortion.

1975 *Taylor v. Louisiana* says both women and men must be available to serve on juries.

1976 The Hyde Amendment limits Medicaid funding for abortion.

1978 Pregnancy Discrimination Act passed by Congress.
Women against Pornography founded in New York City.

1980 Armed Forces are sexually integrated.

1981 President Ronald Reagan cancels the selective service registration of women.

1982 The Equal Rights Amendment dies for lack of ratification by enough states.
Family Protection Act introduced into Congress but fails to pass.

1986 *Meritor Savings Banks, FSB v. Vinson* makes "sexual harassment" the responsibility of employers.
EEOC v. Sears, Roebuck & Co. fails to find evidence of discrimination based on sex at Sears, Roebuck & Co.

1991 Clarence Thomas–Anita Hill testimony on sexual harassment allegations before Senate Judiciary Committee.

1992 *Planned Parenthood of Southeastern Pennsylvania v. Casey* maintains woman's right to abortion but also upholds some restrictions on abortion by the states.

1994 Congress passes the Violence Against Women Act.

2000 Supreme Court strikes down Section 13981 of the Violence Against Women Act.

WOMEN'S RIGHTS

Introduction

Discussions of women's rights have been an integral piece of American politics and culture from the founding of the nation. In a famous exchange, Abigail Adams urged her husband John to "remember the ladies" in the "new code of laws" about to be drafted as the thirteen colonies declared their "independency" from Britain. In her letters to John and her friend Mercy Otis Warren, Abigail touched on several themes pertaining to the position of women in British North America. She argued against the "tyranny of men" that had been encoded in the English common law and that made women non-persons once they married. Following the logic of the male patriots who wished to create a body of rights based on liberal individualism, she hoped to seize this propitious moment and end the "arbitrary power" of husbands and fathers. She also reminded John that women expected protection from men, and by extension, the protection of the state as well, because of what she viewed as their inevitable dependency as the weaker sex. And finally, she promised that unless the grievances of women were heard, they would be likely, someday, to foment rebellion.

John Adams dismissed Abigail's petition as a laughable matter and reminded her pleasantly but condescendingly of the "despotism of petticoats" and claimed that men were generally the subjects, not the tyrants, of women. But in a more thoughtful letter to his friend John Sullivan, he stressed another approach to the political position of women. He was worried that the American Revolution might go too far in establishing the "consent of the people" by allowing even men who did not own property to vote. Adams wrote to Sullivan that if all men might vote, there would be no justifiable argument for excluding women. Like many patriots, Adams believed the firm placement of women inside the family and their exclusion from the public sphere kept social and class relationships in harmony. If gender differences were eradicated, the social fabric of the body politic might be torn to pieces in a United States undergoing political experimentation and rapid social change. Conserving women's traditional position within the family might very well guarantee the ongoing health of the body politic.

The ideas explored by Abigail and John Adams have dominated American discourse on women's rights since the founding of the nation in 1776. The most famous women's rights document of the United States, the 1848 Declaration of Sentiments at Seneca Falls, would call on the principles enunciated in the Declaration of Independence and evoke Abigail's call for an end to the tyranny of men. Reforming the law to end women's second-class citizenship, protecting women from rape, economic exploitation, and violence on the grounds of their physical vulnerability, and using political agitation, sometimes reformist, sometimes radical, to invigorate new feminist causes, have propelled the women's rights' struggle over the course of two centuries. And at every juncture traditionalists such as John Adams have viewed this struggle with alarm.

In the chapters that follow, Americans discuss whether to expand a wide range of women's rights, to return to a more traditional order, or to leave things as they are. Women's rights activists debate the strategies of their cause, and sympathetic allies in other rights movements argue over which political cause should take priority at any historical moment. Underlying this discussion is, often, a political divide over what feminist scholars have described as "equality" versus "difference." Are women so essentially different from men—or their biological roles so important—that they should be granted special protections and/or required to perform certain duties under the law? Should women's and men's physical differences be meaningless when it comes to equality under the law and having access to opportunities for education, employment, or public service? Do women have, as some have suggested, "a constitutional right to be ladies," or should they be called upon to serve their country, as men do, in the jury box and in military combat? Should the law be entirely gender-neutral, and even if such a thing were possible, how would that play out in actual practice in a society with grave racial, sexual and economic inequalities?

From the founding of the nation under the Constitution in 1789, male citizenship and certain obligations were assumed to go hand in hand. Men were to represent dependents and wives in the courtroom and in government, to carry the onerous duty of serving on juries, and in times of war, to be drafted into the armed forces. Women, by virtue of their supposedly more delicate physical constitutions, susceptibility to rape and assault, and sole responsibility for childbearing, were to be protected from these obligations. In its beneficence and respect for womanhood, then, the government protected women from conflict on the battlefield, in the courtroom, in the legislature, and at the polling place. Because women did not serve their country as soldiers, they were not, as any number of social conservatives would repeat, therefore entitled to full rights as citizens. Voting was a right balanced by obligations, obligations that women did not have. This *quid pro quo* argument was usually accompanied by more subjective assertions having to do with sexual difference; men should not be distracted in the courtroom, in legislative bodies, or on the battlefield by the presence of women. Those who made these assertions often claimed that reason, deliberation, and military tactics were for men, and affairs of the heart and of nurturing were for women. It was for women's own good and the preservation of the family that women were spared the consequences of full citizenship and equality. Ending the separation of spheres of influence would undermine the domestic sphere and threaten the national good. Both the suffrage amendment and the equal rights amendment to the Constitution were fought by conservatives on precisely these premises, and while the Nineteenth Amendment giving women equal voting rights was ratified by a narrow margin in 1920, the ERA went down to defeat in 1982, partly due to efforts of conservative women voters.

In the chapters that follow conservatives such as Simon Greenleaf, Catharine Beecher, Lyman Abbott, and Phyllis Schlafly all emphasize gender difference, protection and obligation, but in reference to different issues and across two centuries. Greenleaf and Beecher opposed women speaking in public to mixed audiences of men and women in the 1830s, arguing that erasing such gender lines would create political discord, even anarchy. In the 1890s Lyman Abbott believed that one of the reasons women should not be given the vote was that they were not required to fight for their country and did not want the similar obligation of voting. And in the late twentieth century, lawyer Phyllis Schlafly contended that the ERA would erase special protections for women, force wives and mothers into the job force, and, inevitably, require them to register for the draft.

Women's rights activists have countered these conservative arguments with demands for women's liberation from dependency and their full incorporation into the body politic and the economy. They have assured critics that women are ready to assume the obligations of voting, supporting families, holding political office, serving on juries, and, in modern times, joining the military—and that society will not fall apart as a result. Sarah Grimké and Maria Stewart used the language of Great Awakening Protestantism and the equality of the born-again in Christ to demand that women be allowed to speak on the public issues of the day and to abandon their positions as dependent butterflies for responsible citizenship. Jennie Loitman Barron of the League of Women Voters assured traditionalists that there had been no increase in "the burning of soups" just because women served on juries.

In raising the cry of "the personal is political," the women's liberation movement of the late 1960s articulated an undercurrent of women's rights that did not fit very easily into the framework of eighteenth-century liberalism. Claiming a space for women in the public sphere and demanding the rights accorded to men was one thing; examining the position of women in the family and in sexual relationships both consensual and nonconsensual was another. The assumption that what went on in the family was of little concern to the state and that fathers should rule the domestic sphere had been encoded in the English law. Rape, sexual molestation of children, and other kinds of family violence are now believed to have been commonplace but were largely ignored by law enforcement, the courts, and religious institutions through most of American history. Americans have believed (and often still believe) that women's bodies are a natural resource in need of governance by the state. The supervision of abortion and marriage, the discouragement of homosexuality, and protective legislation in the workplace have disciplined women's bodies in ways thought necessary for family building and the reproduction of future citizens.

The privacy of the domestic sphere and the father's control over it received critical attention from women's rightists from the beginning but remained the most difficult aspect of women's rights to address. Elizabeth Cady Stanton and Susan B. Anthony promoted voluntary motherhood and argued for divorce so that wives could escape marital rape and family violence. In their drive to raise the age of consent and to reform prostitution, women exposed the double sexual standard and tried to make men more accountable for sexual crimes. In the twentieth century lesbians demanded greater tolerance in society for same-sex love, and efforts to secure birth control and then abortion rights challenged traditional religious doctrine and the silence surrounding women's suffering from multiple and unwanted pregnancies. Margaret Sanger insisted on making the connection between women's sexual happiness and their control over their own bodies.

In reply, conservatives such as Anthony Comstock and John T. Noonan have argued that the family takes precedence over reproductive rights for women and that bearing children remains the primary obligation of women in society. George Gilder has suggested that the breakdown in the authority of fathers was responsible for a variety of social ills in American life. The struggle over certain sexual practices, including pornography, same-sex love, abortion and birth control, is still at the heart of the conservative-liberal divide in the United States. Those who think of themselves as "pro-family" have sought to rein in the expansion of women's rights and to restore the power of fathers and husbands as a key element of political stability and morality. Women continue to be, as they were in the late eighteenth century, symbols for both traditionalists and liberationists of what constitutes civilization and the social order. Freed from all restraints of the family and parental control, conservatives argue, women will create social chaos; free women, liberals argue, or Americans will never live up to the promises of liberty and justice for all.

In a complex interplay between political activism, legislative initiative, and quixotic decisions of the Supreme Court, Americans have, for the most part, worked in the direction of expanding rights for women within a liberal rights framework. They have also sought to use the power of the state to protect women on the grounds of their sexual difference and greater sexual vulnerability. Married women's property acts and more liberal divorce and custody laws were enacted in the states in the nineteenth century, as were laws raising the age of consent. In the early twentieth century, protective legislation for some working women met with mixed success in the courts, and in the culmination of the first wave of feminism, women won the right to vote and to run for political office. Struggles to expand educational and professional opportunities for women, except on an individual basis, were not very successful until the passage of Title VII of the Civil Rights Act in 1964 and the enforcement of affirmative action regulations with regard to sex as well as race. In an innovative adaptation of civil rights law to address what had seemed a merely personal matter, feminist theorist Catharine MacKinnon argued that sexual harassment in the workplace was a violation of women's civil rights under the Fourteenth Amendment and that women might bring charges in courts of law against employers who overlooked sexual harassment.

In the nineteenth century, the Supreme Court was entirely on the side of sexual conservatism, pronouncing from the bench as in *Bradwell v. Illinois* in 1873 that "the paramount destiny and mission of woman are to fulfill the noble and benign offices of wife and mother." The court ruled in *Muller v. Oregon* in 1908 that women needed maximum hour laws because "the future well-being of the race" required the protection of maternal health; in *Adkins v. Children's Hospital* in 1923 it overturned a minimum wage law for women because, the majority of justices argued, the Nineteenth Amendment had given women nearly full equality. With a more liberal and activist court in place in the 1970s, decisions such as *Roe v. Wade* seemed to hand abortion rights to women from out of the blue. But it was a more conservative court of the 1980s that once again called upon protectionism by declaring in *Meritor Savings Bank v.*

Vinson that women were a vulnerable sexual class and that preventing sexual harassment against women was the responsibility of employers.

The greatest strides in conceptualizing and agitating for women's rights in the United States came when activists compared sexual discrimination to racial discrimination. The conjoining of the abolitionist and women's rights movements in the mid–nineteenth century created a powerful coalition for human rights. As African Americans mobilized for an end to slavery and for their civil rights, women saw parallels with their own situation. The same momentum fueled the women's liberation movement as it emerged from the civil rights and anti-war movements of the 1960s and launched a second wave of change. The strides in the law made by women and African Americans were in the mainstream of liberalism by expanding individual rights and establishing, at least in theory, equality of opportunity for all. But this approach to both racial and sexual equality assumes that the state will uphold and enforce the law, an assumption that black women knew was violated once Reconstruction ended; it would take nearly another century to bring the federal government back into the struggle for racial equality. Many women in the 1980s and 1990s were dismayed and disappointed as Republican presidents undermined affirmative action, the Equal Employment Opportunity Commission, and reproductive rights. Feminists fear that women's rights will go backward, not forward, in the twenty-first century.

Despite the close-knit relationship between the civil rights and feminist movements, ongoing tensions between women of color and white women have taken their toll on the utopian dream of "sisterhood." The material situation of women of color was and remains far more complicated than that of the middle-class white women who have tended to dominate liberal feminism. Facing racism in employment, housing, health services, and education, women of color have rarely been able to separate feminism from the struggle for racial equality; white women more often have the privilege of focusing completely on their own liberation and ignoring that of class and race. When Ida B. Wells challenged southern racism in her pamphlets on lynching, she attacked a whole range of sexual practices, including the unacknowledged rape of black women and the idealization of white womanhood that underlay a culture of racial violence in the South. The response of Frances Willard and of many suffragists of the day was to characterize both black and immigrant men as potential rapists and as less worthy citizens than middle-class white women. The abandonment of this "feminism of fear" by some suffragists would be a critical factor in the success of votes for women movement before World War I, a success fueled by the expanded participation of Socialist and working-class women as well as middle-class progressives.

Like black feminism, socialist feminism and working-class feminism have more tortured histories in the United States than mainstream liberal feminism. The earliest women's rights protests came from women factory workers who were recruited to labor in the textile mills of New England and who then claimed their rights to fair wages as the "daughters of free men." Quickly dubbed "Amazons" by the newspapers and most labor leaders, "disorderly women" of the working class have been seen as "radicals of the worst sort." Given the resistance among male workers to perceiving of women as individuals with rights in the workplace and in need of strong unions, uprisings by women workers, including black women laundresses in the South, were more episodic in the nineteenth century than productive of real change. As socialists and anarchists, many of them Jewish immigrant women, joined the workforce at the turn of the century, more sustained movements and the creation of industrial unions were possible, sometimes moved along by the help of middle-class allies. In the great New York City shirtwaist strike of 1909, women such as Clara Lemlich, Pauline Newman, and Rose Schneiderman created a mass movement of thousands of striking workers. In the wake of new protective legislation limiting hours of work for women in Lawrence, Massachusetts, in 1912, Polish women struck at the woolen mills over their "short pay." Demanding "bread and roses," women strikers in Lawrence were a critical factor in the Industrial Workers of the World mobilization in Lawrence. Similar demands for bread and roses were made by Chicana women farm workers in California in the 1960s, Chinese sweatshop workers in New York City in 1982, and African-American catfish processing plant workers in Mississippi in 1991. But the infusion of leftist ideology and organizing that was so important to the rise of unions for women in the past has been driven, literally, from the American scene, a scene now dominated by anti-left and centrist-to-right politics.

Although women continue to make strong unionists and to go on strike, the flight of manufacturing jobs from the United States and the decline of the left has left most Americans, including most women, without unions to represent them. An ongoing struggle to establish strong teacher, airline, and white-collar unions does help many women and their families but will continue to face the resistance of employers and advocates of unrestricted capitalism. Class and gender inequality in the workforce continues to concentrate poverty in female-headed families, especially among people of color and immigrants. Although women are supposedly protected from sexual harassment and from sexual discrimination in the workforce, the decline of government funding of civil rights and worker protection agencies and the hostility of the courts to lawsuits has seriously undermined the ability of women and poor people to challenge employer mistreatment.

Women's participation in the armed forces brings women's rights and obligations as citizens full circle and highlights Americans' inability to settle on one approach to women's rights. When the armed services began some sexual integration in the 1970s, a decision that enlisted women had supported for some time, many Americans worried that women might end up being drafted or serving in combat. One of the chief factors in the rejection of the ERA was conservatives' claims that it would force women to be drafted and to serve in combat. Sexual difference, in other words, would be disregarded in the military, abandoning traditional protections for women. With the abolition of the draft in 1973, there was less worry about women in the military, but it was still true that men had to register with the Selective Service on their eighteenth birthdays and women did not. By 1979 the Department of Defense urged Congress to abolish the restrictions on women in combat because sexual integration required similar training for women and men. When President Jimmy Carter suggested in 1980 that both women and men should be registered for the draft, there were outcries from both conservatives and feminists. A representative of the Eagle Forum, a conservative think-tank, claimed that exemption from the draft was a right women had always enjoyed and one symbolic of their "constitutional right to be ladies." President-elect Ronald Reagan quickly announced his opposition to the registration of women, and in 1981 Congress refused to extend registration for the draft to women. The Supreme Court upheld the constitutionality of that decision.

Ideas about sexual difference continue to make women's military service controversial. Many women, both conservative and liberal, believe that women are inherently more peaceful than men. It is therefore a betrayal of women's human natures to force them to fight in war. Opponents of women in the military believe women make inherently bad soldiers because they are overly sentimental and physically weaker than men and that their sexual presence will undermine morale, an argument also made about homosexuals. Historians of rape observe that men in conquering armies often rape enemy women; women in the armed services would be particularly vulnerable.

Meanwhile, young women enlist in the armed services in ever-greater numbers, some of them hoping to fly fighter planes and to use other tools of combat. The armed services engaged in successful affirmative action programs that attracted both people of color and women in the 1980s, but sexual harassment, rape, and violence against homosexuals continue to be problems in the armed services for both women and gays. And with conservatives in the White House, women in the military could not receive abortions on base, a problem that became more acute during the Gulf War when women were stationed in Middle Eastern countries opposed to rights for women that Americans took for granted. These

contradictions among equality of opportunity, beliefs in sexual difference, and the challenges of protecting the sexually vulnerable will create
significant challenges in the American military for years to come and
present difficult dilemmas for conservatives and feminists alike.

The political backlash of the 1990s against feminism has had a sobering
effect on women's rights activists. As a result, some of the long-held faith
in liberalism as a solution to inequality has been shaken. So has faith in
the federal government's commitment to enforcing women's rights. Addressing violence against women raises difficult new questions about the
regulation of free speech and seemingly intractable male behavior. Conservatives and some radical feminists now sometimes overlap in their
insistence on women as the more vulnerable sex and in need of protection from the state. The anti-pornography movement has made for some
interesting bedfellows; radical feminist Andrea Dworkin and conservative Phyllis Schlafly have both called for government restrictions on
pornography. Critics of liberalism point out that new divorce laws, supposedly liberating for women and gender neutral, have impoverished
many ex-wives and denied them custody of their children. Men, some
of them homosexual, have found the courts reluctant to expand the notion of sexual harassment beyond the class of women. The shocking disparity in accessibility of health services and welfare benefits based on
class and race has convinced many feminists that birth control, abortion,
and welfare programs can become tools of the state for modern-day eugenics and the regulation of the bodies of poor women, especially
women of color.

Whatever the future holds for women's rights, it seems likely that
Americans will continue to balance several seemingly contradictory positions: that there are important biological, even psychological, differences between men and women that give them different rights and
obligations in society; that women require protection by the state because
of their sexual vulnerability; and that the gender-neutral, liberal framework of equal rights is the most American of systems and the one most
applicable to women's needs. We can also predict that new women's
movements will arise to reformulate notions of equality and foment new
rebellions. Feminists cannot assume, however, that the next wave of historical change belongs to them; conservatives, both men and women,
believe that reining in expanded rights for women is in the best interests
of American society.

1

Factory Women's Turnouts, Women's Independence, and the Legacy of the American Revolution

At the Continental Congress in Philadelphia in 1776, a small group of white men, most of them well-off owners of land or slaves or both, composed a Declaration of Independence from Great Britain. In a list of rights and grievances they explained why the thirteen North American colonies were justified in establishing a "United States of America." Thomas Jefferson of Virginia, who wrote the first draft of the Declaration and was largely responsible for its language, claimed that all men had "certain unalienable Rights," and that "among these" were "Life, Liberty, and the Pursuit of Happiness," a felicitous phrase that both expanded the traditional notion of political rights from John Locke's original "life, liberty and property" and put something of a film over the new government's commitment to the sacred nature of property. Six years of a difficult war culminated at Yorktown in 1781 in an American victory, and in 1789, the state governments abandoned the weak federal system of governance of the Articles of Confederation and ratified a new Constitution, its authors introducing their system of laws with the authority of "We the People."

The liberalism that swept through England, France, and the United States in the second half of the eighteenth century and that influenced the rhetoric of the American Revolution and the writing of the Constitution is usually referred to as the "Enlightenment." Enlightenment thinkers sought an end to monarchy and aristocratic rule under the "divine right of kings," and advocated representative government, the separation of church and state, and the use of reason to replace tradition and priestly authority. They did so with the argument that human beings were born into a state of nature but could be instructed as children in the virtues of good citizenship and the harmony of the "social contract." But theorists such as John Locke and Jean Jacques Rousseau placed women firmly in the family, where their interests should be represented by fathers and then their husbands, although the unmarried woman, the *feme sole*, was, as in the tradition of British common law, to have many of the property rights of adult men. Governance of the family and the polity was assumed to be beyond the scope of women's mental powers, and any woman who challenged patriarchy in the family or in government was considered to be both "unnatural" and a threat to the civic order.

Those who drafted the federal and state constitutions of the United States and were elected to its congresses and legislatures largely agreed with this conservative interpretation of women's roles. As historian Linda Kerber has said, "restricting women's politicization was one of a series of conservative choices that Americans made in the postwar years as they avoided the full implications of their own revolutionary radicalism."[1] With the assumption that economic and political independence reaffirmed virtue and that dependency created vice, "the dependent status of all women put them in the same lowly category as servants, children, apprentices, slaves and the poor"; their governance could only be entrusted to property-holding men.[2] Only the state constitution of New Jersey, probably due to the influence of Quakers, gave property-holding women the right to vote, but in 1807, New Jersey excluded women, along with blacks and foreigners, on the grounds that barring women from the polls was "highly necessary to the safety, quiet, good order and dignity of the state."[3] The framers of the U.S. Constitution kept slavery but allowed for the end of the foreign slave trade in twenty years. They left voting rights to the states but established a representative system of national government. They limited the powers of the executive branch through a system of checks and balances but in 1791 adopted a far-reaching Bill of Rights in the first ten amendments.

England made some concessions to Enlightenment liberals but kept the monarchy and the House of Lords. France experienced ever more violent stages of revolution after 1790, including the confiscation of property and the public appearance of vociferous and seemingly blood-thirsty women. It was a model that terrified conservatives and liberals on both sides of the Atlantic, and Americans consciously sought a middle way, often congratulating themselves on what appeared to be both their moderation and their radicalism. Mary Wollstonecraft, the British radical who wrote the feminist treatise *A Vindication of the Rights of Women* in 1792 and demanded full equality in education, work, and politics, was familiar to most literate Americans as the epitome of unnatural womanhood. Her death from childbirth fever a few years later seemed a fitting end to her free-love relationship with William Godwin. Deemed a "strumpet" (the eighteenth-century term for a loose woman) and an "Amazon" (a war-like woman from ancient Greece), Wollstonecraft was assumed to be both sexually and politically dangerous because of her independence from male authority and her "bluestocking," or overly educated, persona. Parson Weems, the popular biographer of George Washington, no doubt spoke for many men when he claimed in 1800 that a "mild dove-like temper is . . . necessary to Female beauty," and "A masculine air in woman frightens us."[4]

What might women do as citizens of the United States? They paid taxes, and had, as differential citizens of the Republic, the right to petition their governments for redress. They were not to vote, be office-holders, practice the law, or speak before men. The way in which they might serve the Republic best was to be virtuous and retiring, and to teach their sons patriotism and liberty. This "Republican motherhood" necessitated a modicum of education for women, and between 1750 and 1800 the literacy rate in the United States, especially in New England, rose dramatically, although women's education was later also driven by a shortage of male labor and a growing demand for teachers in schools for boys.

Most ordinary women and men in the United States did not participate in the more lofty debates about the gender ideology of the Revolution. But they did come from an Anglo-American tradition and a material reality that stressed the economic necessity of women's productive labor in the family and the community. In the pre-industrial economy of the seventeenth and eighteenth centuries, men and families could not prosper without the visible hard work of their wives and daughters in spinning and weaving, sewing, nursing, midwifery, and the production of foodstuffs. In the early eighteenth century women sometimes practiced law and medicine and frequently ran small shops and businesses. The colonial division of labor stressed the contributions of "goodwives," whose "economy" helped to manage resources for "the general welfare of both household and community."[5] This traditional division of labor was upset in a dramatic way by the terrible deprivations of the American Revolution: the deaths and desertions of husbands, the impoverishment of farmers and artisans, rising prices for food and rents, a collapsed monetary system. The sufferings of the Revolution, combined with steady post-war immigration from Europe and the British Isles, seemed to create a whole new class of women without men, often in search of poor relief and work in the teeming port cities of New York, Philadelphia, and Baltimore. A growing class disparity intensified the need for "proper" women to separate their wifely duties of child-rearing and domesticity in the privacy of the home from the more degraded—and often public— labor of poor women. Referred to by scholars as "the cult of true womanhood" or "the pastoralization of housework," this ideology, full-blown by the 1830s, insisted that the lives of proper women were somehow removed from the world of physical labor and money making enterprise, though nothing was further from the truth.

At the same time, the early stages of industrialization came to New England and the port cities of the Atlantic coast. A mixed variety of labor systems evolved between 1790 and 1840: the "family system" in textile mills in Rhode Island; artisan workshops in the shoe industry in Lynn and Salem, Massachusetts; outwork (or homework), small factories and family-run shops in the garment industry in New York and Philadelphia; and, in the 1830s, the rise of large integrated textile mills in rural New England and the Delaware Valley. The new mill cities of New England created a sensation in the United States. Foreign dignitaries, including Charles Dickens, visited them and contrasted their early wholesomeness with the degradation of factory work in England. Without a large pool of affordable male labor on which to draw, mill owners turned to farm women from New England to staff the mills and boarding houses of Lowell, Fall River, and Pawtucket.

By the mid-1830s, some women worked alongside other family members at home, others had their pay at the factory collected by their fathers, and some were truly "independent" wage earners, that is, women who were living apart from their families and collecting their wages to spend as they saw fit. Not surprisingly, women who worked in larger groups and lived apart from their families, as in the Lowell "turnout" (or strike) of 1836, were the most militant in protesting cuts in pay and long hours of work. These striking women were the first U.S. women to demand their rights as American citizens in public assembly. Despite their supposed exclusion from full citizenship in the ideology of the Republic, they claimed it anyway. Lowell mill workers "turned out" in spontaneous strikes as the "daughters of free men"; they were not "slaves" but respected workers with the right to the dignity and rewards of honest labor. Fresh from farm homes where women's labor was an uncontested necessity, they mounted a variety of collective protests against their employers, petitioned their state legislatures, and even formed labor organizations.

With the image of Mary Wollstonecraft fresh in the minds of Americans, striking women were characterized in the press as "Amazons." Their efforts were undermined by three factors: the belief that the employer-employee contract was freely entered into by both parties and was therefore immutable; male wage earners' wariness of politicized women; and the divided loyalties of women workers, many of whom refused to turn out or who competed with factory workers in family workshops. The ten-hour movement of the 1840s, which attracted both male and female workers, developed an ideology of labor that would dominate American thinking for decades to come. This ideology put men in charge of both the labor movement and the family, and argued that to take proper charge, they deserved a "family wage." The laboring classes should, then, work to bolster men's wages so that women might retreat to the home. Women factory workers were increasingly depicted as pathetic victims of capitalist greed who needed both the protection of the state and of male labor unionists. Above all, women should not compete with men for the same pay or do "men's work."

A new definition of American citizenship was being claimed by male workers. With so many men no longer the holders of property, with the steady inflow of poor immigrants, especially the Irish, with more free blacks residing in northern communities and competing for jobs, white wage-earning men and their labor unions needed to distinguish themselves from these "others," and especially from slaves and women. "Manliness" and independence was now defined as bread winning for one's family. Women's productive labor, whether in the artisanal workshop, the family farm, or the middle-class urban household, was said to be outside the market economy, a kind of pre-industrial, pastoral labor that did not qualify women for the universal (manhood) voting rights laws that swept the state legislatures in the 1820s. Wage-earning women who lived on their own and claimed a decent wage were viewed as anomalies, "radicals of the worst sort."[6]

READING GUIDE

Blewitt, Mary, *Men Women and Work: Class, Gender, and Protest in the New England Shoe Industry, 1790–1910*. Urbana: University of Illinois Press, 1988. Blewitt demonstrates the complex ways in which both factory employers and male heads of household undermined women's collective attempts to organize as independent wage earners in the nineteenth century. In a clear sexual division of labor, women in Lynn sewed the uppers of shoes, many of them in small household workshops, while men took credit for the "skilled" labor in shoe production and of selling finished goods. Attempts by largely unmarried women wage earners in large factories to make alliances with women in family workshops failed. The shoe labor movement, dominated by men, promoted the "family wage" instead.

Boydston, Jeanne, *Home and Work: Housework, Wages, and the Ideology of Labor in the Early Republic*. New York: Oxford University Press, 1990. A successful attempt to sort out the goods and services produced by women in the pre-industrial economy and why the female gender began to receive less credit for that production in the wake of industrialization. As more and more men in the early nineteenth century were forced to give up farming and self-employment in skilled trades, work for wages came to symbolize "manliness." Women were increasingly associated with the "pastoral" and non-monetary functions of the home, rendering their actual labor invisible.

Cameron, Ardis, *Radicals of the Worst Sort: Laboring Women in Lawrence, Mas-*

sachusetts, 1860–1912. Urbana: University of Illinois Press, 1993. Cameron brings the analysis of textile mill women workers into the early twentieth century, describing the transition in Lawrence from a largely Yankee and Irish community in 1860 to a polyglot of ethnic groups by the time of the great strike of 1912, initiated by a decline in women's wages due to a new maximum hour law in Massachusetts. She stresses that women who challenged textile mill management were seen as "radicals of the worst sort" because they threatened both class and gender hierarchies.

Dublin, Thomas, *Women at Work: The Transformation of Work and Community in Lowell, Massachusetts, 1826–1860*. New York: Columbia University Press, 1979. A classic account of the rise of the large-scale textile mill factory system along the Merrimack River and its transition from an idyllic site of labor for New England women to the speed-up, stretch-out, and decreased wages of the mid–nineteenth century. Dublin's careful research of mill women, both Yankee and Irish, establishes them as real personalities over time, with a variety of motives for working and responses to the factory system.

Dublin, Thomas, ed., *Farm to Factory: Women's Letters, 1830–1860*. New York, Columbia University Press, 1981. A wonderful collection of letters between factory women in New England and their families and a good reminder of how few sources there are of ordinary women's voices.

Faragher, John Mack, *Sugar Creek: Life on the Illinois Prairie*. New Haven: Yale University Press, 1986. Although women's childbearing and hard work were critical to farm life and new settlements on the frontier, their efforts were not assumed to be economic ones. As more farms produced goods for the market economy after the building of the Erie Canal and the railroads, male property-holders were seen as the "breadwinners" of farm families.

Foner, Phillip S., ed., *The Factory Girls*. Urbana: University of Illinois Press, 1977. An indispensable collection of excerpts from working women's newspapers and magazines in New England, with explanatory text and notes.

Kerber, Linda, *Women of the Republic: Intellect and Ideology in Revolutionary America*. Chapel Hill: University of North Carolina Press, 1980. Kerber considers the ideas and political values that shaped gender relationships in the early Republic. She concludes that while the American Revolution was largely a conservative one, seeking to establish the individual liberty of white men while confining women to the domestic sphere, and excluding them from formal politics, the Enlightenment notion that children were malleable social beings gave women important new identities as "Republican mothers."

Murphy, Teresa, *Ten Hours' Labor: Religion, Reform and Gender in Early New England*. Ithaca: Cornell University Press, 1992. Murphy looks at the origins of the ten-hour-day movement in New England and finds that working people often blended the language of labor reform with moral and religious reform. Given the general wariness of politicized women by male heads of households in towns such as Lynn and Fall River, women workers had to force their way into the labor movement and often found more hospitable spaces in the church and temperance movements. The ability of women in Lowell and the shoe towns to speak for themselves rather than to be spoken for was constantly muted but nonetheless often asserted by women labor reformers.

Stansell, Christine, *City of Women: Sex and Class in New York, 1789–1860*. New

York: Alfred A Knopf, 1982. A look at the condition of working-class women and their families in one of the nation's most important port cities. Stansell emphasizes the narrow range of occupations for women, women's economic precariousness, their sexual vulnerability, and early attempts of "factory girls" in the garment trades to organize. New York, like other American cities in this period, was full of women on their own attempting to make their way in a country that assumed that all respectable women were dependents of men. African-American and Irish women, like their male counterparts, were increasingly thrown into competition with each other for jobs as domestic servants, and in general, the condition of black women declined.

NOTES

1. Linda Kerber, *Women of the Republic: Intellect and Ideology in Revolutionary America* (Chapel Hill: University of North Carolina Press, 1980), 287.

2. Christine Stansell, *City of Women: Sex and Class in New York, 1789–1860* (New York: Alfred A. Knopf, 1982), 19.

3. As quoted by Joan Hoff, *Law, Gender and Injustice: A Legal History of U.S. Women* (New York: New York University Press, 1991), 102.

4. Kerber, *Women of the Republic*, 283, 281.

5. Jeanne Boydston, *Home and Work: Housework, Wages, and the Ideology of Labor in the Early Republic* (New York: Oxford University Press, 1990), 22.

6. Ardis Cameron, *Radicals of the Worst Sort: Laboring Women in Lawrence, Massachusetts, 1860–1912* (Urbana: University of Illinois Press, 1993).

DOCUMENTS

1.1. Women at Work in Lowell, Massachusetts, 1831–1834

When Harriet Hanson's father died, her mother moved to Lowell to find work. Mrs. Hanson ran a boarding house, and Harriet went to work in the mills. She was typical of the young women from New England who mounted the first public protests for women's rights as independent wage earners. Her account stresses the importance of women's economic identity outside the family and Yankee women's claims to full citizenship, expressed in public assembly. The Hansons were vulnerable to pressure from the mill owners when Harriet struck because Mrs. Hanson was a boarding-house keeper in a "company town."

HARRIET HANSON GOES ON STRIKE

In 1831, under the shadow of a great sorrow, which had made her four children fatherless,—the oldest but seven years of age,—my mother was left to struggle alone; and, although she tried hard to earn bread enough to fill our hungry mouths, she could not do it, even with the help of kind friends.... [M]y mother's widowed sister,... who kept a factory boarding house in Lowell, advised her to come to that city.... We walked with our mother to the Tremont Corporation, where we were to live, and ... in the first block of tenements then built, I began my life among factory people. My mother kept forty boarders, most of them men, mill-hands, and she did all her housework, with what help her children could give her between schools; for we all, even the baby three years old, were kept at school.

I had been to school constantly until I was about ten years of age, when my mother, feeling obliged to have help in her work besides what I could give, and also needing the money which I could earn, allowed me, at my urgent request (for I wanted to earn *money* like the other little girls), to go to work in the mill. I worked first in the spinning-room as a "doffer." The doffers were the very youngest girls, whose work was to doff, or take off, the full bobbins, and replace them with the empty ones. I can see myself now, racing down the alley, between the spinning-frames, carrying in front of me a bobbin-box bigger than I was.... The working-hours of all the girls extended from five o'clock in the morning

until seven in the evening, with one-half hour for breakfast and for dinner. Even the doffers were forced to be on duty nearly fourteen hours a
day. . . .

When I look back into the factory life of fifty or sixty years ago, I do
not see what is called "a class" . . . I see them as individuals, with personalities of their own. . . . Yet they were a class of factory operatives,
and were spoken of (as the same class is spoken of now) as a set of
persons who earned their daily bread, whose condition was fixed, and
who must continue to spin and to weave to the end of their natural
existence. Nothing but this was expected of them, and they were not
supposed to be capable of social or mental improvement. That they could
be educated and developed into something more than mere work-
people, was an idea that had not yet entered the public mind. So little
does one class of persons really know about the thoughts and aspirations
of another! It was the good fortune of these early mill girls to teach
the people of that time that this sort of labor is not degrading; that the
operative is not only "capable of virtue," but also capable of self-
cultivation. . . .

The law took no cognizance of woman as a money-spender. She was
a ward, an appendage, a relict. Thus it happened, that if a woman did
not choose to marry, or, when left a widow, to re-marry, she had no
choice but to enter one of the few employments open to her, or to become
a burden on the charity of some relative. The cotton-factory was a great
opening to these lonely and dependent women. From a condition ap-
proaching pauperism they were at once placed above want; they could
earn money, and spend it as they pleased; and could gratify their tastes
and desires without restraint, and without rendering an account to anybody. For the first time in this country woman's labor had a money
value. She had become not only an earner and a producer, but also a
spender of money, a recognized factor in the political economy of her
time. And thus a long upward step in our material civilization was taken;
women had begun to earn and hold her own money, and through its
aid had learned to think and to act for herself. . . .

One of the first strikes of cotton-factory operatives that ever took place
in this country was that in Lowell, in October, 1836. When it was announced that the wages were to be cut down, great indignation was felt,
and it was decided to strike, *en masse*. . . . The mills were shut down, and
the girls went in procession from their several corporations to the
"grove" on Chapel Hill, and listened to "incendiary" speeches from early
labor reformers. One of the girls stood on a pump, and gave vent to the
feelings of her companions in a neat speech, declaring that it was their
duty to resist all attempts at cutting down the wages. This was the first
time a woman had spoken in public in Lowell, and the event caused
surprise and consternation among her audience. . . . It was estimated that

as many as twelve or fifteen hundred girls turned out, and walked in procession through the streets. . . .

My own recollection of this first . . . "turn out" . . . is very vivid. I worked in a lower room, where I had heard the proposed strike fully, if not vehemently, discussed; I had been an ardent listener to what was said against this attempt at "oppression" on the part of the corporation, and naturally I took sides with the strikers. When the day came on which the girls were to turn out, those in the upper rooms started first, and so many of them left that our mill was at once shut down. Then, when the girls in my room stood irresolute, uncertain what to do, asking each other, "Would you?" or "Shall we turn out?" and not one of them having the courage to lead off, I . . . became impatient, and started on ahead, saying, with childish bravado, "I don't care what you do, I am going to turn out, whether any one else does or not;" and I marched out, and was followed by the others. . . . The agent of the corporation where I then worked took some small revenges on the supposed ringleaders; on the principle of sending the weaker to the wall, my mother was turned away from her boarding-house, that functionary saying, "Mrs. Hanson, you could not prevent the older girls from turning out, but your daughter is a child, and her you could control."

Source: Harriet H. Robinson, *Loom and Spindle: Or Life Among the Early Mill Girls*, 1898.

1.2.   Women Factory Worker Turnouts of the 1830s

The first known textile mill turnout of women workers occurred at the Samuel Slater factory in Pawtucket, Rhode Island, in 1824. By the mid-1830s, women workers in both the shoe and textile industries were organizing to articulate their grievances. These early protests were usually against decreases in wages and increases in boarding-house rates. Most of the strikes failed, and none of the early women's labor associations survived for long. In these excerpts, women workers describe themselves and their purposes while a few not so friendly observers depict their unladylike resort to political action.

"PREAMBLE TO THE CONSTITUTION OF THE FEMALE SOCIETY OF LYNN . . . FOR THE PROTECTION AND PROMOTION OF FEMALE INDUSTRY"

Equal rights should be extended to all—to the weaker sex as well as to the stronger. The disadvantages which nature and custom have entailed upon females, as to the common transactions and business of life, are sufficiently great of necessity, without the addition of others, which are unnecessary and unjust. Under these circumstances, driven by necessity, to seek relief, a large number of females from this, and neighboring towns, many of whom have families, as well as themselves, dependent on their industry for support; and impressed with the belief, that women as well as men, have certain inalienable rights, among which is the right at all times, of "peaceably assembling to consult upon the common good," have assembled accordingly at the Friends, Meeting house, in Lynn, this thirtieth day of December, ... 1833—

Source: Lynn Record, Jan. 1, 1833.

MARY RUSSELL'S CALL TO SHOEWORKERS

Ladies!—The present state of this Society calls for our serious and candid attention; it seems that but little regard is paid to the rules and regulations; that they have been disregarded and broken by many of its members who have taken work under price. . . . We cannot see the propriety of denying the shoebinders that liberty which other females have, that of setting their own prices upon their own work; and we have but little doubt in saying, that if all the members of this society were to be firm and determined that it would be but a short time ere they might be equally free from oppression. But if we are indifferent to our own interest . . . , we shall soon make prophetic, the language of our oppressors, that women are too fickle minded and vain to accomplish anything of importance. . . . Ladies, let us be alive to our own interests and honor. . . . Let us become a band of sisters; each considering the welfare of the society as her own peculiar interest. . . . Let us be willing to make some sacrifice if necessity require it. . . . If our dress is not quite as fashionable as it was last year, let us be willing to be a little out of date in these trifles, rather than be fashionable slaves. . . .

And in conclusion; Ladies, I beg leave to say, be not discouraged— our prospect daily brightens—we have not made these exertions for nothing—those who have stood foremost in defending and espousing the rights of females, will have the reward of well done.

Source: Lynn Record, June 18, 1834.

A BOSTON PAPER DESCRIBES A LOWELL MILL TURNOUT IN 1834

The number soon increased to nearly eight hundred. A procession was formed and they marched about town. We are told that one of the leaders mounted a pump and made a flaming Mary Woolstonecroft [*sic*] speech on the rights of women and the iniquities of the "*monied* aristocracy," which produced a powerful effect on her auditors, and they determined "to have their own way if they died for it."

Source: Boston Evening Transcript, Feb. 17, 1834.

"UNION IS POWER"

Our present object is to have union and exertion and we remain in possession of our unquestionable rights. We circulate this paper wishing to obtain the names of all who imbibe the spirit of our patriotic Ancestors, who preferred privation to bondage, and parted with all that renders life desirable and even life itself to procure independence for their children. The oppressing hand of avarice would enslave us, and to gain their object, they gravely tell us of the pressure of the times, this we are already sensible of and deplore it. If any are in want, the Ladies will be compassionate and assist them; but we prefer to have the disposing of our charities in our own hands; and as we are free, we would remain in possession of what kind providence has bestowed upon us, and remain daughters of freemen still.

Source: Boston Evening Transcript, Feb. 17, 1834.

1.3.   Male Workers Respond to Women Wage Earners

As more women began to work in factories in the 1830s, men's work as artisans and self-employed manufacturers was undermined by mechanization and falling wages. In 1836 the National Labor Union, made up entirely of male delegates, gathered in Philadelphia and issued this report on "female labor." Note that in the report the women seem as much to blame as their employers for the degradation of men's work and that the ideal place for all women is in the home.

"REPORT OF THE COMMITTEE ON FEMALE LABOR"

The system of Female Labor, as practiced in our cities and manufacturing towns, is surely the most disgraceful escutcheon on the character of American free-men, and one, if not checked by some superior cause, will entail ignorance, misery and degradation on our children, to the end of time. "The physical organization, the natural responsibilities, and the moral sensibility of women, prove conclusively that her labors should be only of a domestic nature." But if the character and attributes of any of God's creatures have been subverted, it has been woman, when forced by adventitious circumstances to become the abused hireling and drudge of the speculator and monopolist. Let the Workingmen of the United States but consider what would become of the rising generation if the almost universal system of Female Labor should not be arrested. The health of the young female, in the majority of cases, is injured by unnatural restraint and confinement, and deprived of the qualities essentially necessary in the culture and bearing of healthy children. Their morals frequently depart before their health, in consequence of being often crowded in such large numbers, with all characters and all sexes; these evils themselves are great, and call loudly for a speedy cure; but still another objection to the system arises . . . [—]the ruinous competition brought in active opposition to male labor, because, when the employer finds, as he surely will, that female assistance will compress his ends, of course the workman is discharged, or reduced to a corresponding rate of wages with the female operative. By these means the parent, the husband, or the brother, is deprived of a sufficient subsistence to support himself and family, when without the auxiliary aid of the female, by his own labor alone he might have supported himself and family in decency, and kept his wife or relative at home, to perform the duties of the household. Females themselves are very blind as to their real interest. . . . One thing, however, must be apparent to every reflecting female, that all her exertions are scarce sufficient to keep her alive; that the price of her labor each year is reduced; and that she in a measure stands in the way of the male when attempting to raise his prices or equalize his labor; and that her efforts to sustain herself and family are actually the same as tying a stone around the neck of her natural protector, Man, and destroying him with the weight she has brought to his assistance. This is the true and natural consequence of female labor, when carried beyond the necessities of the family.

Source: National Laborer, Nov. 12, 1836: 133–34.

1.4.   The Lowell Female Reform Association Petitions for a Ten Hour Day

---

In January 1845, the Female Lowell Reform Association petitioned the Massachusetts legislature for the enactment of a ten-hour-a-day law. The Massachusetts House of Representatives appointed a special committee to examine the claims both men and women made for a shorter day. The ten-hour-day movement claimed that the health of women workers was affected more

*dramatically than that of male workers by long hours and that the
"weaker sex" had a special need for protection from the state.
The petitioners were careful not to be strident, to emphasize their
respectability, and to stress that their leisure time would be devoted to feminine activities. Nonetheless, the Committee dismissed the idea that state regulation should be applied to working
conditions. Massachusetts would be one of the first states in the
United States, however, to pass maximum hour legislation for
women in the early twentieth century.*

"REPORT OF THE SPECIAL COMMITTEE OF THE MASSACHUSETTS HOUSE OF REPRESENTATIVES"

The petitioners declare that they are confined to "from thirteen to fourteen hours per day in unhealthy apartments," and are thereby "hastening
through pain, disease, and privation, down to a premature grave." They
therefore ask the Legislature "to pass a law providing that ten hours
shall constitute a day's work," and that no corporation or private citizen
"shall be allowed, except in cases of emergency, to employ one set of
hands more than ten hours per day."

The whole number of names on the several petitions is 2,139, of which
1,151 are from Lowell. A very large proportion of the Lowell petitioners
are females. . . .

The first petitioner who testified was *Eliza R. Hemmingway* . . . Her employment is weaving, -works by the piece. . . . Her wages average from
$16 to $23 a month exclusive of board. She complained of the hours for
labor being too many, and the time for meals too limited. In the summer
season, the work is commenced at 5 o'clock, A.M., and continued till 7
o'clock, P.M., with half an hour for breakfast and three quarters of an
hour for dinner. During eight months of the year, but half an hour is
allowed for dinner. The air in the room she considered not to be wholesome. . . . Thinks that there is no day when there are less than six of the
females out of the mill from sickness. Has known as many as thirty. She,
herself, is out quite often, on account of sickness. . . . She thought there
was a general desire among the females to work but ten hours, regardless
of the pay. Most of the girls are from the country, who work in the
Lowell Mills. The average time which they remain there is about three
years. She knew one girl who had worked there 14 years. Her health
was poor when she left. . . . There is always a large number of girls at
the gate wishing to get in before the bell rings. . . . They do this to make
more wages. A large number come to Lowell to make money to aid their
parents who are poor. She knew of many cases where married women
came to Lowell and worked in the mills to assist their husbands to pay
for their farms. The moral character of the operatives is good. There was

only one American female in the room with her who could not write her name.

Miss Sarah G. Bagley said she had worked in the Lowell Mills eight years and a half,—six years and a half on the Hamilton Corporation, and two years on the Middlesex. She is a weaver, and works by the piece. She worked in the mills three years before her health began to fail. . . . Last year she was out of the mill a third of the time. She thinks the health of the operatives is not so good as the health of females who do house-work or millinery business. . . . She spoke of the high moral and intellectual character of the girls that many were engaged as teachers in the Sunday schools. That many attended the lectures of the Lowell Institute; and she thought, if more time was allowed, that more lectures would be given and more girls attend. She thought that the girls generally were favorable to the ten hour system. She had presented a petition, same as the one before the Committee, to 132 girls, most of whom said that they would prefer to work but ten hours. . . . Their health would be improved. They would have more time for sewing. Their intellectual, moral and religious habits would also be benefited. . . .

Your Committee have . . . come to the conclusion . . . that legislation is not necessary at the present time, and for the following reasons:

1st. That a law limiting the hours of labor, if enacted at all, should. . . . apply to individuals or copartnerships as well as to corporations. But it will be said . . . that corporations are the creatures of the Legislature, and therefore the Legislature can control them in this . . . This to a certain extent is true, but your Committee go farther than this, and say, that if it should ever appear that the public morals, the physical condition, or the social well-being of society were endangered, . . . it would be in the power and would be the duty of the Legislature to interpose its prerogative to avert the evil.

2d. Your Committee believe that the factory system, as it is called, is not more injurious to health than other kinds of indoor labor. That a law which would compel all of the factories in Massachusetts to run their machinery but ten hours out of the 24, while those in Maine, New Hampshire, Rhode Island and other States in the Union, were not restricted at all, the effect would be to close the gate of every mill in the State.

3d. It would be impossible to legislate to restrict the hours of labor, without affecting very materially the question of wages; and that is a matter which experience has taught us can be much better regulated by the parties themselves than by the Legislature. Labor in Massachusetts is a very different commodity from what it is in foreign countries. Here labor is on an equality with capital, and indeed controls it, and so it ever will be while free education and free constitutions exist. And although we may find fault, and say, that labor works too many hours, and labor is too severely tasked, yet if we attempt by legislation to enter within its orbit and interfere with its plans, we will be told to keep clear and to mind our own business. Labor is intelligent enough to make its own bargains, and look out for its own interests without any interference from us.

Source: Massachusetts General Court, *House of Representatives Documents*: 50, March 12, 1845.

1.5.   Striking Amazons in Pittsburgh, 1845

> *In the 1840s both men and women workers joined the ten-hour-day movement and protested workdays as long as thirteen or fourteen hours. In Pittsburgh, Pennsylvania, women textile workers turned out in 1845 to protest their long hours and tried to persuade other workers to join them. Community leaders, including journalists, characterized the strikers with images that evoked women run amok in the French Revolution.*

"FROM THE PITTSBURGH JOURNAL"

There was a great excitement among the girls on Monday morning. A portion of them . . . determined to go to work. The rest—the real out-and-outers, determined to prevent their refractory sisters from doing so. A large number of them collected around Blackstock's Factory, and began hooting and hissing at those who were going to work. . . .

The mayor was sent for. . . . They would not listen to him patiently, however . . . although he spoke to them in his usual amiable and conciliatory manner. They accused him of being in favor of the employers, and he had to leave without accomplishing anything. The Amazons then proceeded to the upper cotton factory, and commenced a similar assault upon the recusants in that quarter. . . . The police were called; and the mayor and Squire Campbell were on the ground. The girls drew up in front of these two, who were standing on the steps and commenced telling them their notions of matters and things in general, and of the ten hour system in particular. . . .

At length the mayor crossed over to the opposite side of the street, and left Mr. Campbell to face the storm. . . . "He's no 'Squire,' " screamed one of the girls; and a general shout reiterated the sentiment. . . . "Now, ladies," said the squire. . . . Whack! went a handful of mud, missing his squireship's head by an inch or two . . . and here the Squire's harangue was interrupted by another handful of dirt; this time hitting him in the face. . . .

We have seen several rows in our time, but really this mob of women is the most formidable that ever came under our observation. You can do nothing with them; if you attempt to reason with them, they can speak two words to your one.

Source: Young America, October 18, 1845.

1.6.   Women Speak Out in the *Voice of Industry*

The Lowell Female Reform Association continued despite the refusal of the Massachusetts state legislature to restrict hours and published these letters in its periodical. The writers reject the passivity required of women by both employers and working-class men and probe the meaning of the word "protection."

Ellen Munroe, "LETTER TO THE BOSTON BEE"

I have observed that it is a common practice, among Editors, to fill their papers with advice to women, and not infrequently, with ill concealed taunts of woman's weakness. . . . It may be, that most women are so dwarfed and weakened, that they believe that dressing, cooking, and loving . . . , make up the whole of life; But Nature still asserts her rights, and there will always be those too strong to be satisfied, with a dress, a pudding, or a beau, though they may take each in turn, as a portion of life. I speak not now of the distinguished of either sex; they form a bright relief in the otherwise dark picture. Neither do I suppose that there are no exceptions, perhaps many, to the general rule. But to the generality of men, let the question be put. Are you not, thousands of you, as effeminate as the veriest woman of them all? You boast of your manliness; where is it? . . . You boast of the protection you offer to women. Protection! from what? from the rude and disorderly of your own sex—reform them, and women will no longer need the protection you make such a parade of giving. Protect them, do you! let me point you to the thousands of women, doomed to lives of miserable drudgery, and receiving "a compensation which if quadrupled, would be rejected by the man-laborer, with scorn"; are they less worthy of protection because they are trying to help themselves? because they have little inclination and less time to lisp soft nonsense? If you would have the manliness you talk of, seek to raise those poor women from their oppressed, and too often degraded, condition; if you will not do it, go on in your old course, but prate no more of your manliness. . . .

Bad is the condition of so many women, . . . but they have at last learnt the lesson, which bitter experience teaches, that not to those who style themselves their "natural protectors" are they to look for needful help, but to the strong and resolute of their own sex. May all good fortune attend those resolute ones, and the noble cause in which they are engaged. *"She Devils"* as some of them have been elegantly termed by certain persons, calling themselves men; let them not fear such epithets, nor shrink from the path they have chosen.... They are breaking the way; they shall make it smoother for those that come after them, and generations yet unborn shall live to bless them for their courage and perseverance. If we choose to sit down in our indolence, and persuade ourselves that we can do nothing, let us not censure those who are wiser and stronger than we are. It has been said that men and women are "natural enemies," which I do not believe; but if a running fight must be kept up between the two, let women have half the battle-field and fair play. The time will come when both parties will learn that they can be much better friends, when they have more equal rights....

Source: Voice of Industry, March 13, 1846.

"TO THE FEMALE LABOR REFORM ASSOCIATION IN MANCHESTER FROM A LOWELL FACTORY GIRL"

Sister Operatives: As I am now in the "City of Spindles," out of employment, ... pardon me for giving you a few brief hints of my own experience as a factory Operative, before proceeding to make some remarks upon the glorious cause in which you are so arduously engaged. ... I am a peasant's daughter, and my lot has been cast in the society of the humble laborer. I was drawn from the home of my childhood at an early age, and necessity obliged me to seek employment in the Factory. ... It rejoices my heart to see so many of you contending for your rights, and making efforts to elevate the condition of your fellow brethren, and raising them from their oppressed and degraded condition, and seeing rights restored which God and Nature designed them to enjoy. Do you possess the principles of Christianity? Then do not remain silent; but seek to ameliorate the condition of every fellow being.... Let the proud aristocrat who has tyrannized over your rights with oppressive severity, see that there is ambition and enterprise among the "spindles," and show a determination to have your plans fully executed....

Some say that "Capital will take good care of labor," but don't believe it; don't trust them. Is it not plain, that they are trying to deceive the public, by telling them that your task is easy and pleasant, and that there is no need of reform? Too many are destitute of feeling and sympathy, and it is a great Pity that they are not obliged to toil one year, and then they would be glad to see the "Ten Hour Petition" brought before the Legislature. This is plain, but true language....

Read and patronize the *Voice*, and circulate the "Ten Hour Petition" among all classes, and may God strengthen you in your efforts; may you continue on in courage and perseverance until oppression and servitude may be entirely extinguished from our land, and thus, do honor to yourselves, and good to your country.

Source: Voice of Industry, May 15, 1846.

2

Antislavery Women, Public Speaking, and Equal Rights

While the ideas of the Enlightenment shaped the institutions of the early Republic and offered a "rights of man" that might someday be extended to women, it was an outpouring of evangelical religion in the Protestant churches that most influenced the average American at the turn of the eighteenth century. A period of religious enthusiasm lasting from 1790 to 1840 was precipitated by a "second Great Awakening," as Americans of all races and classes, especially women, were born again in Christ and devoted themselves to converting others and to redeeming their own souls through "good works." Between the end of the American Revolution and 1800 most communities "disestablished"—or no longer supported with tax dollars—official churches. Old line faiths such as the Congregationalists, Presbyterians, and Quakers lost ground, and new churches seemed to spring up everywhere, coalescing around several theological tendencies: the new light Presbyterians, the Hicksite Quakers, the Methodists, the African Methodists and Baptists, and the Shakers. Ministers, a few of whom were black or female, were praised for their oratory and their dramatic preaching styles, not for their fancy education. Mother Ann Lee, an impoverished factory worker who emigrated from England at the end of the eighteenth century, left her followers with the conviction that she was a female Christ. She inspired thriving Shaker communities that practiced celibacy and provided women with important religious and economic duties. But Lee was unusual; in nearly all nineteenth-century churches, women might dominate the pews, but men controlled the pulpits.

Enlightenment thought downplayed religion, stressing the separation of church and state and the importance of reason over emotion. But the Second Great Awakening, despite its appeal to piety and emotion, complemented many of the basic tenets of the Enlightenment. Predestination, or the old Calvinist view that only God chose individuals for salvation and that the practice of good works could not insure a place in heaven, was discarded in all but name by the new churches. The revivals stressed that individuals were responsible for their own fate and a loving and forgiving God would accept their repentance and desire to be reborn in Christ. Optimism about individuals' abilities to control their own destinies and create Christian communities paralleled political rhetoric claiming the United States was creating a brand new republicanism free of Europe's mistakes from the past. The Great Awakening's emphasis on prayer and the reading of scripture amplified individualism and personal responsibility while increasing literacy, especially the literacy of white middle-class women, who became great consumers of religions tracts and books.

Closed out of the courthouse, the state house, and the Congress, women joined the Protestant churches in greater numbers than men, and ministers often found that women were their best listeners and most helpful allies in promoting religion. As most of the nation's men became intent on producing goods, amassing capital, and conquering the frontier, women were said to be the repositories of piety, faith, and domesticity, their sphere of influence a refuge from sheer ambition and greed. As historian Nancy Cott has said, "the purpose of women's vocation was to stabilize society by generating and regenerating moral character."[1] In fact, although stripped of any real power in the mainstream denominations, women's moral status in the evangelical churches had been elevated to a higher plane than ever, one that distanced them considerably from the inferior position they had held all through the seventeenth and eighteenth centuries as Biblical "daughters of Eve."

By the 1820s and 1830s there was more talk of "women's sphere" and a clear division in the middle classes between the hurly-burly public world of capitalism and government and the private, sentimentalized, religious world of the home. In the 1830s women strikers were chastised for not remaining in that sphere. But in a steady expansion of their moral influence in society, middle-class women also began, with the encouragement of male ministers and moral reformers, to move beyond the home and into society. Now armed with some female academy education and wide reading in religious periodicals, women first organized themselves into maternal associations to discuss their duties as Christian mothers. They went on to hand out Bibles, perform charitable work, and organize temperance societies. Often originally from small towns in New England and the Mid-Atlantic states, the prostitution and heavy drinking they discovered in their new urban homes appalled them. But none of these reform activities necessarily undermined women's subservient roles. Men often spoke to women in meetings and handled the business matters of female societies. And even though both the temperance and moral reform movements often castigated men for their abuse of women through the liquor trade and prostitution, both movements shied away from any challenge to male authority; instead, they urged men to reform their sinful behavior. Most of these groups were also thinly disguised modes of social control for the middle class, alarmed at the crime, poverty, immigration of Irish Catholics, and challenges to authority that accompanied a rapidly changing and industrializing United States.

The abolitionist movement was a distinct departure from other kinds of reform. Inspired by Boston journalists David Walker and William Lloyd Garrison, radical abolitionists argued that the gradual emancipation of slaves and their colonization in Africa were no longer acceptable to true Christians. Although free blacks had already organized antislavery societies in the major port cities, their numbers were few. Walker, a free black, died suddenly in 1830, probably murdered to silence his incendiary call to revolution and self-defense. It was Garrison's uncompromising demand that slavery should be abolished immediately with no compensation to slaveholders that began to galvanize more white reformers into aggressive action. Reform-minded Quakers, especially converts of Elias Hicks, had long argued against the sinfulness of holding other human beings in bondage, and their emphasis on bearing personal witness through non-violence complemented Garrison's insistence on pacifism. Garrison was remarkably open, moreover, to including women and free blacks in the antislavery movement as writers and speakers, and encouraged women to form their own antislavery societies. Some of the first female antislavery societies in the North were formed by African-American women in Salem and by both white and black women in Boston.

The British radical Frances Wright shocked middle-class Americans by speaking to public audiences of men on the issues of labor and slavery at the end of the 1820s, but Maria Miller Stewart, a Bostonian widow who had known David Walker, was probably the first American woman to speak to a mixed audience of men and women in the United States in a series of lectures in 1832 and 1833. Stewart's position as a free black woman in Boston was always precarious. Cheated out of her husband's inheritance by scheming whites, she had to support herself with domestic service and teaching, although her avocation was preaching and writing about the gospel. Like other northern middle-class blacks, she encountered daily episodes of racism in employment and public accommodations. Black women also faced patriarchal values in their own communities; given the economic and political restrictions placed on their fathers, husbands, and sons, they often "believed it necessary to bolster black men's tenuous claims to social power whenever possible."[2] Stewart claimed the right to speak out against slavery and the exploitation of black women and men as domestic servants in the northern cities, and for their education and self-improvement. Garrison published her lectures and writings in the *Liberator*, but men castigated her in her own community for overstepping the bounds of religious piety. "What if I am a woman?" she responded.[3] Nonetheless, Stewart ended her public speaking career and left Boston for New York City in 1837.

The Quakers had always encouraged women to give personal witness in meetings, and Hicksite Quaker Lucretia Mott spoke to the founding convention of the American Anti-Slavery Society in 1833. But it was Sarah and Angelina Grimké, antislavery refugees from South Carolina and recent converts from Presbyterianism to Quakerism in Philadelphia, who would first appear before large abolitionist audiences. When they visited Boston, the two sisters immediately caught the attention of Garrison, and he recruited them, along with forty men, for public speaking training in 1836. Nothing could have been more sensational. The sisters were from a prominent slave-holding family, spoke with a southern accent, and had personally witnessed the sexual and physical abuse of slaves. Angelina Grimké had even urged slave-holding women to rebel against the institution of slavery in her 1836 publication, *An Appeal to the Christian Women of the South*. By then northern women in antislavery societies had collected thousands of signatures on petitions to abolish slavery in the District of Columbia, and the southern states had responded with a "gag rule" in the House of Representatives, a rule that prevented abolitionist petitions from being read in Congress. John Tyler of Virginia spoke for many southerners when he asserted that the petitions evoked that worst of all specters, women out of bounds and running rampant across the face of civil society: "Woman is to be made the instrument of destroying our political paradise, the Union of these states; she is to be made the presiding genius over the councils of insurrection and discord, she is to be converted into a fiend, to rejoice over the conflagration of our dwellings and the murder of our people."[4]

The Grimkés, who proved to be magnificent public speakers, attracted huge audiences of both men and women in 1836 and 1837. They were immediately criticized by the mainstream Protestant clergy and by an influential proponent of separate spheres, Catharine Beecher, for speaking to "promiscuous audiences" and for raising radical passions that could only be detrimental to political civility. They were remarkably resilient in the face of such devastating criticism. They continued to speak in public, and helped to organize, along with Maria Stewart and Lucretia Mott, the first national Female Anti-Slavery Society (FASS) convention, where they spoke out not only against slavery but the racism of many white women in the movement. The peaceful integration of the female antislavery societies and white women's addresses to mixed audiences of blacks and whites, men and women, horrified northern traditionalists, conjuring up lewd visions of interracial sex. During the second national convention of the FASS in 1838 at the "Freedom Hall" in Philadelphia, a mob attacked the building and burned it to the ground.

Abolitionist women did not abandon their cause in the face of such intimidation. In 1838 Angelina Grimké publicly responded to Catharine Beecher and compared the oppression of women to the slavery of African-American men and women. The only political right of women was the right to petition, which abolitionist women demanded in 1839 as "our only means of direct political action."[5] The antislavery feminists had arrived at the knowledge that they would have to gain some of their own rights before they could effectively argue for the rights of slaves. As the excerpts from their writing in this chapter illustrate, they combined the power of Biblical exegesis, the empowerment of women as moral agents from the Great Awakening, and the Enlightenment principles of republicanism to bolster their claim for political authority. Although a formal women's rights movement would not appear for almost another decade, the theoretical grounding for such a movement had been created.

READING GUIDE

Boydston, Jeanne, Mary Kelley, and Anne Margolis, *The Limits of Sisterhood: The Beecher Sisters on Women's Rights and Woman's Sphere*. Chapel Hill: University of North Carolina Press, 1988. This collection of letters and published works by three of the Beecher sisters documents how one of the most important families of nineteenth-century New England responded to the changing roles of women. While the eldest, Catharine, remained an adamant opponent of women's political advocacy, she and her sister Harriet earned fame and fortune in the United States by publishing novels and domestic advice books. Their half-sister Isabella became an advocate of woman suffrage on the grounds that women, as voters, might save the nation for a higher moral good.

Cott, Nancy F., *The Bonds of Womanhood: "Woman's Sphere" in New England, 1780–1835*. New Haven: Yale University Press, 1977. An indispensable account of how New England women, most of them literate and middle class, used the duties assigned to them in "woman's sphere" to claim new authority as mothers, moral guardians, and models of religious piety. In moving across a spectrum of semi-public groups from maternal circles, the most modest of them, to abolitionism, the most radical and "promiscuous," some women were able to make a logical connection between the bonds of slavery and the "bonds of womanhood."

Ginzberg, Lori D., *Women in Antebellum Reform*. Wheeling, IL: Harlan Davidson, Inc., 2000. A brief and useful summary of the cultural and religious origins of women's reform movements and their connections to class identity in the decades before the Civil War. Ginzberg examines charity for the poor, temperance, "moral reform" (ending prostitution), prison and asylum reform, and the antislavery and women's rights movements.

Kraditor, Aileen, *Means and Ends in American Abolitionism: Garrison and His Critics on Strategy and Tactics, 1834–1850.* New York: Pantheon, 1967. Kraditor explains why Garrison, who rejected the Protestant clergy's views on both slavery and pacifism, made such an important theoretical contribution to the emerging woman's movement, and why women's rights eventually divided the abolitionist movement into conservative and radical factions.

Lerner, Gerda, *The Grimké Sisters from South Carolina: Pioneers for Woman's Rights and Abolition.* Boston: Houghton Mifflin, 1967. A highly readable account of two well-born sisters who left the South in protest against slavery, became Quakers, were recruited by William Lloyd Garrison to lecture for the antislavery movement, and then made a clear connection between the oppression of slaves and the oppression of women.

Richardson, Marilyn, ed., *Maria W. Stewart: America's First Black Woman Political Writer.* Bloomington: Indiana University Press, 1987. A collection of the essays and speeches of Maria W. Stewart of Boston and Philadelphia. Stewart was the first American woman to speak to mixed audiences of men and women and combined intense religious feeling with challenges to both racism in the white community and the inequality of women in the African-American churches.

Sklar, Kathryn Kish, *Catharine Beecher: A Study in American Domesticity.* New Haven: Yale University Press, 1973. Beecher was an example of that seeming paradox of American womanhood; powerful, independent and influential, she nonetheless argued that women should leave politics to men so that women could retain their authority in the home and continue to influence the domestic sphere. Beecher was the chief ideological opponent of the Grimké sisters and their contention that radical causes deserved the attention of middle-class women.

Yellin, Jean Fagan, *Women and Sisters: The Antislavery Feminists in American Culture.* New Haven: Yale University Press, 1989. In her subtle but profoundly important exploration of the use of the antislavery emblems of male and female slaves, Yellin shows how difficult it was for most white women to not read into the cause of abolitionism their own lives and values and thus, in a sense, shift the focus of the cause from slave women to themselves. At the same time, Yellin shows how courageous the antislavery feminists were and how critical their discussion of slavery was to the rise of the first wave of a sustained women's rights movement in the United States. By the late nineteenth century, however, these women had all but been forgotten, their voices silenced by a new wave of conservatism in the representation of "speaking women."

Yellin, Jean Fagan and John C. Van Horne, eds., *The Abolitionist Sisterhood: Women's Political Culture in Antebellum America.* Ithaca: Cornell University Press, 1994. A collection of essays that explore the rise of the women's antislavery movement in Boston, New York, Philadelphia, and Salem, with an emphasis on the interracial aspects of the movement, the struggle of African-American women to combat both paternalism and racism in that movement, and the evolution of the topic of women's rights in the abolitionist cause. A reminder that some abolitionist women were opposed to leaving women's "proper" sphere to agitate for women's rights.

NOTES

1. Nancy F. Cott, *The Bonds of Womanhood: "Woman's Sphere" in New England, 1780–1835* (New Haven: Yale University Press, 1977), 97.

2. Anne M. Boylan, "Benevolence and Antislavery Activity among African American Women in New York and Boston, 1820–1840," in Jean Fagan Yellin and John C. Van Horne, eds., *The Abolitionist Sisterhood: Women's Political Culture in Antebellum America* (Ithaca: Cornell University Press, 1994), 123.

3. "Maria Stewart's Farewell Address to Her Friends in the City of Boston," in Marilyn Richardson, ed., *Maria W. Stewart: America's First Black Woman Political Writer* (Bloomington: Indiana University Press, 1987), 68.

4. As quoted by Jean Fagan Yellin, *Women and Sisters: The Antislavery Feminists in American Culture* (New Haven: Yale University Press, 1989), 3.

5. As quoted by Yellin and Van Horne, "Introduction," *The Abolitionist Sisterhood*, 17.

DOCUMENTS

2.1.   Free Black Women in the North and the Claim for Full Equality

---

In her Boston lecture at Franklin Hall in 1832, Maria Miller Stewart outlined the complexity of the position of free African-American women. They had to seek work to support their families, they were often denied education, and they faced racial discrimination in public facilities. They felt obligated, at the same time, to fight for an end to slavery and for the elevation of black manhood. Calling on women's moral authority in religion, Stewart urged men to take more responsibility for moral and political reform.

"AFRIC'S DAUGHTERS"

Who shall go forward, and take off the reproach that is cast upon the people of color? Shall it be a woman? And my heart made this reply— "if it is thy will, be it even so, Lord Jesus!" . . .

Tell us no more of southern slavery; for with few exceptions . . . I consider our condition but little better. . . . After all, methinks there are no chains so galling as those that bind the soul, and exclude it from the vast field of useful and scientific knowledge. O, had I received the advantages of an early education, my ideas would, ere now, have expanded far and wide; but, alas! I possess nothing but moral capability—no teachings but the teachings of the Holy Spirit. . . .

And such is the powerful force of prejudice. Let our girls possess whatever amiable qualities of soul they may; let their characters be fair and spotless as Innocence itself, let their natural taste and ingenuity be what they may; it is impossible for scarce an individual of them to rise above the condition of servants. Ah! why is this cruel and unfeeling distinction! Is it merely because God has made our complexion to vary? It if be, O shame to soft, relenting humanity! . . .

The whites have so long and so loudly proclaimed the theme of equal rights and privileges, that our souls have caught the name also, ragged as we are. As far as our merit deserves, we feel a common desire to rise above the condition of servants and drudges. I have learnt, by bitter experience, that continual hard labor deadens the energies of the soul, and benumbs the faculties of the mind; the ideas become confined, the mind barren, and, like the scorching sands of Arabia, produces nothing; or like the uncultivated soil, brings forth thorns and thistles.

Again, continual and hard labor irritates our tempers and sours our dispositions; the whole system becomes worn out with toil and fatigue; nature herself becomes almost exhausted, and we care but little whether we live or die. It is true, that the free people of color throughout these United States are neither bought nor sold, nor under the lash of the cruel driver; many obtain a comfortable support; but few, if any, have an opportunity of becoming rich and independent; and the enjoyments we must pursue are as unprofitable to us as the spider's web or the floating bubbles that vanish into air. . . .

Most of our color have dragged out a miserable existence of servitude from the cradle of the grade. And what literary acquirement can be made, or useful knowledge derived, from either maps, books, or charts, by those who continually drudge from Monday morning until Sunday noon! O, ye fairer sisters, whose hands are never soiled, whose nerves and muscles are never strained, go learn by experience! Had we had the opportunity that you have had, to improve our moral and mental faculties, what would have hindered our intellects from being as bright, and our manners from being as dignified as yours? Had it been our lot to have been nursed in the lap of affluence and ease, and to have basked beneath the smiles and sunshine of fortune, should we not have naturally supposed that we were never made to toil? And why are not our forms as delicate, and our constitutions as slender, as yours? Is not the workmanship as curious and complete! Have pity upon us, have pity upon us, O ye who have hearts to feel for other's woes; for the hand of God has touched us. . . .

My beloved brethren, as Christ has died in vain for those who will not accept his offered mercy, so will it be vain for the advocates of freedom to spend their breath in our behalf, unless with united hearts and souls you make some mighty efforts to raise your sons and daughters from the horrible state of servitude and degradation in which they are placed. It is upon you that woman depends; she can do but little besides using her influence; and it is for her sake and yours that I have come forward and made myself a hissing and a reproach among the people . . . for I am also one of the wretched and miserable daughters of the descendants of fallen Africa. . . . Did the pilgrims, when they first landed on these shores, quietly compose themselves and say, "The Britons have all the money and all the power, and we must continue their servants forever?" Did they sluggishly sigh and say, "Our lot is hard, the Indians own the soil, and we cannot cultivate it?" No; they first made powerful efforts to raise themselves, and then God raised up those illustrious patriots, WASHINGTON and LAFAYETTE, to assist and defend them. And, my brethren, have you made a powerful effort? Have you prayed the legislature for mercy's sake to grant you all the rights and privileges of free citizens, that your daughters may rise to that degree of respectability which true merit deserves, and your sons above the servile situations which most of them fill?

Source: Maria W. Stewart, *Productions of Mrs. Maria W. Stewart*. Boston: Friends of Freedom and Virtue, 1835.

2.2.   Catharine Beecher and the Conservatism of Separate Spheres

---

Catharine Beecher was the daughter of the Reverend Lyman Beecher, probably the most influential Protestant minister of the 1830s. If she had been a man, Catharine would have pursued the ministry but claimed the profession of teaching instead and pursued its respectability for women with missionary-like zeal. A lifelong promoter of the idea that women could exercise the greatest influence for good from the domestic sphere, she responded immediately to Angelina Grimké's appeal to southern women to undermine the institution of slavery.

"THE DUTY OF AMERICAN FEMALES"

My Dear Friend,

Your public address to Christian females at the South has reached me, and I have been urged to aid in circulating it at the North. I have also been informed, that you contemplate a tour, during the ensuing year, for the purpose of exerting your influence to form Abolition Societies among ladies of the non-slave-holding States. . . .

The object I have in view, is to present some reasons why it seems unwise and inexpedient for ladies of the non-slave-holding States to unite themselves in Abolition Societies; and thus, at the same time, to exhibit the inexpediency of the course you propose to adopt. . . .

The distinctive peculiarity of the Abolition Society is this: it is a voluntary association in one section of the country, designed to awaken public sentiment against a moral evil existing in another section of the country. . . .

The best way to make a person like a thing which is disagreeable, is to try in some way to make it agreeable. . . . If the friends of the blacks had quietly set themselves to work to increase their intelligence, their usefulness, their respectability, their meekness, gentleness, and benevolence, and then had appealed to the pity, generosity, and Christian feelings of their fellow citizens, a very different result would have appeared.

Instead of this, reproaches, rebukes, and sneers, were employed to convince the whites that their prejudices were sinful and without any just cause. . . . This tended to irritate the whites, and to increase their prejudice against the blacks. . . . Then, on the other hand, the blacks extensively received the Liberator, and learned to imbibe the spirit of its conductor.

They were taught to feel that they were injured and abused, the objects of a guilty and unreasonable prejudice—that they occupied a lower place in society than was right—that they ought to be treated as if they were whites; and in repeated instances, attempts were made by their friends to mingle them with whites, so as to break down the existing distinctions of society. Now, the question is not, whether these things, that were urged by Abolitionists, were true. The thing maintained is, that the method taken by them to remove this prejudice was neither peaceful nor Christian in its tendency, but, on the contrary, was calculated . . . to generate anger, pride, and recrimination, on one side, and envy, discontent, and revengeful feelings, on the other. . . .

It is Christianity that has given to woman her true place in society. And it is the peculiar trait of Christianity alone that can sustain her therein. "Peace on earth and good will to men" is the character of all the rights and privileges, the influence, and the power of woman. A man may act on society by the collision of intellect, in public debate; he may urge his measures by a sense of shame, by fear and by personal interest; he may coerce by the combination of public sentiment; he may drive by physical force, and he does not outstep the boundaries of his sphere. But all the power, and all the conquests that are lawful to woman, are those only which appeal to the kindly, generous, peaceful and benevolent principles. Woman is to win every thing by peace and love; by making herself so much respected, esteemed and loved, that to yield to her opinions and to gratify her wishes, will be the free-will offering of the heart. But this is to be all accomplished in the domestic and social circle. The moment woman begins to feel the promptings of ambition, or the thirst for power, her aegis of defense is gone. All the sacred protection of religion, all the generous promptings of chivalry, all the poetry of romantic gallantry, depend upon woman's retaining her place as dependent and defenseless, and making no claims, and maintaining no right but what are the gifts of honour, rectitude and love. . . .

If these general principles are correct, they are entirely opposed to the plan of arraying females in any Abolition movement; because . . . it brings them forward as partisans in a conflict that has been begun and carried forward by measures that are anything rather than peaceful in their tendencies; because it draws them forth from their appropriate retirement, to expose themselves to the ungoverned violence of mobs, and to sneers and ridicule in public places; because it leads them into the arena of political collision, not as peaceful mediators to hush the opposing elements, but as combatants to cheer up and carry forward the measures of strife. If it is asked, "May not woman appropriately come forward as a suppliant for a portion of her sex who are bound in cruel bondage?" It is replied, that, the rectitude and propriety of any such measurer, depend entirely on its probable results. If petitions from females will operate to exasperate; if they will be deemed obtrusive, indecorous, and unwise, by those to whom they are addressed; . . . if they will be the opening wedge, that will tend eventually to bring females as petitioners and partisans into every political measure that may tend to injure and oppress their sex . . . then it is neither appropriate nor wise, nor right, for a woman to petition for the relief of oppressed females. . . .

In this country, petitions to [C]ongress, in reference to the official duties of legislators, seem IN ALL CASES, to fall entirely without the sphere of female duty. Men are the proper persons to make appeals to the rulers whom they appoint, and if their female friends, by arguments and persuasions, can induce them to petition, all the good that can be done by such measures will be secured. But if females cannot influence their nearest friends, to urge forward a public measure in this way, they surely are out of their place, in attempting to do it themselves. . . .

But it may be asked, is there nothing to be done to bring this national sin of slavery to an end? . . .

To this it may be replied, that Christian females may, and can say and do much to bring these evils to an end; and the present is a time and an occasion when it seems most desirable that they should know, and appreciate, and exercise the power which they do possess for so desirable an end. . . .

And is there not a peculiar propriety in such an emergency, in looking for the especial agency and assistance of females, who are shut out from the many temptations that assail the other sex,—who are the appointed ministers of all the gentler charities of life,—who are mingled throughout the whole mass of the community,—who dwell in those retirements where only peace and love ought ever to enter,—whose comfort, influence, and dearest blessings, all depend on preserving peace and good will among men?

In the present aspect of affairs among us, when everything seems to be tending to disunion and distraction, it surely has become the duty of every female instantly to relinquish the attitude of a partisan, in every matter of clashing interests, and to assume the office of a mediator, and an advocate of peace. . . .

Source: Catharine E. Beecher, *An Essay on Slavery and Abolitionism, with Reference to the Duty of American Females*, 1837.

2.3.   Angelina Grimké and Human Rights

> *Angelina Grimké responded to Catharine Beecher's pamphlet with a series of letters to the abolitionist newspaper* The Liberator. *She used the doctrine of evangelical Protestantism to claim the moral equality of women, then the principles of republicanism to argue for their irrevocable right to petition. She also makes the assumption that, as a woman in "bonds," she can understand what it must be like to be a slave.*

A REPLY TO CATHARINE BEECHER

Letter XI: "The Sphere of Woman and Man As Moral Beings The Same"

Thou sayest ... [woman] must "make no claims, and maintain no rights, but what are the gifts of honor, rectitude and love." From whom does woman receive her rights? From God, or from man?. ... One would really suppose that man, as her lord and master, was the gracious giver of her rights, and that these rights were bestowed upon her by "the promptings of chivalry, and the poetry of romantic gallantry"—out of the abundance of his honor, rectitude and love. Now, if I understand the real state of the case, woman's rights are not the gifts of man—no! nor the gifts of God. His gifts to her may be recalled at his good pleasure—but her rights are an integral part of her moral being; they cannot be withdrawn; they must live with her forever. Her rights lie at the foundation of all her duties; and, so long as the divine commands are binding upon her, so long must her rights continue. ...

According to what thou sayest, the women of this country are not to be governed by principles of duty, but by the effect their petitions produce on the members of Congress, and by the opinions of these men. If they deem them "obtrusive, indecorous, and unwise," they must not be sent. ...

Another objection to woman's petition is, that they may "tend to bring females, as petitioners and partisans, into every political measure that may tend to injure and oppress their sex." As to their ever becoming partisans, i.e., sacrificing principles to power or interest, I reprobate this under all circumstances, and in both sexes. But I trust my sisters may always be permitted to petition for a redress of grievances. Why not? The right of petition is the only political right that women have. ... If, then, we are taxed without being represented, and governed by laws we have no voice in framing, then, surely, we ought to be permitted at least to remonstrate against "every political measure that may tend to injure and oppress our sex in various parts of the nation, and under the various public measures that may hereafter been forced." Why not! Art thou afraid to trust the women of this country with discretionary power as to petitioning! Is there not sound principle and common sense enough among them, to regulate the exercise of this right? I believe they will always use it wisely. I am not afraid to trust my sisters—not I. Thou sayest, "In this country, petitions to Congress, in reference to the official duties of legislators, seem, IN ALL CASES, to fall entirely without the sphere of female duty. Men are the proper persons to make appeals to the rulers whom they appoint," etc. Here I entirely dissent from thee. The fact that women are denied the right of voting for members of Congress, is but a poor reason why they should also be deprived of the right of petition. If their numbers are counted to swell the number of Representatives in our State and National Legislatures, the very least that can be done is to give them the right of petition in all cases whatsoever; and without any abridgment. If not, they are mere slaves, known only through their masters.

Letter XII: "Human Rights Not Founded On Sex"

The investigation of the rights of the slave has led me to a better understanding of my own. I have found the Anti-Slavery cause to be the high school of morals in our land—the school in which human rights are more fully investigated, and better understood and taught, than in any other. Here a great fundamental principle is uplifted and illuminated, and from this central light, rays innumerable stream all around. Human beings have rights, because they are moral beings; the rights of all men grow out of their moral nature; and as all men have the same moral nature, they have essentially the same rights. These rights may be wrested from the slave, but they cannot be alienated. . . . Now if rights are founded in the nature of our moral being, then the mere circumstance of sex does not give to man higher rights and responsibilities, than to woman.

When human beings are regarded as moral beings, sex, instead of being enthroned upon the summit, administering upon rights and responsibilities, sinks into insignificance and nothingness. My doctrine then is, that whatever is morally right for man to do, it is morally right for woman to do. Our duties originate, not from difference of sex, but from the diversity of our relations in life, the various gifts and talents committed to our care, and the different eras in which we live.

The regulation of duty by mere circumstance of sex, rather than by the fundamental principle of moral being, has led to all that multifarious train of evils flowing out of the anti-Christian doctrine of masculine and feminine virtues. By this doctrine, man has been converted into the warrior, and clothed with sternness . . . whilst woman has been taught to lean upon an arm of flesh, to sit as a doll arrayed in "gold, and pearls, and costly array," to be admired for her personal charms, and caressed and humored like a spoiled child, or converted into a mere drudge to suit the convenience of her lord and master. . . . This principle has given to man a charter for the exercise of tyranny and selfishness, pride and arrogance, lust and brutal violence. It has robbed woman of essential rights, the right to think and speak and act on all great moral questions, just as men think and speak and act; the right to share their responsibilities, perils and toils; the right to fulfill the great end of her being, as a moral, intellectual and immortal creature, and of glorifying God in her body and her spirit which are His. Hitherto, instead of being a help meet to man, in the highest, noblest sense of the term as a companion, a co-worker, an equal; she has been a mere appendage of his being, an instrument of his convenience and pleasure, the pretty toy with which he wiled away his leisure moments, or the pet animal whom he humored into playfulness and submission. . . . I believe I speak forth the words of truth and soberness when I affirm, that woman never was given to man. She was created, like him, in the image of God, and crowned with glory and honor; created only a little lower than the angels,—not, as is almost universally assumed, a little lower than man. . . .

I recognize no rights but human rights—I know nothing of men's rights and women's rights; for in Christ Jesus, there is neither male nor female.

Source: Angelina Grimké, "Letters to Catharine Beecher in Reply to an Essay on Slavery and Abolitionism," *Liberator*, June 23–Nov. 3, 1837.

2.4.   The Orthodox Protestant Ministry Responds

Protestant ministers had encouraged women to assume moral responsibility outside the home, but in this denunciation of "promiscuous audiences," they sought to curb a powerful movement that had gone far beyond their original expectations. As most conservative critics of women's rights continue to do, they made an "essentialist" or "biological" argument for differences between women and men, and predicted dreadful consequences, including female infertility, if women overthrew their God-given roles.

PASTORAL LETTER

We invite your attention to the dangers which at present seem to threaten the female character with wide-spread and permanent injury.

The appropriate duties and influence of woman are clearly stated in the New Testament. Those duties and influence are obtrusive and private, but the source of mighty power. When the mild, dependent, softening influence of woman upon the sternness of man's opinions is fully exercised, society feels the effects of it in a thousand forms. The power of woman is her dependence, flowing from the consciousness of that weakness which God has given her for her protection, (!) and which keeps her in those departments of life that form the character of individuals, and of the nation. There are social influences which females use in promoting piety and the great objects of Christian benevolence which we cannot too highly commend. We appreciate the unostentatious prayers and efforts of woman in advancing the cause of religion at home and abroad; in Sabbath-schools; in leading religious inquirers to the pastors (!) for instruction; and in all such associated effort as becomes the modesty of her sex: and earnestly hope that she may abound more and more in these labors of piety and love. But when she assumes the place and tone of man as a public reformer, our care and protection of her seem unnecessary; we put ourselves in self-defense (!) against her; she yields the power which God has given her for her protection, and her character becomes unnatural. If the vine, whose strength and beauty is to lean upon the trellis-work, and half conceal its clusters, thinks to assume the independence and the overshadowing nature of the elm, it will not only cease to bear fruit, but fall in shame and dishonor into the dust. We cannot, therefore, but regret the mistaken conduct of those who encourage females to bear an obtrusive and ostentatious part in measures or reform, and countenance of any that sex who so far forget themselves as to itinerate in the character of public lecturers and teachers. We especially deplore the intimate acquaintance and promiscuous conversation of females with regard to things which ought not to be named; by which that modesty and delicacy which is the charm of domestic life, and which constitutes the true influence of woman in society, is consumed, and the way opened, as we apprehend, for degeneracy and ruin.

Source: General Association of Massachusetts to the Churches Under Their Care, *New England Spectator*, July 12, 1837.

2.5.   Angelina Grimké and Theodore Dwight Weld Exchange Views on the Priority of Women's Rights

---

Theodore Dwight Weld, an abolitionist, supported the Grimkés' public speaking on abolitionism. In this exchange of letters with Angelina, Angelina defends the sisters' claim to speak for the rights of woman as well as those of the slave, and also conveys how frightening it was for a woman to speak in public in the 1830s. Weld argued that women's rights, while a legitimate cause, was less important at the time than ending slavery. Weld married Angelina in 1838, and both Sarah and Angelina withdrew from their public roles.

ANGELINA GRIMKÉ TO THEODORE DWIGHT WELD,
Aug. 8, 1837

Dear Brother: No doubt thou hast heard by this time of all the fuss . . . about our stepping so far out of the bounds of female propriety as to lecture to promiscuous assemblies. My auditors literally sit some times with "mouths agape and eyes astare," so that I cannot help smiling in the midst of "rhetorical flourishes" to witness their perfect amazement at hearing a woman speak in the churches. . . . We are placed very unexpectedly in a very trying situation, in the forefront of an entirely new contest—a contest for the rights of woman as a moral, intelligent and, responsible being. . . . I cannot help feeling some regret that this sh'd have come up before the Anti Slavery question was settled, so fearful am I that it may injure that blessed cause, and then again I think this must be the Lord's time and therefore the best time, for it seems to have been brought about by a concatenation of circumstances over which we had no control. The fact is it involves the interests of every minister in our land and therefore they will stand almost in a solid phalanx against woman's rights and I am afraid the discussion of this question will . . . also touch every man's interests at home, in the tenderer relation of life; it will go down into the very depths of his soul and cause great searchings of heart. . . . I must confess my womanhood is insulted, my moral feelings outraged when I reflect on these things, and I am sure I know just how the free colored people feel towards the whites when they pay them more than common attention; it is not paid as a RIGHT, but given as a BOUNTY. . . .

As to our being Quakers being an excuse for our Speaking in public, we do nor stand on this ground at all; we ask no favors for ourselves, but claim rights for our sex. If it is wrong for woman to lecture or preach, then let the Quakers give up their false views, and let other sects refuse to hear their women, but if it is right then let all women who have gifts, "mind their calling" and enjoy "the liberty wherewith Christ hath made them free." . . .

How dost thou think I felt at those great meetings in Lowell? 1,500 city people in the blaze of a chandelier. Sister says that before I rose I looked as if I was saying to myself "the time has come and the sacrifice must be offered." Indeed I often feel in our meeting as if I was "as a lamb led to the slaughter," sometimes so sick before I rise that it seems

impossible for me to speak 10 minutes; but the Lord is at my right hand,
. . . and fills my mouth as soon as I open it in faith for the dumb.

Thy sister in the bonds of woman and the slave, A.E. Ge.

THEODORE DWIGHT WELD TO SARAH AND ANGELINA GRIMKÉ, Aug. 15, 1837

My dear sisters:

. . . As to the rights and wrongs of women, it is an old theme with
me. . . . What I advocated in boyhood I advocate now, that woman in
EVERY particular shares equally with man's rights and responsibilities.
Now I have made this statement of my creed on this point to show you
that we fully agree in Principle. . . . Now not withstanding this, I do most
deeply regret that you have begun a series of articles in the Papers on
the rights of woman. Why, my dear sisters, the best possible advocacy
which you can make is just what you are making day by day. Thousands
hear you every week who have all their lives held that woman must not
speak in public. Such a practical refutation of the dogma as your speaking furnishes has already converted multitudes. Leading abolitionists,
male and female, everywhere are under responsibilities that cover all
their time, powers and opportunities. . . . How few must do the work!
How much to be done! How very short the "accepted time" in which to
do it. Besides you are Southerners, have been slaveholders; your dearest
friends are all in the sin and shame and peril. All these things give you
great access to [the] northern mind, great sway over it. . . .

Devote, consecrate your whole bodies, souls and spirits to the greater
work which you can do far better . . . than anybody else. Again, the abolition question is most powerfully preparative and introductory to the
other question. By pushing the former with all our might we are most
effectually advancing the latter. By absorbing the public mind in the
greatest of all violations of rights, we are purging its vision to detect
other violations.

Let us all first wake up the nation to lift millions of slaves of both
sexes from the dust, and turn them into MEN and then when we all
have our hand in, it will be an easy matter to take millions of females
from their knees and set them on their feet, or in other words transform
them from babies into women.

Your brother T.D. Weld

2.6.   Women Petition Congress

---

*Women abolitionists could not vote, but they arduously pur-
sued their right to petition, collecting signatures urging the ending
of the domestic slave trade in Washington, D.C., and in 1838,
condemning the annexation of Texas. With a "gag rule" in effect,*

these petitions could not be read in the House of Representatives, and ex-President John Quincy Adams, now a Representative from Massachusetts, became the chief opponent of this silencing. Adams did not claim any further extension of women's rights from the right of petition, but he did argue that the political effort to end slavery was a legitimate extension of women's moral responsibilities in the home. The gag rule was finally lifted in 1842.

"THE RIGHT OF THE PEOPLE, MEN AND WOMEN, TO PETITION"

When I last addressed the House I was engaged in discussing the principle asserted by the chairman of the Committee on Foreign Affairs; the practical effect of which must be to deprive one half the population of these United States of the right of petition before this House. I say it goes to deprive the entire female sex of all right of petition here. . . . I will read [the report of his remarks] again; it is highly important, and well deserving of the attention of this House, and its solemn decision. It referred to all petitions on the Subject of the annexation of Texas to this Union which come from women.

Many of these petitions were signed by women. He always felt regret when petitions thus signed were presented to the House relating to political matters. He thought that these females could have a sufficient field for the exercise of their influence in the discharge of their duties to their fathers, their husbands, or their children, cheering the domestic circle, and shedding over it the mild radiance of the social virtues, instead of rushing into the fierce struggles of political life. He felt sorrow at this departure from their proper sphere, in which there was abundant room for the practice of the most extensive benevolence and philanthropy, because he considered it discreditable, not only to their own particular section of the country, but also to the national character, and thus giving him a right to express this opinion . . .

Why does it follow that women are fitted for nothing but the cares of domestic life?. . . . I admit that it is their duty to attend to these things. . . . But I say that the correct principle is, that women are not only justified, but exhibit the most exalted virtue when they do depart from the domestic circle, and enter on the concerns of their country, of humanity, and of their God. The mere departure of woman from the duties of the domestic circle, far from being a reproach to her, is a virtue of the highest order, when it is done from purity of motive, by appropriate means and towards a virtuous purpose.

Now, I aver, further, that in the instance to which his observation

refers, . . . the act of petitioning against the annexation of Texas to this
Union, the motive was pure, the means appropriate, and the purpose
virtuous, in the highest degree. As an evident proof of this, I recur to
the particular petition from which this debate took its rise, . . . the first
petition I presented here against the annexation—a petition consisting
of three lines, and signed by 238 women of Plymouth, a principal town
in my own district. Their words are:

> The undersigned, women of Plymouth, (Mass.,) thoroughly aware
> of the sinfulness of slavery, and the consequent impolicy and dis-
> astrous tendency of its extension in our country, do most respect-
> fully remonstrate, with all our souls, against the annexation of
> Texas to the United States, as a slave-holding territory.

Those are the words of their memorial. . . . They petitioned under a
conviction that the consequence of the annexation would be the advancement of that which is sin in the sight of God, slavery. I say, further, that
the means were appropriate, because it is Congress who must decide on
the question; and, therefore, it is proper that they should petition Congress if they wish to prevent the annexation. And I say, in the third place,
that the end was virtuous, pure, and of the most exalted character . . . to
prevent the perpetuation and spread of slavery through America. I say,
moreover, that I subscribe, in my own person, to every word the petition
contains. . . .

Source: John Quincy Adams, *The Right of the People, Men and Women to Petition:
On the Freedom of Speech and of Debate*, 1838.

3

The Seneca Falls Convention and the Rise of the Women's Rights Movement

Historians agree that the first formal meeting of the women's rights movement took place in a small Methodist chapel in Seneca Falls, New York, in 1848. The Seneca Falls meeting is nearly always associated with its most flamboyant and self-promoting speaker, Elizabeth Cady Stanton. The daughter of a prominent and well-to-do upstate New York judge, Elizabeth and her husband Henry Stanton spent their honeymoon in 1840 attending the World Anti-Slavery Convention in London, but discovered, to Elizabeth's outrage, that the British abolitionists would not seat the six American women delegates on the floor. Consigned to the balcony, they were joined by American abolitionist William Lloyd Garrison in a show of protest. As they walked the streets of London, Elizabeth and sister delegate Lucretia Mott explored the idea of holding a women's rights convention in the United States upon their return.

Elizabeth Cady Stanton was soon the mother of three small children, and did not follow up on her plans until she moved from Boston to Seneca Falls, a small New York village near Utica on the Erie Canal, deep in the heart of the "burned over district" of revivalism and reform. Although the "Declaration of Sentiments" that emerged from the Seneca Falls Convention is one of the most eloquent statements of human freedom ever written in English, the convention itself should not be seen as a unique occurrence, but as one of a series of growing murmurs of protest by middle-class women. Like so many other meetings of the 1830s and 1840s, it was primarily a gathering of abolitionists but the first, as far as is known, whose organizers issued a public call to discuss women's rights. The first national convention of women's rights was held in Worcester two years later, and between 1848 and 1860 ten local and national conventions were held in the Northeast and the Midwest. While Elizabeth Cady Stanton is often given credit for first claiming the right to vote for women, it had, in fact, been proposed by Sarah and Angelina Grimké ten years earlier, and in 1846, six women from Jefferson County in upstate New York had petitioned the New York State constitutional convention for "equal, and civil and political rights with men," including the suffrage.[1] The Declaration of Sentiments at Seneca Falls was not a cry in the wilderness, but a set of ideas whose time had come, despite its unpopularity with most of American society.

Gerda Lerner, a pioneer in women's history, asked a significant question in a 1969 essay. Why was it "the lady" rather than "the mill girl" who first articulated a claim to full rights for her sex? While subsequent work by historians has shown that most women's rightists were not wealthy but from the "middling sorts," class and ethnicity were significant factors in the drafting of the Sentiments. The sixty-eight women and thirty-two men who attended the meeting were well-educated for their time, all Protestants and native-born. Most were from upstate New York and connected in some way to the bustling commerce and industrialization that accompanied the building of the Erie Canal. Only journalist and antislavery orator Frederick Douglass, from nearby Rochester, was black. Despite Douglass's enthusiasm for the Sentiments, its omission of any discussion of African-American women under slavery is striking.

Like the Declaration of Independence on which it was modeled, the Sentiments is a claim to the universality of rights for an entire class of individuals, not an exposition on the differences among them and the implication of those differences for oppression. Surely it was a significant theoretical step to describe all women as a class and to set forth the long list of discriminatory practices in the law, education, the professions, and politics that affected that class; it is difficult, even from the perspective of the twenty-first century, to add much to the Sentiments list in the way of legal rights. Nonetheless, it continued to be the case that poor, Native American, and slave women were not usually in a position to think mainly of themselves as individuals entitled to rights as citizens of the political state. Their problems were more acutely those of earning a living, protecting themselves from rape and abuse, and keeping families intact. While there were African-American women speaking up for both the antislavery and women's rights movements, none of their speeches before the Civil War have been recorded, except for unauthenticated recollections of talks by Sojourner Truth. Scholar Nell Irwin Painter has shown how important Truth's "primitivism" as an illiterate ex-slave was to the white women who dominated the public voice of the women's rights movement; more educated and middle-class black women were largely ignored or taken for granted.

Why did women such as Elizabeth Cady Stanton and her cohort of feminists, including Lucy Stone and Susan B. Anthony, neither of whom attended the Seneca Falls Convention but who became life-long activists for women's equality, feel entitled to claim their rights? Why were they indignant with the system as it was?

For one thing, free women's legal status in American society had deteriorated between the American Revolution and the 1840s. The law and the courts were dominated, not by the lofty and expansive principles of the Constitution, but by narrow statutes and the crabbed confines of English common law. The common law's chief expositor, William Blackstone, argued that married women's legal status was negated by marriage in coverture; husbands not only represented their wives in all lawsuits and legal matters, but held ownership of their property and wages. Most states allowed for the "reasonable" physical punishment of wives, discouraged divorce, even in the most dreadful of circumstances, and rarely granted women custody of their children unless husbands had deserted their families. There had been an erosion of women's dower rights (the entitlement of widows to the use of one third of their husband's property until their own deaths); in the new economy of fluid capital and frequent financial panics dower rights encumbered real estate. While some women had represented themselves in the courts and practiced lay medicine in the eighteenth century, new licensing regulations and the professionalization of medicine and the law raised impossible educational and apprenticeship barriers for women after 1800. Colleges were closed to them, and most female academies did not offer women students good training in science and mathematics. Even the new state property acts, which allowed women to keep title to the property they brought into marriage, including a measure passed in New York State in 1848, were as much designed to protect the holdings of fathers from the debts of their sons-in-law as to give married women new property rights.

But it was also the case that many native-born white women led more comfortable and self-directed lives than had their mothers, making these restrictions even more abhorrent. Women such as Lucy Stone and Elizabeth Cady Stanton joined the women's rights movement before the Civil War partly because they had rising expectations. Although they were closed out of most of the higher paying professions, they were better educated than ever, and could earn livings, meager as they were, through teaching, writing, and public speaking. Some were inheriting significant amounts of money. For the first time, women might postpone marriage or avoid it altogether, choosing "liberty, a better husband." A few bold women demanded higher education and training in the professions. Elizabeth Blackwell entered Geneva Medical College, a few miles from Seneca Falls, New York, in 1847 and became the first woman doctor in the United States. Lucy Stone, a farmer's daughter from West-brook, Massachusetts, was determined to attend college and graduated in 1847 from Oberlin College in Ohio, the first college in the United States to admit both blacks and women. If even "the most ignorant and de-graded men—both native and foreigners" could vote, sit on juries, and hold public office, why not women, especially these women, they asked?

In the 1850s, pioneering women's rightists proved their mettle. Eliza-beth Cady Stanton and Susan B. Anthony formed a fortuitous personal and political friendship when they left the Daughters of Temperance because its directors would not condone divorce. In a particularly bold move, women in upstate New York adopted Amelia Bloomer's costume of Turkish pantaloons and a tunic. Despite the fact that "bloomer" wear-ers were covered from wrist to neck to ankle, they were ridiculed and caricatured in the press, accused of wearing the pants in the family and forcing men to nurse the babies and do the dishes. The goal of the cos-tume was far more simple: freedom of movement and from fear of catch-ing voluminous dresses on fire, a significant cause of injury and death for women in the nineteenth century. Although they abandoned the cos-tume within a few years, women's rights activists continued to rail against the savagery of corsets and confining clothing for women and to urge what they delicately described as "voluntary motherhood," or leav-ing the decision to have children up to the wife. Alternating abolitionist work with women's rights organizing, Lucy Stone, Susan B. Anthony, and Sojourner Truth traveled across the Northeast and the old Midwest to speak for women's rights, sometimes encountering rotten tomatoes and worse. Lucy Stone was once "deluged with ice cold water" and "put on a shawl and went on with her lecture."[2] Truth was asked at one lecture to open her dress to prove she was a woman. Antoinette Brown Blackwell, Lucy Stone's college friend at Oberlin, became the first or-dained Presbyterian woman minister in the United States. Attempting to speak at the World Temperance Society meeting in New York City in 1853, she was hissed and booed for an hour and forced from the platform by male delegates, many of whom were clergymen. When Lucy Stone married Henry Blackwell in 1855, kept her own name, and gave birth to a daughter Alice, Susan B. Anthony was left virtually alone in the lecture field, nurtured by Elizabeth Cady Stanton, who, confined at home with a steady stream of small children, described herself as "a caged lioness."[3] This was a period when women could not combine motherhood and a career or travel on lecture tours with nursing infants. But these women made their political mark later in life, energetic old ladies who never gave up the fight. Even the steady ridicule they garnered did the cause good; there were few free people in the United States who did not know of them by 1860, and the very fear they had aroused showed that they had struck a chord that would not stop reverberating.

READING GUIDE

Basch, Norma, *In the Eyes of the Law: Women, Marriage, and Property in Nineteenth-Century New York*. Ithaca: Cornell University Press, 1982. This careful examination of the married women's property acts documents the glacial pace of actual reform. Despite new legislation that seemed to give women more authority over their property, Basch shows that the courts' interpretation of individual cases continued to re-enforce men's control over women's wages, income and property, and that these court cases became a major spur to the women's rights movement in the state of New York.

Collier-Thomas, Bettye, "Frances Ellen Watkins Harper: Abolitionist and Feminist Reformer, 1815–1911," in Ann D. Gordon, et al., eds, *African American Women and the Vote, 1837–1965*. Amherst: University of Massachusetts Press, 1997. A figure of renown in the African-American civil rights movement, Frances Ellen Watkins Harper has been discovered by historians of women as well. This essay is a helpful introduction to Harper, who was a powerful public speaker, an activist in the Woman's Christian Temperance Union, a novelist, and, after the Civil War, a suffragist. Harper's 1877 address, "The Colored Women of America," laid out an agenda that was later incorporated into the work of the National Association of Colored Women's Clubs.

DuBois, Ellen Carol, *Feminism and Suffrage: The Emergence of an Independent Women's Movement in America, 1848–1869*. Ithaca: Cornell University Press, 1978. DuBois examines the political progression of the first women's movement and argues that Anthony and Stanton's break with the temperance movement over the issue of divorce and their alliance with the abolitionists were critical theoretical steps. DuBois has continued to argue that suffrage was the most radical of the demands of the antebellum women's rights movement. In this early work, however, she gives women's rights advocates outside the Anthony and Stanton circle almost no attention.

Flexner, Eleanor, *Century of Struggle: The Woman's Rights Movement in the United States*. Cambridge: Harvard University Press, [1959] 1968. Flexner combed archives in the 1950s for a history of women's rights in a decade when feminism had fallen out of favor completely and there was no such field as women's history. Flexner discusses the plight and protests of female workers and African Americans as well as middle-class women's struggles for autonomy. No other scholar did more to revive interest in women's history and to put political struggle at its heart than Flexner, and this book remains a readable classic.

Gordon, Ann D., ed., *The Selected Papers of Elizabeth Cady Stanton and Susan B. Anthony*. New Brunswick, NJ: Rutgers University Press, 1997. This condensed collection of correspondence documents a long and fruitful relationship between two women over the long course of their lives. The papers show Stanton and Anthony as good writers, acerbic critics, and witty commentators, and their correspondence deserves a primary place in the canon of American letters.

Isenberg, Nancy, *Sex and Citizenship in Antebellum America*. Chapel Hill: University of North Carolina Press, 1998. This study of the discussion of women's rights between 1830 and 1860 goes beyond Seneca Falls and its organizers to similar conventions and clusters of activists in Ohio, Massachusetts, and New York. Isenberg demonstrates that what she calls the issue of co-equality was widespread. Rather than simply claiming the same rights as men or focusing mainly on suffrage, women's rightists before the Civil War almost always asked for an extensive societal and political co-equality based on women's and men's different but equally important contributions to American democracy. Claiming that women had the same moral and intellectual capacities as men, the rightists continued to find their most fundamental opposition in the mainstream Protestant churches. Nearly all women's rightists were forced, as a consequence, to become religious dissidents, disputing the (male) ministers' domination of the pulpit, and by extension, the political platform as well.

Lerner, Gerda, "The Lady and the Mill Girl: Changes in the Status of Women in the Age of Jackson," *American Studies* 10 (Spring, 1969), 5–15, and "The Meanings of Seneca Falls, 1848–1998," *Dissent* (Fall, 1998), 35–41. These two essays by an eminent U.S. historian of women span nearly a thirty-year period and contribute fresh thinking to the motivations behind the Declaration of Sentiments. "The Lady and the Mill Girl" remains one of the most important pieces of U.S. women's history ever written.

Painter, Nell Irvin, *Sojourner Truth: A Life, A Symbol*. New York: W.W. Norton and Company, 1996. A profound and masterful biography of a critical figure in the nineteenth-century women's movement and the African-American community. Painter shows how ex-slave Isabella Baumfree ("Sojourner Truth") was taken up by white women in the antislavery movement as a kind of exotic African "primitive," while the illiterate Truth eked out a living addressing both blacks and whites and selling her dictated autobiography and "spirit cards" (photographs of herself). This book sheds new light on the complex racial dynamics in a movement that spoke up for black women but also, often subconsciously, used them to promote white women's interests.

Rossi, Alice, ed., *The Feminist Papers: From Adams to de Beauvoir*. Boston: Northeastern University Press, 1988. The heart of this book of readings with helpful critical commentary spans the nineteenth-century women's movement in the United States, with particular attention paid to the upstate New York feminists and the Blackwell family. Rossi also includes some of the important British and European thinkers who influenced the Americans, including John Stuart Mill, Frances Wright, and Friedrich Engels.

Stanton, Elizabeth Cady, Susan B. Anthony, and Matilda Joslyn Gage, *History of Woman Suffrage*, vol. I. New York: Fowler and Wells, 1881. A first-hand account of the rise of the women's rights movement edited by three of its most important activists. Personal accounts, newspaper editorials, petitions, and biographical sketches comprise this first attempt to narrate a history of American women. Not surprisingly, Stanton and Anthony place the themselves at center stage, a bias that dominates twentieth-century scholarship of the women's rights movement as well.

Sterling, Dorothy, ed., *We Are Your Sisters: Black Women in the Nineteenth Century*. New York: W.W. Norton and Company, 1984. Defying the dictum that it was impossible to find materials documenting the lives of black women, Sterling combed archives for accounts and created this rich and inspiring collection of autobiographical and first-hand accounts. Her documents show how, at least before the Civil War, most African-American women remained focused, not on abstract notions of women as a legal class, but on struggles against segregation, racial discrimination, sexual abuse, and the all-consuming battle to end slavery.

NOTES

1. As quoted by Lori D. Ginzberg, *Women in Antebellum Reform* (Wheeling, IL: Harlan Davidson, Inc., 2000), 104.

2. Alice Stone Blackwell, "The Right of Women to Speak in Public—What They Have Done with It," n.d., Maud Wood Park Papers, Library of Congress.

3. Elizabeth Cady Stanton to Susan B. Anthony, in Ida Husted Harper, ed., *The Life and Work of Susan B. Anthony* (Indianapolis: Bowen-Merrill, 1898), vol. 1: 142.

DOCUMENTS

3.1. Sarah Grimké Urges Women to Assume Their Political Responsibilities, 1837

Sarah Grimké's Letters on the Equality of Sexes and the Condition of Women, *which appeared in the* Spectator *in 1837 and in* The Liberator *in 1838 were the first published "feminist" treatises in the United States, making many of the same claims for female equality made by Mary Wollstonecraft in 1792. While Wollstonecraft stressed secular ideas of liberty and equality, Grimké took her rationale from the parity of Christians in God's salvation and the moral obligation of women to challenge social inequities such as slavery.*

"WHAT ARE THE DUTIES OF WOMAN AT THE PRESENT TIME?"

Until we comprehend the design of God in the creation of woman; until we take our stand, side by side with our brother; until we . . . lose, in our moral, intellectual, and immortal nature, the consciousness of sex, we shall never fulfil the end of our existence. . . . Duties belong to *situation*, not to sex; a mother has duties totally different from a single woman; but the rights and responsibilities of men and women as moral beings are identical, and must necessarily be so, if their nature is the same, and their relations to the supreme Being precisely similar. With regard to all moral reformations, men and women have the same duties and the same rights. The ground I take on this is very plain. . . .

The present is a deeply interesting and important period in the history of woman. . . . Can woman turn from so much wretchedness, and suppose that when she has seen well to the ways of her household, and prepared a well spread table for her family, all her duties are performed and the end of her existence is answered? . . . In the present state of Christendom, every woman is acting for, or against the great work of moral reformation; every woman, . . . is retarding, or accelerating the spread of truth and righteousness on the earth, by her example and conversation. . . . There is so much to do, no one need be at any loss. Some have time, others have money, others can write, others can speak. . . . I would say, emancipate yourselves from every kind of bondage, if the Lord require it, and this *you* only can decide. . . . Remember, to God your account has been rendered, and no man, or body of men, can answer for us. . . . Whilst I earnestly desire that women may come up to their duties in the great work of regenerating a fallen world, I entreat them to do it openly fearless, trusting in the Lord. I have known some women sign petitions for the abolition of slavery in the District of Columbia, secretly, because their husbands forbade their doing it, or disapprove of it. . . . Never deceive a man by a *show* of submission. Tell him that you cannot obey him, rather than God, and that it is your intention to sign that petition. . . . Such an open and Christian course of conduct will secure the esteem and confidence of almost any man, while it will take from him the charter he now fancies he holds. . . . I am persuaded, if we did not love our chains, man would, after a short resistance, yield to the power of truth, and unbind our fetters, but we love to be idolized. . . . We would rather be the playthings of man, than to stand on an equality with him, because if we assume the dignified station of free agents, of moral beings, we at once avow ourselves liable to the same responsibilities which rest upon him.

Source: Sarah M. Grimké, *Letters on the Equality of the Sexes and the Condition of Woman, Addressed to Mary S. Parker, President of the Boston Female Antislavery Society*, October 10, 1837.

3.2.   Simon Greenleaf Responds to *Letters on the Equality of the Sexes*

Simon Greenleaf was a preeminent professor of law at Harvard Law School and was also well known for his erudition in Protestant literary circles. Greenleaf believed that the protection of women in the family under coverture was an indication of the superiority of Christian societies over more "primitive" cultures that supposedly "exploited" women's labor and failed to protect them from sexual abuse. In 1838 and 1839 he gave several lectures in New England that were, in all probability, a direct response to the challenge posed by Sarah Grimké's publication. This anonymous article in a Protestant periodical has been attributed to him.

"ON THE LEGAL RIGHTS OF WOMAN"

The public ear has been filled with declamation upon the wrongs of woman, —her political and legal non-existence, —her natural equality, —her inalienable rights, and her degrading servitude; as though the sex, at some early period, had been conquered and subjugated by man, and were still held in a state of bondage. Disquietudes, deep and distressing,

are thus created, where peace and confidence ought to prevail. . . . Our
first step . . . is to disabuse ourselves of existing prejudices, by inquiring
into the true and actual position of woman. . . . We shall better understand the value of her position in this country . . . by . . . considering her
condition in other nations, both in ancient and modern times, and the
depths from which she has been raised to her present most just elevation
of rank in the Christian world. . . . It is remarkable that the influence of
Christianity, wherever it has been felt in any nation, has given woman
a new station in society, releasing her from bondage, and rendering her
at once the companion, the equal, and the friend of man. . . .

The experience of all nations has shown that the state of society has
been rendered miserable whenever both sexes have mingled in party
politics. . . . It is for the preservation of social peace, therefore, and of
domestic happiness, that our law has assigned to the labor of moving
the *political* machine to *men*. In this division of labor, the rights of woman
are not infringed. . . . Should she feel inclined to murmur because she is
bound by laws in the making of which she had no active participation,
let her remember that the blood shed in her defense, on the battle field
was not her own. . . . But subject to those restrictions in *political* matters,
. . . we are not aware of any distinction between the legal rights of unmarried women, and of men. . . . Should she *choose* to violate the propri-
eties of her station, whether by travelling in the character of public
lecturer, by engaging with masculine energy in the distracting controversies of the day, . . . the *law* merely consigns her to the tribunal of *public
opinion*, and condemns her only to its withering rebuke. From the cradle
to the grave, the law watches over her with untiring vigilance, and
guards her *rights* with paternal care. . . .

But, *it is objected*, that "*after* marriage, woman becomes a mere *cipher
in the eye of the law*". . . . This most delicate and interesting of all human
relations . . . is treated by our law, with the greatest degree of care, since
it affects all classes of society, and is the principal source of domestic
and social happiness. This is the object for which the parties unite themselves, inseparably, and for ever. . . . As the union of husband and wife
is thus intimate, indissoluble and perpetual, there is little occasion for
any distinction in the ownership of their common property. As it is a
common fund, . . . it can make but little difference, in the results, by
whose name it is called. . . .

Restless spirits, may raise discontents with the system; for it is always
easier to point out faults, than to correct them. But a fair survey of
[Woman's] position will evince the liberal policy and extreme care of the
law, in guarding her rights, and promoting her welfare. And happy will
it be for our land, if, instead of following modern agitators and reform-

ers, in their visionary schemes of fancied improvement, we prefer, with better reason, to enjoy the advantages already secured by our own familiar and well-tried institutions.

Source: Christian Review, 5, June 1840: 269–89.

3.3.   Keziah Kendall Disagrees with Simon Greenleaf

This remarkable letter from a woman who may have lived on a Massachusetts farm was recently discovered in the papers of Simon Greenleaf at Harvard Law School. Kendall had heard a Greenleaf lecture and wrote to complain about its content. According to Kendall, she and her two sisters ran a prosperous farm, but the laws of coverture and the prospect of a younger sister's flighty decision to marry in haste made Kendall fear for their future. She shows a keen interest in the law as it applies to women, argues that women who are taxed should have equal property rights, and defends the connection made by the Grimké sisters between the slavery of blacks and the bonds of womanhood.

KEZIAH KENDALL TO SIMON GREENLEAF [1839?]

I take the liberty to write to you on the subject of the Lyceum lecture you delivered last Feb. but as you are not acquainted with me I think I will introduce myself. My name is Keziah Kendall. I live not many miles from Cambridge, on a farm with two sisters, one older, one younger than myself. I am thirty two. Our parents and only brother are dead -we have a good estate -comfortable house -nice barn, garden, orchard &c and money in the bank besides. Jemima is a very good manager in the house, keeps everything comfortable—sees that the milk is nicely prepared for market—looks after everything herself, and rises before day, winter and summer,—but she never had any head for figures, and always expects me to keep all accounts, and attend to all business concerns. Keranhappuck, (who is called Kerry) is quite young, only nineteen, and as she was a little girl when mother died, we've always petted her, and let her do as she pleased, and now she's courted. Under these circumstances the whole responsibility of our property, not less than twenty five thousand dollars rests upon me. I am not over fond of money, but I have worked hard ever since I was a little girl, and tried to do all in my power to help earn, and help save, and it would be strange if I did not think more of it than those who never earned anything, and never saved anything they could get to spend, and you know Sir, there are many such girls nowadays.

Well—our milkman brought word when he came from market that you were a going to lecture on the legal rights of women, and so I thought I would go and learn. Now I hope you wont think me bold when I say, I did not like that lecture much. I dont speak of the manner, it was pretty spoken enough, but there was nothing in it but what every body knows. We all know about a widow's thirds, and we all know that a man must maintain his wife, and we all know that he must pay her debts, if she has any—but I never heard of a yankee woman marrying in debt. What I wanted to know, was good reasons for some of those laws that I cant account for. I do hope if you are ever to lecture at the Lyceum again, that you will give us some. I must tell my story to make you understand what I mean.

One Lyceum lecture that I heard in C.[ambridge] stated that the Americans went to war with the British because they were taxed without being represented in Parliament. Now we are taxed every year to the full amount of every dollar we possess—town, county, state taxes—taxes for land, for movables, for money and all. Now I dont want to go representative or any thing else, any more that I do to be a "constable or a sheriff," but I have no voice about public improvements, and I dont see the justice of being taxed any more than the "revolutionary heroes" did. You mention that woman [sic] here, are not treated like heathen and Indian women—we know that—nor do I think we are treated as Christian women ought to be, according to the Bible rule of doing to others as you would others should do unto you. I am told (Not by you) that if a woman dies a week after she's married that her husband takes all her personal property and the use of her real estate as long as he lives—if a man dies his wife can have her thirds—this does not come up to the Gospel rule.

Now the young fellow that is engaged to our Kerry, is a pleasant clever fellow, but he is not quite one and twenty, and I dont s'pose he ever earned a coat in his life. Uncle told me there was a way for a woman to have her property trustee'd, and I told it to Kerry—but she, poor girl has romantic notions owing to reading too many novels, and when I told her of it, she would not hear of such a thing—"What take the law to keep my property away from James before I marry him—if it was a million of dollars he should have it all." So you see I think the law is in fault here—to tell you the truth I do not think young men are near so careful about getting in debt as girls, and I have known more than one that used their wife's money to pay off old scores. . . .

Another thing—you made some references upon women following the Anti's. Women have joined the Antislavery societies, and why? Women are kept to slaves as well as men—it is a common cause, deny the justice of it, who can! To be sure I do not wish to go about lecturing like the Misses Grimkie [sic], but I have not the knowledge they have, and I verily believe that if I had been brought up among slaves as they were, and knew all that they know, and felt a call from humanity to speak, I should run the venture of your displeasure, and that of a good many others like you. . . .

Yours with regard
Keziah Kendall.

Source: Papers of Simon Greenleaf, Harvard Law School Library.

3.4.   Lucy Stone and Her Sister-in-Law Discuss Woman's Place

---

Lucy Stone, born in 1818, grew up in West Brookfield, a small village in western Massachusetts, and was dismayed by her mother's difficult life of domestic labor and never-ending pregnancies. After teaching in a district school for nine years, she used her savings to attend female seminaries and, in 1843, entered Oberlin College in Ohio. Invited to prepare a commencement address to be read by a male proxy in 1847, she refused, and instead decided to go on the lecture circuit as a speaker for women's rights. This letter from Sarah Stone, her brother William's wife, is a reminder that most women in the 1840s still opposed the idea of voting. Sarah Stone's comments on wages must have especially rankled Lucy, because she had protested during her teaching years about the disparity in wages for male and female teachers with equal qualifications.

LETTER FROM SARAH STONE TO LUCY STONE,
November 28, 1846

My dear Sister,

I don't know as I was very much surprised at the content of your letter. I have *half-believed* for a long time that you were preparing for a public speaker, though I hoped I might be mistaken. Not that I think it wrong in itself, but because I think it an employment a great many grades *below*, what I believe my *only* and *dearly loved sister* qualified to engage in. I don't hardly know what you mean by "laboring for the restoration and salvation of our sex" but I conclude you mean a salvation from some thralldom imposed by man. . . . I don't believe a woman is groaning under half so heavy a yoke of bondage as you imagine. I am sure I do not feel burdened by anything man has laid upon me, be sure

I can't vote, but what care I for this, I *would* not if I could. I know there is a distinction made in the wages of males and females when they perform the same labor, this I think is unjust, and it is the only thing in which woman is oppressed, that I know of, but women have no one to blame, but themselves in this matter. If as a general thing they had qualified themselves, as men have they would command the same price, but they have not. . . . I think my sister if you would spend the remainder of your life in *educating* our sex, you would do a *far greater* good than you will if you spend your *noble energies* in forever *hurling* "back the insults and indignities that men heap upon us." This I am sure you can never do "by the grace of God" for it is entirely contrary to his spirit and teachings.

Your sister, Sarah

Source: Stone Blackwell Papers, Library of Congress.

3.5.   The Declaration of Sentiments, 1848

The drafters of the Declaration of Sentiments articulated publicly what many women's rights advocates had been writing and thinking about for more than a decade. Abandoning the religious context that had informed Sarah Grimké's Letters on the Equality of the Sexes, *the drafters chose the liberal humanism of the Declaration of Independence and of Mary Wollstonecraft's radicalism instead, but borrowed heavily from the Grimkés' idea that sexual inequality had a devastating psychological impact on women.*

"THE DECLARATION OF SENTIMENTS AT SENECA FALLS,"
July 20, 1848

When, in the course of human events, it becomes necessary for one portion of the family of man to assume among the people of the earth a position different from that which they have hitherto occupied, but one to which the laws of nature and of nature's God entitle them, a decent respect to the opinion of mankind requires that they should declare the causes that impel them to such a course.

We hold these truths to be self-evident: that all men and women are created equal; that they are endowed by their Creator with certain unalienable rights; that among these are life, liberty, and the pursuit of happiness; that to secure these rights governments are instituted, deriving their just powers from the consent of the governed. Whenever any form of government becomes destructive of these ends, it is the right of those who suffer from it to refuse allegiance to it, and to insist upon the institution of a new government, laying its foundation on such principles, and organizing its powers in such form, as to them shall seem most likely to effect their safety and happiness. Prudence, indeed, will dictate that governments long established should not be changed for light and transient causes; and accordingly all experience hath shown that mankind are more disposed to suffer, while evils are sufferable, than to right themselves by abolishing the forms to which they were accustomed. But when a long train of abuses and usurpations, pursuing invariably the same object evinces a design to reduce them under absolute despotism, it is their duty to throw off such government, and to provide new guards for their future security. Such has been the patient sufferance of the women under this government, and such is now the necessity which constrains them to demand the equal station to which they are entitled.

The history of mankind is a history of repeated injuries and usurpations on the part of man toward woman, having in direct object the establishment of an absolute tyranny over her. To prove this, let facts be submitted to a candid world.

He has never permitted her to exercise her inalienable right to the elective franchise.

He has compelled her to submit to laws, in the formation of which she had no voice.

He has withheld from her rights which are given to the most ignorant and degraded men—both native and foreigners.

Having deprived her of this first right of a citizen, the elective franchise, thereby leaving her without representation in the halls of legislation, he has oppressed her on all sides.

He has made her, if married, in the eye of the law, civilly dead.

He has taken from her all right in property, even to the wages she earns.

He has made her, morally, an irresponsible being, as she can commit many crimes with impunity, provided they be done in the presence of her husband. In the covenant of marriage, she is compelled to promise obedience to her husband, he becoming, to all intents and purposes, her master—the law giving him power to deprive her of her liberty, and to administer chastisement.

He has so framed the laws of divorce, as does accord to woman moral superiority, it is preeminently his duty to encourage her to speak and teach, as she has an opportunity, in all religious assemblies.

Resolved, That the same amount of virtue, delicacy, and refinement of behavior that is required of woman in the social state, should also be required of man, and the same transgressions should be visited with equal severity on both man and woman.

Resolved, That the objection of indelicacy and impropriety, which is so often brought against woman when she addresses a public audience, comes with a very ill-grace from those who encourage, by their attendance, her appearance on the stage, in the concert, or in feats of the circus.

Resolved, That woman has too long rested satisfied in the circumscribed limits which corrupt customs and a perverted application of the Scriptures have marked out for her, and that it is time she should move in the enlarged sphere which her great Creator has assigned her.

Resolved, That it is the duty of the women of this country to secure to themselves their sacred right to the elective franchise.

Resolved, That the equality of human rights results necessarily from the fact of the identity of the race in capabilities and responsibilities.

Resolved, therefore, That, being invested by the Creator with the same capabilities, and the same consciousness of responsibility for their exercise, it is demonstrably the right and duty of woman, equally with man, to promote every righteous cause by every righteous means; and especially in regard to the great subjects of morals and religion, it is self-evidently her right to participate with her brother in teaching them, both in private and in public, by writing and by speaking, by any instrumentalities proper to be used, and in any assemblies proper to be held; and this being a self-evident truth growing out of the divinely implanted principles of human nature, any custom or authority adverse to it, whether modern or wearing the hoary sanction of antiquity, is to be regarded as a self-evident falsehood, and at war with mankind.

At the last session Lucretia Mott offered and spoke to the following resolution:

Resolved, That the speedy success of our cause depends upon the zealous and untiring efforts of both men and women, for the overthrow of the monopoly of the pulpit, and for the securing to woman an equal participation with men in the various trades, professions, and commerce.

3.6.   Newspapers Respond to the Declaration of Sentiments

Except for Frederick Douglass in his abolitionist paper North Star, *editors of the northeastern newspapers responded with derision to the Seneca Falls platform.*

"INSURRECTION AMONG THE WOMEN"

A female Convention has just been held at Seneca Falls, N.Y., at which was adopted a "declaration of rights," setting forth, among other things, that "all men and *women* are created equal, and endowed by their Creator with certain inalienable rights." The list of grievances which the *Amazons* exhibit, concludes by expressing a determination to insist that woman shall have "immediate admission to all the rights and privileges which belong to them as citizens of the United States." . . . This is *bolting* with a vengeance.

Source: Worcester *Telegraph,* July, 1848.

"THE WOMEN OF PHILADELPHIA"

Our Philadelphia ladies not only possess beauty, but they are celebrated for discretion, modesty, and unfeigned diffidence, as well as wit, vivacity, and good nature. Whoever heard of a Philadelphia lady setting up for a reformer, or standing out for woman's rights, or assisting to *man* the election grounds, raise a regiment, command a legion, or address a jury? Our ladies glow with a higher ambition. They soar to rule the hearts of their worshipers, and secure obedience by the sceptre [*sic*] of affection. The tenure of their power is a law of nature, not a law of man, and hence they fear no insurrection, and never experience the shock of a revolution in their dominions. But all women are not as reasonable as ours of Philadelphia. The Boston ladies contend for the rights of women. The New York girls aspire to mount the rostrum, to do all the voting, and, we suppose, all the fighting too. . . . Our Philadelphia girls object to fighting and holding office. . . . Women have enough influence over human affairs without being politicians. Is not everything managed by female influence? Mothers, grandmothers, aunts, and sweethearts manage everything. Men have nothing to do but to listen and obey to the "of course, my dear, you will, and of course, my dear, you won't." Their rule is absolute; their power unbounded. Under such a system men have no claim to rights, especially "equal rights."

A woman is nobody. A wife is everything. A pretty girl is equal to ten thousand men, and a mother is, next to God, all powerful. . . . The ladies of Philadelphia, therefore, "under the influence of the most serious sober second thoughts," are resolved to maintain their rights as Wives, Belles, Virgins, and Mothers, and not as Women.

Source: Public Ledger and Daily Transcript, July, 1848.

AN EDITORIAL BY FREDERICK DOUGLASS

One of the most interesting events of the past week, was the holding of what is technically styled a Woman's Rights Convention at Seneca Falls. The speaking, addresses, and resolution of this extraordinary meeting was wholly conducted by women; and although they evidently felt themselves in a novel position, it is but simple justice to say that their whole proceedings were characterized by marked ability and dignity.

No one present, we think, however much he might be disposed to differ from the views advanced by the leading speakers on that occasion, will fail to give them credit for brilliant talents and excellent dispositions. . . . Several interesting documents setting forth the rights as well as the grievances of women were read. Among these was a Declaration of Sentiments, to be regarded as the basis of a grand movement for attaining the civil, social, political, and religious rights of women. We should not do justice to our own convictions, or to the excellent persons connected with this infant movement, if we did not in this connection offer a few remarks on the general subject which the Convention met to consider and the objects they seek to attain. . . . A discussion of the rights of animals would be regarded with far more complacency by many of what are called the "wise" and the "good" of our land, than would a discussion of the rights of women. It is, in their estimation to be guilty of evil thoughts, to think that woman is entitled to equal rights with man. Many who have at last made the discovery that the negroes have some rights as well as other members of the human family, have yet to be convinced that women are entitled to any. Eight years ago a number of persons of this description actually abandoned the anti-slavery cause, lest by giving their influence in that direction they might possibly be giving countenance to the dangerous heresy that woman, in respect to rights, stands on an equal footing with man. In the judgment of such persons the American slave system, with all its concomitant horrors, is less to be deplored than this "wicked" idea. It is perhaps needless to say, that we cherish little sympathy for such sentiments or respect for such prejudices. Standing as we do up on the watchtower of human freedom, we cannot be deterred from an expression of our approbation of any movement, however humble, to improve and elevate the character of any members of the human family. . . . In respect to political rights, we hold woman to be justly entitled to all we claim for man. We go farther, and express our conviction that all political rights which it is expedient for man to exercise, it is equally so for woman. All that distinguishes man as an intelligent and accountable being, is equally true of woman, and if that government only is just which governs by the free consent of the governed, there can be no reason in the world for denying to woman the exercise of the elective franchise, or a hand in making and administering the laws of the land. Our doctrine is that "right is of no sex." We therefore bid the women engaged in this movement our humble God-speed.

Source: Rochester *North Star*, July 28, 1848.

3.7.   Frances Ellen Watkins Describes the Concerns of African-American Women

Although African-American women must have spoken about the rights of women before the Civil War, none of the texts of these speeches have survived. Frances Ellen Watkins was born free in Baltimore, Maryland, and although well-educated and the author of a book of poetry, could only find work as a domestic servant or a dress-maker. A militant abolitionist who worked in the Underground Railroad to help slaves escape from the South, Watkins was a supporter of John Brown and admired his armed raid on Harper's Ferry, West Virginia, in 1859. In these letters to her friend William Still, an organizer of the Underground Railroad in Philadelphia, she identifies herself not so much as a speaker in need of women's rights, but as a member of an oppressed race whose interests she might advance through lecturing and boycotting slave-produced goods.

LETTERS OF FRANCES ELLEN WATKINS

1852: What would you do if you were in my place? Would you give up and go back and work at your trade (dress-making)? There are no people that need all the benefits resulting from a well-directed education more than we do. The condition of our people, the wants of our children, and the welfare of our race demand the aid of every helping hand. It is a work of time, a labor of patience, to become an effective school teacher, and it should be a work of love in which they who engage should not abate heart or hope until it is done.

1854: Well, I am out lecturing. I have lectured every night this week; besides addressed a Sunday-school, and I shall speak, if nothing prevent, to-night. My lectures have met with success. Last night I lectured in a white church in Providence. Mr. Gardener was present, and made the estimate of about six hundred persons. Never, perhaps was a speaker, old or young, favored with a more attentive audience. My voice is not wanting in strength as I am aware of, to reach pretty well over the house. My maiden lecture was Monday night in New Bedford on the Elevation and Education of our People.

The agent of the State Anti-Slavery Society of Maine travels with me, and she is a pleasant, dear sweet lady. I do like her so. We travel together, eat together and sleep together. (She is a white woman). In fact

I have not been in one colored person's house since I left Massachusetts; but I have a pleasant time. I have met with some of the kindest treatment up here that I have ever received.

I spoke on Free Produce, and now by the way I believe in that kind of Abolition. Oh, how can we pamper our appetites upon luxuries drawn from reluctant fingers? Oh, could slavery exist long if it did not sit on a commercial throne? I have reason to be thankful that I am able to give a little more for a Free labor dress, if it is coarser. I can thank God that upon its warp and woof I see no stain of blood and tears; that to procure a little finer muslin for my limbs no crushed and broken heart went out in sighs. If the liberation of the slave demanded it, I could consent to part with a portion of the blood from my own veins if that would do him any good.

1858: Now let me tell you about Pennsylvania. I have been in every New England state, in New York, Canada and Ohio, but of all these places, this is about the meanest of all, as far as the treatment of colored people is concerned. The other day I, in attempting to ride in one of the city cars, after I had entered, the conductor came to me and wanted me to go out on the platform. Now, was not that brave and noble? As a matter of course, I did not. Someone asked that I be permitted to sit in a corner. I did not move but kept the same seat. When I was about to leave, he refused my money and I threw it down on the car floor and got out, after I had ridden as far as I wished. Such impudence!

On the Carlisle road I was interrupted and insulted several times. Two men came after me in one day. I have met, of course, with kindness among individuals and families; all is not dark in Pennsylvania, but the shadow of slavery, oh, how drearily it hangs.

Source: William Still, *The Underground Railroad*. Philadelphia, 1872: 755–80.

3.8.   A Utica Newspaper Scolds Susan B. Anthony

In the difficult decade of the 1850s, Anthony often managed to speak on women's rights while ostensibly lecturing on temperance or antislavery. She was also wearing the Bloomer costume and encouraging women to take more control over their own bodies. The response elicited here is a nearly timeless derogatory attack, implying that feminists are sex-starved and promiscuous at the same time, unattractive, and misanthropic, encouraging other women to hate men.

EDITORIAL IN THE UTICA *TELEGRAPH*

We conceived a very unfavorable opinion of this *Miss* Anthony when she performed in this city on a former occasion, but we confess that, after listening attentively to her discourse last evening, we were inexpressibly disgusted with the impudence and impiety evinced in her lecture. Personally repulsive, she seems to be laboring under feelings of strong hatred toward men, the effect, we assume, of jealousy and neglect. . . . With a degree of impiety which was both startling and disgusting, this shrewish *maiden* counseled the numerous wives and mothers present to separate from their husbands whenever they became intemperate, *and particularly not to allow the said husbands to add another child to the family.* . . . Think of such advice given in public by one who claims to be a *maiden* lady!

She announced quite confidently that wives don't de facto love their husbands if they are dissipated. Everyday observation proves the utter falsity of this statement, and if there is one characteristic of the sex which more than another elevates and ennobles it, it is the *persistency* and intensity of woman's love for man. But what does Miss Anthony know of the thousand delights of married life; of the sweet stream of affection, of the golden ray of love which ever beams through life's ills? Bah!. . . . Miss Anthony concluded with a flourish of trumpets . . . after which she gathered her short skirts about her tight pants, sat down and wiped her spectacles.

Source: Ida Husted Harper, *The Life and Work of Susan B. Anthony*, vol. I. Indianapolis: Merrill, 1898.

4

The Fourteenth Amendment and the "New Departure"

In the spring of 1865 advocates of racial and sexual equality looked to the future with renewed hope. The nation's dreadful Civil War was over. Susan B. Anthony, the meagerly paid director of the Women's National Loyal League in New York City, had coordinated the collection of 100,000 signatures on petitions for universal emancipation. The Loyal League presented a petition to the Congress of the United States drafted by Elizabeth Cady Stanton demanding woman suffrage.

But voting rights for women was the last thing on the agenda of Congress. With Abraham Lincoln now dead and southern sympathizer Andrew Johnson installed as president in the White House, protecting ex-slaves became a national emergency, despite the speedy ratification of the Thirteenth Amendment in 1865. Conservative whites in the yet unreconstructed South drafted Black Codes that limited freed-people's basic rights and reintroduced virtual slavery. Violence against African Americans was commonplace, and in 1866 race riots of whites attacking blacks culminated in murder and mayhem in Memphis and New Orleans.

With most southern senators and representatives still out of the U.S. Congress, the Republicans launched a program of Reconstruction in the South. Although limited in numbers and stretched thin across the South, the U.S. Army and the Freedmen's Bureau were to provide federal civil rights protection for blacks and enforce voting rights for black men, encouraged in the southern legislatures by a Fourteenth Amendment to the U.S. Constitution in 1868. Because voting qualifications for citizens and the civil protection of their inhabitants had been left to the states in the U.S. Constitution, the Fourteenth Amendment represented a bold new attempt, as many northern Democrats and ex-Confederates claimed, to assert federal jurisdiction in the states.

From the 1820s on, the ideal of universal adult (white) male suffrage was a widely accepted marker of full citizenship in the states, a trend often noted by women's rights advocates. Unlike their eighteenth-century counterparts, mid-nineteenth-century politicians knew they had to address the issue of woman suffrage; however illegitimate they thought it might be, it had been raised for public discussion in the 1840s and was the subject of petitions to Congress thereafter. In an increasingly diverse nation of ethnic groups, religions, and foreign-born citizens, there were other categories of citizens whose exclusion by white elites in the states needed reaffirming as well: the Chinese in California, for example, who were barred specifically by the state constitution from voting or holding property. In New England, large numbers of the foreign-born, even if they were naturalized citizens, might be disqualified from voting on the basis of their religion, education, or property-holding.

The Fourteenth Amendment decreed that states that excluded adult "male inhabitants" who were citizens of the United States from the polls would have their representation in the House of Representatives reduced in proportion to the number of eligible excluded voters. Senator Charles Sumner, who had presented the Women's Loyal League petition for suffrage to Congress but then spoke against its timing as "inopportune," claimed later that he had covered nineteen pages of paper with crossed out phrases "to get rid of the word 'male' and yet keep 'negro suffrage' . . . but it could not be done."[1]

The Fourteenth Amendment was submitted to the states in June 1866, and fully ratified in 1868. Some ex-slaves had voted under the protection of the U.S. Army in 1868 and 1870, infuriating white southerners, but also making the ratification of the Reconstruction amendments by key state legislatures possible. The first section of the Fourteenth Amendment was designed to guarantee the civil rights of ex-slaves. In what would later be hotly contested and malleable language, the states were forbidden to "abridge the privileges or immunities of citizens of the United States" or to "deprive any person of life, liberty, or property without due process of law," or to "deny any person within its jurisdiction the equal protection of the law." Perhaps no other piece of the Constitution had as much future import for expanding the rights of American citizens as the first section of the Fourteenth Amendment. One thing was immediately clear: while the drafters of the amendment intended that black women be viewed as citizens and persons to be protected by the federal government, they did not intend to impose universal suffrage on the states, and said so explicitly in the second section of the amendment by introducing the word "male," for the first time, into the Constitution. The fullest discussion of the gendered language of the Fourteenth Amendment in Congress erupted in December of 1866 over an amendment, introduced by a Democratic party senator hostile to voting rights for blacks, to end the barring of persons from the polls on the basis of either sex or race in the District of Columbia. Senators made clear in public debate that woman suffrage was either untimely or ludicrous, and certain to wreck the voting prospects of black men—along with the political fortunes of the Republican party. The Fourteenth Amendment emblazoned that "one little word" *male* in the Constitution for the foreseeable future, but for naught; the contorted language of the second section did nothing to spur the unreconstructed southern states into changing their constitutions until compelled to do so by federal law.

It would take the more positive and simple language of the Fifteenth Amendment, ratified in 1870, to bring universal black male suffrage, at least for the time being, to the entire nation. Congressmen from the Mid-Atlantic and New England states quickly defeated a version of it that would have added naturalized citizenship, property, education, or religion as conditions that could not be used by the states to make citizens ineligible to vote. A provision to list the condition of sex as well received only a handful of votes, leaving only race, color, and previous condition of servitude. The Fifteenth Amendment thus reaffirmed the Fourteenth's exclusion of voting rights on the basis of sex and left the door open for continued exclusion by the states on particular grounds as long as they were not those of race or color.

How did advocates of equality for both women and African Americans respond to these measures? While the import of the first section of the Fourteenth Amendment was not grasped immediately by leaders of women's rights, the language of the second section was painfully clear and forced all abolitionists to confront a choice between half a loaf or none. Nearly all African-American leaders and most women's rightists endorsed the Fourteenth Amendment as an emergency measure necessary to the present and future safety of ex-slaves. They agreed with Frederick Douglass that this had to be "the Negro's hour." But a small number of women's rights leaders, most notably Elizabeth Cady Stanton and Susan B. Anthony, refused to go along with the Fourteenth Amendment and argued for its defeat. Stanton had claimed already in 1860 that "the prejudice against sex is more deeply rooted and more unreasonably maintained than that against color," and she, in particular, responded to the Fourteenth Amendment with "overtly racist" language, expressing "white women's special fury that men they considered their inferiors had been enfranchised before them."[2] Beginning as early as her 1865 petition to Congress and extending over the rest of the century, Stanton underscored the voting credentials of native-born, Protestant, educated women in contrast to those of illiterate immigrants, "primitive" ex-slaves, Asians, and Catholics. Stanton and Susan B. Anthony joined forces with the notorious racist Democrat George Train in Kansas to promote a state referendum on woman suffrage in 1868, and a year later Anthony and Stanton left the Equal Rights Association to create the National Woman Suffrage Association.

Stanton and Anthony have been heralded in recent biographies as valiant women who refused to compromise on the principle of women's equality; Lucy Stone and Henry Blackwell, who opted for political pragmatism and civil rights for blacks, have been labeled conservatives. The truth is more complex. Women who had claimed their own rights before the Civil War all recognized the disastrous effect of the Fourteenth and Fifteenth Amendments for women's equality, whether they supported them or not. Whether or not they supported the amendments, they mobilized in a variety of ways to mount what they described as a "New Departure" claiming, unequivocally, the right to vote. Historian Joan Hoff has argued that the amendments galvanized a new and more vigorous women's movement but also narrowed that movement's political purpose to obtaining woman suffrage. In contrast to Hoff, Ellen DuBois believes that the ideology of woman suffrage and militancy of the new departure had radical implications. Proponents of woman suffrage in the Reconstruction years emphasized woman's potential autonomy in the workplace and in the family once she was an independent citizen with the same rights as a man. The possibility of claiming her own living and controlling her own body would be amplified if she had the power of citizenship the vote bestowed. In their discussions of the vote in the 1860s, at least, women's rightists were careful to emphasize that possession of the vote would also be critical to black women's autonomy. This idea was succinctly expressed by Sojourner Truth: "If colored men get their rights, and not colored women theirs, you see the colored men will be masters over the women, and it will be just as bad as it was before."[3]

During the decade of the New Departure from 1868 to 1878, woman suffrage activists spoke to legislative committees, disrupted the polls by attempting to vote, and engaged in civil disobedience. In 1868 women in a variety of places tried to register to vote, and some succeeded in voting. In the spiritualist community of Vineland, New Jersey, women voted in 1868, and a year later, Lucy Stone and her mother attempted, unsuccessfully, to vote in nearby Roseville. The territory of Wyoming gave its small population of women the vote in 1869, and in 1870, there was a wave of attempted voting by groups of women in localities across the nation, including African-American women in South Carolina. In 1872 Susan B. Anthony was arrested by a federal agent after voting in Rochester, New York, and in St. Louis, Missouri, Virginia Minor and her husband Francis sued the registrar for not allowing her to vote. (As a married woman, Virginia Minor could not initiate a lawsuit on her own behalf.) In her dramatic criminal trial of 1873, Susan B. Anthony was convicted of the crime of voting but refused to pay her fine. Minor called on the first section of the Fourteenth Amendment to justify her claim that her rights had been violated by the state of Missouri.

The Minors' lawsuit culminated in a unanimous U.S. Supreme Court ruling in 1875 in *Minor v. Happersett*. The opinion reiterated that women were citizens and persons as defined by the Fourteenth Amendment, but that this status did not automatically entitle them to the vote. The founders of the American government did not intend, the decision argued at great length, to bestow the full rights of citizenship upon women. Women citizens, however, could still be said to live in a democracy. They were represented by male voters in their families and by elected officials of their communities. The implication was that suffragists would have to obtain an amendment to the U.S. Constitution or enact new state voting laws in order to vote.

The arguments presented by male politicians and judges in the 1860s and 1870s against women's voting echoed those of the clergy ten years before. Women's primary contributions to the Republic were domestic and maternal and best carried out in the private sphere. Women would either disrupt the sanctity of the polling place with their distracting presence, or the clamor of the polling place would corrupt women's morality. Only "strong-minded" women, assumed by the public to be "men in women's garb," sought the vote; natural women, submissive and retiring, didn't really want to vote. John Boyle O'Reilly argued in the Boston *Pilot* that "Women's suffrage is an unjust, unreasonable, unspiritual abnormality. It is a hard, undigested, tasteless, devitalized proposition . . . to reduce masculinity even by the obliteration of femininity. . . . It is the antithesis of that highest and sweetest mystery—conviction by submission, and conquest by sacrifice."[4] The most substantive argument was that women did not have the obligation to serve in the army or the navy, and were therefore not entitled to voting rights; the fact that black men had served in the Civil War with valor had been an important argument in favor of their suffrage.

By the time a woman suffrage amendment to the Constitution, a so-called "Sixteenth Amendment," was presented to the House Committee on Privileges and Elections in 1878, the moment for equal treatment under the law for both ex-slaves and women had passed. Federal Reconstruction had come to an end in the South. The federal courts refused to interpret the first section of the Fourteenth Amendment broadly, and by 1873 had limited federal intervention in the states to matters of due process involving race. In an ironic turn of events, the Supreme Court issued a series of decisions in the 1870s that defined business corporations as persons with "privileges and immunities" that could not be violated by state regulation, but allowed for new voting restrictions that were mere surrogates for racial bias. The rights of African Americans had been seriously compromised, and women were no closer than they had been in 1848 to voting except in a few scantily populated western territories. The country was moving, in the words of Ellen DuBois, into "an age in which political democracy was contracting rather than expanding," and the New Departure was over.[5]

READING GUIDE

Davis, Angela Y., *Women, Race and Class*. New York: Random House, 1981. Davis, a philosophy student who became a militant leader of the Black Power movement in the 1970s, was among the first students of the woman suffrage movement to document the Stanton and Anthony wing's persistent racism and mixed record on racial equality. Although Davis's account is somewhat polemical, it perhaps needed to be in the context of claiming a space for women of color in the feminist movement of the 1970s. The quotations are accurate, the judgments harsh, and the writing clear and accessible.

DuBois, Ellen, *Woman Suffrage and Women's Rights*. New York: New York University Press, 1998. DuBois was among the first to rethink the importance of the Reconstruction period for the women's rights movement in several pivotal essays republished in this collection. See, in particular, "Outlawing the Compact of the Fathers: Equal Rights, Woman Suffrage, and the United States Constitution, 1820–1878," and "Taking the Law into Our Own Hands: Bradwell, Minor and Suffrage Militance in the 1870s" (81–138).

Harper, Ida Husted, ed., *The Life and Work of Susan B. Anthony*, 2 vols. Indianapolis: Bowen-Merrill, 1898. These rich volumes contain Anthony's speeches and letters and can be read with profit for an understanding of the dedication and passion she brought to the crusade for women's equality, a crusade that lasted into the twentieth century. Anthony's refusal to back down in the face of persistent dismissal by male politicians, reformers, and lawyers remains remarkable.

Hoff, Joan, *Law, Gender and Injustice: A Legal History of U.S. Women*. New York: New York University Press, 1991: 143–91. Hoff probes the ways in which those she identifies as the "first feminists" responded to the political events of the Civil War and Reconstruction during the years she terms the transition from "constitutional neglect" to "constitutional discrimination." Extensively researched and carefully argued, her account emphasizes what she sees as the damage done to the vision of the women's rights movement with a narrowed focus on voting rights.

McFeely, William S., *Frederick Douglass*. New York: Touchstone, 1992. This powerful biography of the nineteenth century's most famous African American documents his painful parting of the ways with his old comrades from upstate New York over the Fourteenth Amendment. Douglass teamed up with Anna Dickinson to promote the Fifteenth Amendment in the Republican party and never saw himself as abandoning women's rights. (Dickinson, a popular orator and abolitionist, in 1864 was the first woman to speak to both houses of Congress.)

Stanley, Amy Dru, "Conjugal Bonds and Wage Labor: Rights of Contract in the Age of Emancipation," *Journal of American History* 75 (Sept. 1988): 471–500. Stanley shifts the examination of women's property rights away from middle- and upper-class women to the working-class woman whose only "property" was her body and its capacity to labor for wages and "earn" her husband's support with domestic work, including sexual work. Although emancipation and the Fourteenth Amendment spurred greater emphasis on freely made contracts, especially for wages, married women remained in an ambiguous situation because of their continued inability to make other kinds of contracts, to represent themselves legally, and to leave abusive marriages. Although the new statutes gave the wife "a contractual right to her wages, her husband retained his proprietary claim both to her person and to her domestic labor" (495).

Stanton, Elizabeth Cady, Susan B. Anthony, and Matilda Joslyn Gage, eds., *History of Woman Suffrage*, vol. II. New York: Fowler and Wells, 1882. A rich compendium of speeches, convention proceedings, biographical sketches, and a detailed account of the discussion of the Thirteenth, Fourteenth, and Fifteenth Amendments in the equal rights community and its split into two factions, the National Woman Suffrage Association, led by Stanton and Anthony, and the American Woman Suffrage Association, headed by Lucy Stone and Henry Blackwell. The volume, of course, endorses the Stanton and Anthony perspective but provides rich materials for evaluating both positions.

NOTES

1. Elizabeth Cady Stanton, Susan B. Anthony, and Matilda Joslyn Gage, eds., *History of Woman Suffrage*, vol. II (New York: Fowler and Wells, 1882), 91, 120.

2. Elizabeth Cady Stanton, "Address to the New York State Legislature," *Feminism: The Essential Historical Writings*, ed. Miriam Schneir (New York: Vintage, 1994), 119; Ellen DuBois, *Woman Suffrage and Women's Rights* (New York: New York University Press, 1998), 96.

3. Stanton, Anthony and Gage, *History of Woman Suffrage*, vol. II, 193.

4. Hasia Diner, *Erin's Daughters in America: Irish Immigrant Women in the Nineteenth Century* (Baltimore: Johns Hopkins University Press, 1983), 146.

5. DuBois, *Woman Suffrage and Women's Rights*, 107.

DOCUMENTS

4.1.   Elizabeth Cady Stanton Responds to the Fourteenth Amendment

> *As news of the language of the Fourteenth Amendment spread through the abolitionist community, several male reformers, including Wendell Phillips and Frederick Douglass, argued that woman suffrage had to be postponed because it was "the Negro's hour." Elizabeth Cady Stanton responded with ferocious language that argued white women were more qualified, on average, to the vote than black men. Her use of the term "Sambo" was particularly offensive to black abolitionists.*

"THIS IS THE NEGRO'S HOUR"

The representative women of the nation have done their uttermost for the last thirty years to secure freedom for the negro, and so long as he was lowest in the scale of being we were willing to press *his* claims; but now, as the celestial gate to civil rights is slowly moving on its hinges, it becomes a serious question whether we had better stand aside and see "sambo" walk into the kingdom first. As self-preservation is the first law of nature, would it not be wise to keep our lamps trimmed and burning, and when the constitutional door is open, avail ourselves of the strong arm and blue uniform of the black soldier to walk in by his side, and thus make the gap so wide that no privileged class could ever again close it against the humblest citizen of the republic?

"This is the negro's hour." Are we sure that he, once entrenched in all his inalienable rights, may not be an added power to hold us at bay? Have not "black male citizens" been heard to say they doubted the wisdom of extending the right of suffrage to women? Why should the African prove more just and generous than his Saxon compeers? If the two millions of Southern black women are not to be secured in their rights of person, property, wages, and children, their emancipation is but another form of slavery. In fact, it is better to be the slave of an educated white man, than of a degraded, ignorant black one. . . .

It is all very well for the privileged order to look down complacently and tell us, "This is the negro's hour; do not clog his way; do not embarrass the Republican party with any new issue; be generous and magnanimous; the negro once safe, the woman comes next." Now, if our prayer involved a new set of measures, or a new train of thought, it would be cruel to tax "white male citizens" with even two simple questions at a time; but the disfranchised all make the same demand, and the same logic that secures suffrage to one class gives it to all.

Source: Elizabeth Cady Stanton to the *New York Antislavery Standard*, December 26, 1865.

4.2.   Congressmen Debate the Language of the Fourteenth Amendment

---

The Fourteenth Amendment was easily passed in Congress in June of 1866 and sent on to the states for ratification with no discussion of women's rights. In December of 1866 the Senate debated a suffrage bill for the District of Columbia, over which it has jurisdiction. In an attempt to torpedo black male suffrage, Senator Edgar Cowan, a Democrat of Pennsylvania, added an amendment to strike the word male from the main bill. The ensuing debate demonstrates how ludicrous and dangerous most senators, with the exception of Benjamin Wade, believed woman suffrage to be and why those who said they supported woman suffrage did not want to do so at the price of losing suffrage for black men.

DEBATE ON A VOTING RIGHTS BILL FOR THE DISTRICT OF COLUMBIA

Senator Johnson of Maryland:

I have seen the elections in Baltimore, where they are just as orderly as they are in other cities; but we all know that in times of high party excitement it is impossible to preserve that order which would be sufficient to protect a delicate female from insult, and no lady would venture to run the hazard of being subjected to the insults that she would be almost certain to receive.

They do not want this privilege. As to protecting themselves, . . . if they govern those who govern, is not that protection enough? And who does not know that they govern us? Thank God they do. But what more right has a woman . . . to suffrage than a boy who is just one day short of twenty-one? You put him in your military service when he is eighteen; you may put him in it at a younger age if you think proper; but you will not let him vote. Why? . . . Not because that boy may not be able to exercise the right, but because . . . there must be some general rule. . . .

I like to learn wisdom from the men of 1776. . . . Down to the present hour no such proposition as this has received . . . any support, unless it was for a short time in the State of New Jersey. It has nothing to do with the right of negroes to vote. That is perfectly independent.

Senator Benjamin Wade of Ohio:

The Senator tells us that the community in which he lives is so barbarous and rude that a lady could not go to the polls to perform a duty which the law permitted without insult and rudeness. . . . I do not believe that our communities have got to that degree of depravity. . . . On the other hand, I have always found wherever I have gone that the rude and the rough in their conduct were civilized and ameliorated by the presence of females; for I do believe . . . that, take the world as it is, the female part of it are really more virtuous than the males.

As I can see no good reason to the contrary, I shall vote for this proposition. . . . I do not expect that public opinion will be so correct at this time that my vote will be effective; but nevertheless it would be no excuse for me that I did not do my part toward effecting a reform that I think the community requires, because I did not see that the whole world was going with me.

Senator Frelinghuysen of New Jersey:

Sir, I confess a little surprise at the remark . . . that there is no difference between granting suffrage to colored citizens and extending it to the women of America. The difference, to my mind, is as wide as the earth. As I understand it, we legislate for classes, and the women of America as a class do vote now . . . The women of America vote by their faithful and true representatives, their husbands, their brothers, their sons. . . . More than that, sir, ninety-nine out of a hundred, I believe nine hundred and ninety-nine out of a thousand, of the women in America do not want the privilege of voting in any other manner. . . . In both these regards there is a vast difference between the situation of the colored citizen and the women of America.

Senator Pomeroy of Kansas:

I shall vote against the amendment. . . . There are other measures that I would be glad to support in their proper place and time; but this is a great measure of itself. Since I have been a member of the Senate, there was a law in this District [of Columbia] authorizing the selling of colored men. To have traveled in six years from the auction-block to the ballot with these people is an immense stride, and if we can carry this measure alone of itself we should be contented for the present. I am for this measure religiously and earnestly, and I would vote down and vote against everything, that I thought weakened or that I thought was opposed to it.

Source: Congressional Globe, December 11–13, 1866.

4.3.   The American Equal Rights Association Debates the Reconstruction Amendments

In the conventions of the American Equal Rights Association, abolitionists and women's rightists gathered to discuss the progress of their goal of equal suffrage and civil rights for both African Americans and women. A painful choice had to be made; was this "the Negro's hour" or should the Fourteenth and Fifteenth Amendments be opposed? Male voters in Kansas voted in 1867 on referenda that would have given the suffrage to both women and blacks; Susan B. Anthony and Elizabeth Cady Stanton campaigned for woman suffrage in Kansas alongside the notorious racist Democrat, George Francis Train. As violence against African Americans and northern Reconstructionists in the South mounted, tensions ran high. Rebuffed at the 1869 convention, Elizabeth Cady Stanton and Susan B. Anthony broke away to publish their newspaper Revolution *and to found the National Woman Suffrage Association.*

EQUAL RIGHTS ASSOCIATION DEBATE

Stephen Foster:

I only wanted to tell you why the Massachusetts society cannot coalesce with the party here, and why we want these women [Stanton and Anthony] to retire and leave us to nominate officers who can receive the respect of both parties. . . . If you choose to put officers here that ridicule the negro, and pronounce the Amendment infamous, why I must retire: I can not work with you.

Henry B. Blackwell:

In regard to the criticisms of our officers, I will agree that many unwise things have been written in *The Revolution* by [George Francis Train]. . . . But that gentleman has withdrawn, and you, who know the real opinions of Miss Anthony and Mrs. Stanton on the question of negro suffrage, do not believe that they mean to create antagonism between the negro and the woman question.

Frederick Douglass:

There is no name greater than that of Elizabeth Cady Stanton in the matter of woman's rights and equal rights, but my sentiments are tinged a little against *The Revolution*. There was . . . the employment of certain names, such as "Sambo," and the gardener, and the bootblack, and the daughters of Jefferson and Washington. I have asked what difference there is between the daughters of Jefferson and Washington and other daughters. I must say that I do not see how any one can pretend that there is the same urgency in giving the ballot to woman as to the negro. With us, the matter is a question of life and death. . . . When women, because they are women, are hunted down through the cities of New York and New Orleans, when they are dragged from their houses and hung upon lamp-posts; when their children are torn from their arms, and their brains dashed out upon the pavement; when they are objects of insult and outrage at every turn; when they are in danger of having their homes burnt down over their heads; when their children are not allowed to enter schools; then they will have an urgency to obtain the ballot equal to our own.

Susan B. Anthony:

The old anti-slavery school say women must stand back and wait until the negroes shall be recognized. But . . . there is not the woman born who desires to eat the bread of dependence, no matter whether it be from the hand of father, husband, or brother; for any one who does so eat her bread places herself in the power of the person from whom she takes it. Mr. Douglass talks about the wrongs of the negro; but with all the outrages that he to-day suffers, he would not exchange his sex and take the place of Elizabeth Cady Stanton.

Lucy Stone:

Mrs. Stanton will, of course, advocate the precedence for her sex, and Mr. Douglass will strive for the first position for his, and both are perhaps right. If it be true that the government derives its authority from the consent of the governed, we are safe in trusting that principle to the uttermost. If one has a right to say that you can not read and therefore can not vote, then it may be said that you are a woman and can not vote. We are lost if we turn away from the middle principle and argue for one class. . . . Let no man speak of an educated suffrage. . . . The gentleman [Douglass] who addressed you claimed that the negroes had the first right to the suffrage, and drew a picture which only his great word-power can do. . . . But woman suffrage is more imperative than his own; and I want to remind the audience that when he says what the Ku-Kluxes did all over the south, the Ku-Kluxes here in the North in the shape of men, take away the children from the mother, and separate them as completely as if done on the block of the auctioneer. . . . Woman has an ocean of wrongs that can not be fathomed. There are two great oceans; in the one is the black man, and in the other is the woman. But I thank God for the XV Amendment, and hope that it will be adopted in every State. I will be thankful in my soul if *any*body can get out of the terrible pit. But I believe that the safety of the government would be more promoted by the admission of woman as an element of restoration and harmony than the negro. I believe that the influence of woman will save the country before every other power. I see the signs of the times pointing to this consummation, and I believe that in some parts of the country women will vote for the President of the United States in 1872.

Source: Elizabeth Cady Stanton, Susan B. Anthony, and Matilda Joslyn Gage, eds., *History of Woman Suffrage*, vol. II. New York: Fowler and Wells, 1882: 382–84.

4.4.   Justice Morrison Waite's Decision in *Minor v. Happersett*

As women attempted to vote in the federal election of 1872, some cast their votes, others were turned away, and some were arrested. After attempting to register in St. Louis, Missouri, Virginia Minor could not sue the registrar, Reese Happersett, because, as a married woman, she was not a legal agent; her husband Francis did so on her behalf. By the time the Supreme Court issued its decision in the Minor case in 1875, several other cases had established the Court's unwillingness to interpret the Fourteenth Amendment broadly, and so the Court's position on Minor was predictable. Justice Waite, however, took considerable time in his opinion to establish the "fact" that women are "persons" and "citizens" but not "voters" under the rubric of the Constitution.

MINOR V. HAPPERSETT

The question is presented in this case, whether, since the adoption of the XIV Amendment, a woman, who is a citizen of the United States and the State of Missouri, is a voter in that State, notwithstanding the provision of the Constitution and laws of the State, which confine the right of suffrage to men alone. . . .

The argument is, that as a woman, born or naturalized in the United States and subject to the jurisdiction thereof, is a citizen of the United States and of the State in which she resides, she has the right of suffrage as one of the privileges and immunities of her citizenship, which the State can not by its laws of constitution abridge.

There is no doubt that women may be citizens. They are persons, and, by the XIV Amendment, "all persons born or naturalized in the United States and subject to the jurisdiction thereof" are expressly declared to be "citizens of the United States and of the State wherein they reside." But, in our opinion, it did not need this Amendment to give them that position. Before its adoption, the Constitution of the United States did not in terms prescribe who should be citizens of the United States or of the several States, yet there were necessarily such citizens without such provision. . . .

Sex has never been made one of the elements of citizenship in the United States. In this respect men have never had an advantage over women. The same laws precisely apply to both. The XIV Amendment did not affect the citizenship of women any more than it did of men. In this particular, therefore, the rights of Mrs. Minor do not depend upon the Amendment. She has always been a citizen from her birth, and entitled to all the privileges and immunities of citizenship. . . .

The Constitution does not define the privileges and immunities of citizens. For that definition we must look elsewhere. In this case we need not determine what they are, but only whether suffrage is necessarily one of them.

It can not for a moment be doubted that, if it had been intended to make all citizens of the United States voters, the framers of the Constitution would not have left it to implication. So important a change in the condition of citizenship as it actually existed, if intended, would have been expressly declared.

Women were excluded from suffrage in nearly all the States by the express provision of their constitutions and laws. If that had been equivalent to a bill of attainder, certainly its abrogation would not have been left to implication. Nothing less than express language would have been employed to effect so radical a change. So also of the Amendment which declares that no person shall be deprived of life, liberty, or property, without due process of law; adopted as it was as early as 1791. If suffrage was intended to be included within its obligations, language better adapted to express that intent would most certainly have been employed. The right of suffrage, when granted, will be protected. He who has it can only be deprived of it by due process of law; but, in order to claim protection, he must first show that he has the right. . . .

Certainly if the courts can consider any question settled, this is one. For near ninety years the people have acted upon the idea that the Constitution, when it conferred citizenship, did not necessarily confer the right of suffrage. If uniform practice long continued can settle the construction of so important an instrument as the Constitution of the United States confessedly is, most certainly it has been done here. Our province is to decide what the law is, not to declare what it should be.

Source: 88 U.S. 162.

4.6.   The "Sixteenth Amendment" and the U.S. Congress, 1878

With no redress in the courts, woman suffragists proposed a "sixteenth amendment" to the U.S. Constitution that would make suffrage universal for women voters in the United States. (Soon dubbed the "Susan B. Anthony" Amendment, the simple language of the measure was used in the Nineteenth Amendment of 1920.) Victoria Woodhull presented the proposed amendment to the Committee on Privileges and Elections in 1878. The Committee's reply stressed "an experiment so novel" would bring near revolutionary change to American society, but argued that woman suffrage might emerge over time in the states.

A PROPOSED AMENDMENT TO THE CONSTITUTION OF THE UNITED STATES (January 10, 1878)

Resolved by the Senate and House of Representatives of the United States of America in congress assembled, two-thirds of each House concurring therein. That the following article be proposed to the legislatures of the several States as an amendment to the Constitution of the United States, which, when ratified by three-fourths of the said legislatures, shall be valid as part of the said constitution, namely:

Article 16, Sec. 1.—The right of citizens of the United States to vote shall not be denied or abridged by the United States or by any State on account of sex.

Sec. 2.—Congress shall have power to enforce this article by appropriate legislation.

REPORT OF THE COMMITTEE ON PRIVILEGES AND ELECTIONS ON SENATE RESOLUTION 12 (June 14, 1878)

This proposed amendment forbids the United States, or any State to deny or abridge the right to vote on account of sex. If adopted, it will make several millions of female voters, totally inexperienced in political affairs, quite generally dependent upon the other sex, all incapable of performing military duty and without the power to enforce the laws which their numerical strength may enable them to make, and comparatively very few of whom wish to assume the irksome and responsible political duties which this measure thrusts upon them. An experiment so novel, a change so great, should only be made slowly and in response to a general public demand, of the existence of which there is no evidence before your committee.

Petitions from various parts of the country, containing by estimate about 30,000 names, have been presented to congress asking for this legislation. They were procured through the efforts of woman suffrage societies, thoroughly organized, with active and zealous managers. The ease with which signatures may be procured to any petition is well known. The small number of petitioners, when compared with that of the intelligent women in the country, is striking evidence that there exists among them no general desire to take up the heavy burden of governing, which so many men seek to evade. It would be unjust, unwise and impolitic to impose that burden on the great mass of women throughout the country who do not wish for it, to gratify the comparatively few who do.

It has been strongly urged that without the right of suffrage, women are, and will be, subjected to great oppression and injustice.

But every one who has examined the subject at all knows that, without female suffrage, legislation for years has improved and is still improving the condition of woman. The disabilities imposed upon her by the common law have, one by one, been swept away, until in most of the States she has the full right to her property and all, or nearly all, the rights which can be granted without impairing or destroying the marriage relation. These changes have been wrought by the spirit of the age, and are not, generally at least, the result of any agitation by women in their own behalf.

Nor can women justly complain of any partiality in the administration of justice. They have the sympathy of judges and particularly of juries to an extent which would warrant loud complaint on the part of their adversaries of the sterner sex. Their appeals to legislatures against injustice are never unheeded, and there is no doubt that when any considerable part of the women of any State really wish for the right to vote, it will be granted without the intervention of congress.

Any State may grant the right of suffrage to women. Some of them have done so to a limited extent, and perhaps with good results. It is evident that in some States public opinion is much more strongly in favor of it than it is in others. Your committee regard it as unwise and inexpedient to enable three fourths in number of the States, through an amendment to the national constitution, to force woman suffrage upon the other fourth in which the public opinion of both sexes may be strongly adverse to such a change.

For these reasons, your committee report back said resolution with a recommendation that it be indefinitely postponed.

5 _____

Bradwell v. Illinois and *Taylor v. Louisiana*: Women in the Courtroom

When Susan B. Anthony was tried for the crime of voting in 1873, she entered a courtroom with somber walls covered with portraits of what today's feminists might half-jokingly describe as "dead white men." A male judge presided, the lawyers who argued the case were male, and the jury was male. The judge refused to allow her to testify and had written his instructions to the jury before her attorney had argued her case. (Anthony could not have found a lawyer of her own sex to defend her because the state of New York did not admit women to the bar, even if they had the required education and training.) The judge made the mistake, however, of asking Anthony if she wished to say anything to the court before sentence was pronounced. In an impassioned response, Anthony, who had argued in speeches before the trial that she was qualified to vote on the basis of the Fifteenth Amendment because as a woman she was in "legal servitude," challenged the entire basis of the system of "forms of law made by men, administered by men, in favor of men, and against women" by which she had been found "guilty." Anthony had hoped to take her case through the courts on appeal, but because her lawyer had posted her bail and because the judge refused to enforce any sentence, she could not carry her case any further.

Susan B. Anthony's case encapsulated a critical issue in the history of women's rights. Did it make a difference for female (and male) defendants to have women lawyers, judges, and jurors in the courtroom? Was jury duty and testifying in court an imposition on, as Linda Kerber as phrased it, "women's constitutional right to be ladies," or were they obligations of citizenship worth achieving through the women's rights movement? Would poor women and women of color be treated the same way as more privileged white women such as Anthony? Who opposed women in the courtroom and why?

The disappointments of the Reconstruction-era amendments and the growing number of college-educated women probably sparked the first attempts by women to pass the bar; many of these pioneers were active in the suffrage movement, had been gravely disappointed by the courts' dismissal of women's claims to equal protection under the law, and saw women's access to the legal profession as a critical step in assailing hoary tradition. The western state bars were the most likely to license women, and in 1869 suffragist Arabella Mansfield of Iowa became the first professional woman lawyer in the United States. That same year, Myra Bradwell, another suffragist, passed the Illinois bar exam but was denied a license on the grounds that she was married; as a woman she was said to suffer from a "legal disability" that might impede her ability to make contracts and represent clients. But in 1872, a single woman was also denied admission to the Illinois bar simply on the grounds that she was a woman.

Bradwell had, meanwhile, appealed her case all the way to the Supreme Court, arguing that the Fourteenth Amendment guaranteed citizens of the United States due process under the privileges and immunities of citizenship clause and that the state of Illinois had violated that due process by denying her a license. The Supreme Court's decision in *Bradwell* was issued the day after the *Slaughter House* decision in 1873, and the two cases were closely related. In the *Slaughter House* suit, filed by independent butchers of Louisiana against a state monopoly, the Supreme Court argued that the Fourteenth Amendment did not obligate the federal government to intervene in the states' regulation of occupations, except if that regulation had to do with race. The *Bradwell* decision used the *Slaughter House* case as precedent for excluding Bradwell from the legal profession, and the import of *Slaughter House* and *Bradwell* for future cases involving women was clear; until the Supreme Court changed its mind, women could not argue as a class, as African Americans could supposedly do, against sexual discrimination on the basis of the Fourteenth Amendment. In a separate concurring opinion, Justice Joseph Bradley reiterated the importance of barring women, whether married or not, from the courtroom altogether. Allowing women to practice law would constitute nothing less than a sexual and "judicial revolution."

Nonetheless, women struggled to take up the law. While the courts, often bastions of entrenched male privilege, remained hostile, state legislatures, more subject, perhaps, to popular opinion, were more receptive, and by the time the Bradwell case was decided in Washington, an

Illinois law permitted women to qualify for the bar. It was most difficult for women to be licensed in the Northeast. Law schools slowly opened to women, with state universities and the newer private universities, notably Boston University, University of Chicago, Stanford University, and New York University admitting women first. Charlotte E. Ray, the first African-American woman lawyer, disguised her sex on her application to Howard University Law School in Washington, D.C., was allowed to attend, and emerged with a degree in 1872. By 1917 women were still banned from the bar in four states, and the Rhode Island and Delaware bars did not license women until 1920. Yale Law admitted token numbers of (white) women in 1918, as did Columbia in 1927. Harvard Law did not admit women until 1950.

Women frequently found that even with degrees and licenses, they could not practice law. Clients, especially those who could afford to pay, often refused to hire women lawyers. Women were often barred from higher courts of appeal on the basis of sex. The more lucrative business and criminal law cases were dominated by all-male firms. When they did practice law, women lawyers often worked in family law, for impoverished clients, for city and state agencies, and in labor and factory inspection law. Underdogs themselves, they frequently took up the causes of other underdogs. Lena O. Smith did pioneer work in civil rights law for the black community in Minneapolis in the 1920s. An exceptional group of reformist women lawyers came out of New York University Law School in the early twentieth century. Crystal Eastman, a prominent feminist and a founder of the American Civil Liberties Union, wrote the classic *Accidents and the Law*, which sparked major reform in worker compensation and factory regulation in New York state. Carol Weiss King defended immigrants and radicals in the deportation cases of the "Red Scare" that followed World War I. Dorothy Kenyon, appointed by Mayor Fiorello LaGuardia as Deputy Commissioner of Licenses in New York City, protested against the courts' treatment of prostitutes and refused to ban burlesque in the city's nightclubs. When it came to serving on the bench, women lawyers were at the bottom of the legal hierarchy. By 1910 only ten women in the United States had served in a judicial capacity, and by 1930 only twelve states had at least one woman judge.

One of the most famous woman judges of the twentieth century was Florence Ellinwood Allen, who attended the University of Chicago Law School and graduated second in her class in 1913. Her career demonstrated the still important connection between agitation for women's rights and joining the legal profession. Allen began as a Legal Aid lawyer and was elected, with the help of women voters, to a judgeship in 1920; she was elected to the Ohio Supreme Court in 1922 and reelected in 1928 by a huge majority. She was the first woman to be appointed a federal judge and in 1949 was forwarded to President Harry S Truman as a candidate for the Supreme Court. Truman reputedly interviewed justices of the Supreme Court and found that they "don't want a woman. They say they couldn't sit around with their robes off and their feet up."[1]

When women entered the courtroom as defendants, plaintiffs, or lawyers, they were likely to find all-male juries well into the twentieth century. Although British common law and its application in state courts of the United States had established the tradition of a trial by a "jury of one's peers," no such language appears in the U.S. Constitution; the Sixth Amendment requires only a speedy and public trial in the federal courts by an impartial jury. The interpretation of what constituted an impartial jury or a jury of one's peers remained a fluid one. In an important case that further underscored the masculinity of citizenship as defined in the Fourteenth Amendment, the Supreme Court ruled in *Strauder v. West Virginia* (1879) that the states might "confine the selection [of jurors] to males, to freeholders, to persons within certain ages, or to persons having educational qualifications," as long as they did not exclude male citizens on the basis of race or color. Traditionalists argued that jury duty was an onerous obligation, similar to military service, that only men could be forced to bear; exempting women from jury duty was a way of protecting them from the conflict of both the battlefield and the courtroom. Other apologists for all-male juries argued that women were too emotional and uncritical of spurious arguments to serve on juries and that they were needed at home by their husbands and children. Feminists countered that single women, childless women, and women who could obtain domestic help might very well serve on juries, with no "recorded increase in the burning of soups." Utah was the first state to allow women to volunteer for jury duty, in 1898, but New York did not allow women to volunteer for jury duty until 1937 and Massachusetts until 1946.

Voluntary registration did not make women's jury duty equivalent to men's. It was widely assumed, by both the courts and women themselves, that most women would remain out of the jury box. Exemptions from jury duty for women, on the basis of their sex alone, were widespread. The 1946 Massachusetts law establishing women's right to register for jury duty allowed judges to dismiss women who were "likely to be embarrassed by hearing the testimony or by discussing [it] in the jury room."[2] Very few women ever registered for jury duty. In Florida in the 1950s, for example, less than 5 percent of all women who were eligible were registered for jury duty and almost no women were ever impaneled on juries.

Making the case for mandatory jury duty for women continued to be difficult. Feminist organizations like the League of Women Voters had argued for sex-blind mandatory jury duty but were unsuccessful in portraying jury duty as a positive right rather than an onerous obligation.

Another tactic was to argue that women defendants did not receive a fair trial if there were no women on their juries. But this approach was fraught for feminists; it implied that women and men were so different from each other that women defendants required "special treatment" and that only women could understand other women. In any event, in *Hoyl v. Florida* (1961) the Supreme Court agreed that Gwendolyn Hoyt, who had admitted to killing her husband in 1957, had received a fair trial from an all-male jury. As long as some women were registered and available to serve on juries, the courts ruled, the fact that an actual jury was all male did not make it an unrepresentative or partial one. But with a renewed civil rights movement and a second wave of feminism in the 1970s, advocates of women's mandatory jury duty returned to a focus on gender equality equivalent to racial equality and the questions of exclusion that had been raised in *Strauder*. Building on cases carried through the courts by the legal funds of the NAACP and the ACLU, Ruth Bader Ginsburg convinced the Supreme Court in *Taylor v. Louisiana* (1975) that a murder defendant—in this case a man—had received an unfair trial because he had an-all male jury. Legal scholar Leslie Fried-man Goldstein argues that *Taylor* constituted a reinterpretation not only of "the general phrases 'due process' and 'equal protection' but also the more precise term 'an impartial jury.' "[3]

By 1972 an Equal Rights Amendment passed by Congress was em-boldening many more women to challenge their exclusion from the courtroom and discrimination in the legal profession. Both voluntary and federally enforced affirmative action programs for women in higher ed-ucation and employment were resulting in much higher proportions of women entering law school and being admitted to the bar. Although only 4.7 percent of all lawyers in the United States were women in 1970, the number rose to 12 percent a decade later. By 1987, 40 percent of all the law students were women, an extraordinary transformation in a sin-gle generation.

Although women now serve on juries routinely, their appointment to the bench is still limited, with most women serving in family court, a tendency reified in a popular television program of the turn of the twen-tieth century, *Judging Amy*. President Jimmy Carter laid the basis for more men of color and women in the federal court system by enforcing the Omnibus Judgeship Act of 1978, which established merit, not political patronage, as the basis for appointments to the federal bench. Ronald Reagan, a Republican party president opposed to abortion rights and the Equal Rights Amendment, nominated the first woman to the Supreme Court, Sandra Day O'Connor, who was confirmed by the Senate in 1981. O'Connor went on to write the affirmative opinion upholding *Roe v. Wade* in *Planned Parenthood of Southeastern Pennsylvania v. Casey* in 1992, and in so doing, referred to both *Bradwell v. Illinois* and *Hoyt v. Florida*, as legal artifacts "no longer consistent with our understanding of the family, the individual, or the Constitution." O'Connor was joined on the bench by a William Jefferson Clinton nominee, Ruth Bader Ginsburg, in 1993.

Does having women in the courtrooms as counsel, judge, or juror make a difference? While some observers argue that women behave pretty much as men do when confronted by the law, others insist that "a woman's perspective" brings gender balance to the legal process and insures that women's interests will be better protected in the courtroom.

READING GUIDE

DeCrow, Karen, *Sexist Justice*. New York: Random House, 1974. DeCrow's lively critique of the law reflects the outrage felt by women in the legal profession in the early years of the women's liberation movement. DeCrow began law school at the age of 31 in New York and was the only woman in her class. Half analytical and half autobiographical, this account of constitutional law as it was applied to women "in the dark ages" is sobering indeed.

Drachman, Virginia G., *Sisters in Law: Women Lawyers in Modern American History*. Cambridge: Harvard University Press, 1998. This lively study of women in the legal profession focuses on the period from 1860 to 1940; women made, she argues, almost no significant progress in the profession between the 1930s and the 1970s. She provides individual portraits of women pioneers in the law, helpful tables, and an investigation of the discrimination women faced in law school, at the bar, and in the larger community.

Epstein, Cynthia Fuchs, *Women in Law*. New York: Basic Books, 1981. Although Epstein gives a brief description of women's history in the law profession, her main focus in on the progress women have made in the law since the rise of affirmative action programs in the 1970s; 4.7 percent of all lawyers were women in 1970, but by 1980, 12 percent were. In this sociological profile of women lawyers, Epstein argues that "law is one of the most traditional and exclusive professions in the United States." She also believes that it makes a difference "that women become lawyers . . . Not only is the entry of women in the legal profession an important indicator of their general equality in American life, but it constitutes a broadening of the profession's responsiveness to the needs of all sectors of society" (7).

Gilliam, Nancy T., "A Professional Pioneer: Myra Bradwell's Fight to Practice Law," *Law and History Review* 5 (Spring, 1987): 105–33. This essay describes the *Bradwell* case and its connection to *Slaughter House* in detail, but also fleshes out Bradwell's remarkable history. Although she never practiced law, Bradwell edited the influential *Chicago Legal News*, an important forum for the discussion of the law's evolution at the local, state, and federal level, as well as for Bradwell's efforts to achieve sexual equality and other progressive reforms.

Kerber, Linda K., *No Constitutional Right to Be Ladies: Women and the Obligations of Citizenship*. New York: Hill and Wang, 1998. A sophisticated analysis of what political thinkers describe as the "obligations" of citizenship and the dilemmas both reformers and conservatives faced in thinking about the consequences of obligations for gender difference and equality in the nineteenth and twentieth centuries. Kerber's chapter, "Woman Is the Center of Home and Family Life: Gwendolyn Holt and Jury Service in Twentieth Century America" (124–220), is a penetrating account of the historical and conceptual issues involved in women's jury duty service and the efforts to bring women into the jury box. Kerber also describes the pioneering work of Dorothy Kenyon, Pauli Murray, and Ruth Bader Ginsburg in changing the law for African Americans and women. There is no doubt that the progress of women in the United States in the law was based on work done by civil rights and civil liberties lawyers.

Morello, Karen Berger, *The Invisible Bar: The Woman Lawyer in America 1638 to the Present*. New York: Random House, 1986. A thinly documented but clearly written narrative of women lawyers and their access to law school education, hiring in major firms, and presence on the bench. Morello includes a very helpful chapter on black women lawyers.

Murray, Pauli. *Song in a Weary Throat: An American Pilgrimage*. New York: HarperCollins, 1987. Turned away from the University of North Carolina law school on the basis of her race and from Harvard Law School on the basis of her sex, Pauli Murray became a social justice activist. She gained national attention when she worked to obtain clemency for a black sharecropper on the grounds that his murder trial verdict should be thrown out because blacks were excluded from jury service. She entered Howard Law School in 1941, and in this autobiography, describes her growing awareness of both racism and sexism in the legal profession. Murray and other law students at Howard "sat-in" at segregated cafeterias in Washington, D.C., 20 years before similar sit-ins in North Carolina by black students gained national attention. After a long and influential legal career, Murray became the first ordained woman Episcopal priest, in 1977.

NOTES

1. As quoted by Karen Berger Morello, *The Invisible Bar: The Woman Lawyer in America 1638 to the Present* (New York: Random House, 1986), 235.

2. As quoted by Linda Kerber, *No Constitutional Right to Be Ladies: Women and the Obligations of Citizenship* (New York: Hill and Wang, 1998), 143.

3. Leslie Friedman Goldstein, *The Constitutional Rights of Women: Cases in Law and Social Change*, 2d edition (Madison: University of Wisconsin Press, 1988), 142.

DOCUMENTS

5.1. Susan B. Anthony Reprimands the Courts

After voting in 1872 in Rochester, New York, for presidential candidate Ulysses S. Grant, Susan B. Anthony was arrested and tried in a New York State court. Asked whether she had anything to say in response to her sentence, a fine of $100, she lambasted the court in this exchange with Judge Ward Hunt on June 18, 1873. She made clear that she was willing to commit civil disobedience and be arrested in order to uphold her refusal to obey "an odious aristocracy" shored up by the legal profession, the law, and the courts.

"THIS SO-CALLED REPUBLICAN GOVERNMENT"

The Court:

The prisoner will stand up. Has the prisoner anything to say why sentence shall not be pronounced?

Miss Anthony:

Yes, your honor, I have many things to say; for in your ordered verdict of guilty, you have trampled under foot every vital principle of our government. My natural rights, my civil rights, my political rights, are all alike ignored. Robbed of the fundamental privilege of citizenship, I am degraded from the status of a citizen to that of a subject; and not only myself individually, but all of my sex, are, by your honor's verdict, doomed to political subjection under this so-called Republican government.

Judge Hunt:

The Court can not listen to a rehearsal of arguments the prisoner's counsel has already consumed three hours in presenting.

Miss Anthony:

May it please your honor, I am not arguing the question, but simply stating the reasons why sentence can not, in justice, be pronounced against me. Your denial of my citizen's right to vote is the denial of my right of consent as one of the governed, the denial of my right of representation as one of the taxed, the denial of my rights to a trial by a jury of my peers as an offender against law, therefore, the denial of my sacred rights of life, liberty, property, and—

Judge Hunt:

The Court can not allow the prisoner to go on.

Miss Anthony:

But your honor will not deny me this one and only poor privilege of protest against this high-handed outrage upon my citizen's rights. May it please the Court to remember that since the day of my arrest last November, this is the first time that either myself or any person of my disfranchised class has been allowed a word of defense before judge or jury—

Judge Hunt:

The prisoner must sit down; the Court can not allow it.

Miss Anthony:

All my prosecutors, from the 8th Ward corner grocery politician, who entered the complaint, to the United States Marshal, Commissioner, District Attorney, District Judge, your honor on the bench, not one is my peer, but each and all are my political sovereigns; and had your honor submitted my case to the jury, as was clearly your duty, even then I should have had just cause of protest, for not one of those men was my peer; but, native or foreign, white or black, rich or poor, educated or ignorant, awake or asleep, sober or drunk, each and every man of them was my political superior; hence, in no sense, my peer. Even, under such circumstances, a commoner of England, tried before a jury of lords, would have far less cause to complain than should I, a woman, tried before a jury of men. Even my counsel, then Hon. Henry R. Selden, who has argued my cause so ably, so earnestly, so unanswerably before your honor, is my political sovereign. Precisely as no disfranchised person is entitled to sit upon a jury, and no woman is entitled to the franchise, so, none but a regularly admitted lawyer is allowed to practice in the courts, and no woman can gain admission to the bar—hence, jury, judge, counsel, must all be of the superior class.

Judge Hunt:

The Court must insist—the prisoner has been tried according to the established forms of law.

Miss Anthony:

Yes, your honor, but by forms of law all made by men, interpreted by men, administered by men, in favor of men, and against women; and hence, your honor's ordered verdict of guilty, against a United States citizen for the exercise of "that citizen's right to vote," simply because that citizen was a woman and not a man. But, yesterday, the same man-made forms of law declared it a crime punishable with $1,000 fine and six months' imprisonment, for you, or me, or any of us, to give a cup of cold water, a crust of bread, or a night's shelter to a panting fugitive as he was tracking his way to Canada. And every man or woman in whose veins coursed a drop of human sympathy violated that wicked law, reckless of consequences, and was justified in so doing. As then the slaves who got their freedom must take it over, or under, or through the unjust forms of law, precisely so now must women, to get their right to a voice in this Government, take it; and I have taken mine, and mean to take it at every possible opportunity.

Judge Hunt:

The Court orders the prisoner to sit down. It will not allow another word.

Miss Anthony:

When I was brought before your honor for trial, I hoped for a broad and liberal interpretation of the Constitution and its recent amendments, that should declare all United States citizens under its protecting aegis—that should declare equality of rights the national guarantee to all persons born or naturalized in the United States. But failing to get this justice—failing, even, to get a trial by a jury *not* of my peers—I ask not leniency at your hands—but rather the full rigors of the law.

Judge Hunt:

The Court must insist—(Here the prisoner sat down.)

Judge Hunt:

The prisoner will stand up. (Here Miss Anthony arose again.) The sentence of the Court is that you pay a fine of one hundred dollars and the costs of the prosecution.

Miss Anthony:

May it please your honor, I shall never pay a dollar of your unjust penalty. And I shall earnestly and persistently continue to urge all women to practical recognition of the old revolutionary maxim, that "Resistance to tyranny is obedience to God."

Source: Elizabeth Cady Stanton, Susan B. Anthony, and Matilda Joslyn Gage, eds., *History of Woman Suffrage*, vol. II. New York: Fowler and Wells, 1882: 687–89.

5.2.   Myra Bradwell Protests Her Exclusion from the Illinois State Bar Association

Myra Colby Bradwell's case, legal scholars believe, was the first case to go before the Supreme Court that based its argument on the Fourteenth Amendment. In his argument before the Court, Bradwell's lawyer presented an evocative and clear-cut case for using the privileges and immunities, equal protection, and due process clauses of the Fourteenth Amendment to defend her right to enter the profession of the law, a case that Justice Samuel F. Miller simply referred back to the narrow ruling in Slaughter

House, *decided just the day before. In his more expansive opin-*
ion, Justice Joseph Bradley emphasizes married women's inability
to represent themselves or others.

MYRA BRADWELL v. STATE OF ILLINOIS

Opinion of Justice Samuel Miller:

In regard to [the Fourteenth] Amendment counsel for the plaintiff in this court truly says that there are certain privileges and immunities which belong to a citizen of the United States as such; otherwise it would be nonsense for the Fourteenth Amendment to prohibit a state from abridging them, and he proceeds to argue that admission to the bar of a state, of a person who possesses the requisite learning and character, is one of those which a state may not deny.

In this latter proposition we are not able to concur with counsel. We agree with him that there are privileges and immunities belonging to citizens of the United States, in that relation and character, and that it is these and these alone which a state is forbidden to abridge. But the right to admission to practice in the courts of a state is not one of them. This right in no sense depends on citizenship of the United States. It has not, as far as we know, ever been made in any state or in any case to depend on citizenship at all. Certainly many prominent and distinguished lawyers have been admitted to practice, both in the state and Federal courts, who were not citizens of the United States or of any state. But, on whatever basis this right may be placed, so far as it can have any relation to citizenship at all, it would seem that, as to the courts of the state, it would relate to citizenship of the state, and as to Federal courts, it would relate to citizenship of the United States.

The opinion just delivered in the *Slaughter-House Cases*, from Louisiana . . . renders elaborate argument in the present case unnecessary; for, unless we are wholly and radically mistaken in the principle on which those cases are decided, the right to control and regulate the granting of license to practice law in the courts of a state is one of those powers which are not transferred for its protection to the Federal government, and its exercise is in no manner governed or controlled by citizenship of the United States in the party seeking such license.

Justice Joseph Bradley:

I concur in the judgment of the Court in this case, by which the judgment of the supreme court of Illinois is affirmed, but not for the reasons specified in the opinion just read.

The claim of the plaintiff, who is a married woman, to be admitted to practice as an attorney and counselor at law, is based upon the supposed right of every person, man or woman, to engage in any lawful employment for a livelihood.

It certainly cannot be affirmed, as a historical fact, that this has ever been established as one of the fundamental privileges and immunities of the sex. On the contrary, the civil law, as well as nature herself, has always recognized a wide difference in the respective spheres and destinies of man and woman. Man is, or should be, woman's protector and defender. The natural and proper timidity and delicacy which belongs to the female sex evidently unfits it for many of the occupations of civil life. The constitution of the family organization, which is founded in the divine ordinance, as well as in the nature of things, indicates the domestic sphere as that which properly belongs to the domain and functions of womanhood. The harmony, not to say identity, of interests and views which belong or should belong to the family institution, is repugnant to the idea of a woman adopting a distinct and independent career from that of her husband. So firmly fixed was this sentiment in the founders of the common law that it became a maxim of that system of jurisprudence that a woman had no legal existence separate from her husband, who was regarded as her head and representative in the social state; and, notwithstanding some recent modification to this civil status, many of the special rules of law flowing from and dependent upon this cardinal principle still exists in full force in most states. One of these is, that a married woman is incapable, without her husband's consent, of making contracts which shall be binding on her or him. This very incapacity was one circumstance which the supreme court of Illinois deemed important in rendering a married woman incompetent fully to perform the duties and trusts that belong to the office of an attorney and counselor.

It is true that many women are unmarried and not affected by any of the duties, complications, and incapacities arising out of the married state, but these are exceptions to the general rule. The paramount destiny and mission of woman are to fulfill the noble and benign offices of wife and mother. This is the law of the Creator. And the rules of civil society must be adapted to the general constitution of things, and cannot be based upon exceptional cases.

The humane movements of modern society, which have for their object the multiplication of avenues for woman's advancement, and of occupations adapted to her condition and sex, have my heartiest concurrence. But I am not prepared to say that it is one of her fundamental rights and privileges to be admitted into every office and position, including those which require highly special qualifications and demanding special responsibilities. In the nature of things it is not every citizen of every age, sex, and condition that is qualified for every calling and position. It is the prerogative of the legislator to prescribe regulations founded on nature, reason, and experience for the due admission of qualified persons to professions and callings demanding special skill and confidence.

Source: 83 U.S. 130, 1873.

5.3.   Making a Claim for Women to Serve on Juries

Having won the right to vote in 1920, women found that most states continued to bar them from the jury box. In this publication for the League of Women Voters, Massachusetts lawyer Jennie Loitman Barron argues that women should be able to serve on juries as long as those with demanding duties can be exempted. Her most pointed remarks are aimed at the idea that the home will be neglected if women leave it for jury duty. She also contends that the roles of women in modern life have admirably suited them to serve as jurors.

"WHY WOMEN SHOULD SERVE ON JURIES"

The right of a trial by jury is one of the most firmly rooted of the fundamental principles of our nation and of all our states. It is considered more important than any other one guarantee of liberty because it protects the common people from the power of their officials. Juries have always been an essential part of our administration of justice. The Constitution of the United States and of every state in the Union guarantees the right to public trial by an impartial jury. . . .

Appropriate exemptions from jury service should be provided for women, as appropriate exemptions for men are now provided. Among the men who are exempted are doctors, lawyers, dentists, pharmacists, veterinarians, preachers, school teachers, city officials, ship captains, and engineers. In addition to these classes, the following women should be exempt: women trained nurses, women assistants in hospitals, women attendant nurses, women nursing sick members of their own family, and mothers having a child or children under twelve years of age, or women having the legal custody of such children. Of course all persons, whether men or women, if ill or otherwise physically incapacitated, are exempt. . . .

It is significant that about one-fifth of the women in the United States are engaged in gainful occupations. In addition, several million women, composed largely of women not engaged in gainful occupations, are members of and active in, the women's clubs. "Women have left the sidewalks where they have so long been spectators, and have joined the procession." There is no reason why this procession should not lead to the jury box. . . .

Justice to women, and even to the community, demands that women should be eligible to sit as jurors, for if women are like men, they surely should serve; and if women are unlike men, then their point of view, different from that of the men, should be represented on our juries. Jury service, whether a privilege or a duty, is an incident of citizenship. Women certainly do not want to be denied it if a privilege, nor evade it if a duty. Every advance in civilization means responsibility as well as privilege. Citizenship implies responsibility. Women are ready to assume the burdens as well as the benefits of citizenship. . . .

The right of trial by jury was intended to give every citizen a trial by an impartial jury and judgment by one's peers. Can we say that a woman or girl on trial is receiving a trial by an impartial jury, when women are not eligible as jurors? To say that a woman before the Bar is entitled to judgment by her peers, and then to exclude women from the jury room, is to misinterpret the spirit which underlies our institutions. Jury service for women is another step toward the attainment of that universal justice for which the American nation stands. . . .

It is contended by some that women do not want to serve as jurors. Since serving on a jury is a civic duty, one should not question whether the women want to serve. Men drafted for military service were not asked whether that duty was convenient or agreeable to them. Persons conscripted for this much safer, better paid, and easier branch of the civil service, and chosen only for brief periods, and then only very infrequently, should cheerfully render this service. . . .

As regard the women in the home, "Who is going to look after the baby?" The "babies" of many women are school teachers, clerks, doctors, and in our stores and factories. These babies probably would not miss mother's care more than usual, and, of course, the compensation received from jury duty they could easily hire others to do their housework. To these women jury service, with its short hours and reasonable compensation, would be an educational and an interesting diversion from the monotonous routine of household drudgery. It is better that the sweeping and dishwashing should suffer temporarily at the hands of the high school girl next door, than that the state should be deprived of splendid jury material.

Those with household help can easily find time for jury service. . . . The home has not suffered because of thousands of women's clubs of every possible political and humanitarian complexion, nor because women have sat on city councils, or on boards of directors. Grace and charm have not departed from the American home; family life has not been destroyed; . . . children have not gone, in greater numbers than before, breakfastless to school. There is no recorded increase in the burning of soups. Indeed, women's outside interests have helped to develop the home. Homemaking is something more than housekeeping. Many homes are hurt by the trivialities and lack of interest of mothers in the affairs of life.

Source: Jennie Loitman Barron, *Jury Service for Women*. Washington, D.C.: League of Women Voters, 1924.

5.4.   The Supreme Court Considers Florida's Jury Duty Law

In the summer of 1957 Gwendolyn Holt hit her husband with a baseball bat in a domestic dispute; he later died of his injuries. She was found guilty of second-degree murder, and her lawyers were unable to reduce the charge to manslaughter. Although there were 46,000 female voters in Holt's county in Florida, only 218 had come forward to volunteer for jury duty, and of those only about 35 had been declared eligible; no women were impaneled for the Holt trial. When Holt's lawyers, including civil liberties lawyer Dorothy Kenyon, claimed that Holt had not been given equal protection under the law because women jurors might have understood her case better than men, the Supreme Court ruled that because women could volunteer for jury duty, Florida's juries could be considered unbiased.

HOYT v. FLORIDA

[Mrs. Hoyt's] premises misconceive the scope of the right to an impartially selected jury assured by the Fourteenth Amendment. That right does not entitle one accused of crime to a jury tailored to the circumstances of the particular case, whether relating to the sex or other condition of the defendant, or to the nature of the charges to be tried. It requires only that the jury be indiscriminately drawn from among those eligible in the community for jury service, untrammeled by any arbitrary and systematic exclusions. . . .

We of course recognize that the Fourteenth Amendment reaches not only arbitrary class exclusions from jury service based on race or color, but also all other exclusions which "single out" any class of persons "for different treatment not based on some reasonable classification." . . .

Where, as here, an exemption of a class in the community is asserted to be in substance an exclusionary device, the relevant inquiry is whether the exemption itself is based on some reasonable classification and whether the manner in which it is exercisable rests on some rational foundation.

In the selection of jurors Florida has differentiated between men and women in two respects. It has given women an absolute exemption from jury duty based solely on their sex, no similar exemption obtaining as to men. And it has provided for its effectuation in a manner less onerous than that governing exemptions exercisable by men: women are not to be put on the jury list unless they have voluntarily registered for such service; men, on the other hand, even if entitled to an exemption, are to be included on the list unless they have filed a written claim of exemption.

In neither respect can we conclude that Florida's statute is not "based on some reasonable classification," and that it is thus infected with unconstitutionality. Despite the enlightened emancipation of women from the restrictions and protections of bygone years, and their entry into many parts of community life formerly considered to be reserved to men, woman is still regarded as the center of home and family life. We cannot say that it is constitutionally impermissible for a State, acting in pursuit of the general welfare, to conclude that a woman should be relieved from the civic duty of jury service unless she herself determines that such service is consistent with her own special responsibilities. . . .

This case in no way resembles those involving race or color in which the circumstances shown were found by this Court to compel a conclusion of purposeful discriminatory exclusions from jury service. . . . There is present here neither the unfortunate atmosphere of ethnic or racial prejudices which underlay the situations depicted in those cases, nor the long course of discriminatory administrative practice which the statistical showing in each of them evinced.

Source: 368 U.S. 57, 1961.

5.5.   The Louisiana Jury Law Is Declared Unconstitutional

Billy Taylor was accused and found guilty of aggravated kidnapping and appealed his guilty decision on the grounds that no women had served on his jury. In Louisiana every woman was exempted by the state from jury duty unless she filed a written affidavit declaring her intention to serve. In the brief filed with the Supreme Court, Taylor's chief lawyer, Ruth Bader Ginsburg, argued on the basis of the Sixth Amendment that women should be obligated to serve on juries because defendants would not receive a fair trial otherwise. In 1975, the Supreme Court ruled that Taylor had not received a fair trial because his jury was not

*chosen from a cross-section of the community and thus mandated
jury duty service for women throughout the United States.*

BILLY TAYLOR v. LOUISIANA

The Louisiana jury selection system does not disqualify women from jury service, but in operation its conceded systematic impact is that only a very few women, grossly disproportionate to the number of eligible women in the community, are called for jury service. In this case no women were on the venire from which the petit jury was drawn. . . .

We accept the fair cross-section requirement as fundamental to the jury trial guaranteed by the Sixth Amendment and are convinced that the requirement has solid foundation. The purpose of a jury is to guard against the exercise of arbitrary power—to make available the common-sense judgment of the community as a hedge against the overzealous or mistaken prosecutor and in preference to the professional or perhaps over-conditioned or biased response of a judge. . . . This prophylactic vehicle is not provided if the jury pool is made up of only special segments of the populace or if large, distinctive groups are excluded from the pool. . . . Restricting jury service to only special groups or excluding identifiable segments playing major roles in the community cannot be squared with the constitutional concept of jury trial. . . .

We are also persuaded that the fair cross section requirement is violated by the systematic exclusion of women, who in the judicial district involved here amounted to 53 percent of the citizens eligible for jury service. This conclusion necessarily entails the judgment that women are sufficiently numerous and distinct from men that if they are systematically eliminated from jury panels, the Sixth Amendment's fair cross section requirement cannot be satisfied. . . .

Accepting as we do, however, the view that the Sixth Amendment affords the defendant in a criminal trial the opportunity to have the jury drawn from venires representative of the community, we think it is no longer tenable to hold that women as a class may be excluded or given automatic exemptions based solely on sex if the consequence is that criminal jury venires are almost totally male. To this extent we cannot follow the contrary implications of the prior cases, including *Holt v. Florida*. If it was ever the case that women were unqualified to sit on juries or were so situated that none of them should be required to perform jury service, that time has long since passed. If at one time it could be held that Sixth Amendment juries must be drawn from a fair cross section of the community but that this requirement permitted the total exclusion of women, this is not the case today. Communities differ at different times and places. What is a fair cross section at one time or place is not necessarily a fair cross section at another time or a different place.

Source: 419 U.S. 522, 1975.

6

Women's Sexuality Before World War I: Rape, Prostitution, and Reform

The history of the law's response to rape, the age of consent, prostitution, and cross-dressing (women or men disguised in opposite-sex clothing) in North America is a long and tortured one. As women struggled to define their sexual needs and identity, the clergy, the medical profession, and political traditionalists often viewed women's sexuality as a dangerous and disruptive force in society, in need of being held in check by fathers, husbands, and the state. Women were often accused of inviting sexual assault because of their dress, their so-named seductive behavior, and their venturing out beyond the home. Although most men sought to protect women of their own class and race from sexual exploitation, men and women often refused to acknowledge the sexual violence or misconduct of men from their own groups. The weight of the law and the stereotyping of men as rapists fell most heavily on American "outsiders": poor men, immigrants, and men of color. Women from these groups were most vulnerable to rape and the necessity of earning wages through prostitution.

The rape of a white woman was considered a heinous crime in North American colonial law; for example, a defendant found guilty of rape in Puritan Massachusetts or Connecticut could, theoretically, receive a death sentence. But even where punishment for rape was less severe, very few crimes of rape ever reached the courts, and when they did, men of good class standing were usually found innocent. Indians, servants, slaves, and free blacks were much more likely to be found guilty than white male property holders. In the eighteenth century prosecutors

began to charge male defendants with attempted rape, a crime subject
to a less serious sentence but one more likely to result in conviction.
Whether the charge was rape or attempted rape, female victims of rape
rarely came forward with accusations, and for good reason; whatever
the circumstances they were almost always put on trial themselves, a
practice that continues today and still discourages women from reporting rape.

At the turn of the eighteenth century, women in British North America
were often depicted in popular songs and printed matter as lusty, seductive, and incapable of controlling their own passions. The age of consent, or the age at which a female was legally considered adult enough
to consent to sexual relations, was commonly set at ten. Even though the
age of consent was raised in New York State in 1813 to fourteen,
working-class girls and women received almost no cooperation from the
judicial system in cases of sexual assault. Scholar Marybeth Hamilton
Arnold found that in 48 rape cases prosecuted in New York City between
1790 and 1820, one third of the alleged victims were under the age of
fourteen and of the 48 cases only 18 resulted in conviction. A lawyer
who defended a client accused of raping a thirteen-year-old in 1800 argued that she had consented to sex and that "passions may be as warm
in a girl of her age as in one of advanced years."[1] Unless a victim fought
back, was badly injured, had a pristine reputation, and was accompanied
in court by her father or husband, she had little chance of making charges
stick.

Both white indentured servants and African-American slaves were
subject to coercive sex because of their powerless status, a status re-
enforced by the rationalization that they were more bawdy and passionate than wives and daughters of the free-holding classes. Although the
rape of an indentured servant might technically be viewed as a crime, it
was rarely prosecuted, and slave women, who could not testify in court
or bring charges against their masters, had no legal recourse against rape.
Celia, who at the age of fourteen was purchased in a slave market, transported by her widowed master to a small farm in Missouri, and then
raped and made pregnant twice by him, killed him in her one-room
cabin when he refused to leave her alone after years of abuse. Remarkably, a white slave-holding lawyer defended her on the grounds that,
even though a slave, as a woman she was entitled to defend her body
from sexual violence. The defense was too radical for a slave-holding
society that had to preserve the absolute power of the master class at all
costs. Celia was found guilty and hanged in 1855.

Middle-class women were also victims of rape, but bringing charges
of rape against perpetrators brought dishonor to a victim's family and
put a woman's reputation in doubt, so few women reported the crime.
As the country became more urban, as young men needed more time to

prepare for occupations, and as Protestant piety spread among the middle classes, the pre-marital pregnancy rate and the birth rate declined. An ethos of what historian Nancy Cott has described as "passionlessness" for women was in place. Proper women were supposedly modest, inherently pure beings who did not enjoy the crude sexual advances of men. As women joined moral reform and abolitionist groups in the 1830s and 1840s, they used this ideology to discuss sexual matters more openly and to attack men's sexual behavior for what they labeled a "double standard." They argued that men might seduce or rape innocent daughters and slave women as well as purchase sex from prostitutes, but women had to pay for men's sexual proclivities with unmarried pregnancies, and sometimes, ruined lives. Moral reformers sought to protect their daughters from seduction in the city, to shun husbands who visited houses of prostitution, and to train their sons to postpone sex until marriage. They launched campaigns to convert those they perceived as victims of male lust to both upright living and to Christianity, but ultimately had to face the fact that most women chose prostitution as the only option they had for supporting themselves and their families.

Many women read the first American equivalent of pornography in the abolitionist accounts of slave abuse that circulated in the northern press of the 1840s. Rife with gory details of whippings, beatings, sexual coercion, and the sale of mulatto women into "fancy houses" in New Orleans and Charleston, many of these accounts were based on true stories. But they also echoed popular ideas about middle-class women's notions of what constituted proper sexual behavior. Women in middle-class novels were expected to live in utter shame or die once seduction or rape had sullied them. Enslaved women, like prostitutes, faced a complicated task in explaining to polite society their recovery and survival. An interesting example of that task is depicted in Harriet Jacobs's *Incidents in the Life of a Slave Girl*, published under the pseudonym of Linda Brent. Jacobs resisted her master's advances but had two children by another white man who had promised her freedom. How might she explain such an action to middle-class abolitionists who believed in passionlessness?

Many women also experienced sexual abuse from their husbands. Wives might not secure husbands' cooperation in the use of abstinence or withdrawal to space pregnancies, and still others found sexual intercourse painful as a result of childbirth injuries or gynecological infections. According to legal precedent, married women could not be raped because they had consented to conjugal relations with their husbands when they married; indeed, failure of either husbands or wives to have sexual intercourse was, dating back to the colonial period, one of the few legitimate grounds for divorce. As the nineteenth century progressed, however, women began to sue for separation or divorce on the grounds of sexual cruelty. By 1886 only six states, most of them in the South, did not grant divorce on the grounds of cruelty. But whatever the law, plaintiffs found their treatment in the courts to be capricious, dependent on judges' readings of evidence and precedent. Many judges continued to believe that the abuse of wives was less important than keeping marriages intact and that men were entitled to have sex with their wives no matter what the circumstances. In *English v. English*, the New Jersey Supreme Court overturned an 1876 lower court's decision granting Abigail English a divorce, despite her husband's brutal sexual treatment of her, on the grounds that women could expect sexual intercourse to be painful and because protecting the institution of marriage was paramount. By 1891 a Connecticut court was willing to concede that "marital sex . . . required the duty of forebearance on the part of the husband at the reasonable request of the wife, as well as the duty of submission on the part of the wife at the reasonable request of the husband."[2] Not until the rise of the women's liberation movement in the late 1960s did a serious discussion about making marital rape a crime ensue, but changing the law was no easy matter. One California state senator "joked" to a group of feminists in 1980, "If you can't rape your wife, who can you rape?"[3] By 1991, however, only four states continued to exempt marital sexual coercion from definitions of rape. Making charges of marital rape, "date rape," and father-daughter incest stick, however, continues to be difficult because most of these alleged crimes have no witnesses other than defendants and plantiffs.

By the second half of the nineteenth century prostitution, or what radicals such as Emma Goldman called "the traffic in women," was a widely discussed phenomenon not only among moral reformers but also in state legislatures and the U.S. Congress. Prostitution was most visible in the West, where there was a critical shortage of female sexual partners for men pouring into the region to mine, ranch, homestead, and in the case of many Chinese men, work as contract laborers on the transcontinental railroad. Some women were able to amass property and make handsome livings as madams. A Denver entrepreneur said that she had gone "into the sporting life for business reasons and for no other. It was a way for a woman in those days to make money, and I made it."[4] Latin American, Mexican, and Chinese women were subject to the most degrading conditions as prostitutes. The federal Page Act of 1875 forbade the immigration of Chinese contract labor and prostitutes, and legitimate immigration was made even more difficult with the Chinese Exclusion Act of 1882.

Chinese *tongs* (organized gangs or clans) conspired with U.S. customs officials, merchants, and Chinese madams to smuggle Chinese women into West Coast ports and to subject them to slave-like conditions. Some women were either kidnapped or lured onto ships with promises of legitimate employment in the United States, but poverty, famine, and the cultural inferiority of daughters in China contributed to the direct sale of women into prostitution or arranged marriage by Chinese families. Although some women were placed in arranged marriages, most were confined to the "cribs," virtual cages along the back alleys of city streets, forced to sell sexual services day and night to the roughest men of all races and classes. Escape was nearly impossible because the average prostitute produced a profit of $2,500 a year and the *tongs* made certain that runaways were recaptured.

By the turn of the twentieth century, middle-class outrage over prostitution, dubbed the "white slave trade" in the eastern press, was at a peak. A series of shocking exposés of U.S. prostitution rings in the Midwest and the East produced the Mann Act of 1910, which forbade the transportation of women across state lines for immoral purposes. Italians and Jews were stereotyped as the pliers of the white slave trade and a rash of semi-pornographic literature reinforced proper Americans' convictions that virtuous young white women were being drugged, kidnapped, and placed in houses of ill repute by dark-skinned foreigners. Prostitution, however, continued to thrive, and every city had its "red light" district by the time of World War I.

Reformers' attempts to raise the age of consent made some progress in the nineteenth century, and by 1895 it was between fourteen and eighteen in twenty-nine states. Black and white women's chapters of the Woman's Christian Temperance Union and other progressive women's groups focused next on the South, where "women's" age of consent was still ten. Women reformers' attempts were largely met with disdain or silence by white male state legislators, who feared traditional forms of community control over interracial sex and sociability might be undermined if rape laws were changed. A double standard continued to be applied to victims of rape by the dominant white community. While white women who were said to be victims of black rapists became objects of public sympathy and their alleged rapists often targets of lynch mobs, little concern was ever expressed when the rapists were white and the victims black. Disdainful of blacks generally, white authorities provided little protection for black women attacked by black men.

Although sexual coercion was far too common a woman's lot, some women tried to imagine what sexual freedom and fulfillment might mean. Dr. Elizabeth Blackwell, the first woman physician, argued that women felt the "immense power of sexual attraction" and suggested that women needed gentle physical affection from men as well as vaginal penetration to make sex pleasurable. A few medical guides said explicitly that the clitoris was the site of women's sexual pleasure, although most focused on women's supposed lack of sexual desire. Clelia Mosher, a female physician, interviewed women patients about their sex lives in the 1890s and found that many couples had achieved satisfactory sex lives, especially when husbands cooperated in family planning.

By the end of the Civil War, a number of women had experimented with cross-dressing, often to enlist in the army or to go west, but also to find jobs that would support their families or a female partner in a lesbian "marriage." A host of city laws that made cross-dressing a crime, especially in western cities such as San Francisco, reflected society's concern that women and men properly identify themselves through dress and that they remain heterosexual. Nonetheless, the East seemed full of "Boston marriages," two middle- or upper-class women living together and foregoing heterosexual relationships. Scholars have documented that some of these same-sex partnerships were sexual ones. With the birth of psychology at the turn of the century, more attention was paid to "sexual inversion," and gay women found themselves, along with gay men, categorized as "abnormal" by the experts.

Victoria Woodhull, who proclaimed herself a candidate for president of the United States in 1872, was demonized for her public declaration of the philosophy of free love. By 1900 Emma Goldman, an anarchist immigrant Russian Jew who was frequently arrested for her incendiary speeches, and socialist Charlotte Perkins Gilman echoed early reformers' belief that women should choose sexual partners on the basis of mutual love and desire. Goldman and Gilman argued that marriage was a form of prostitution; the married woman traded her reproductive, domestic, and sexual labor for economic support. Although Gilman thought marriage might be redeemed if women earned their own livings and were freed from domestic chores, Goldman insisted that the institution was inherently stifling for both women and men. Gilman, who had argued in her 1898 book *Women and Economics* that the sex instinct would become less dominant as women became more independent economically, could not have been more wrong about the sexual proclivities of the next century. Nonetheless, both women had a critical influence on generations of women who were willing to look at love, sex, and marriage in a more critical light.

READING GUIDE

Carby, Hazel V., *Reconstructing Womanhood: The Emergence of the Afro-American Woman Novelist*. New York: Oxford University Press, 1987. This important work probes the difficulties that African American women writers such as Harriet Jacobs had in depicting their lives in the face of a middle-class ideal that stressed women's passivity, piety, and chastity and that failed to address the question of what women might do—other than perish—once they had been seduced or raped.

Cohen, Patricia Cline, *The Murder of Helen Jewitt: The Life and Death of a Pros-

titute in Nineteenth Century New York. New York: Vintage Books, 1999. A fascinating account of the nation's first "tabloid" murder, but also a well-researched study of a young woman's decision to support herself with prostitution. Cohen evokes a fascinating world in New York City in the 1830s of sex for sale, especially to young men seeking to establish themselves in the business world before they married. In this incident, a jury chose a respectable man's story over the obvious evidence that he had murdered Helen Jewitt.

D'Emillo, John and Estelle B. Freedman, *Intimate Matters: A History of Sexuality in America*. New York: Harper and Row, 1988. This useful summary covers American sexual practice and the representation of sex in medical circles, popular culture, and advice books from 1600 to the present.

Faderman, Lillian, *Odd Girls and Twilight Lovers: A History of Lesbian Life in Twentieth-Century America*. New York: Penguin Books, 1992. Faderman uses diaries, letters, novels, advice from "sexologists," and newspapers to establish a rich history of lesbian culture in the United States. While love between women went virtually unnoticed before 1910, the "crackdown" on same-sex love of all sorts with the rise of psychology put lesbians under new scrutiny and helped to transform women's identity as lesbians.

McCunn, RuthAnn Lum, *Thousand Pieces of Gold*. Boston: Beacon Press, 1988. Based on the life of a real person, Lalu Nathoy, *Thousand Pieces of Gold* is a novelistic impression of a Chinese woman sold into prostitution who was transported to a mining town in Idaho to work in the saloon of a Chinese businessman. She gained her freedom through the kindness and devotion of a white miner; the unbalanced sex ratio of the mining towns made her valuable not only as a prostitute but as a wife. This book could be assigned in both high school and college classrooms.

McLaurin, Melton, *Celia, A Slave*. Athens: University of Georgia Press, 1991. McLaurin uncovered the Celia case while doing his doctoral research and in this fine monograph uses the behavior of the members of a white family and that of their slaves on a small farm in Missouri to elucidate how the personal relationships of slavery reflected politics, law, and culture in the South.

Palmieri, Patricia Ann, *In Adamless Eden: The Community of Women Faculty at Wellesley*. New Haven: Yale University Press, 1995. Palmieri looks at the rich women's culture of the faculty at Wellesley College between 1875 and 1910, a culture built on women's friendship, love relationships, and female households that often included mothers. Several generations of students and faculty at Welleseley created a world of social activism, academic scholarship, and fine teaching that drew sustenance from women's same-sex relationships, some of them, clearly, lesbian.

Pascoe, Peggy, *Relations of Rescue: The Search for Moral Authority in the American West, 1874–1939*. New York: Oxford University Press, 1990. Pascoe was one of the first scholars to take a fresh look at the efforts of middle class Protestant women to intervene in the lives of those they saw as the victims of sexual abuse in "heathen" societies: the Chinese, Native-Americans, and the Mormons, for instance. In the case of missionary homes created in the West to "rescue" Chinese women from prostitution, she finds that while the "victims" were subjected to heavy proselytizing, they were also able to use the homes to find new jobs and arrange marriages.

Smith-Rosenberg, Carroll, "Beauty, the Beast, and the Militant Woman: A Case Study in Sex Roles and Social Stress in Jacksonian America," in *Disorderly Conduct: Visions of Gender in Victorian America.* New York: Oxford University Press, 1985: 109–28. This classic essay, first published in 1971, explores the energetic attempts of middle class women to reform prostitution in New York City in the 1830s and 1840s. Smith-Rosenberg successfully dissects the class dynamics of a contradictory movement that wished to rescue women but could not declare itself unequivocally for women's rights.

Stansell, Christine, *City of Women: Sex and Class in New York, 1789–1860.* Urbana: University of Illinois Press, 1987. Stansell's account of working-class women's lives and moral reformers' attempts to influence them is the best treatment of the dynamics of prostitution in an urban setting before the Civil War. Stansell shows that the sale or exchange of sexual services was common, and that women and girls who did so were not stigmatized by their families or neighbors and might very well make a transition into respectable marriage. On the other hand, the harrowing task of supporting families in the tenements of New York meant that every woman was but a small step away from having to sell her body to feed herself and her children. Sexual battering and rape of both unmarried and married women was fairly common with little recourse for women except fighting back, often in alliance with other women, however they could.

Weisberg, D. Kelly, ed., *Applications of Feminist Legal Theory to Women's Lives: Sex, Violence, Work and Reproduction.* Philadelphia: Temple University Press, 1993: 405–532. These reprinted selections from recent feminist literature provide the latest thinking on why rape occurs, the judicial system's response to rape, and what might be done to protect women more fully, as well as specific essays on date rape, rape and racism, and marital rape.

Yung, Judy, *Unbound Feet: A Social History of Chinese Women in San Francisco.* Berkeley: University of California Press, 1995. Written by a young scholar whose own extended family had a fascinating history of migration between China and the United States, this history describes the largest population of Chinese women in the United States and changes in those women's lives to the end of World War II. Between 1860 and 1945, working-class Chinese women moved from prostitution and domestic slavery into the laundry, dress making, and restaurant trades, and by the 1940s into office and sales jobs. With Chinese husbands often feeling demoralized and closed out of decent jobs and barred from owning real estate, women often ran family businesses and kept families together. Yung interviewed a wide variety of women and provides their names in Chinese characters and in English.

NOTES

1. As quoted by Marybeth Hamilton Arnold, " 'The Life of a Citizen in the Hands of a Woman': Sexual Assault in New York City, 1790–1820," in *Passion and Power: Sexuality in History* (Philadelphia: Temple University Press, 1989), 42.

2. As quoted by Robert L. Griswold, "Law, Sex, Cruelty and Divorce in Victorian America, 1840–1900," *American Quarterly* 38 (Winter, 1986): 735.

3. As quoted by Kathleen C. Berkeley, *The Women's Liberation Movement in America* (Westport, CT: Greenwood Press, 1999), 69.

4. As quoted by Estelle B. Freedman and John D'Emillio, *Intimate Matters: A History of Sexuality in America* (New York: Harper and Row, 1988), 138.

DOCUMENTS

6.1. Dr. William Sanger Discusses Women's Sexual Desire

Dr. William Sanger worked as a physician at Blackwell's Island, where most New York City prostitutes were incarcerated or treated for disease. Sanger interviewed them, attempting to discover what had driven them to sell sex. He was surprised to learn that some women said, simply, that they had an "inclination" for prostitution, although nearly all had faced poverty and ill-paying jobs. He could not help editorializing, despite their answer of inclination, on what he believed to be women's true sexual nature.

"INCLINATION AND DESIRE"

In itself such an answer would imply an innate depravity, a want of true womanly feeling, which is actually incredible. The force of desire can neither be denied nor disputed, but still in the bosoms of most females that force exists in a slumbering state until aroused by some outside influences. No woman can understand its power until some positive cause of excitement exists. What is sufficient to awaken the dormant passions is a question that admits innumerable answers. Acquaintance with the opposite sex, particularly if extended so far as to become a reciprocal affection, will tend to this; so will the companionship of females who have yielded to its power; and so will the excitement of intoxication. But it must be repeated, and most decidedly, that without these or some other equally stimulating cause, the full force of sexual desire is seldom known to a virtuous woman. In the male sex nature has provided a more susceptible organization than in females, apparently with the beneficent design of repressing those evils which must result from mutual appetite equally felt by both. In other words, man is the *aggressive* animal, so far as sexual desire is involved. Were it otherwise, and the passions in both sexes equal, illegitimacy and prostitution would be far more rife in our midst than at present.

Source: William W. Sanger, *The History of Prostitution: Its Extent, Causes, and Effects Throughout the World*. Boston: Crowley, Nichols, and Company, 1855: 488–89.

6.2.   "Oversexed Women" and the Medical Establishment

While mid-nineteenth-century physicians and parents seemed to be obsessed with "onanism," or masturbation, in both men and women, women who were suspected of masturbation or sexual "promiscuity" came in for special criticism, and occasionally, sexual surgery, including clitoridectomy or ovarotomy. David T. Gilliam, a proponent of female castration, claimed that "patients are improved, some of them cured; [and] the moral sense of the patent is elevated. . . . She becomes tractable, orderly, industrious, and cleanly." In this medical analysis of 1883 Dr. Joseph Howe describes "nymphomania" and its cure. (Dr. Isaac Baker Brown was reputed to be the inventor of clitoridectomy.)

"NYPHOMANIA"

Nymphomania, sometimes called *furor uterinus*, is a disease peculiar to females. It often arises from masturbation, or excessive sexual indulgence. . . . Sometimes it manifests itself in healthy young women who have never masturbated, and who are innocent of any practical knowledge of the sexual relation. Such persons are naturally passionate, and their unsatisfied desires, their continence, is the real exciting cause of the affliction.

Nymphomania is apt to occur between the ages of sixteen and twenty-five. Blondes are more frequently subject to it than brunettes. It is characterized by an uncontrollable appetite for lascivious pleasures, exhibited (in its worst forms) in public and private, without regard to time, place, or surroundings. . . .

The only cure for the affliction is marriage, or amputation of the clitoris, according to the plan recommended by Baker Brown, who has reported numerous cures by the operation. In this connection it may be well to mention that Dr. Brown incurred the enmity of his professional brethren for a too free use of the operation . . . and was, I think, compelled to leave some of the London medical societies, of which he was a prominent member.

Source: Joseph W. Howe, *Excessive Venery, Masturbation, and Continence.* New York: Birmingham and Company, 1883: 108.

6.3.   An Advocate of Women's Rights Condemns Sexual Coercion in Marriage

Mary Gove lectured on women's physiology in the 1840s, and after leaving her first husband, married T.D. Nichols, a physician, and co-authored with him a book on marriage. The Nichols believed that women had less sensual desire than men but might enjoy sex under the proper circumstances. They attributed masturbation, or "diseased amativeness," and a host of other ills, including abortion, to loveless marriages and the economic dependence of wives.

PROMOTING VOLUNTARY MOTHERHOOD AND CONDEMNING SEXUAL COERCION

People are constantly asking the question, What would become of children if married persons were allowed to separate? *Let me tell conservatively that nine-tenths of the children that now burden the world would never be born.* Couples are held together by their own prejudices and the pressure of public opinion till a child is born. This child belongs to the father, and he wants a housekeeper and a nurse for it; he wants some one to reputably supply the amative want; perhaps the woman may be attractive to him—besides, the whole social mechanism holds this couple as in a vice together. The wife may have an utter indifference to the husband, or a loathing and abhorrence of him; but she must bear more children as a condition of support, and for the privilege of keeping the babe of her love in her bosom—of having something to fill her poor, desolate heart, and compensate her for a life of impurity which her spirit revolts against, till its oft violated instincts are unable to distinguish good from evil. . . .

The general idea and feeling, whether we know it or not, is that woman is property. She has no right to herself if she is married. Nine-tenths of the children born in marriage are not desired by the mother, often not by the father, though it is a great blessing that great love is born with them. Women have not, as a universal fact, the passion that asks the sexual indulgence. Vast numbers of the women of civilization have neither the sexual nor maternal passion. All women want love and support. They do not want to bear children, or to be harlots for this love or this support. . . .

When marriage becomes what it must be in a true freedom, *union in love*, it will be divinely beautiful. When it is a bargain, a sacrifice, made from other motives than affection, and, besides, is indissoluble, it is shocking to all true moral sense. When we consider love as alone sanctifying the union of the sexes, then we see the necessity of divorce, to prevent people living in adultery, who have married without love, or who have ceased to love after marriage.

Source: T.D. Nichols and Mary S. Gove Nichols, *Marriage: Its History, Character and Results; Its Sanctities, and Its Profanities: Its Science and Its Facts*. New York: T.D. Nichols, 1854.

6.4.   A Slave Girl Tries to Defend Herself from Sexual Assault

---

> *Harriet Jacobs was born a slave in Edenton, North Carolina, in 1813. Her first mistress taught her to read and write, but died when Harriet was twelve years old, leaving her in a will to a niece. In her new household, Jacobs encountered Dr. Norcom, who began a campaign to seduce her. The jealousy of Norcom's wife protected Jacobs for a time, but Norcom built a cottage where he intended to keep Jacobs as a mistress. Jacobs claimed to have resisted Norcom's advances but gave in to the sexual entreaties of a prominent lawyer, who later reneged on his promise to purchase the freedom of Harriet and their two children. Like many victims of childhood sexual abuse, Jacobs was afraid to confide in an adult, even her adored grandmother, but when she became pregnant, had no choice. She fled to Boston in 1843 and was reunited with her children but could only find meager wages as a seamstress; in 1861, she published her narrative at her own expense. Dependent on the sale of her book to white abolitionists, especially women abolitionists, Jacobs attempted to explain her behavior to an audience that believed women's sexual purity before marriage was of paramount importance. Dr. Flint is a pseudonym for Dr. Norcom.*

"THE TRIALS OF GIRLHOOD"

I now entered on my fifteenth year—a sad epoch in the life of a slave girl. My master began to whisper foul words in my ear. Young as I was, I could not remain ignorant of their import. I tried to treat them with indifference or contempt. The master's age, my extreme youth, and the fear that his conduct would be reported to my grandmother, made him bear this treatment for many months. . . . He tried his utmost to corrupt the pure principles my grandmother had instilled. He peopled my young mind with unclean images, such as only a vile monster could think of. I turned from him with disgust and hatred. But he was my master. I was compelled to live under the same roof with him—where I saw a man forty years my senior daily violating the most sacred commandments of nature. He told me I was his property; that I must be subject to his will in all things. My soul revolted against the mean tyranny. But where could I turn for protection? No matter whether the slave girl be as black as ebony or as fair as her mistress. In either case, there is no shadow of law to protect her from insult, from violence, or even from death; all these are inflicted by fiends who bear the shape of men. The mistress, who ought to protect the helpless victim, has no other feelings towards her but those of jealousy and rage. The degradation, the wrongs, the vices, that grow out of slavery, are more than I can describe. They are greater than you would willingly believe. . . .

I longed for some one to confide in. I would have given the world to have laid my head on my grandmother's faithful bosom, and told her all my troubles. But Dr. Flint swore he would kill me, if I was not as silent as the grave. Then, although my grandmother was all in all to me, I feared for her as well as loved her. I had been accustomed to look up to her with a respect bordering upon awe. I was very young, and felt shamefaced about telling her such impure things, especially as I knew her to be very strict on such subjects. . . .

O, ye happy women, whose purity has been sheltered from childhood, who have been free to choose the objects of your affection, whose homes are protected by law, do not judge the poor desolate slave girl too severely! If slavery had been abolished, I also, could have married the man of my choice; I could have had a home shielded by the laws; and I should have been spared the painful task of confessing what I am now about to relate; but all my prospects had been blighted by slavery. . . . I felt as if I was forsaken by God and man; as if all my efforts must be frustrated; and I became reckless in my despair. . . .

It chanced that a white unmarried gentlemen had obtained some knowledge of the circumstances in which I was placed. He knew my grandmother, and often spoke to me in the street. He became interested for me, and asked questions about my master, which I answered in part. He expressed a great deal of sympathy, and a wish to aid me. He constantly sought opportunities to see me, and wrote to me frequently. I was a poor slave girl, only fifteen years old.

So much attention from a superior person was, of course, flattering; for human nature is the same in all. I also felt grateful for his sympathy, and encouraged by his kind words. It seemed to me a great thing to have such a friend. By degrees, a more tender feeling crept into my heart. He was an educated and eloquent gentleman; too eloquent, alas, for the poor slave girl who trusted in him. Of course I saw whither all this was tending. I knew the impassable gulf between us; but to be an object of interest to a man who is not married, and who is not her master, is agreeable to the pride and feelings of a slave, if her miserable situation has left her any pride or sentiment. It seems less degrading to give one's self, than to submit to compulsion. There is something akin to freedom in having a lover who has no control over you, except that which he gains by kindness and attachment. A master may treat you as rudely as he pleases, and you dare not speak; moreover, the wrong does not seem so great with an unmarried man, as with one who has a wife to be made unhappy. There may be sophistry in all this; but the condition of a slave confuses all principles of morality, and in fact, renders the practice of them impossible. . . .

Of a man who was not my master I could ask to have my children well supported; and in this case, I felt confident I should obtain the boon. I also felt quite sure that they would be made free. With all these thoughts revolving in my mind, and seeing no other way of escaping the doom I so much dreaded, I made a headlong plunge. Pity me, and pardon me O virtuous reader! . . . The painful and humiliating memory will haunt me to my dying day. Still, in looking back, calmly, on the events of my life, I feel that the slave woman ought not to be judged by the same standard as others. . . .

I thought I could bear my shame if I could only be reconciled to my grandmother. I longed to open my heart to her. I thought if she could know the real state of the case, and all I had been bearing for years, she would perhaps judge me less harshly. My friend advised me to send for her. I did so; but days of agonizing suspense passed before she came. Had she utterly forsaken me? No. She came at last. I knelt before her, and told her the things that had poisoned my life; how long I had been persecuted; that I saw no way of escape; and in an hour of extremity I had become desperate. She listened in silence. I told her I would bear any thing and do any thing, if in time I had hopes of obtaining her forgiveness. I begged of her to pity me, for my dead mother's sake. And she did pity me. She did not say, "I forgive you;" but she looked at me lovingly, with her eyes full of tears. She laid her old hand gently on my head, and murmured, "Poor child! Poor child!"

Source: Linda Brent [Harriet Jacobs], *Incidents in the Life of a Slave Girl, Written by Herself*. Boston: 1861.

6.5.   A Case of Marital Rape

In 1876 Abigail English filed for divorce on the grounds of "extreme cruelty" in the state of New Jersey. She claimed that her husband John had subjected her to repeated sexual intercourse despite the fact that she experienced acute pain; when she re-

fused sex, her husband battered and raped her. Two physicians
corroborated her painful condition. A lower court granted her a
divorce, but suggested that if the couple reconciled the order
would be set aside. The New Jersey Court of Errors and Appeals
agreed to review the case, and set aside the lower court's divorce
decree. Citing John English's declaration of repentance and a
physician's advice, the higher court ruled that Abigail English
must return to her husband and submit to sexual intercourse, no
matter how painful, because marriage was too sacred a sacra-
ment to be overthrown so lightly.

ENGLISH V. ENGLISH

Our statute enacts that for extreme cruelty in either of the parties, the
Court of Chancery may decree a divorce from bed and board forever
thereafter, or for a limited time, as shall seem just and reasonable . . . and
this decree of perpetual separation has been made, unless the parties
shall voluntarily apply for a discharge. So far as the action of the court
is concerned, it is a separation of this husband and wife forever.

The act of separation is so important in its consequences to the parties
and to their children; it is so contrary to the policy of the law, which
rather seeks to "set the solitary in families," and keep them thus united
for their own good and for the welfare of society, that it is important in
every case to examine carefully whether those cogent reasons are to be
found which constrain the court to allow and order such separation.

We shall adopt the specific definition of extreme cruelty which has
been approved in this case, and inquire whether there has been a gross
abuse of marital rights. Such abuse must be attended with suffering,
injury to the health, and be against the will of the wife.

The case shows that from the time of the marriage, on August 21st
1867, to June, 1873, there is no complaint that she was abused in this
respect. But from that date up to the 6th day of November, 1875, when
she left her husband's house, taking with her their two little children,
she says that he has thus injured her. On June 3d, 1873, the third child
was born, and in the long and difficult delivery, which was effected with
instruments, she sustained such hurt that she was a sufferer until after
she left her home, and may be so still. She so testifies, and although her
husband denies all knowledge of any disorder, she is corroborated by
two physicians, who have examined her since the separation, and describe her condition. Since June 3d, 1873, the husband had access to her
frequently, when he must have known that she suffered, and was weakened by his acts. It is not requisite to give the particulars. Much of the
case on this point depends, necessarily, upon her own evidence, which
is sustained by the family physician to the extent that she needed rest

for her recovery from the delivery, the disorder that followed it, and a subsequent miscarriage in November, 1874. The wife made no complaint to any one excepting her husband, and continued to occupy the bed with him until within three days of her leaving. The evidence of Theodore G. Thomas, a physician who has made women's diseases a specialty, is that while in the situation in which he found her, soon after the separation, moderate indulgence would not damage her, yet the excessive indulgences would. He further says, although there would be pain, that a large proportion of married women assent under exactly those circumstances.

It is obvious that there should be an affectionate forbearance on the part of the husband when the wife is thus affected, and a selfish, lustful persistence, without regard to consequences, is unkind, even where no decided objection is made. But, in this case, it is charged that objections have been made, and considerable rudeness, if not force, used at times, to effect the purpose. This is the wife's statement, but it is denied by the husband, who says that the complaints were that she did not wish to have more children. She is a woman of a nervous and rather delicate constitution, and while her account may be exaggerated, we are satisfied that it is substantially correct. This evidence does not stand upon the wife's testimony alone: it is corroborated by other facts in the case, founded mainly on the defendant's own qualifications and denials of her statements.

On the night of November 3d, 1875, she complains that he was persistent and violent in his efforts, and as she arose from the bed, after his failure to succeed, he struck her in the back with his fist. She says that her cries awoke the children, and were heard by the servant. . . . On Saturday, November 6th, she left, taking with her the two little children, and went to her father's house, where she has since remained. . . .

It is important to consider the relations of the parties during their marriage, and some facts since their separation, to arrive at a just conclusion in this peculiarly delicate and painful case.

After the marriage, he was always kind and affectionate, with the exception of the matters of this complaint. He provided a good home for her, and gave her every reasonable indulgence and allowance . . . The relatives, friends and servants who have been called as witnesses, all testify that they were fond in their endearments, even in the presence of others, and that they were remarkably affectionate. The wife says that she loved him until the day after November 2d, when he was morose and sullen in his conduct. His affection for her appears to have been always strong, and continues, so that he describes himself as miserable in his separation from his wife and children, and he says he is willing to make any reasonable concessions if she will return. . . .

The point of determination is not whether the husband, in his rudeness, has injured his wife without sufficient thought or care of her physical health, while doing an act which, in ordinary cases, is not unlawful, injurious or dangerous, for it must be conceded under the facts of this case that he has thus abused his martial rights; but the true inquiry is whether the conduct of the husband has been such as to raise a reasonable apprehension that further acts of the same abuse will be committed if the wife should return to him. The court must be satisfied that the wife is in danger of bodily harm if she go back to him, or that he has done and will continue to do such acts as will endanger her health, or render her life one of such extreme discomfort and wretchedness as to incapacitate her to discharge the duties of a wife. It is not the question whether she will live more comfortably at her father's house, with a liberal allowance for alimony, but whether she is released from her duty as a wife by the extreme cruelty of her husband, and the reasonable apprehension that it will continue. The principle which must decide this case does not affect these parties alone: it is of the utmost importance to all, that these bonds should not be lightly severed.

A separation from bed and board is not decreed only as a punishment for past misconduct, but mainly as a protection against future probable acts of cruelty. . . . It is not necessary, if we were disposed, to go so far in this case, for we see no reasonable ground to apprehend that this defendant, whose disposition appears to be affectionate towards his family, and who has been already subjected to distress, exposure and expense, as the consequences of his misconduct, will again transgress, with the certainty that he will, with such aggravation, be perpetually separated from his wife. . . . We are of the opinion that this divorce should now be refused.

Source: New Jersey Equity Reports, June Term, 1876, 27: 580–86.

6.6.   A Chinese Immigrant Woman's "Contract"

This is a typical "contract," usually signed with an X, by Chinese women lured, kidnapped, or sold into prostitution in China and then transported to the United States. Enforced by the long arm of the "tongs," and generally ignored by U.S. legal authorities, few women could escape their indentured servitude as prostitutes. On the other hand, as scholar Judy Yung observes, the contracts were often used as evidence of the need to exclude Chinese immigrants altogether.

CHINESE IMMIGRATION: THE SOCIAL, MORAL, AND POLITICAL EFFECT

An agreement to assist the woman, Ah Ho, because coming from China to San Francisco she became indebted to her mistress for passage. Ah Ho herself asks Mr. Yee Kwan to advance for her six hundred and thirty dollars, for which Ah Ho distinctly agrees to give her body to Mr. Yee for service of prostitution for a term of four years. There shall be no interest on the money. An Ho shall receive no wages. At the expiration of four years, Ah Ho shall be her own master. Mr. Yee Kwan shall not hinder or trouble her. If Ah Ho runs away before her time is out, her mistress shall find her and return her, and whatever expense is incurred in finding and returning her, Ah Ho shall pay. On this day of agreement Ah Ho, with her own hands, has received from Mr. Yee Kwan six hundred and thirty dollars. If Ah Ho shall be sick at any time for more than ten days, she shall make up by an extra month of service for every ten days' sickness. Now this agreement has proof—this paper received by Ah Ho is witness, dated 1873.

Source: Judy Yung, *Unbound Feet: A Social History of Chinese Women in San Francisco*. Berkeley: University of California Press, 1995: 27.

6.7.   Emma Goldman Analyzes the "White Slave Trade"

In 1910 the anarchist Emma Goldman published her lectures and included "The Traffic in Women," an analysis of prostitution in large American cities. Like other radicals, Goldman argued that prostitution was an inevitable result of women's exploitation in the labor force. Goldman observed that women of color, not just white women, were commodities in the sex trade; a twentieth-century "modernist" and advocate of free love, she argued for sex education and woman's right to express sexual passion without recrimination. Her reference to "Mrs. Warren" comes from George Bernard Shaw's play comparing marriage and prostitution, Mrs. Warren's Profession.

"THE TRAFFIC IN WOMEN"

Our reformers have suddenly made a great discovery—the white slave traffic. The papers are full of these "unheard-of conditions," and law-makers are already planning a new set of laws to check the horror. . . .

What is really the cause of the trade in women? Not merely white

women, but yellow and black women as well. Exploitation, of course;
the merciless Moloch of capitalism that fattens on underpaid labor, thus
driving thousands of women and girls into prostitution. With Mrs. Warren these girls feel, "Why waste your life working for a few shillings a
week in a scullery, eighteen hours a day?" . . .

Nowhere is woman treated according to the merit of her work, but
rather as a sex. It is therefore almost inevitable that she should pay for
her right to exist, to keep a position in whatever line, with sex favors.
Thus it is merely a question of degree whether she sells herself to one
man, in or out of marriage, or to many men. Whether our reformers
admit it or not, the economic and social inferiority of woman is responsible for prostitution.

Just at present our good people are shocked by the disclosures that in
New York City alone one out of every ten women works in a factory,
that the average wage received by women is six dollars per week for
forty-eight to sixty hours of work, and that the majority of female wage
workers face many months of idleness which leaves the average wage
about $280 a year. In view of these economic horrors, is it to be wondered
at that prostitution and the white slave trade have become such dominant factors? . . .

It is a conceded fact that woman is being reared as a sex commodity,
and yet she is kept in absolute ignorance of the meaning and importance
of sex. Everything dealing with that subject is suppressed, and persons
who attempt to bring light into this terrible darkness are persecuted and
thrown into prison. Yet it is nevertheless true that so long as a girl is
not to know how to take care of herself, not to know the function of the
most important part of her life, we need not be surprised if she becomes
an easy prey to prostitution, or to any other form of a relationship which
degrades her to the position of an object for mere sex gratification.

We have long ago taken it as a self-evident fact that the boy may
follow the call of the wild; that is to say, that the boy may, as soon as
his sex nature asserts itself, satisfy that nature; but our moralists are
scandalized at the very thought that the nature of a girl should assert
itself. To the moralist prostitution does not consist so much in the fact
that the woman sells her body, but rather that she sells it out of wedlock.
That this is no mere statement is proved by the fact that marriage for
monetary considerations is perfectly legitimate, sanctified by law and
public opinion, while any other union is condemned and repudiated. Yet
a prostitute, if properly defined, means nothing else than "any person
for whom sexual relationships are subordinated to gain." . . .

Fully fifty per cent of married men are patrons of brothels. It is through
this virtuous element that the married women—nay, even the children—
are infected with venereal diseases. Yet society has not a word of con-
demnation for the man, while no law is too monstrous to be set in motion

against the helpless victim. She is not only preyed upon by those who use her, but she is also absolutely at the mercy of every policeman and miserable detective on the beat, the officials at the station house, the authorities in every prison.

Much stress is laid on white slaves being imported into America . . . but I absolutely deny that prostitution is recruited to any appreciable extent from Europe. It may be true that the majority of prostitutes of New York City are foreigners, but that is because the majority of the population is foreign. The moment we go to any other American city, to Chicago or the Middle West, we shall find that the number of foreign prostitutes is by far a minority. . . .

Equally exaggerated is the belief that the majority of street girls in this city were engaged in this business before they came to America. Most of the girls speak excellent English, are Americanized in habits and appearance,—a thing absolutely impossible unless they had lived in this country many years. That is, they were driven into prostitution by American conditions, by the thoroughly American custom of excessive display of finery and clothes, which of course, necessitates money,—money that cannot be earned in shops or factories. . . .

Just as absurd is it to proclaim the myth that the Jews furnish the largest contingent of willing prey. No one but the most superficial will claim that Jewish girls migrate to strange lands, unless they have some tie or relation that brings them there. The Jewish girl is not adventurous. Until recent years she had never left home, not even so far as the next village or town, except it were to visit some relative. Is it then credible that Jewish girls would leave their parents or families, travel thousands of miles to strange lands, through the influence and promises of strange forces? Go to any of the large incoming steamers and see for yourself if these girls do not come either with their parents, brothers, aunts, or other kinsfolk. There may be exceptions, of course, but to state that large numbers of Jewish girls are imported for prostitution, or any other purpose, is simply not to know Jewish psychology. . . .

Source: Emma Goldman, *Anarchism and Other Essays*. New York: Mother Earth Publishing Company, 1910: 177–92.

6.8.   Cross-Dressing Women

> *By the late nineteenth century social critics commented on the number of women living together in marriage-like arrangements. Scholars have described these as "woman-identified" relationships, and we know that some of them were sexual. While*

women of means or women in the professions might support
themselves and their families, working-class women could rarely
support themselves without men. Some working-class lesbians
dressed as men, particularly in occupations such as mining,
ranching, and heavy industrial work, and took women partners
as "wives."

"WOMAN WHO POSED AS MAN 60 YEARS, DEAD: ONLY REASON WAS TO SECURE MAN'S WORK"

Katherine Vosbaugh, who for sixty years posed as a man, wearing male garb, living the rough life of the pioneers in the Southwest and who even "married" another woman, died yesterday morning. . . . Born nearly forty years ago in France of a good family, this remarkable woman donned male garb when but a slip of a girl, came to America and worked as a bank clerk, bookkeeper, restauranteur, cook and sheep herder . . . without her sex being known. . . . Two years ago, "Frenchy" . . . was taken with pneumonia and brought to the hospital where her secret was revealed. Even then, this strange woman refused to wear skirts. Clad in regulation man's attire, she has since worked about the hospital and was known by the nickname of "Grandpa. . . ."

The name of her "wife" was never learned, but the ceremony seems to have taken place for the purpose of saving the woman's good name. A few months after the marriage a child was born to the wife, which died after a few months. Shortly after the death of the child the two women came to this city and opened a restaurant on Commercial street. . . . The establishment was one of the most popular restaurants in the southwest. What became of "Frenchy's" wife is not known. She drifted away and her "husband" refused until the time of her death to reveal the woman's name. . . .

The eccentricities of youth became more pronounced as she grew older and more and more she came to look like a man. For years she lived with men on the ranch cooking for them assisting them in the ranch work and sleeping in the same rooms, but her secret was never suspected.

Source: Trinidad [Colorado] Advertiser, November 11, 1907.

6.9.   Women Identified Women

By 1900 the "sexologists," early psychologists who wrote about
sexuality and sexual practice, had condemned female partner-
ships as deviant or "perverse," and their views had begun to
spread to college administrators and those who gave advice to

*young women. From an older generation, Frances Willard had
several such relationships and no misgivings about the healthi-
ness of love relationships between women. The "maids of Llangollen" is a reference to two aristocratic women of Ireland and
Wales who ran away in 1778 and lived together for more than
fifty years.*

"THE FRIENDSHIPS OF WOMEN"

The loves of women for each other grow more numerous each day,
and I have pondered much why these things are. That so little should
be said about them surprises me, for they are everywhere. Perhaps the
"Maids of Llangollen," (in Wales) afford the most conspicuous example;
two women, young and fair, with money and position, who ran away
together, refusing all offers to return, and spent their happy days in each
other's calm companionship. . . . In these days, when any capable and
careful woman can honorably earn her own support, there is no village
that has not its examples of "two hearts in counsel," both of which are
feminine. Oftentimes these joint proprietors have been unfortunately
married, and so have failed to "better their condition" until, clasping
hands, they have taken each other "for better or for worse." These are
the tokens of a transition age. Drink and tobacco are to-day the great
separatists between women and men. Once they used these things together, but woman's evolution has carried her beyond them; man will
climb to the same level some day, but meanwhile . . . the fact that he
permits himself fleshly indulgences . . . make their planes different. . . .
Among the leading advocates of woman's advancement, and of an equal
standard of chastity for both sexes, we do not find tobacco users or drink-
ers of beer and wine. The friendships of women are beautiful and
blessed.

Source: Frances Willard, *Glimpses of Fifty Years: The Autobiography of an American
Woman*. Chicago: H.J. Smith, 1889: 641–42.

7

The Atlanta Laundresses' Strike, Self-Help, and Anti-Lynching: African-American Women's Rights Between Emancipation and World War I

With the defeat of the Confederacy in 1865, the South faced revolutionary change. African Americans expected to gain specific freedoms: reestablishing families or dissolving nonconsensual relationships arranged by slaveholders, earning wages for their labor, moving about freely, and obtaining land and the right to vote. With plantation owners desperate for workers to harvest cash crops, city councils and state legislatures imposed stringent new restrictions on what they termed (black) "vagrancy" and prohibited moving about on public roads and city streets in search of food, shelter, and jobs. Assumed to be prostitutes if not at work in kitchens or on plantations, black women were subject to imprisonment and to sexual assault by policemen and jailers. Without any cash on hand and banks in chaos, plantation owners were unable, even if they had been willing, to pay wages to ex-slaves, and every southern city was inundated with poor migrants, black and white, more of them women than men, seeking employment and shelter. The Freedmen's Bureau, a federal agency appointed to protect ex-slaves but also to keep them in the South doing plantation farming, assumed that black families, with men in charge, should contract their labor for the next year's crop.

The Republican party sought to protect black male suffrage with the Fifteenth Amendment but save for a few Radicals did not consider overturning the property rights of plantation owners with land reform. African Americans discussed the political resolution of their plight in large mass meetings in which the line between religious worship and politics blurred. Men and women had their say, and during Reconstruction, some women went to the polls to participate in elections. Historians of African-American women's history disagree over the extent to which women continued to exercise autonomy within their communities. They do agree, however, that by 1880 or so, a black male professional and middle class had assumed governance over civic organizations and in the churches, easing women out of the decision making process and into separate women's associations, a fact upon which women such as Anna J. Cooper and Frances Watkins Harper commented.

A series of poor cotton crops and bad weather following the Civil War pushed an already devastated region into economic catastrophe. A new labor system developed in the South that had many elements of the old. While African-American land ownership grew slowly but steadily, most families were forced to work for whites. White landowners had expected to return to a gang labor system with women and men working alongside each other in the fields from dawn to dusk. But African Americans wanted to remove women from the double duty labor they had performed as field hands and mothers and to spare them from the sexual abuses they might face when supervised by white men. Tenant farming and share cropping was the result. Black (and many white) farmers worked the land of plantation owners on borrowed seed, implements, and mules in expectation of payment on the next year's crop, plunging themselves deep in debt to landowners and country stores. Black women were rarely able to stay out of the fields for long, but at least they might intermingle domestic and field responsibilities on their own time and under the supervision of their husbands rather than white overseers. This system left women enmeshed in the nuclear family and with few recognizable individual rights, their husbands' authority re-enforced by the black churches.

Black women who lived in cities tried to work out similar arrangements in domestic work, almost always their only choice of occupation beyond field work. By 1880, for example, 98 percent of all African-American women wage earners in Atlanta, Georgia, were domestics in this steadily growing city of the "New South," with its railroad connections, factories, cotton brokerages, and commercial establishments. Black domestics tried to avoid live-in servant arrangements, which kept them trapped in white homes in work days that never ended and unable to care for their own children, and made them vulnerable to sexual assault by white men. They preferred day work, and, if possible, sewing or taking in laundry, which allowed them to work collectively in their own neighborhoods while supervising their children. White women employers and black women servants engaged in day-to-day warfare over wages, work schedules, and the size of something southerners called the "service pan" (leftovers or food supplies from the kitchen carried by black women home to their families). Black women servants fought back by refusing to do some kinds of work, malingering, and leaving jobs they considered unacceptable, a practice known to both employers and servants as "quitting." Scholar Tera Hunter argues that despite the excess of women looking for domestic work in Atlanta, "quitting" allowed black women some control over working conditions and created the false impression of a servant shortage.

Doing laundry remained the most arduous task of housework well into the twentieth century, requiring heavy lifting, building hot fires, and back-breaking work over washtubs and ironing boards. Even poor southern white women who did their own cooking and cleaning sent their laundry out; between 1880 and 1890 in Atlanta, for example, washerwomen had increased by 150 percent and general domestics by only 15 percent. Laundresses organized "secret societies" in urban communities, paying in small dues and pledging to work together for higher rates. They went on strike in Jackson, Mississippi, in 1866, in Galveston, Texas, in 1877, and in Atlanta in 1881. During these strikes they attacked Chinese and other commercial laundries, claiming the right to set rates and to monopolize the laundry trade. Gains from these strikes were ephemeral, but they reminded white women employers that laundresses and servants could stand up to poor treatment. Many whites, however, assumed that black women were destined to serve them. During World War I, when "work or fight" laws were passed to force strikers back to work, a few southern cities used the stratagem to coerce black women to work as servants and arrested some of those who refused for vagrancy.

Factory jobs, with the exception of the tobacco industry, remained closed to black women well into the twentieth century, and the desperate poverty of the South continued to pit black women and white women against each other, not only in the mistress-servant relationship, but as neighbors struggling for survival in working-class communities. Thousands of whites, many of them women and children, found work in the cotton mills of the South, and they guarded those jobs with ferocity. When twenty black women were hired by the Fulton Bag and Cotton mill in 1897 in Atlanta to fold bags, two hundred white women workers walked out and demanded the black women be fired. (Some of these women protestors sent their laundry out to black women.) A strike by both men and women at the mill forced Fulton to restrict black employment to janitorial work.

Although there was a brief flurry of interracial cooperation among white and black farmers in the Populist movement of the 1890s, the presidential election of 1896 signaled the doom of a progressive racial politics in the South for decades to come. With "Jim Crow" and disenfranchisement firmly in place and sanctioned by Supreme Court decisions in *Plessy v. Ferguson* (1896) and *Williams v. Mississippi* (1898), southern states enacted segregation laws everywhere and forced black men from the voting rolls with grandfather clauses, literacy tests, and poll taxes. The federal government had turned its back on ex-slaves and allowed the "race question" to be settled by white conservatives in the South.

While segregation, exclusion from most occupations, and disenfranchisement were bad enough, black women and men faced the constant threat of violence. As more blacks created small businesses, bought land, and formed political organizations, they were assaulted by gang rapists and lynch mobs. The "myth of the black rapist," the southern claim that white women's virtue was in danger from sexual assault by brutish black men, was used to justify the lynching of black men and to ignore the lynching and rape of black women. Ida B. Wells's pioneering investigative journalism of lynching in the South, drawn almost entirely from white southern newspapers, proved that attempted rape was almost never the real cause of lynching and that economic competition with whites was a more likely one. Rumors of rape were used to mobilize white vigilantes who executed black men without benefit of a trial, sometimes mutilating or burning their bodies as well. Rather than admit that white women sometimes had love affairs or consensual sexual relations with black men, most whites constructed black male/white female sex as rape. Although many black women in the South had joined the Woman's Christian Temperance Union, its president, Frances Willard, defended lynching as a form of social control over drunken black men. The "protection" of white womanhood from the "black rapist" put white women at the center of what white southerners defined as their "way of life." White women and children attended lynchings, which were often "festive" affairs, and by the 1910s and 1920s women had joined the Ku Klux Klan in large numbers.

As black women faced their situation, they adopted a strategy that novelist Alice Walker and historian Elsa Barkley Brown have described as "womanism." Womanism confronted the complicated nexus of racism directed at men as well as women, the connections among race, sex, and violence, discrimination in public services, and reaffirmed the dictum that "women's issues may be race issues, and race issues may be women's issues."[1] Black women addressed widespread poverty and ill health among blacks, the necessity of community development and self-help, and the reclaiming and expansion of political rights. In Richmond, Virginia, Maggie Lena Walker, a former laundress and teacher, argued that black women were particularly important in community organizing and that they should exercise "every talent that God had given them" in order to "raise the race to higher planes of living."[2] She welcomed both working-class and middle-class women into the Independent Order of Saint Luke, a mutual benefit and insurance society, and with their help founded educational institutions, a penny savings bank, a newspaper, and a department store. Women members of Saint Luke protested against segregated streetcars, lynching, and inferior schools for black children. When male leaders claimed that women's club work was "decadent" and drew wives and mothers away from the home, she argued their activism was indispensable to elevating the race and, like many other African-American women leaders, saw no contradiction in combining motherhood, paid work, and volunteer activism.

Walker is but one example of the many middle-class woman who mobilized in the 1890s against deteriorating political and social conditions for black people. They organized women's clubs all over the country and created a National Association of Colored Women's Clubs in 1896. Middle-class black women were forced to reconcile a number of contradictions in doing their political work. They had to be militant but ladylike, claim a public space for women without undermining their sexual integrity, and attack poverty and discrimination in employment while also suggesting that the "race" might advance if working-class blacks adopted middle-class values of temperance, thrift, and hard work, an argument that sometimes echoed white criticisms of blacks. In order to defend black men against potential charges of rape and the whole race against charges of promiscuity, these women downplayed the sexual abuse and rape of black women by black men and harped on what they viewed as promiscuous behavior in some black women. (Such a political tendency reappeared in some sectors of the African-American community during Anita Hill's testimony concerning Supreme Court nominee Clarence Thomas's alleged sexual harassment in 1991.)

Black women were also on the defensive in dealing with white women's movements. They faced race discrimination in their own communities but also in the woman suffrage, anti-lynching, and temperance movements; race-segregated chapters in national movements were nearly the universal rule. Some of the most important interracial work in the early twentieth century was accomplished in the Young Women's Christian Association, the Baptist conventions, and the Methodist Episcopal Church, using the ethos of Protestant benevolence and women's volunteer work to justify race cooperation. Nonetheless, black women were always cast in the role of supplicants in these white maternalist organizations.

In addition to Walker, two women stand out as national leaders in black women's rights before World War I. Ida B. Wells Barnett, a daughter of Mississippi slaves who became a teacher and a journalist, made protests against the rape of black women and the lynching of blacks her life's crusade when three close friends were killed by a mob in Memphis in 1892. Forced to leave the South after her newspaper *Free Speech* was raided and destroyed, she settled in Chicago, married a lawyer, had children, and recruited black voters in Chicago. Never apologetic, always direct, her firebrand radicalism on the race question sparked criticism from both blacks and whites. She often clashed with Mary Church Terrell of Washington, D.C., an Oberlin College graduate and an upper-class-conscious clubwoman, over which one of them would speak for black clubwomen and the anti-lynching movement. Walker, Barnett, and Terrell were also active in the suffrage movement and the National Association for the Advancement of Colored People (NAACP), an interracial civil rights movement formed in 1909.

African-American women leaders often found themselves marginalized in national civil rights organizations and the black churches, and some of them said publicly that black ministers and politicians, in particular, were unable to acknowledge women as co-equals in the struggle. But women's steady and indispensable presence in the civil rights struggle became apparent in the Montgomery Bus Boycott of 1955–1956, for instance, when the Women's Political Council of Montgomery used its church networks to convince riders, most of them black women domestic workers, to stay off the buses. Best known for the emergence of Martin Luther King, Jr., the boycott in Montgomery also signaled a new mass movement that crossed class lines and that depended on the political activism of women for its success. More than sixty years after the laundry strike in Atlanta, working-class black women in Montgomery launched a city-wide boycott of the buses that led to the demise of Jim Crow segregation in the South.

READING GUIDE

Brown, Elsa Barkley, "Negotiating and Transforming the Public Sphere: African American Political Life in the Transition from Slavery to Freedom," *Public Culture* 7 (1994), 107–46, and "Womanist Consciousness: Maggie Lena Walker and the Independent Order of Saint Luke," *Signs* 14 (no. 3, 1989), 610–33. Brown has overturned traditional thinking about African-American women's political consciousness, showing that feminism *per se* was inappropriate to their situation and that in looking for and not finding it, scholars have ignored "womanism," a version of black women's rights that addressed the complexities of race and class as well as gender. In her painstaking research of Richmond sources, Brown documents the political activism of black women from the moment of emancipation into the 1920s and also tackles the difficult question of how the oppression of black women has sometimes been lost in the struggle to empower black men in the civil rights movement.

Giddings, Paula, *When and Where I Enter: The Impact of Black Women on Race and Sex in America*. New York: William Morrow, 1984. This well-written narrative of black women's history focuses on important women leaders in the civil rights movement from the anti-lynching movement through the 1970s and is a useful introduction to the subject.

Hall, Jacquelyn Dowd, " 'The Mind That Burns in Each Body': Women, Rape and Racial Violence," in Ann Snitow, Christine Stansell, and Sharon Thompson, eds., *Powers of Desire: The Politics of Sexuality*. New York: Monthly Review Press, 1983: 328–49. In this graceful essay, Hall explores the dark layers of lynching and rape in the South and their reverberations for contemporary feminism. She reminds white women that definitions of rape and the prosecution (or non-prosecution) of rape have often been used by powerful white men to justify lynching and the jailing of black men while ignoring the rape of black women entirely and continuing their own freedom to "predation" on black and white women alike. These factors present complications for black and white women's relationships with each other that are still ongoing.

Hewitt, Nancy A. and Suzanne Lebsock, eds., *Visible Women: New Essays on American Activism*. Urbana: University of Illinois Press, 1993. A number of essays in this volume explore middle-class community activism in the South, some of it interracial. See Deborah Gray White, "The Cost of Club Work, The Price of Black Feminism," Marion W. Roydhouse, "Bridging Chasms: Community and the Southern YWCA," and Mary E. Frederickson, " 'Each One Is Dependent on the Other': Southern Church Women, Racial Reform, and the Process of Transformation, 1900–1930" (243–324).

Higginbotham, Evelyn Brooks, *Righteous Discontent: The Women's Movement in the Black Baptist Church, 1880–1920*. Cambridge: Harvard University Press, 1993. More African Americans in the United States belonged to the National Baptist Convention than any other denomination. Higginbotham characterizes the black churches as "public space," where social welfare, anti-lynching and Jim Crow campaigns, and "race uplift" work were organized by women. Despite their "separate and unequal status . . . women were crucial to broadening the public arm of the church and making it the most powerful institution of racial self-help in the African American community" (2–3).

Hine, Darlene Clark, Wilma King, and Linda Reed, eds., *"We Specialize in the Wholly Impossible": A Reader in Black Women's History*. Brooklyn: Carlson Publishing, 1995. This reader contains a variety of up-to-date essays on black women's history, many of them devoted to post-emancipation topics.

Hine, Darlene Clark, ed., *Black Women in United States History*, 16 vols. Brooklyn: Carlson Publishing, 1990. This invaluable collection of original source material, scholarly articles, and monographs is a gold mine of information and interpretation. Volumes 1–4 cover colonial times through the nineteenth century, volumes 5–8 through the twentieth century, volumes 9–10 "Theory and Practice," and volumes 11–14 monographs on attitudes toward black women, 1880–1920, as well as black women in organized reform and the civil rights movement, and biographies and the original works of Jane E. Hunter, Mary Church Terrell, and Ida B.Wells Barnett.

Hunter, Tera W., *To 'Joy My Freedom: Southern Black Women's Lives and Labors After the Civil War*. Cambridge: Harvard University Press, 1997. This rich study of working-class women's lives in Atlanta from emancipation through the Great Migration to the North during World War I presents black women as active agents of their own destinies, determined to have a say in the use of public space and negotiating labor conditions. The work of Hunter and Brown challenges Jones's supposition of a clear separation between the private and the public spheres of African-American life and does not subsume black women into the family. In Jones's defense, however, the urban-rural divide was a large one in the nineteenth century, and it is doubtful that either white or black rural women had the options Hunter and Brown find for women in Richmond and Atlanta.

Jones, Jacqueline, *Labor of Love, Labor of Sorrow: Black Women, Work and the Family from Slavery to the Present*. New York: Vintage Books, 1986. Jones was among the first scholars to write about the black family after emancipation without the negative characterizations of social scientists such as E. Franklin Frazier and Daniel Patrick Moynihan, characterizations that cast black families as "emasculated," broken, and passive in the wake of poverty and discrimination. The bulk of Jones's book covers southern rural and urban black women in the years from 1865 through 1930. She argues that tenant farming was a mixed blessing for black women, releasing them from the worst excesses of slavery but plunging them into a patriarchal nuclear family structure that, along with poverty, made them subject to the control of their husbands and fathers.

Kerber, Linda K., " 'I Am Just as Free and Just as Good as You Are': The Obligation Not to Be a Vagrant," *No Constitutional Right to Be Ladies*. New York: Farrar, Straus and Giroux, 1998: 47–80. In this stunning essay, Kerber explores the evolution of American ideas about vagrancy, and concludes that it "obligates" poor women, and men, "not to be idle," but "not to be idle" in certain ways: black women, for instance, have been assumed to be "idle" when they were not at work for whites or were visible in public places. Older notions of idleness based on race and gender were inscribed in New Deal and Great Society policies and have recently shown up again in the welfare reform policies of the states and the federal government in the 1990s.

Royster, Jacqueline Jones, *Southern Horrors and Other Writings: The Anti-Lynching Campaign of Ida B. Wells, 1892–1900*. Boston: Bedford Books, 1997. This small reader contains the most important writings of Wells and a helpful biography and bibliography and should be useful in both high school and college level classes.

NOTES

1. Elsa Barkley Brown, "Womanist Consciousness: Maggie Lena Walker and the Independent Order of Saint Luke," *Signs* 14 (no. 3, 1989), 611.

2. As quoted by Brown, "Womanist Conciousness," 627.

DOCUMENTS

7.1.   **Laundry Strikes by Black Women in Galveston and Atlanta**

Accounts of African-American women's laundry strikes that have survived come from white-run newspapers. Two such accounts follow, one from Galveston, Texas, in 1877, and one from Atlanta in 1881. The "amused" tone of both of these articles emphasizes the often-employed stereotype of the assertive black woman making a public disgrace of herself by assaulting non-striking workers and Chinese competitors. In Atlanta the City Council considered a licensing fee on personal as well as commercial laundries to break the strike. Already working long hours and with no discretionary income to spare, the licensing fee discouraged some washerwomen but steeled others in their cause. They presented their demands to the City Council in a defiant letter that presents the solidarity of husbands and wives in the black working class in a quite different way than the Atlanta Constitution *did. Historians do not know what the outcome of these strikes was, except that both cities used arrests for vagrancy and the threat of the chain gang to intimidate strikers.*

"SO-CALLED WASHERWOMEN, ALL COLORED, GO FOR EACH OTHER AND THE HEATHEN CHINESE"

Monday night colored women, emboldened by the liberties allowed their fathers, husbands and brothers, during Monday, and being of a jealous nature, determined to have a public hurrah yesterday of their own, and as the men had demanded two dollars for a day's labor they would ask $1.50, or $9 per week. As women are generally considered cleansers of dirty linen, their first move was against the steam laundry, corner of Avenue A and Tenth street, owned by Mr. J.N. Harding, who has in his employ several women, as it happened yesterday all white.

About 6:30 A.M. colored women began collecting about his house, until they numbered about twenty-five, seven men being with them. The laundry women were soon seen coming to work. When met and told that they should not work for less than $1.50 per day, four cursed back; but, one, a Miss Murphy went into the house and began working. Seeing this, the women rushed in, caught her and carried her into the street, and by threats forced her to leave. As no other laborers were found, a council of war was being held, when a colored woman passed by and entered the house to collect money for Monday's labor. The cry was raised that Alice had gone back on them. . . . A rush was made for her, but Alice is not slow in her motions, therefore the first who got in reach went to grass from a well-directed blow, but they were too many for Alice, who was literally covered with women, clawing and pulling, until Alice's clothes were torn from her body and they could get no hold, then the poor woman was let up and driven off.

This success again emboldened the women to further demonstrations. The cry was raised, "Let's lock them out for good; here's nails I brought especially." An axe lying in the wood pile was grabbed, and the laundry house doors and windows secured. Then off they started for the heathen Chinese. . . . So down Market street they went, led by a portly colored lady. . . .

On the way many expressions as to their intentions were heard, such as "We will starve no longer." "Chinese got no business coming here taking our work from us." Each California laundry was visited in turn . . .

At these laundries all the women talked at once, telling Sam Lee, Slam Sing, Wau Loong and the rest that "they must close up and leave this city within fifteen days, or they would be driven away," each Chinaman responding "Yees, yees," "Alice rightee," "Me go, yees," and closed their shops. The women proceeded through Market street to Eighteenth where they scattered after avowing they would meet again at 4 o'clock on the corner of Market and Eleventh streets and visit each place where women were hired, and if they receive less than $1.50 per day or $9 per week they would force them to quit.

Source: Galveston News, August 1, 1877.

"WASHERWOMEN STRIKE"

A reporter for the Atlanta Constitution presents a police officer's account of the strike:

Three weeks ago twenty negro women and a few negro men met in Summer Hill Church and discussed the matter. The next night the negro preachers in all the churches announced a mass meeting of the washerwomen. The meeting was a big one and the result was an organization. Officers were elected, committees appointed and time and places for meetings read out. Since then there has been meetings every night or two, and now there is a society or club in every ward in the city.

"What do they do at these meetings?"

Make speeches and pray. They swear they never will wash another piece for less than a one dollar a dozen, but they will never get it and will soon give in.

"They are trying to prevent those who are not members from washing, are they not?"

Yes. The committee first goes to those who have no connection with the organization and try to persuade them to join. Failing in this they then threaten them with cowhides, fire and death, if they disobey. The men are as bad as the women. When a woman refuses to join the society, their men threaten to 'whip 'em and the result is that the ranks are daily swelling. Why, last night there was a big meeting at New Hope church and fifty additions were made to the list. They passed resolutions informing all women not members of the society to quit work or stand the consequences. I tell you, this strike is a big thing.

Letter to the Jim English, Mayor of Atlanta, from 486 members of the Washerwomen Society:

Atlanta, Georgia, August 1 [1881]

Dear Sir:

We, the members of our society, are determined to stand to our pledge and make extra charges for washing, and we have agreed, and are willing to pay $25 or $50 for licenses as a protection, so we can control the washing for the city. We can afford to pay these licenses, and will do it before we will be defeated, and then we will have full control of the city's washing at our own prices, as the city has control of our husbands' work at their prices. Don't forget this. We hope to hear from your council Tuesday morning. We mean business this week or not washing.

Yours, respectfully, From 5 societies, 486 members

Source: Atlanta *Constitution*, July 29 and August 2, 1881.

7.2.   An African-American Servant Describes Her Employment in 1912

This anonymous article was published in a northern magazine that had been sympathetic to African-American emancipation, suffrage, and civil rights. The writer, a widow, reminds her readers that the black woman servant has trouble caring for her own family when she must work as a live-in caretaker of another woman's children. She also underscores the disrespect shown to black women by most whites.

"MORE SLAVERY AT THE SOUTH, BY A NEGRO NURSE"

I am a negro woman, and I was born and reared in the South. I am now past forty years of age and am the mother of three children. My husband died nearly fifteen years ago, after we had been married about five years. For more than thirty years—or since I was ten years old—I have been a servant in one capacity or another in white families in a thriving Southern city, which has at present a population of more than 50,000. In my early years I was at first what might be called a "house-girl," or better, a "house-boy." I used to answer the doorbell, sweep the yard, go on errands, and do odd jobs. Later on I became a chambermaid and performed the usual duties of such a servant in a home. Still later I was graduated into a cook, in which position I served at different times for nearly eight years in all. During the last ten years I have been a nurse. I have worked for only four different families during all these thirty years. But, belonging to the servant class, which is the majority class among my race at the South, and associating only with servants, I have been able to become intimately acquainted not only with the lives of hundreds of household servants, but also with the lives of their employers. I can, therefore, speak with authority on the so-called servant question; and what I say is said out of an experience which covers many years.

To begin with, then, I should say that more than two-thirds of the negroes of the town where I live are menial servants of one kind or another, and besides that more than two-thirds of the negro women here, whether married or single, are compelled to work for a living,—as nurses, cooks, washerwomen, chambermaids, seamstresses, hucksters, janitresses, and the like. I will say, also, that the condition of this vast host of poor colored people is just as bad as, if not worse than, it was during the days of slavery. Though today we are enjoying nominal freedom, we are literally slaves. And, not to generalize, I will give you a sketch of the work I have to do—and I'm only one of many.

I frequently work from fourteen to sixteen hours a day. I am compelled by my contract, which is oral only, to sleep in the house. I am allowed to go home to my own children, the oldest of whom is a girl of 18 years, only once in two weeks, every other Sunday afternoon—even then I'm not permitted to stay all night. I not only have to nurse a little white child, now eleven months old, but I have to act as playmate or "handy-andy," not say governess, to three other children in the home, the oldest of whom is only nine years of age. . . . I am not permitted to rest. It's "Mammy, do this," or "Mammy, do that," or "Mammy, do the other," from my mistress, all the time. So it is not strange to see "Mammy" watering the lawn in front with the garden hose, sweeping the sidewalk, mopping the porch and halls, dusting around the house, helping the cook, or darning stockings. . . . I don't know what it is to go to church; I don't know what it is to go to a lecture or entertainment or anything of the kind; I live a treadmill life; and I see my own children only when they happen to see me on the streets when I am out with the children, or when my children come to the "yard" to see me, which isn't often, because my white folks don't like to see their servants' children hanging around their premises. You might as well say that I'm on duty all the time—from sunrise to sunrise, every day in the week. I am the slave, body and soul, of this family. And what do I get for this work—this lifetime bondage? The pitiful sum of ten dollars a month! And what am I expected to do with these ten dollars? With this money I'm expected to pay my house rent, which is four dollars per month, for a little house of two rooms, just big enough to turn round in; and I'm expected, also to feed and clothe myself and three children. . . .

Of course, nothing is being done to increase our wages, and the way things are going at present it would seem that nothing could be done to cause an increase in wages. We have no labor unions or organizations of any kind that could demand for us a uniform scale, . . . and if some negroes did here and there refuse to work for seven and eight and ten dollars a month, there would be hundreds of other negroes right on the spot ready to take their places and do the same work. . . . The truth is, we have to work for little or nothing or become vagrants! And that, of course, in this State would mean that we would be arrested, tried, and dispatched to the "State Farm," where we would surely have to work for nothing or be beaten with many stripes!

Source: Independent 72, January 15, 1912: 196–200.

7.3.   Anna J. Cooper Articulates the Concept of "Womanism" in 1892

Anna J. Haywood Cooper was the daughter of a slave woman and a white man. She attended a freedman's teacher training school in Raleigh, North Carolina, after emancipation, and after her husband died in 1881, went to Oberlin College. She later became the principal of a college preparatory school in Washington, D.C. In her 1892 work, A Voice from the South, *she discusses in frank terms the discouragement assertive black women faced from ministers and self appointed "race men" such as Booker T. Washington.*

"THE COLORED WOMAN OF TODAY"

The colored woman of to-day occupies, one may say, a unique position in this country. In a period of itself transitional and unsettled, her status seems one of the least ascertainable and definitive of all the forces which make for our civilization. She is confronted by both a woman question and a race problem, and is as yet an unknown or an unacknowledged factor in both. While the women of the white race can with calm assurance enter upon the work they feel by nature appointed to do, while their men give loyal support and appreciative countenance to their efforts, recognizing in most avenues of usefulness the propriety and the need of woman's distinctive co-operation, the colored woman too often finds herself hampered and shamed by a less liberal sentiment and a more conservative attitude on the part of those for whose opinion she cares most. That this is not universally true I am glad to admit. There are to be found both intensely conservative white men and exceedingly liberal colored men. But as far as my experience goes the average man of our race is less frequently ready to admit the actual need among the sturdier forces of the world for woman's help or influence. That great social and economic questions await her interference, that she could throw any light on problems of national import, that her intermeddling could improve the management of school systems, or elevate the tone of public institutions, or humanize and sanctify the far reaching influence of prisons and reformatories and improve the treatment of lunatics and imbeciles,—that she has a word worth hearing on mooted questions in political economy, that she could contribute a suggestion on the relations of labor and capital, or offer a thought on honest money and honorable trade, I fear the majority of "Americans of the colored variety" are not yet prepared to concede. It may be that they do not yet see these questions in their right perspective, being absorbed in the immediate needs of their own political complications. A good deal depends on where we put the emphasis in this world; and our men are not perhaps to blame if they see everything colored by the light of those agitations in the midst of which they live and move and have their being. The part they have had to play in American history during the last twenty-five or thirty years has tended rather to exaggerate the importance of mere political advantage, as well as to set a fictitious valuation on those able to secure such advantage. It is the astute politician, the manager who can gain preferment for himself and his favorites, the demagogue known to stand in with the powers at the White House and consulted on the bestowal of government plums, whom we set in high places and denominate great. It is they who receive the hosannas of the multitude and are regarded as leaders of the people. . . .

As woman's influence as a political element is as yet nil in most of the commonwealths of our republic, it is not surprising that with those who place the emphasis on mere political capital she may yet seem almost a nonentity so far as it concerns the solution of great national or even racial perplexities.

Source: Anna J. Cooper, *A Voice from the South, By a Black Woman of the South.* Xenia, OH, 1892: 134–37, 142–45.

7.4.   "Lifting as We Climb": The National Association of Colored Women's Clubs Defines Its Role

Mary Church, another graduate of Oberlin College, was fired from her high school teaching position in Washington, D.C., when she married Robert Terrell, the first African-American judge of the Washington Municipal Court. The National Association of Colored Women was formed in 1896 as an umbrella organization for local black women's clubs but quickly became an instrument for prominent black women's influence; Mary Terrell was its first president. In this 1902 essay, she takes a strong position on civil rights but also endorses vocational instruction and a higher moral standard for poor black women to improve the reputation of the race.

"WHAT ROLE IS THE EDUCATED NEGRO WOMAN TO PLAY IN THE UPLIFTING OF HER RACE?"

The National Association [of Colored Women] has chosen as its motto: Lifting as We Climb. In order to live strictly up to this sentiment, its members have determined to come into the closest possible touch with the masses of our women, through whom the womanhood of our people is always judged. It is unfortunate, but it is true, that the dominant race in this country insists upon gauging the Negro's worth by his most illiterate and vicious representatives than by the more intelligent and worthy classes. Colored women of education and culture know that they cannot escape altogether the consequences of the acts of their most depraved sisters. They see that even if they were wicked enough to turn a deaf ear to the call of duty, both policy and self-preservation demand that they go down among the lowly, the illiterate and even the vicious, to whom they are bound by the ties of race and sex, and put forth every possible effort to reclaim them. By coming into close touch with the masses of our women it is possible to correct many of the evils which militate so seriously against us and inaugurate the reforms, without which, as a race, we cannot hope to succeed.

Through the clubs we are studying the labor question and are calling the attention of our women to the alarming rapidity with which the Negro is losing ground in the world of labor. If this movement to withhold employment from him continues to grow, the race will soon be confronted by a condition of things disastrous and serious, indeed. We are preaching in season and out that it is the duty of every wage-earning colored woman to become thoroughly proficient in whatever work she engages, so that she may render the best service of which she is capable, and thus do her part toward establishing a reputation for excellent workmanship among colored women.

Our clubs all over the country are being urged to establish schools of domestic science. It is believed that by founding schools in which colored girls could be trained to be skilled domestics, we should do more toward solving the labor question as it affects our women, than by using any other means it is in our power to employ.... Colored women are asking the white mothers of the land to teach their children that when they grow to be men and women, if they deliberately prevent their fellow creatures from earning an honest living by closing their doors of trade against them, the Father of all men will hold them responsible for the crimes which are the result of their injustice and for the human wrecks which the ruthless crushing of hope and ambition always makes.

Through our clubs colored women hope to improve the social atmosphere by showing the enormity of the double standard of morals, which teaches that we should turn the cold shoulder upon a fallen sister, but greet her destroyer with open arms and a gracious smile. The duty of setting a high moral standard and living up to it devolves upon colored women in a peculiar way. False accusations and malicious slanders are circulated against them constantly, both by the press and by the direct descendants of those who in years past were responsible for the moral degradation of their female slaves.

Carefully and conscientiously we shall study the questions which affect the race most deeply and directly. Against the convict lease system, the Jim Crow car laws, lynchings and all other barbarities which degrade us, we shall protest with such force of logic and intensity of soul that those who oppress us will either cease to disavow the inalienability and equality of human rights, or be ashamed to openly violate the very principles upon which this government was founded.

And so lifting as we climb, onward and upward we go, struggling and striving and hoping that the buds and blossoms of our desires will burst into glorious fruition ere long. With courage born of success achieved in the past, with a keen sense of the responsibility which we must continue to assume we look forward to the future, large with promise and hope. Seeking no favors because of our color or patronage because of our needs, we knock at the bar of justice and ask for an equal chance.

Source: Mary Church Terrell in D.W. Culp, ed., *Twentieth Century Negro Literature.* Toronto: 1902, 172–77.

7.5.   Ida B. Wells on "Self-Help"

All African-American leaders stressed some form of "self-help" in order to provide the black community with community services, schools, and banks, as well as to encourage upward mobility through hard work, temperance, and thrift. In her South-ern Horrors Ida B. Wells also used the term to advocate boycotts, migration, black newspaper circulation, and armed-self defiance to combat lynching, press censorship, and Jim Crow segregation.

"SELF-HELP"

In the creation of . . . healthier public sentiment, the Afro-American can do for himself what no one else can do for him. The world looks on with wonder that we have conceded so much and remain law-abiding under such great outrage and provocation.

To Northern capital and Afro-American labor the South owes its re-habilitation. If labor is withdrawn capital will not remain. The Afro-American is thus the backbone of the South. A thorough knowledge and judicious exercise of this power in lynching localities could many times effect a bloodless revolution. The white man's dollar is his god, and to stop this will be to stop outrages in many localities.

The Afro-American of Memphis denounced the lynching of three of their best citizens, and urged and waited for the authorities to act in the matter and bring the lynchers to justice. No attempt was made to do so, and the black men left the city by thousands, bringing about great stag-nation in every branch of business. Those who remained so injured the business of the street car company by staying off the cars, that the su-perintendent, manager and treasurer called personally on the editor of the "Free Speech," asked them to urge our people to give them their patronage again. Other business men became alarmed over the situation and the "Free Speech" was run away that the colored people might be more easily controlled. A meeting of white citizens . . . passed resolutions for the first time, condemning [the lynching]. *But they did not punish the lynchers. . . .*

The appeal to the white man's pocket has ever been more effectual than all the appeals ever made to his conscience. Nothing, absolutely nothing, is to be gained by a further sacrifice of manhood and self-respect. By the right exercise of his power as the industrial factor of the

South, the Afro-American can demand and secure his rights, the punishment of lynchers, and a fair trial for accused rapists.

Of the many inhuman outrages of this present year, the only case where the proposed lynching did *not* occur, was where the men armed themselves . . . and prevented it. The only times an Afro-American who was assaulted got away has been when he had a gun and used it in self-defense.

The lesson this teaches and which every Afro-American should ponder well, is that a Winchester rifle should have a place of honor in every black home, and it should be used for that protection which the law refuses to give. When the white man who is always the aggressor knows he runs as great risk of biting the dust every time his Afro-American victim does, he will have greater respect for Afro-American life. The more the Afro-American yields and cringes and begs, the more he has to do so, the more he is insulted, outraged, and lynched.

The assertion has been substantiated throughout these pages that the press contains unreliable and doctored reports of lynchings, and one of the most necessary things for the race to do is to get these facts before the public. The people must know before they can act, and there is no educator to compare with the press.

The Afro-American papers are the only ones which will print the truth, and they lack means to employ agents and detectives to get at the facts. The race must rally a mighty host to the support of their journals, and thus enable them to do much in the way of investigation.

Source: Ida B. Wells, *Southern Horrors: Lynch Law in All Its Phases*. New York: The New York Age Printing Company, 1892.

7.6.   An Exchange Between Ida Wells and Frances B. Willard on Race, Sex, and Lynching, 1890–1894

One of the most provocative arguments Wells made in her exposés of lynching was that most liaisons between black men and white women were consensual, and that it was black women who were mostly likely to be victims of interracial rape, claims heatedly denied by white southerners. Wells took her anti-lynching cause to England in 1893 and 1894, where she argued that white women reformers in the United States, and in particular the Woman's Christian Temperance Union, had been unwilling to condemn lynching. Thousands of women from both the North and the South, black and white, were members of the WCTU.

*Willard defended "white womanhood" and implied that lynching
was necessary for its protection. Like other advocates of a "feminism of fear" she argued that northern immigrant and southern
black men should be barred from the ballot box.*

FRANCES WILLARD ADDRESSES THE WCTU IN ATLANTA
IN 1890

Now, as to the "race problem" in its minified current meaning, I am
a true lover of the southern people—have spoken and worked in, perhaps, 200 of their towns and cities; have been taken into their love and
confidence at scores of hospitable firesides; have heard them pour out
their hearts in the splendid frankness of their impetuous natures. And I
have said to them at such times: "When I go North there will be wafted
to you no word from pen or voice that is not loyal to what we are saying
here and now." Going South, a woman, a temperance woman, and a
Northern temperance woman—three great barriers to their good will
yonder—I was received by them with a confidence that was one of the
most delightful surprises of my life. I think we have wronged the South,
though we did not mean to do so. The reason was, in part, that we had
irreparably wronged ourselves by putting no safeguards on the ballot
box at the North that would sift out alien illiterates. They rule our cities
today; the saloon is their palace, and the toddy stick their sceptre. It is
not fair that they should vote, nor is it fair that a plantation Negro, who
can neither read nor write, whose ideas are bounded by the fence of his
own field and the price of his own mule, should be entrusted with the
ballot. We ought to have put an educational test upon the ballot from
the first. The Anglo-Saxon race will never submit to be dominated by
the Negro so long as his altitude reaches no higher than the personal
liberty of the saloon, and the power of appreciating the amount of liquor
that a dollar will buy. New England would no more submit to this than
South Carolina. "Better whisky and more of it" has been the rallying cry
of great dark-faced mobs in the Southern localities where local option
was snowed under by the colored vote. Temperance has no enemy like
that, for it is unreasoning and unreasonable. Tonight it promises in a
great congregation to vote for temperance at the polls tomorrow; but
tomorrow twenty-five cents changes that vote in favor of the liquor-
seller.

I pity the southerners, and I believe the great mass of them are as
conscientious and kindly-intentioned toward the colored man as an
equal number of white church-members of the North. Would-be dema-
gogues lead the colored people to destruction. Half-drunken white
roughs murder them at the polls, or intimidate them so that they do not
vote. But the better class of people must not be blamed for this, and a

more thoroughly American population than the Christian people of the South does not exist. They have the traditions, the kindness, the probity, the courage of our forefathers. The problem on their hands is immeasurable. The colored race multiplies like the locusts of Egypt. The grogshop is the center of power. "The safety of woman, of childhood, of the home, is menaced in a thousand localities at this moment, so that the men dare not go beyond the sight of their own roof-tree." How little we know of all this, seated in comfort and affluence here at the North, descanting upon the rights of every man to cast one vote and have it fairly counted; that well-worn shibboleth invoked once more to dodge a living issue.

Source: Ida B. Wells, *A Red Record*. Chicago: Ida B. Wells, 1894.

"THE BLACK AND WHITE OF IT"

Nobody in this section of the country believes the old threadbare lie that Negro men rape white women. If southern white men are not careful, they will over-reach themselves and public sentiment will have a reaction; a conclusion will then be reached which will be very damaging to the moral reputation of their women. . . .

The editor of the "Free Speech" . . . asserts . . . that there are many white women in the south who would marry colored men if such an act would not place them at once beyond the pale of society and within the clutches of the law. The miscegenation laws of the South only operate against the legitimate union of the races; they leave the white man free to seduce all the colored girls he can, but it is death to the colored man who yields to the force and advances of a similar attraction in white women. White men lynch the offending Afro-American, not because he is a despoiler of virtue, but because he succumbs to the smiles of white women. . . .

There is a growing demand among Afro-Americans that the guilt or innocence of parties accused of rape be fully established. They know the men of the section of the country who refuse this are not so desirous of punishing rapists as they pretend. The utterances of the leading white men show that with them it is not the crime but the *class*. Bishop Fitzgerald has become apoligist for lynchers of the rapists of *white* women only. Governor Tillman, of South Carolina, . . . standing under the tree in Barnwell, S.C., on which eight Afro-Americans were hung last year, declared that he would lead a mob to lynch a *negro* who raped a *white* woman. So say the pulpits, officials and newspapers of the south. But when the victim is a colored woman it is different.

Source: Ida B. Wells, *Southern Horrors: Lynch Law in All Its Phases*. New York: The New York Age Printing Company, 1892.

FRANCES WILLARD ADDRESSES THE WCTU IN 1894

The zeal for her race of Miss Ida B. Wells, a bright young colored woman, has, it seems to me, clouded her perception as to who were her friends and well-wishers in all high-minded and legitimate efforts to banish the abomination of lynching and torture from the land of the free and the home of the brave. It is my firm belief that in the statements made by Miss Wells concerning white women having taken the initiative in nameless acts between the races she has put an imputation upon half the white race in this country that is unjust, and, save in the rarest exceptional instances, wholly without foundation. This is the unanimous opinion of the most disinterested and observant leaders of opinion whom I have consulted on the subject, and I do not fear to say that the efforts she is making are greatly handicapped by statements of this kind, nor to urge her as a friend and well-wisher to banish from her vocabulary all such allusions as a source of weakness to the cause she has at heart.

Source: Ida B. Wells, *A Red Record: Lynchings in the United States*. Chicago, Privately printed, 1894.

IDA B. WELLS CONDEMNS THE WCTU'S POSITION ON LYNCHING

The charge has been made that I have attacked Miss Willard and misrepresented the W.C.T.U.

I said now and I repeat now, that in all the ten terrible years of shooting, hanging and burning of men, women and children in America, the Women's [*sic*] Christian Temperance Union never suggested one plan or made one move to prevent those awful crimes. If this statement is untrue the records of that organization would disprove it before the ink is dry. . . . The W.C.T.U. had no word, either of pity or protest; its great heart which concerns itself about humanity the world over, was, toward our case, pulseless as a stone. Let those who deny this speak by the record. Not until after the first British campaign, in 1893, was even a resolution passed by the body which is the self constituted guardian for "God, home and native land."

In 1894 . . . , when the committee on resolutions reported their work, not a word was said against lynching. . . . A resolution against lynching was introduced by Mrs. Fessenden [from the floor] and read, and then that great Christian body, which in its resolutions had expressed itself in opposition to the social amusement of card playing, athletic sports and promiscuous dancing; had protested against the licensing of saloons, inveighed against tobacco, . . . wholly ignored the seven millions of colored people of this country whose plea was for a word of sympathy and support for the movement in their behalf. The resolution was not adopted, and the convention adjourned.

Source: Ida B. Wells, *A Red Record: Lynchings in the United States*. Chicago: Privately printed, 1894.

8

Muller v. Oregon, Adkins v. Children's Hospital, and Drafting an Equal Rights Amendment: The Equality-Difference Debate

The equality-difference debate is at the heart of most discussions about women in society. As it expanded over time, the American liberal tradition moved in the direction of stressing individual rights to equal treatment under the law without reference to property holding, race, or gender. The Seneca Falls Declaration of Sentiments of 1848 struck just this note by underscoring the barriers to women's equality in the professions, the workplace, religion, and politics. But scholars also stress some hidden assumptions behind this demand for equal rights: few women of the nineteenth century would have challenged ideas that women needed special protections based on their physical characteristics and reproductive capacities, nor would they have agreed that men and women had exactly the same responsibilities in society. Age of consent laws, for instance, were designed to protect young women from sexual assault, and no one doubted the premise that women should be exempted from military conscription.

As more women entered the workforce in the second half of the nineteenth century, advocates of women's rights faced a new set of dilemmas in addressing difference and equality. Women were, clearly, exploited as workers on the basis of their sex. By 1890, 19 percent of all women were working for wages outside the household. The vast majority of them were young women between the ages of 16 and 25, and most of those in the lowest paying manufacturing jobs were immigrants. Confined to a few kinds of work in textiles, the sewing trades, the food industry, and commercial laundries, women's factory work was characterized by long hours, speed-up assembly lines, and unhealthy work environments. Although there were a few middle-class "career women" by the early twentieth century, it was mostly desertion, widowhood, and poverty that drove women over twenty-five to seek employment. In the early twentieth century the move toward shorter working hours and the rise of office, retail, and telephone operating jobs created new options for white women workers, some of them married. By 1920 about 23 percent of all women workers were married, and this proportion would grow steadily through the twentieth century. African-American women, single and unmarried, were always more likely to work than white women, mostly because race discrimination made two incomes essential to the support of black families.

Whatever their marital status, women workers were concentrated in a very small number of occupations, most of them categorized as "unskilled," and wages for women were, on average, less than one-half those of men. The most dominant labor union of the time, the American Federation of Labor (AFL), viewed women workers as a threat to men's wages and control of the skilled trades. The AFL supported protective legislation for women but opposed minimum wage laws as a damper on men's efforts to demand better pay. AFL president Samuel Gompers argued that the main focus of the labor movement should be to negotiate a "family wage" for men sufficient to keep mothers at home and children in school. "In our country," Gompers said in 1906, "there is no necessity for the wife contributing to the support of the family by working. . . . The wife as a wage-earner is a disadvantage economically considered, and socially is unnecessary."[1] Gompers assumed, as did employers, that the average woman worker was a young dependent who would leave the workforce after she married.

Every year, however, the proportion of women in the labor force continued to grow, and in an era when employers had a free hand in determining wages, working conditions, and hours for all workers whatever their sex, the plight of the working class began to be reported widely in the press by "Progressive" reformers. Dramatic strikes of steel workers in Homestead, Pennsylvania, coal miners in Ludlow, Colorado, textile workers in Lawrence, Massachusetts, and garment workers in New York City and Chicago made clear that employers would use every means at their disposal, including armed violence, to beat back labor reforms and unions. Progressives believed that the federal and state governments should step in to provide a more reasonable balance between labor and capital, and they made new use of social science surveys and statistical evidence to support their claims. But it was difficult to convince the courts to uphold maximum hour and minimum wage laws for men. The "right" of both workers and employers to negotiate contracts without any interference from the state remained a tenet of American constitutional law.

Progressives had better luck in arguing for government intervention when they addressed the workplace needs of the "unmanly," notably women and children. The drive for protective legislation for both women and children was often led by middle-class women reformers, many of them coming out of the urban social settlement movement of the late nineteenth century and defining themselves as practitioners of a new profession they called "social work." Inspired by Illinois activist Jane Addams, social welfare reformers devoted themselves to community service and created a number of organizations that they hoped would bridge the gap between the middle class and working class by reining in the excesses of employers. Florence Kelley, a young divorced mother of three, came to live at Addams's Hull House in Chicago in 1891, fresh from her encounter with socialism at the University of Zurich and a failed marriage in New York City. She lobbied for an Illinois factory act that prohibited child labor and limited working hours for women in manufacturing, and Governor John Altgeld made her Illinois's first factory inspector. Addams and Kelley worked with trade union women rebuffed by the AFL to form the Women's Trade Union League (WTUL), and in 1899 Kelley became president of a national Consumers' League (CL). Both organizations stressed cross-class alliances to bolster working women's voices in their unions and the workplace. But middle-class women reformers dominated both the WTUL and the CL, and they assumed that working-class women would eventually marry and leave the workforce, even though they themselves were often unmarried and had professional careers. They agreed with Gompers that motherhood and work outside the home did not mix.

The CL promoted the "union label" among women consumers, a guarantee that products they purchased had been manufactured in union shops. Kelley propelled the CL into public policy as well. By 1910 a number of states had passed maximum hour laws for children and women on the grounds that they required special protection in the workplace. Such laws were invariably struck down, except in *Holden v. Hardy*, an 1898 Supreme Court case involving Utah miners. The Court agreed in *Hardy* that mining was an occupation dangerous enough to health and safety that it required an eight-hour day. But in 1905, the Court ruled in *Lochner v. New York* that bakers did not require limited hours because no one had shown baking to be damaging to their health and safety. In 1907 laundry owner Curt Muller sued the state of Oregon on the grounds that Oregon's maximum ten-hour day law for women, passed in 1903, violated freedom of contract rights for women under the equal protection clause of the Fourteenth Amendment. Women who worked in his laundry, Muller contended, should be able to work as many hours as they chose to, especially those who were supporting families.

The CL seized the *Muller* opportunity to promote the constitutional validity of protective legislation for women. Social scientists Josephine and Pauline Goldmark were hired to compile information documenting the condition of women in industry, and Louis Brandeis, a young Jewish-American lawyer who would be appointed to the Supreme Court a few years later, prepared the legal arguments. Brandeis used the rationale for state intervention into matters of health and safety as defined in *Holden v. Hardy* to argue that women were a special class in need of shorter hours. The Goldmark-Brandeis brief played up the reproductive roles of women, arguing that the state had a vested interested in preserving the national resource of women's bodies for the creation of future citizens of the nation. Instead, then, of stressing that long hours were exploitative and dangerous for all workers, the brief underscored difference as a means of promoting women's special needs.

The Supreme Court upheld Oregon's law in 1908 and used language that echoed the Brandeis brief. Over the next ten years, a number of states passed laws providing protective legislation for women and children, and in 1917, in *Bunting v. Oregon*, the Supreme Court upheld a ten-hour day law for men. Protective legislation for all workers seemed a real possibility until after World War I.

In the 1920s, when President Calvin Coolidge's maxim that "what's good for business is good for the country" ruled the marketplace, union organizers and Progressive reformers faced tough sledding. Employers used the courts in sophisticated ways to gain injunctions against strikes and to make employment a strict matter of freedom of contract between individual workers and their employers. In a five-to-four decision in 1923, the Supreme Court struck down a District of Columbia minimum wage law for women workers in *Adkins v. Children's Hospital*. The majority argued that the Nineteenth Amendment granting women suffrage had erased the remaining barriers to women's equality in the United States and that no such special protections for women were required. In a chilling historical development, it seemed to reformers that both the Fourteenth and the Nineteenth Amendments had been corrupted, taken out of their original egalitarian context, and used to uphold employers' power over defenseless workers.

Another threat to protective legislation loomed on the horizon, this time from the ranks of the National Woman's Party, led by Alice Paul. Having won the vote, Paul believed the next crusade of the feminist movement should be an equal rights amendment to the U.S. Constitution. Paul and Florence Kelley argued over just what language should be incorporated into the amendment. Paul was promoting a liberal notion of equality that emphasized removing restrictions to liberty of all kinds. Kelley, a translator of Marx and Engels who had been inspired by European socialism, believed that economic equality required protections from the state. "The realities of industrial life," says scholar Joan G. Zimmerman, had convinced Kelley and other progressives that unrestricted liberty of contract was "the basis of an empty freedom."[2] Not persuaded by Kelley, Paul decided to use the simplest possible language for her proposed amendment: "Men and Women shall have equal rights throughout the United States and every place subject to its jurisdiction."

The split in the women's movement over the language of the equal rights amendment was profound and long lasting. Most women reformers supported protective legislation and condemned the position of the Woman's Party as selfish and narrow-minded. But there were women workers in the 1920s who found that protective restrictions, especially on night work for women, got in the way of good wages and advancement in their occupations. AFL locals used night work provisions to exclude women from bartending, the printing trades, and streetcar conducting. Women printers founded a group called the League for Equal Opportunity, which visited state legislative committees to oppose restrictions on women's night work and to promote an eight-hour day for all workers regardless of sex. The League used the 1920s cultural icon of the flapper to point up the absurdity of banning night work for women: "Strange, isn't it, that dancing, card-playing, autoing, etc. in the deadly night hours is harmless, but earning a good wage by honest work is dangerous to the future generation if performed in the same night hours?"[3]

With the arrival of the Great Depression, the stage was finally set for protective legislation that would apply to all workers regardless of sex. A lobby of women reformers convinced President Franklin D. Roosevelt to make Frances Perkins of New York State the Secretary of Labor (and thereby, the first woman cabinet member). The Roosevelt administration attempted to draft minimum wage and maximum hour laws that would pass the scrutiny of the Supreme Court, finally doing so in the National Fair Labor Standards Act of 1938. The law made an eight-hour day with paid overtime standard for most workers and initiated a minimum wage of 25 cents an hour. By omitting agricultural, migrant, clerical, service, and domestic workers, however, the bill left many occupations with large numbers of women beyond the aegis of federal protection. New social security benefits were based on participation in the workforce, thus excluding adult women, except those married to former workers or those who had been widowed, from old age insurance.

Although an equal rights amendment made little headway over the ensuing decades, the Civil Rights Act of 1964 and its Title VII banning discrimination in employment on the basis of sex provided women's rights activists with a means of challenging protective legislation. Dozens of state laws regulating women's work were removed from the books in the 1960s and 1970s. But how far would ignoring difference go? Many employers still refused to hire women for jobs on the grounds that they might become pregnant, and they often fired women who became pregnant, holding up the male life-cycle as the norm.

In a series of Supreme Court cases, a majority of the justices refused to protect the right of pregnant women to retain their jobs until Lillian Garland's case appeared before them. Garland took a leave from her position at California Federal Savings and Loan for a difficult pregnancy. A 1978 California law required employers to grant up to four months of unpaid maternity leave to women and to allow them to return to their jobs. California Federal did not allow Garland to return to work, and when the state of California upheld her claim, California Federal, backed by the state's Chamber of Commerce, sued on the grounds that the state law violated Title VII by treating women workers differently than men. In *California Federal Savings and Loan v. Guerra* in 1987, the Supreme Court ruled that pregnancy and other such "temporary disabilities" could receive special protection and were not in violation of Title VII.

The debate over difference and equality will continue among feminists, traditionalists, and makers of public policy. For the foreseeable future, gender-neutral workplace guidelines for family leave, pregnancy, illness, and health and safety conditions likely will be the best guarantee of all workers' rights, including women. At the same time, gender-neutral decisions in the courts, for instance in child custody and divorce cases, have in recent years given men new rights, some feminists argue, at the expense of women. In the end, using an equality or difference argument is more likely to be a strategic decision than a fixed principle.

READING GUIDE

Baer, Judith, *The Chains of Protection: The Judicial Response to Women's Labor Legislation*. Westport, CT: Greenwood Press, 1978. Written in the midst of attempts to ratify the Equal Rights Amendment, this account by a legal feminist argues that protective legislation has hampered women's participation and advancement in the workforce and should be erased. Baer includes helpful information on some of the absurdities of protective legislation facing women after World War II such as the barring of women from "night work" and bartending, and demonstrates that it took extensive litigation by plaintiffs to enforce equal protection aspects of Title VII in the workplace after 1963.

Brandeis, Louis A., assisted by Josephine Goldmark, *Women in Industry: Decision of the United States Supreme Court in* Curt Muller vs. State of Oregon. New York: Arno Press, 1969. Although Louis Brandeis received most of the credit for the crafting of the argument in defense of the Oregon state maximum hour law, Josephine Goldmark wrote most of the text. The case is important not only for its defense of protective legislation but also for its pioneering "sociological" approach to constitutional law that used European fatigue and efficiency studies to document the harmful effects of industrialization on all workers, but especially on women.

Erickson, Nancy, "*Muller V. Oregon* Reconsidered: The Origins of a Sex-Based Doctrine of Liberty of Contract," *Labor History* 30 (Spring, 1989): 228–50. Erickson argues that despite its status in case law as a major turning point, *Muller* in fact continued long understood notions of contract law for women based on women's special legal status as members of families rather than as independent citizens.

Kessler-Harris, Alice, *In Pursuit of Equity: Women, Men, and the Quest for Economic Citizenship in 20th-Century America.* New York: Oxford University Press, 2001. Kessler-Harris examines the roots of what she describes as "economic citizenship," a citizenship rooted in wage-earning that favored white men through social security provisions, job discrimination, and income tax law drafted in the mid–twentieth century. Economic citizenship assumed that women were different than men, best defined as dependent members of families with relatively short work lives. In a United States where more and more people are not members of traditional families and where more and more women work most of their adult lives, "an equal opportunity framework" demands reform of many twentieth-century parameters of economic citizenship.

Lehrer, Susan, *Origins of Protective Labor Legislation for Women, 1905–1925.* Albany: State University of New York Press, 1987. A careful account of why protective legislation came into being in the Progressive period. Lehrer demonstrates that Progressives' acceptance of a sex-segregated labor market and their consignment of all women to motherhood influenced, inevitably, their responses to the growing employment of women in industry. She includes helpful chapters on how working women, employers' associations, feminists, and organized labor responded to such laws, and argues that, in the long run, protective legislation did more to promote the interests of a "capitalist state" than it did to promote social change.

Skocpol, Theda, "Safeguarding the 'Mothers of the Race': Protective Legislation for Women Workers," in *Protecting Soldiers and Mothers: The Political Origins of Social Policy in the United States.* Cambridge: Harvard University Press, 1992: 373–423. In this highly acclaimed analysis of special legislation for special classes of citizens in the United States, Skockpol compares legislation benefiting veterans and mothers and potential mothers. Such legislation preserves gender hierarchies and sexual difference, and Skocpol argues that reformers' reliance on litigation in the courts made protective legislation particularly vulnerable to the vagaries of historical change, as seen in *Adkins v. Children's Hospital* in 1923.

Vogel, Lise, *Mothers on the Job: Maternity Policy in the U.S. Workplace.* New Brunswick, NJ: Rutgers University Press, 1993. Vogel examines the equality-difference debate and concludes that neither approach has provided full safeguards for women workers in the past. Although the courts have, for the moment, reaffirmed anti-discrimination laws with regard to pregnancy, these laws might be overturned on the basis of equal protection at any time. Vogel believes that pregnancy should be treated as a temporary disability, and that all workers with disabilities should benefit from protective legislation. This approach does not ignore pregnancy, but defines it as a more "ordinary" condition similar to other temporary incapacities and thus incorporates both equality and difference.

Woloch, Nancy, Muller v. Oregon: *A Brief History with Documents*. New York: Bedford Books, 1996. A compilation of the most important court cases regarding maximum hour and minimum wage law before and after *Muller v. Oregon*, along with contemporaneous debate about the issues. Complete with photographs and bibliography, this short reading would be useful as a classroom text.

Zimmerman, Joan G., "The Jurisprudence of Equality: the Women's Minimum Wage, the First Equal Rights Amendment, and *Adkins v. Children's Hospital*, 1905–1923," *Journal of American History* 79 (June, 1991): 188–225. Using the papers of Florence Kelley and Alice Paul, Zimmerman illustrates the debate over the wording of a proposed equal rights amendment. Although Paul attempted to incorporate safeguards for protective laws into the wording of the amendment, she could not draft suitable language, and, in phrasing a simple statement simply banning discrimination based on sex, alienated Kelley and the protectionists. The ensuing divide over the ERA among feminists was long lasting and bitter.

NOTES

1. As quoted by Susan Lehrer, *Origins of Protective Labor Legislation for Women, 1905–1925* (Albany: State University of New York Press, 1987), 149.

2. Joan G. Zimmerman, "The Jurisprudence of Equality: The Women's Minimum Wage, the First Equal Rights Amendment, and *Adkins v. Children's Hospital*, 1905–1923," *Journal of American History* 79 (June, 1991): 195.

3. As quoted by Lehrer, *Origins of Protective Labor Legislation*, 165.

DOCUMENTS

8.1.   A Laundry Owner Challenges the Oregon Ten-Hour Day For Women

In 1907 Curt Muller challenged Oregon's statute limiting women factory and laundry workers to a ten-hour day. Muller's lawyers noted that no one had established that such work was dangerous to the health of workers, a critical factor in a favorable ruling on a Utah law limiting the work of miners to eight hours a day. Arguing that women were as much citizens as men, the brief claimed that women's rights to contract the hours of their labor with employers had been violated.

CURT MULLER SUPREME COURT BRIEF

The employment of women may be forbidden entirely. This, however, is a very different thing from regulation of such employment in a perfectly moral and healthful vocation. Under the statute under review, the employment of women is expressly recognized as proper, and the business in which they are to be employed is not hazardous, dangerous, or immoral. The right to employ women is assumed, but in so far as the law restricts the hours of service it must be sustained if at all upon the ground that employment of women for a greater length of time than ten hours in any one day endangers the public health. There is no question of morals or general welfare involved. It is not a labor statute as such, and is not promulgated or sought to be sustained upon any economic theory of wages. It is purely and simply a limitation of the hours of service of an adult woman, whether married or single, in a healthful employment, and in a business not condemned as immoral or dangerous. It is not within the police power of the state to deprive her of the right to dispose of her labor in such an employment at pleasure, and for such length of time and under such conditions as she may desire. Upon what theory can the state become her guardian and interfere with her freedom of contract and the right of her employer to contract with her freely and voluntarily, as if she were a man? This is the question for decision. . . .

But conceding that it is now settled in accordance with the rule laid down in *Holden v. Hardy*, . . . that where the employment is peculiarly dangerous to the health of the employees, and many citizens are thereby endangered, the legislature may, under the police power of the state, limit the hours of service, it does not follow that the hours of service of all employees in all employments, may be limited. If any limitation is sought to be imposed, it must rest upon the inherent dangers of the particular service, independent of the nationality, race, or sex of the employees. The employment must be such as to justify supervision, regulation, and police control. The employees of adult age, whether men or women, in the same service, are alike entitled to equal protection and freedom of contract. It is difficult to imagine any employment that may be dangerous to women employees that would not be equally dangerous to men. The health of men is not less entitled to protection than that of women. For reasons of chivalry, we may regret that all women may not be sheltered in happy homes, free from the exacting demands upon them in pursuit of a living, but their right to pursue any honorable vocation, any business not forbidden as immoral, or contrary to public policy, is just as sacred and just as inviolate as the same right enjoyed by men.

Source: Phillip B. Kurland and Gerhard Casper, eds., *Landmark Briefs and Arguments of the Supreme Court of the United States*, Vol. 16. Arlington, VA: University Publications of America, 1975: 8, 13–31.

8.2.   The Consumers' League Demonstrates That Women Require Shorter Hours Than Men

---

For its 1907 brief defending the 1903 Oregon law, the Consumers' League used the pro bono *services of lawyer Louis D. Brandeis. Using information assembled by Josephine and Pauline Goldmark, Brandeis argued that under certain circumstances freedom of contract under the equal protection clause might be abrogated by government. Although the Goldmarks demonstrated that long hours were detrimental to the health of all workers, Brandeis called on the testimony of physicians and industrial health experts to show that not only women's health but also the health of their future children might be jeopardized by long hours; the brief also claimed that long hours undermined women's morality and their ability to maintain proper homes.*

BRIEF FOR CONSUMERS' LEAGUE

The legal rules applicable to this case are few and are well established, namely: *First*: The right to purchase or to sell *labor* is a part of the "liberty" protected by the Fourteenth Amendment of the Federal Constitution. *Second*: This right to "liberty" is, however, subject to such reasonable restraint of action as the State may impose in the exercise of the police power for the protection of health, safety, morals, and the general welfare. . . .

Long hours of labor are dangerous for women primarily because of their special physical organization. In structure and function women are differentiated from men. Besides these anatomical and physiological differences, physicians are agreed that women are fundamentally weaker than men in all that makes for endurance: in muscular strength, in nervous energy, in the powers of persistent attention and application. Overwork, therefore, which strains endurance to the utmost, is more disastrous to the health of women than of men, and entails upon them more lasting injury. . . .

The fatigue which follows long hours of labor becomes chronic and results in general deterioration of health. Often ignored, since it does not result in immediate disease, this weakness and anæmia undermines the whole system; it destroys the nervous energy most necessary for steady work, and effectually predisposes to other illness. The long hours of standing, which are required in many industries, are universally denounced by physicians as the cause of pelvic disorders. . . .

The effect of overwork on morals is closely related to the injury to health. Laxity of moral fibre follows physical debility. When the working day is so long that no time whatever is left for a minimum of leisure or home-life, relief from the strain of work is sought in alcoholic stimulants and other excesses. . . .

The experience of manufacturing countries has illustrated the evil effect of overwork upon the general welfare. Deterioration of any large portion of the population inevitably lowers the entire community physically, mentally, and morally. When the health of women has been injured by long hours, not only is the working efficiency of the community impaired, but the deterioration is handed down to succeeding generations. Infant mortality rises, while the children of married working-women, who survive, are injured by inevitable neglect. The overwork of future mothers thus directly attacks the welfare of the nation.

History, which has illustrated the deterioration due to long hours, bears witness no less clearly to the regeneration due to the shorter working day. To the individual and to society alike, shorter hours have been a benefit wherever introduced. The married and unmarried working woman is enabled to obtain the decencies of life outside of working hours. With the improvement in home life, the tone of the entire community is raised. Wherever sufficient time has elapsed since the establishment of the shorter working day, the succeeding generation has shown extraordinary improvement in physique and morals.

Source: Louis D. Brandeis and Josephine Goldmark, *Women in Industry*. New York: National Consumers' League, n.d. [1908].

8.3.   The Supreme Court Upholds the Oregon Law

The Brandeis approach, perhaps the most conservative possible, appealed to traditionalists on the Supreme Court. In his opinion for the Court, Justice David J. Brewer carried the Brandeis brief conclusions even further, and also indicated that the justices had been impressed by the extent of the expert testimony of the Consumers' League.

MULLER V. OREGON

It is the law of Oregon that women, whether married or single, have equal contractual and personal rights with men.... "The current runs steadily and strongly in the direction of the emancipation of the wife, and the policy, as disclosed by all recent legislation upon the subject in this State, is to place her upon the same footing as if she were a *feme sole*, not only with respect to her separate property, but as it affects her right to make binding contracts; and the most natural corollary to the situation is that the remedies for the enforcement of liabilities incurred are made co-extensive and co-equal with such enlarged conditions."

It thus appears that, putting to one side the elective franchise, in the matter of personal and contractual rights they stand on the same plane as the other sex. Their rights in these respects can no more be infringed than the equal rights of their brothers.... But this assumes that the difference between the sexes does not justify a different rule respecting a restriction of the hours of labor.

In patent cases counsel are apt to open the argument with a discussion of the state of the art. It may not be amiss, in the present case, before examining the constitutional question, to notice the course of legislation as well as expressions of opinion from other than judicial sources. In the brief filed by Mr. Louis D. Brandeis, for defendant in error, is a very copious collection of all these matters, an epitome of which is found in the margin....

The legislation and opinions referred to in the margin may not be, technically speaking, authorities, and in them is little or no discussion of the constitutional question presented to us for determination, yet they are significant of a widespread belief that women's physical structure, and the functions she performs in consequence thereof, justify special legislation restricting or qualifying the conditions under which she should be permitted to toil. Constitutional questions, it is true, are not

settled by even a consensus of present public opinion, for it is the peculiar value of a written constitution that it places in unchanging form
limitations upon legislative action, and thus gives a permanence and
stability to popular government which otherwise would be lacking. At
the same time, when a question of fact is debated and debatable, and
the extent to which a special constitutional limitation goes is affected
by the truth in respect to that fact, a widespread and long continued
belief concerning it is worthy of consideration. We take judicial cognizance of all matters of general knowledge. . . .

That woman's physical structure and the performance of maternal
functions place her at a disadvantage in the struggle for subsistence is
obvious. This is especially true when the burdens of motherhood are
upon her. Even when they are not, by abundant testimony of the medical
fraternity continuance for a long time on her feet at work, repeating this
from day to day, tends to injurious effects upon the body, and as healthy
mothers are essential to vigorous offspring, the physical well-being of
woman becomes an object of public interest and care in order to preserve
the strength and vigor the race.

Still again, history discloses the fact that woman has always been dependent upon man. He established his control at the outset by superior
physical strength, and this control in various forms, with diminishing
intensity, has continued to the present. . . . Though limitations upon personal and contractual rights may be removed by legislation, there is that
in her disposition and habits of life which will operate against a full
assertion of those rights. She will still be where some legislation to protect her seems necessary to secure a real equality of right. . . . Differentiated by these matters from the other sex, she is properly placed in a
class by herself, and legislation designed for her protection may be sustained, even when like legislation is not necessary for men and could
not be sustained. It is impossible to close one's eyes to the fact that she
still looks to her brother and depends upon him. Even though all restrictions on political, personal, and contractual rights were taken away, and
she stood, so far as statutes are concerned, upon an absolutely equal
plane with him, it would still be true that she is so constituted that she
will rest upon and look to him for protection; that her physical structure
and a proper discharge of her maternal functions—having in view not
merely her own health, but the well-being of the race—justify legislation
to protect her from the greed as well as the passion of man. The limitations which this statute places upon her contractual powers, upon her
right to agree with her employer as to the time she shall labor, are not
imposed solely for her benefit, but also largely for the benefit of all. Many
words cannot make this plainer. The two sexes differ in structure of
body, in the functions to be performed by each, in the amount of physical
strength, in the capacity for long-continued labor, particularly when

done standing, the influence of vigorous health upon the future well-being of the race, the self-reliance which enables one to assert full rights, and in the capacity to maintain the struggle for subsistence. This difference justifies a difference in legislation and upholds that which is designed to compensate for some of the burdens which rest upon her.

We have not referred in this discussion to the denial of the elective franchise in the State of Oregon, for while that may disclose a lack of political equality in all things with her brother, that is not of itself decisive. The reason runs deeper, and rests in the inherent difference between the two sexes, and in the different functions in life which they perform. . . . The judgment of the Supreme Court of Oregon is *Affirmed*.

Source: 208 U.S. 412, February 24, 1908.

8.4.   The Supreme Court Redefines Due Process

The decade of the 1920s began with suffrage for women, but a more conservative atmosphere settled over Washington and the Supreme Court. In 1923 the court considered Adkins v. Children's Hospital, *a case in which the plantiff sought to overturn a minimum wage law for women in Washington, D.C. The* Adkins *brief cited two examples of the ill effects of the minimum wage law: at Children's Hospital, it overrode higher wages negotiated by nurses, and at the Congress Hall Hotel Company, an elevator operator was fired because the employer would not raise her wage to the minimum. Despite a massive brief in favor of the law financed by the Consumers' League, the Court concluded that because women had won the suffrage they no longer needed as many special protections and should be freer to compete with men in the marketplace of employment.*

ADKINS V. CHILDREN'S HOSPITAL

There is, of course, no such thing as absolute freedom of contract. It is subject to a great variety of restraints. But freedom of contract is, nevertheless, the general rule and restraint the exception, and the exercise of legislative authority to abridge it can be justified only by the existence of exceptional circumstances. Whether these circumstances exist in the present case constitutes the question to be answered. . . .

In the *Muller* Case the validity of an Oregon statute, forbidding the employment of any female in certain industries more than ten hours during any one day, was upheld. The decision proceeded upon the theory that the difference between the sexes may justify a different rule respecting hours of labor in the case of women than in case of men. . . . But the ancient inequality of the sexes, otherwise than physical, . . . has continued "with diminishing intensity." In view of the great—not to say revolutionary—changes which have taken place since that utterance, in the contractual, political, and civil status of women, culminating in the Nineteenth Amendment, it is not unreasonable to say that these differences have now come almost, if not quite, to the vanishing point. In this aspect of the matter, while the physical differences must be recognized in appropriate cases, and legislation fixing hours or conditions of work may properly take them into account, we cannot accept the doctrine that women of mature age require or may be subjected to restrictions upon their liberty of contract which could not lawfully be imposed in the case of men under similar circumstances. To do so would be to ignore all the implications to be drawn from the present-day trend of legislation as well as that of common thought and usage, by which woman is accorded emancipation from the old doctrine that she must be given special protection or be subjected to special restraint in her contractual and civil relationships. . . .

If now, in the light furnished by the foregoing exceptions to the general rule forbidding legislative interference with freedom of contract, we examine and analyze the statute in question, we shall see that it differs from them in every material respect. . . . It is simply and exclusively a price-fixing law, confined to adult women . . . who are legally as capable of contracting for themselves as men. It forbids two parties having lawful capacity—under penalties as to the employer—to freely contract with one another in respect of the price for which one shall render service to the other in a purely private employment. . . .

The relation between earnings and morals is not capable of standardization. It cannot be shown that well-paid women safeguard their morals more carefully than those who are poorly paid. Morality rests upon other considerations than wages, and there is, certainly, no such prevalent connection between the two as to justify a broad attempt to adjust the latter with reference to the former. As a means of safeguarding morals the attempted classification, in our opinion, is without reasonable basis. . . .

The ethical right of every worker, man or woman, to a living wage may be conceded. One of the declared and important purposes of trade organizations is to secure it. And with that principle and with every legitimate effort to realize it in fact, no one can quarrel; but the fallacy of the proposed method of attaining it is that it assumes that every employer is bound at all events to furnish it.

Source: 261 U.S. 525, April 23, 1923.

8.5.   Florence Kelley Critiques an Equal Rights Amendment

Most of the women's movement, ranging from the League of Women Voters to the National Federation of Women's Clubs, opposed the equal rights amendment drafted by Alice Paul of the Woman's Party in 1923. In these "twenty questions," Florence Kelley of the Consumers' League tries to balance women's equality with their need for protection by the state. In so doing, she went far beyond the world of employment, evoking women's vulnerability to rape and desertion, their dependency in marriage, and arguing that the proposed equal rights amendment could result in the drafting of women for the armed services. Kelley also interjected an old argument of anti–woman suffrage Southerners—that any further moves toward constitutional equality would undermine white supremacy in the South. (Several repetitive questions have been deleted.)

"TWENTY QUESTIONS"

All modern-minded people desire, of course, that women should have full political equality and be free from the old exclusions from the bench, the bar, the pulpit, the highest ranges of the teaching profession, and of the civil service. Obviously all elective and appointive offices should be open to women and they should have every opportunity for jury duty and the right to equal guardianship of their children.

Ostensibly the new draft of the Woman's Party for an amendment to the United States Constitution is to assure to all women the foregoing rights—and many others. At first sight it may seem adapted to this end. It reads: "Men and women shall have equal rights throughout the United States and all places subject to its jurisdiction."

Before accepting it, however, the following questions have to be carefully considered.

1. Will husbands need to continue to support their wives?
2. Can deserting husbands be brought back and compelled to support wife and child? (They can now, in many states.)
3. May not mothers be compelled to work for the maintenance of their children, as the fathers must do?
4. The laws providing for widows' pensions are clearly discriminations in favor of women. Shall widowers have pensions—or

shall widowed mothers be deprived of theirs? Will any third choice be possible under the amendment?

5. What will become of the dower rights that women now have in many states?

6. Will women be subject to conscription?

7. What will be the effect upon the age for marriage? Will girls remain minors to the 21st birthday? Will all the age of consent laws be wiped out?

8. Will fathers become jointly responsible with mothers of illegitimate children?

9. What will become of the penalties . . . for seduction? for violation of the Mann Act? for rape?

10. Will not those women wage-earners who now have the benefit of the statutory eight-hours day, rest at night and one day's rest in seven, lose these advantages?

11. What safeguards will wage-earning women have, to compensate the disadvantages which they everywhere tend to suffer in competing with men—i.e., longer hours and lower wages?

16. Equal rights with whom? It is still ambiguous.

17. Are the rights of Colored women in the South to be equal, as in Illinois and New York, with the rights of White men and women? If not, should it not be modified to read "White men and women shall have equal rights throughout the United States and all places subject to its jurisdiction?"

Source: Florence Kelley, *Twenty Questions about the Proposed Equal Rights Amendment of the Woman's Party*. New York: National Consumers' League, 1924.

8.6.   A Social Scientist Comments on Protective Legislation for Women

---

Dr. Elizabeth Faulkner Baker, an assistant professor of economics at Barnard College, evaluated protective legislation in 1929. She was particularly cognizant of the new opportunities in the workforce that World War I had created for women and the deleterious effects of protective legislation on special categories of women workers. She arrives at what would become a new consensus during the New Deal—that it was best to provide mini-

mum wage and maximum hour law to both genders. She also
foreshadows the argument for deleting protective legislation that
would be articulated by a variety of women's groups in the 1970s.

"AT THE CROSSROADS"

Why are there special laws for women in industry and to what extent
have they accomplished their aim? These have been seething questions
since the World War—a far cry from those days at the turn of the century
when pitying friends of over-worked women pleaded with legislatures
to pass bills for their relief. Year after year as women poured into store
and factory these pleadings were heard. Laws were enacted in one state
after another reducing inhumanly long hours in the working day, limiting or forbidding night work or all employment in mines, saloons, and
certain other specific occupations, demanding seats and decent dressing
rooms, and, in a number of states, minimum wages. Public sentiment
was aroused in favor of these laws and they largely stood the tests of
the courts. . . .

However, after full suffrage was won for women and through
women's revealing work experiences during the war, opposition to these
laws arose. The objection has not been to the theory of protection for
workers, but to its exclusive application to women. The protestants explain that these laws do not always protect—that they too often shackle
instead. They urge that women have small chance before their profit
seeking employers to secure desirable occupation when there are restrictions placed upon what they can offer, while men can give their services
on their own terms. Other things being equal, they say, men will always
be preferred if these laws prevail, leaving women to earn a scanty living
out of the left-over jobs—a part of the luckless mass of underpaid, unskilled and unorganized workers who toil long and hope little.

If society is to be protected against the raids of power-driven machinery, the critics of discriminatory legislative protection say, *all* of the human victims must be guarded—the men as well as the women, the
fathers as well as the mothers. All of those who cannot protect themselves whoever they may be must be guarded. In this way only can
weaker bargainers, men or women, have an equal opportunity before
employers . . .

The women printers in New York state offer an example which has
come to be known as a "cause célèbre."

Since newspaper offices fall into the category of factories under the
law, the maximum fifty-hour week for women in factories passed in 1913
and the prohibition against night work applied to women printers. The
most conspicuous effect of this application of the law was its repeal in
1921, resulting from the persistent contention of the women it affected

that it was pushing them down. They pleaded that they were losing their places on the seniority lists, and that the chances for day work are only one in ten as compared to those for the night (because of the preponderance of morning papers that are printed at night). Exploitation of night workers is impossible, they urged, for by union agreement shifts are shorter and wages higher for the night than for the day. Also it was agreed that life may easily have more attractions when one can work in the cool of the evening and be off duty for rest and recreation during the day.

In November, 1921, after these women had won their case against the law, and again in 1926, the New York Bureau of Women in Industry investigated the printing trades to ascertain the effects of the greater freedom upon women printers. Considerable prejudice against women on the part of union men and foremen was discovered, so that women were not being employed in large numbers. In 1921 no changes in their employment had been made among the sixty-eight women in up-state newspaper offices, but in 1926 the number employed had increased 43 per cent, to ninety-seven in all, and eleven were working at night. The change in New York City was much more immediate. Six months after the withdrawal of the law and in the face of union prejudice, one-half of the thirty-five women proofreaders, linotypists and hand compositors had changed the nature of their employment. In 1926 this number had increased 50 per cent, to fifty three in all, and twenty seven instead of seventeen were working at night. . . .

The case of women street car conductors is scarcely less known than that of the printers. In New York state in 1919 the factory law again had been applied without regard to the peculiarities of the industry, and the astonishing findings were that of the nearly three thousand women employed, the work of but seventeen was such as could be continued under the new law. In other words, 83 percent of the women had to be entirely prohibited from work or be shifted. An analysis showed that only 4 percent of these women *could* be shifted to bring them within the law. . . .

Thus were hundreds of women in transportation service thrown out when the law was enacted; although it must be remembered that the law in this instance merely hastened a shift which was certain to take place upon the return of the men from the war. The women had enjoyed their transportation experience, the fresh air work had increased health and happiness according to an authoritative report, and their hours of labor were no longer than those worked by women for years. Furthermore a small number of these women had permanent positions which, as with the printers, the law alone forced them to leave. . . .

To the protectionists these minorities of women who are hurt by legal protection have been unimportant. Their loss of opportunities is but the usual sacrifice made for the optimum good. To the anti-protectionists, these minorities are at women's industrial frontiers. They are so valuable to the advance of the majorities that their need for greater freedom from the law must be met. . . .

We appear, then, to have arrived at the crossroads in the legal protection of women in industry. Which way shall be our next turn? One road is toward more and more laws for women; another leads to none—to the abrogation of laws which to not apply alike to men and women. Should the opposing forces prove equally potent we seem doomed to stand still.

But there is still another way. In the long pull women have had to free themselves from the hold of tradition, it is impossible to say how much they have been hindered by special labor laws—although we know they have been hindered. On the other hand, we have the best evidence that we shall have for a long time of good that these laws have done. Moreover, improved working conditions which they encouraged have also become a part of the new code of industrial leaders.

Is not our direction, then, clear? Let the present statutes for women remain for the present at least, with some necessary exceptions for the victimized minorities. Drive hard for the extension of these laws to include men as well. Aim as rapidly as possible to wipe out sex discrimination in the labor law by raising the status of all sub-level workers to the level of those better off. Present a program of legislation for men and women workers with solid economic foundation, one which is abreast of the time. Let this program be developed by an informed and industrious commission with the progress of women at heart. . . . If we sincerely desire to advance the position of women in industry, is not this the road to take?

Source: Elizabeth Faulkner Baker, "At the Crossroads in the Legal Protection of Women in Industry," *Annals of the American Academy of Political and Social Science*, 143 (May, 1929): 265–79.

**8.7.   A Woman Worker and Unionist Comments on the Equal
            Rights Amendment**

In 1961 President John F. Kennedy, at the urging of women Democrats, appointed a Commission on the Status of Women and asked the venerable Eleanor Roosevelt to be its director. Mary Callahan, an International Union of Electrical Workers official and long-time worker in the electrical products industry, describes here the controversy that developed in the Commission over ending protective legislation.

MARY CALLAHAN COMMENTS ON THE ERA

On that very first commission we did a lot of work. . . . We started out with schools, child care, social security, the ERA, anything and everything that had to do with the status of a woman in the United States, from the cradle to the grave. It was very interesting. There were people with whom I had never expected to sit down at a roundtable. Like Mrs. Roosevelt, who in herself was just incomparable. . . .

I was on the protective labor legislation subcommittee. I was opposed to the ERA, because I thought it would remove the legal protections for women that took fifty years to get. The position that IUE and some of the women on our committee took was that all this protective labor legislation should be reviewed. Those laws that were discriminatory and obsolete should be abolished. We should keep all those that were good and make them applicable to anybody that works, not just sex-wise. Then the ERA would be okay.

We were not opposed to ERA as such, but because of what it was going to do to the protective legislation that we wanted to have extended to men. . . . But if you go for the ERA now, that's going to be the end of the laws and we are going to be back where we were fifty years ago. Then we would discuss it and discuss it. . . . I don't think that anybody should work eight hours without a break or a lunch hour. We in the unions are protected. We did this for ourselves. But unions always stood for social justice, and some of the things that were rescinded seemed to me to be very, very unfair. These benefits should have just been extended to men. My concern is for all people.

Source: Brigid O'Farrell and Joyce L. Kornbluh, *Rocking the Boat: Union Women's Voices, 1915–1975*. New Brunswick, NJ: Rutgers University Press, 1996: 126–28.

9

"The Uprising of the 20,000": Working Women, Unions, and Feminism

Working-class women in the United States face the double burden of class and gender disadvantage, and often of racism as well. They have struggled to articulate their grievances as women through complex layers of family, ethnicity, and patterns of immigration. Often viewed as unorganizable by male union leaders, they have waged a dual battle in unions and the workplace for attention to their grievances. There were many working women's strikes in the twentieth century that reflected these struggles: Polish women launching the great Lawrence textile mill strike in 1912 over "short pay"; African-American pecan shellers in St. Louis on strike in 1933 over terrible working conditions and low pay; Puerto Rican and African-American hospital workers walking out with demands for a union in New York City in 1959. The thirteen-week strike of shirtwaist workers in New York City in 1909 is a good example of the tenacity of working-class women strikers and the resistance they have met from both employers and male unionists.

Much of the garment industry moved south of the U.S. border and to Asia in the late twentieth century, but for two centuries it was a major employer of U.S. workers. In the early twentieth century two unions, the International Ladies Garment Workers Union (ILGWU) and the Amalgamated Clothing Workers of America (ACWA), began to organize workers in the women's and men's clothing industries. Women held low-paid sewing machine jobs, while men performed what was characterized as more skilled and arduous work: pressing, the tracing and cutting of pattern pieces of cloth, or in men's clothing, the tailoring of fitted suits and coats. Although a wave of strikes in the ten years before World War I were often initiated by women, many of the gains in the garment industry went to male workers—the husbands and brothers, often—of women who went on strike.

Strikes in the garment industry raised important issues for families who counted on the earnings of those who made clothes, the entrepreneurs who organized their manufacture, and the unions who assisted strikers. Male unionists often called for a "family wage," pay large enough for male breadwinners to keep their wives at home. They assumed women workers were unskilled, young, and in the workforce only until they married and that women made unreliable union members. Thus "working girls" had to wage a two-front battle against the garment industry bosses and their male co-workers. In doing so they often called on political movements beyond unionism that might unite strikers, inspire endurance for the long haul, and win the support of the wider community. In the shirtwaist strike socialism and woman suffrage provided striking women with allies and a sense of fighting for a "higher cause." Striking women raised the specter of what historian Jacquelyn Dowd Hall has described as the "disorderly woman," a woman who threatens to escape the boundaries of family and gender submission by picketing and protesting in public space, a specter that returned, for instance, in the Farah pants factory strike by Chicana workers in El Paso in 1972.

Often referred to as "the uprising of the 20,000," the 1909 strike in the shirtwaist industry in New York City was one of the most dramatic strikes of the early twentieth century. The ubiquitous shirtwaist, or white blouse, was the emblem of the new working women of the turn of the century. Worn with a dark skirt, it could be laundered separately and recycled for another day's wear to the factory, the office, or the schoolroom. An industry in transition, shirtwaist production took place in a variety of settings: crowded one-room sweatshops in the tenements, upper-story lofts of cast-iron buildings, and a few large factories with rows and rows of sewing machines. Many of the employers and the factory supervisors, some of them women, were German Jews and Yankees. The industry was characterized by perpetually low wages, mandatory overtime during the busy season, and lay-offs during the slack months. Workers were paid by the piece, that is the number of items they completed in a day; many had to rent sewing machines from employers or carry their own sewing machines to work. An eleven- or twelve-hour day was likely to yield five or six dollars a week. The speeded-up pace of foot treadle sewing machines was the enemy of youth and of peace of mind. The working conditions were noisy, unsanitary, and dangerous; dirty sweatshops strewn with fabric, thread, and dust were combustible fire hazards awaiting disaster.

A relatively new sector of the garment industry, the shirtwaist trade employed many of the newest women immigrants, who were pouring into the Northeast from eastern and southern Europe during the open-door immigration decades before World War I. About 10 percent of the workers were native-born Americans, 35 percent were Italian, and 55 percent were Russian Jewish; most were young women between the ages of fifteen and twenty-five. Native-born workers were often the daughters of so-called "labor aristocrats," skilled workers who had gained the best benefits from the organizing of the American Federation of Labor (AFL) and who looked down on the Jews and Italians hired in recent years. Italian women, most of them daughters of artisans and tenant farmers from small villages in southern Italy, were reluctantly sent to work by parents who worried about their sexual virtue and emphasized women's submission to the authority of fathers. But Jewish women had typically worked to support their families in the Old World, and many were political dissidents and socialists. They came to America with some education, strategies of group resistance, ethnic solidarity, and radical ideas about the rights of women and working people.

Crowded into ghetto-like conditions on the Lower East Side of Manhattan, Russian Jewish immigrants forged a community life that encouraged sacrifice for family and the common good of the Jewish people in a new land. But young Russian Jewish women also found the urban environment liberating to themselves as individuals; they attended night school, shopped for hats and inexpensive clothing with hard-earned wages, went to dance halls, and joined radical political groups. Pauline Newman, who emigrated in 1901, and Clara Lemlich, who arrived in 1903, had already participated in neighborhood rent strikes and the Kosher meat boycott of 1902 before the Triangle shirtwaist walkout in 1909. Clara Lemlich worked at Triangle as a seamstress before she was fired for attempting to organize workers into a union—one in a series of jobs she lost for her defiance of the shirtwaist bosses. Lemlich found organizing shirtwaist workers in locals of the ILGWU rough going. The AFL dominated the garment industry and ignored women workers, forming small craft unions of male pressers and cutters instead. Italian women had ignored appeals to organize, and both Jewish and Yankee fathers assured their daughters that union business was for men.

In September 1909, Jewish workers at several shirtwaist factories in New York, including Triangle, walked off their jobs and went on strike to protest low wages and poor working conditions. Employers hired prostitutes and male thugs to join the picket line and discredit the reputation of the strikers. Subject to sexual harassment from supervisors and male workers in the shops, women factory workers fought to distinguish themselves from women who sold their bodies to earn a living. Fistfights broke out on the picket line, and both strikers and prostitutes were arrested, sometimes sharing jail cells; the result was that the striker gained a greater understanding of the prostitute's dilemma. This claiming of public space on the sidewalks fronting the shops was only the first indication that the "disorderly women" of the shirtwaist strike would have to assume new identities, and not necessarily respectable ones. As one judge put it, they seemed to be "on strike against God and nature."

Clara Lemlich's Local 25 of the ILGWU called for a general strike of all shirtwaist workers in solidarity with Triangle and other shops but was rebuffed by the ILGWU leadership and by AFL president Samuel Gompers. But at a strike meeting on November 22, after male union leaders, including Gompers, attempted to deflect the audience from the idea of a general strike, Lemlich took the platform and proclaimed in Yiddish: "I am a working girl, one of those who are on strike against intolerable conditions. I am tired of listening to speakers who talk in general terms. What we are here for is to decide whether we shall or shall not strike. I offer a resolution that a general strike be declared—now." The audience was captivated, and, substituting the word union for Jerusalem, took the ancient Jewish oath of faith, sweeping the leadership into approval of a general strike. Discouraged by the attitude of male unionists, middle-class Progressive women and working-class women trade unionists used the recently formed Women's Trade Union League (WTUL) to promote the strike. The WTUL and the Socialist Party proved to be the most effective supporters of the waist workers, taking the strike beyond simple unionism and into struggles for women's rights and working-class solidarity.

The strike lasted into 1910, an incredible achievement for the workers, who spent the harsh winter picketing, being arrested, going to jail, and allocating meager strike funds to their hard-pressed families. Middle and upper-class allies of the strikers from the WTUL and the New York suffrage movement joined the picket lines of the strikers, and that caught the attention of the press. The result was ambivalence on the part of the strikers: gratitude for the help, and resentment that their own sacrifices had meant so little to New York reporters. Male unionists resented that women, most of them mere teenagers, were center-stage in the strike and accused them of being romantic and impractical. Well-to-do suffragists such as Alva P. Belmont were often insensitive to the class dominance they evidenced toward the waist workers, and Socialist women feared that women workers would be diverted from unionism to suffrage work by the upper class. But the presence of socialites on the picket line helped the strikers; as the number of arrests increased, the cross-class drama of the picketing caught on in nationally distributed publications, and the plucky strikers became, at best heroines, or at the very least, objects of curiosity. Some Italian women joined the strike, despite the deep strictures of Italian culture against any mixed-sex public activities for women before marriage. African-American women, who were never hired in the shops before the strike and had been ignored by the WTUL, were among those brought in as strikebreakers. Because shirtwaist shops were embedded in the immigrant neighborhoods of New York, however, strikers and their families had some control over public space. The police and the employers' hired thugs could not, in the end, contain the strike or break down the solidarity of the workers.

Another factor in the winning of the strike was a new kind of ILGWU, an industrial, not a craft, union that reached out to Italian workers and that recognized all garment workers, including women, as members of bargaining units. The reconstructed ILGWU became the most important site of union membership for women workers in the United States before World War II, but one that was still dominated by male officers and male concerns. Women were assumed to be foot soldiers in the greater war to achieve breadwinner salaries for men. As Annilese Orleck has explained, "from the very start of the [ILGWU] . . . its male officers were caught in a bind. Though they subscribed to a vision of unionism very close to that of the AFL—a muscular fraternity of skilled workers—their power as a union depended on being able to organize an industry of unskilled women."[1]

The strike petered out in early 1910, as male cutters and pressers in the larger shops signed contracts and went back to work. Women workers were left with a union that their employers did not have to bargain with on the shop floor and who simply ignored the safety and sanitary regulations demanded in the strike. A year later, a fire broke out at the Triangle Shirtwaist Company. The fire escapes had been locked to prevent workers from leaving early or taking unauthorized breaks. One-hundred-forty-six workers, most of them women, were killed in the fire, many of them jumping from upper-story windows to escape the flames. Pauline Newman lost many of her oldest friends and spent a year mourning—and organizing new ILGWU workers in Boston, Cleveland, and Philadelphia. The WTUL, fearing that male unionists would never incorporate women into their unions, turned to protective legislation for women and to worker education. The shirtwaist striker was now a pathetic victim rather than a brave heroine.

Gains by workers in the garment industry have always been difficult to sustain. In New York, working conditions declined in the 1920s as factory owners moved sweatshops to other cities and sent manufacturing out to subcontractors. Today, most garments bought by Americans are made outside the United States. But with legal and illegal immigration to the United States at new highs at the end of the twentieth century, sweatshops continue to proliferate. In the 1960s, for example, immigrant women from rural China were employed in small sweatshops in New York's Chinatown, and with the sometimes reluctant help of the male leadership of the ILGWU, began to organize. Chinese women garment workers staged a successful strike in 1982, but found themselves in competition with higher-paid Puerto-Rican, African-American, and Jewish workers.

In the Texas border towns of El Paso and San Antonio, women garment workers at the Farah garment manufacturing company grew restive over their pay and working conditions in the 1960s and 1970s. Farah produced pants and slacks for the consumer retail trade, selling to chain stores such as J.C. Penney and Sears and Roebuck. Of its workers, 95 percent were of Mexican descent, and 85 percent were women. Having sought opportunity in the United States, sometimes decades earlier, workers at Farah thought of their jobs as "good jobs"; they were an alternative to domestic service or migrant labor, the only other major forms of employment for Chicanas in Texas. But in contrast to the shirtwaist workers of New York sixty years earlier, Chicanas were not always young and temporary workers. A significant proportion were married and had children; some were the sole breadwinners in their families.

Farah boasted of periodic raises and a retirement fund, but most workers were paid the minimum wage for years, and no one had been able to keep a job long enough to retire. Management used a quota system to encourage rapid production, and employed Anglo supervisors to drive the women's pace. Rosa Flores, an early organizer for the ACWA at Farah, could produce sixty bundles a day and earned $1.80 an hour. Told she must go faster, she raised her quota to ninety bundles a day but received no increase in salary. The factory floors were often unventilated and dirty, many workers had respiratory and other health problems, and workers who were receptive to sexual advances of Anglo supervisors received special treatment. The company provided no maternity benefits despite the large proportion of married women workers with children.

In 1969 unhappy workers at Farah began a union drive to affiliate with the ACWA, but Farah refused to recognize the union and in 1972, workers in San Antonio and El Paso walked off the job when they learned that union organizers had been fired. The walkout quickly spread and produced a long list of grievances. Chicanas demanded a reasonable work pace along with salary increases and better benefits. The company imported Mexicans with green cards from Juarez as strikebreakers. Fights on the picket line ensued. Some of those who crossed the line were long-time employees of Farah who viewed union organizers as troublemakers and Farah as a paternalistic employer. Families and neighbors were divided over whether to strike, and women who walked out found that they had to claim a new and more assertive identity. "Alma" remembered that she wore pants instead of a dress to work the day she thought she might join the picket line. The picketers pleaded with her not to go inside, and the supervisors tried to persuade her to stay at her table. Gathering up her courage, she walked out with her shopmates: "I really knew we were going to do something. That we were really going to fight for our rights."[2]

Inspired by the United Farm Workers (UFW) national boycott of grapes, the ACWA launched a similar boycott of Farah pants that was remarkably effective. Women now had public roles, sometimes speaking to supporters in far-off cities, for instance, that were in contradiction with the Mexican perception of *la familia* and women's roles within it. The strike took up time that women had usually spent on domestic duties. Some strikers' marriages ended in divorce, but in others, women negotiated a new and more independent role for themselves. As one Chicana said: "For years I wouldn't do anything without asking my husband's permission. . . . Of course, I don't do this anymore. [The time of the strike was] when it started changing. . . . I was able to begin to stand up for myself, and I began to feel that I should be accepted for the person that I am."[3]

Like the New York City shirtwaist strikers of 1909, the Farah strikers gained legitimacy by turning their struggle into something more than the demand for a union—in their case *la raza*, the demand for Mexican-American dignity and civil rights. In early 1974, Farah was ordered by the National Labor Relations Board to reinstate striking workers and to hold an election to decide on union affiliation. On February 23, 1974, Farah recognized the union as a bargaining agent and the ACWA ended the boycott.

Characterized by low overhead, the subcontracting system and a relentless search for the cheapest labor, the garment industry has moved from one impoverished labor site to another over the course of the twentieth century. Farah never recovered from the combination of the strike and its own bad business decisions; thousands of Farah workers had been laid off by the late 1970s and most of the contract gains of 1974 lost. Rural workers continue to flock to garment work in the hope of surviving—even thriving—in urban settings and more modern economies. But garment industry work pits struggling immigrants of different ethnicities against each other and, while offering entrepreneurial and managerial opportunities to some (mostly men), does so at the cost of ordinary workers (mostly women) struggling to make a decent wage. Men still hold the better-paying and more-skilled jobs in the industry, but women workers hold the key to successful unionization. To the extent that unions have succeeded in the garment industry they have been "industrial unions," unions that incorporate all workers regardless of skill, age, ethnicity or gender. Women have often had to lead the way in these unions, sparking strikes, taking the risk of being "disorderly," and, in the process, negotiating new identities for themselves in the family, the workplace, and the union.

READING GUIDE

Bao, Xiaolan, *Holding Up More than Half the Sky: Chinese Women Garment Workers in New York City, 1948–92.* Champaign: University of Illinois Press, 2001. Bao explores the lives of Chinese women garment workers in New York City after the wave of migration following World War II. Bao finds that although they were hard-pressed to combine their dual roles of raising children and working long hours in sweatshops, Chinese women gained a new sense of self-confidence along with their paychecks, laying the groundwork for a 1982 strike of 20,000 workers.

Dye, Nancy Schrom, *As Equals and as Sisters: Feminism, the Labor Movement, and the Women's Trade Union League of New York.* Columbia: University of Missouri Press, 1980. Dye examines the fraught alliance between middle-class women reformers and working-class organizers in the Women's Trade Union League and determines that although the "allies" were critical to the early stages of garment workers' organization, they were often paternalistic and domineering, suspicious of the Socialists, and intent on mobilizing union women for the suffrage movement. Whatever their motives, the work of the WTUL remained frustrating. Male unionists excluded women from positions of leadership, dismissed women workers as frivolous, and put almost no money into their organizing. Middle-class allies and union women turned, increasingly, to protective legislation, especially after the Triangle Shirtwaist Company fire of 1911, a strategy that male unionists were willing to support.

Glenn, Susan A., *Daughters of the Shtetl: Life and Labor in the Immigrant Generation.* Ithaca: Cornell University Press, 1990. This account of Jewish women who came to the United States in the early twentieth century explores the continuity and changes in the roles of mothers and daughters in New York and Chicago. Building on several decades of labor and immigration history scholarship, Glenn also makes use of garment worker union records, oral histories, and a rich array of photographs. Glenn concludes that "the garment workers' uprising transformed the industry, . . . [t]hey transformed the immigrant community; and equally important, they transformed the lives of women workers" (206).

Hall, Jacquelyn Dowd, "Disorderly Women: Gender and Labor Militancy in the Appalachian South," *Journal of American History* 73 (1986): 354–82. This critical essay conceptualizes the "disorderly woman" in the context of a 1929 textile strike in Elizabethtown, North Carolina, in 1929. The great value of Hall's essay is to show that women strikers inevitably raise questions about gender identities in family and society.

Jensen, Joan M. and Sue Davidson, eds., *A Needle, a Bobbin, a Strike: Women Needleworkers in America.* Philadelphia: Temple University Press, 1984. This collection of essays is a must-read for anyone interested in the history of the sewing trades and women's participation in them. Topics include needlework before 1900, "the great uprisings" between 1900 and 1920 in Rochester, Chicago, Cleveland, and New York, and the dispersion of the garment industry through runaway shops and the labor mobilization of new ethnic groups between 1920 and 1980. The essays underscore the basic characteristics of sweatshop organization, the difficulties of winning union representation for women, and the circumstances under which workers will demand better conditions and pay, despite the wide variety of ethnic groups, geographical places or kinds of garments involved. The volume also contains one of the few published accounts of the Farah strike.

Malkiel, Theresa S., *The Diary of a Shirtwaist Worker*. Ithaca: ILR Press of Cornell University, 1990. Francoise Basch provides a helpful introductory essay on the shirtwaist strike of 1909 to this work of "history, fiction and propaganda" by Socialist and WTUL organizer Theresa Malkiel. Malkiel uses the device of a Yankee woman's "diary" to explore the ethnic and class complexities of the strike and the evolution of a labor aristocrat's daughter's consciousness from snobbery and dependency to independence and labor union radicalism. Highly readable and brief, this text is a good classroom reading.

Moses, Claire Goldberg and Heidi Hartmann, eds., *U.S. Women in Struggle: A Feminist Studies Anthology*. Champaign: University of Illinois Press, 1995. This collection of essays reprinted from the journal *Feminist Studies* includes several important pieces on women's labor history and the gender dynamics of union organizing. See, in particular, Alice Kessler-Harris, "Where Are the Organized Women Workers?" 110–33; Sharon Hartman Strom, "Challenging 'Woman's Place': Feminism, the Left, and Industrial Unionism in the 1930s," 145–65; and Dorothy Sue Cobble, "Rethinking Troubled Relations between Women and Unions: Craft Unionism and Female Activism," 166–88.

Orleck, Annelise, *Common Sense and a Little Fire: Women and Working-Class Politics in the United States, 1900–1965*. Chapel Hill: University of North Carolina Press, 1995. This rich social and labor history intertwines the lives of four remarkable Jewish women organizers in the garment trades: Fannia Cohn, Pauline Newman, Clara Lemlich, and Rose Schneiderman. All firebrands in their youth, they came to New York from Russia early in the twentieth century with Socialist ideas, a desire to read and learn, and eager to mobilize their class and their gender. They staged rent strikes, organized Jewish workers, and devoted their lives to working people. After playing a critical role in the shirtwaist strike of 1909, organizing for the ILGWU and speaking for woman suffrage, Lemlich married and joined the Communist Party. Newman raised a child with a woman partner, dressed like a man, and traveled the country organizing for the ILGWU. Fannia Cohn pioneered in worker education, and Rose Schneiderman was an eloquent speaker for both woman suffrage and the WTUL. A friend of Eleanor Roosevelt and Frances Perkins, Schneiderman would have a significant impact on Franklin D Roosevelt's thinking about labor issues.

Ruiz, Vicki L., *From Out of the Shadows: Mexican Women in Twentieth-Century America*. New York: Oxford University Press, 1998. Ruiz, a scholar of Mexican and Mexican women's history on both sides of the border, has been instrumental in bringing Chicana history into the field of women's studies. Here she shows how border-crossing women in the Southwest adapted to changes in work and family responsibilities in the twentieth century. Rooted in a proud and family-based culture that celebrates women's religious and community roles but nonetheless expects their subservience to fathers and husbands, women of Mexican descent in the United States have struggled for a more expansive public sphere and a larger voice in community struggles. Canneries, migrant field work, and the garment industry have often been the sites of Mexican strikes and the kinds of gender and ethnic dynamics that emerged in the Farah strike of 1972. She argues that "Chicanas share a topography of multiple identities, and definitions of Chicana feminism remain contested" (125).

NOTES

1. Annelise Orleck, *Common Sense and a Little Fire: Women and Working-Class Politics in the United States, 1900–1965* (Chapel Hill: University of North Carolina Press, 1995), 65.

2. As quoted by Laurie Coyle, Gail Hershatter, and Emily Honig, "Women at Farah: An Unfinished Story," in Joan M. Jensen and Sue Davidson, eds., *A Needle, a Bobbin, a Strike: Women Needleworkers in America* (Philadelphia: Temple University Press, 1984), 249.

3. Ibid., 258.

DOCUMENTS

9.1. A Male Unionist Comments on Women Workers

The most dominant union before the Great Depression of the 1930s was the American Federation of Labor. The AFL organized "brotherhoods" of skilled male workers and viewed working women with alarm, arguing they undermined men's wages and that unions should strive for a "family wage" for men that would enable men to support their wives at home. A Boston union official articulated this view.

Edward O'Donnell, "WOMEN AS BREADWINNERS: A NATURAL PHENOMENON?"

The invasion of the crafts by women has been developing for years amid irritation and injury to the workman. The right of the woman to win honest bread is accorded on all sides, but with craftsmen it is an open question whether this manifestation is of a healthy social growth or not. The rapid displacement of men by women in the factory and workshop has to be met sooner or later, and the question is forcing itself upon the leaders and thinkers among the labor organizations of the land. Is it a pleasing indication of progress to see the father, the brother and the son displaced as the bread winner by the mother, sister and daughter? Is not the evolutionary backslide, which certainly modernizes the present wage system in vogue, a menace to prosperity—a foe to our civilized pretensions? . . .

The growing demand for female labor is not founded upon philanthropy, as those who encourage it would have sentimentalists believe; it does not spring from the milk of human kindness. It is an insidious assault upon the home; it is the knife of the assassin, aimed at the family circle—the divine injunction. It debars the man, through financial embarrassment from family responsibility, and physically, mentally and socially excludes the woman equally from nature's dearest impulse. Is this the demand of civilized progress; is it the desires of Christian dogma? . . .

Capital thrives not upon the peaceful, united, contented family circle; rather are its palaces, pleasures and vices fostered and increased upon the disruption, ruin or abolition of the home, because with its decay and ever glaring privation, manhood loses its dignity, its backbone, its aspirations. . . .

To combat these impertinent inclinations, dangerous to the few, the old and well-tried policy of divide and conquer is invoked, and to our own shame, it must be said, one too often renders blind aid to capital in its warfare upon us. The employer in the magnanimity of his generosity will give employment to the daughter, while her two brothers are weary because of their daily tramp in quest of work. The father, who has a fair, steady job, sees not the infamous policy back of the flattering propositions. Somebody else's daughter is called in in the same manner, by and by, and very soon the shop or factory are full of women, while their fathers have the option working for the same wages or a few cents more, or take their places in the large army of unemployed. . . .

The wholesale employment of women in the various handicrafts must gradually unsex them, as it most assuredly is demoralizing them, or stripping them of that modest demeanor that lends a charm to their kind, while it numerically strengthens the multitudinous army of loafers, paupers, tramps and policemen, for no man who desires honest employment, and can secure it, cares to throw his life away upon such a wretched occupation as the latter.

The employment of women in the mechanical departments is encouraged because of its cheapness and easy manipulation, regardless of the consequent perils; and for no other reason. The generous sentiment enveloping this inducement is of criminal design, since it comes from a thirst to build riches upon the dismemberment of the family or the hearthstone cruelly dishonored.

Source: American Federationist 4, October 1897: 186–87.

9.2.   Pauline Newman Goes to Work in a Sweatshop

> *In this recollection, Pauline Newman describes her migration to the United States from a small Russian village and her introduction to the Triangle Shirtwaist Company. The tight-knit familial and ethnic connections in the Jewish community and Newman's passion for learning kept her life from being one of sheer drudgery and inspired her to agitate for unions.*

"PAULINE NEWMAN FROM LITHUANIA, 1901"

That was the time, you see, when America was known to foreigners as the land where you'd get rich. There's gold on the sidewalk—all you have to do is pick it up. So people left that little village and went to America. My brother first and then he sent for one sister, and after that, a few years after that, my father died and they sent for my mother and my other two sisters and me. I was seven or eight at the time. I'm not sure exactly how old, because the village I came from had no registration of birth, and we lost the family Bible on the ship and that was where the records were. . . .

A cousin of mine worked for the Triangle Shirtwaist Company and she got me on there in October of 1901. It was probably the largest shirtwaist factory in the city of New York then. They had more than two hundred operators, cutters, examiners, finishers. Altogether more than four hundred people on two floors. The fire took place on one floor, the floor where we worked. You've probably heard about that. But that was years later.

We started work at seven-thirty in the morning, and during the busy season we worked until nine in the evening. They didn't pay you any overtime and they didn't give you anything for supper money. Sometimes they'd give you a little apple pie if you had to work very late. That was all. Very generous.

What I had to do was not really very difficult. It was just monotonous. When the shirtwaists were finished at the machine there were some threads that were left, and all the youngsters—we had a corner on the floor that resembled a kindergarten—we were given little scissors to cut the threads off. . . .

Well, of course, there were [child labor] laws on the books, but no one bothered to enforce them. The employers were always tipped off if there was going to be an inspection. "Quick," they'd say, "into the boxes!" And we children would climb into the big boxes the finished shirts were stored in. Then some shirts were piled on top of us, and when the inspector came—no children. The factory always got an okay from the inspector, and I suppose someone at City Hall got a little something, too.

The employers didn't recognize anyone working for them as a human being. You were not allowed to sing. . . . We weren't allowed to talk to each other. Oh no, they would sneak up behind if you were found talking to your next colleague. You were admonished: "If you keep on you'll be fired." If you went to the toilet and you were there longer than the floor lady thought you should be, you would be laid off for half a day and sent home. And of course, that meant no pay. You were not allowed to have your lunch on the fire escape in the summertime. The door was locked to keep us in. That's why so many people were trapped when the fire broke out.

My pay was $1.50 a week no matter how many hours I worked. My sisters made $6.00 a week; and the cutters, they were the skilled workers, they might get as much as $12.00. The employers had a sign in the elevator that said: "If you don't come in on Sunday, don't come in on Monday." You were expected to work every day if they needed you and the pay was the same whether you worked extra or not. You had to be there at seven-thirty, so you got up at five-thirty, took the horse car, then the electric trolley to Greene Street to be there on time.

At first I tried to get somebody who could teach me English in the evening, but that didn't work out. . . . I joined the Socialist Literary Society. Young as I was and not very able to express myself, I decided that it wouldn't hurt if I listened. There was a Dr. Newman, no relation of mine, who was teaching in City College. He would come down to the Literary Society twice a week and teach us literature. . . . He gave me a list of books to read, and, as I said, if there is a will you can learn. We read Dickens, George Eliot, the poets. . . .

Conditions were dreadful in those days. We didn't have anything. If the season was over, we were told, "You're laid off. Shift for yourself." How did you live? After all, you didn't earn enough to save any money. Well, the butcher trusted you. He knew you'd pay him when you started work again. Your landlord, he couldn't do anything but wait, you know. Sometimes relatives helped out. There was no welfare, no pension, no unemployment insurance. There was nothing. We were much worse off than the poor are today because we had nothing to lean on; nothing to hope for except to hope that the shop would open again and that we'd have work. . . .

I stopped working at the Triangle Factory during the strike in 1909 and I didn't go back. The union sent me out to raise money for the strikers. I apparently was able to articulate my feelings and opinions about the criminal conditions, and they didn't have anyone else who could do better, so they assigned me. And I was successful getting money. After my first speech before the Central Trade and Labor Council I got front-page publicity, including my picture. I was only about fifteen then. Everybody saw it. Wealthy women were curious and they asked me if I would speak to them in their homes. I said I would if they would contribute to the strike, and they agreed. So I spent my time from November to the end of March upstate in New York, speaking to the ladies of the Four Hundred. . . .

We didn't gain very much at the end of the strike. I think the hours were reduced to fifty-six a week or something like that. We got a 10 percent increase in wages. I think that the best thing that the strike did was to lay a foundation on which to build a union. There was so much feeling against unions then. The judge, when one of our girls came before him, said to her: "You're not striking against your employer, you know, young lady. You're striking against God," and sentenced her to two weeks on Blackwell's Island, which is now Welfare Island. And a lot of them got a taste of the club. . . .

After the 1909 strike I worked with the union, organizing in Philadelphia and Cleveland and other places, so I wasn't at the Triangle Shirtwaist Factory when the fire broke out, but a lot of my friends were. I was in Philadelphia for the union and, of course, someone from here called me immediately and I came back. It's very difficult to describe the feeling because I knew the place and I knew so many of the girls. The thing that bothered me was the employers got a lawyer. How anyone could have *defended* them!—because I'm quite sure that the fire was planned for insurance purposes. And no one is going to convince me otherwise. And when they testified that the door to the fire escape was open, it was a lie! It was never open. Locked all the time. One hundred and forty-six people were sacrificed, and the judge fined Blank and Harris seventy-five dollars!

Conditions were dreadful in those days. But there was something that is lacking today and I think it was the devotion and the belief. We *believed* in what we were doing. We fought and we bled and we died.

Source: Joan Morrison and Charlotte Fox Zabusky, *American Mosaic: The Immigrant Experience in the Words of Those Who Lived It*. New York: E.P. Dutton, 1980: 8–14.

9.3.   The 1909 Shirtwaist Strike

> *Helen Marot, a middle-class organizer for the Women's Trade Union League, believed that male unionists had impeded effective organizing of women but that the cross-class coalition of allies and shirtwaist workers in the strike had been politically effective. She also believed that women made the "best" strikers.*

Helen Marot, "A WOMAN'S STRIKE—AN APPRECIATION OF THE SHIRTWAIST MAKERS OF NEW YORK"

The strike or lockout occurred out of the busy season, with a large supply at hand of workers unorganized and unemployed. Practical trade unionists believed that the manufacturers felt certain of success on account of their ability to draw to an unlimited extent from an unorganized labor market and to employ a guard sufficiently strong to prevent the strikers from reaching the workers with their appeals to join them. But the ninety girls and sixty men strikers were not practical, they were Russian Jews who saw in the lockout an attempt at oppression. . . . The men strikers were intimidated and lost heart, but the women carried on the picketing, suffering arrest and abuse from the police and the guards employed by the manufacturers. At the end of the third week they appealed to the women's trade union league to protect them, if they could, against false arrest. . . .

A brief inspection by the league of the action of the pickets, the police, the strike breakers and the workers in the factory showed that the pickets had been intimidated, that the attitude of the police was aggressive and that the guards employed by the firm were insolent. The league acted as complainant at police headquarters and cross-examined the arrested strikers; it served as witness for the strikers in the magistrates' court and became convinced of official prejudice in the police department against the strikers and a strong partisan attitude in favor of the manufacturers. The activity and interest of women, some of whom were plainly women of leisure, was curiously disconcerting to the manufacturers and every effort was used to divert them. At last a young woman prominent in public affairs in New York and a member of the league, was arrested while acting as volunteer picket. Here at last was "copy" for the press.

During the five weeks of the strike, previous to the publicity, the forty thousand waist makers employed in the several hundred shops in New York were with a few exceptions here and there unconscious of the struggle of their fellow workers in the Triangle. There was no means of communication among them, as the labor press reached comparatively few. . . .

The arrests of sympathizers aroused sufficient public interest for the press to continue the story for ten days, including in the reports the treatment of the strikers. This furnished the union its opportunity. . . . After three weeks of newspaper publicity and shop propaganda the reports came back to the union that the workers were aroused. It was alarming to the friends of the union to see the confidence of the union officers before issuing the call to strike. Trade unionists reminded the officers that the history of general strikes in unorganized trades was the history of failure. They invariably answered with a smile of assurance, "Wait and see."

The call was issued Monday night, November 22nd, at a great mass meeting in Cooper Union addressed by the president of the American Federation of Labor. "I did not go to bed Monday night"; said the secretary of the union, "our Executive Board was in session from midnight until six A.M. I left the meeting and went out to Broadway near Bleecker street. I shall never again see such a sight. Out of every shirtwaist factory, in answer to the call, the workers poured and the halls which had been engaged for them were quickly filled." In some of these halls the girls were buoyant, confident; in others there were girls who were frightened at what they had done. . . .

The feature of the strike which was as noteworthy as the response of thirty thousand unorganized workers, was the unyielding and uncompromising temper of the strikers. This was due not to the influence of nationality, but to the dominant sex. The same temper displayed in the shirtwaist strike is found in other strikes of women, until we have now a trade-union truism, that "women make the best strikers." . . . Working women have been less ready than men to make the initial sacrifice that trade-union membership calls for, but when they reach the point of striking they give themselves as fully and as instinctively to the cause as they give themselves in their personal relationships. It is important, therefore, in following the action of the shirtwaist makers, to remember that eighty per cent were women, and women without trade-union experience. . . .

It was after the new year that the endurance of the girls was put to the test. During the thirteen weeks benefits were paid out averaging less than $2 for each striker. Many of them refused to accept benefits, so that married men could be paid more. The complaints of hardships came almost without exception from the men. Occasionally it was discovered that a girl was having one meal a day and even at times none at all.

In spite of being underfed and often thinly clad, the girls took upon themselves the duty of picketing, believing that the men would be more severely handled. . . . These striking girls underwent as well the nervous strain of imminent arrest, the harsh treatment of the police, insults, threats and even actual assaults from the rough men who stood around the factory doors. During the thirteen weeks over six hundred girls were arrested; thirteen were sentenced to five days in the workhouse and several were detained a week or ten days in the Tombs. . . .

Before the strike every shop was "open" and in most of them there was not a union worker. In thirteen short weeks three hundred and twelve shops had been converted into "closed" or full union contract shops.

But the significance of the strike is not in the actual gain to the shirtwaist makers of three hundred union shops, for there was great weakness in the ranks of the opposition. . . . The strike at times seemed to be an expression of the woman's movement rather than the labor movement. This phase was emphasized by the wide expression of sympathy which it drew from women outside the ranks of labor.

It was fortunate for strike purposes but otherwise unfortunate that the press, in publishing accounts of the strike, treated the active public expression of interest of a large body of women sympathizers with sensational snobbery. It was a matter of wide public comment that women of wealth should contribute sums of money to the strike, that they should admit factory girls to exclusive club rooms, and should hold mass meetings in their behalf. If, as was charged, any of the women who entered the strike did so from sensational or personal motives, they were disarmed when they came into contact with the strikers. Their earnestness of purpose, their complete abandon to their cause, their simple acceptance of outside interest and sympathy as though their cause were the cause of all, was a bid for kinship that broke down all barriers. Women who came to act as witnesses of the arrests around the factories ended by picketing side by side with the strikers. These volunteer pickets accepted, moreover, whatever rough treatment was offered, and when arrested, asked for no favors that were not given the strikers themselves.

The strike brought about adjustments in values as well as in relationships. Before the strike was over federations of professional women and women of leisure were endorsing organization for working women.

Source: Proceedings of the Academy of Political Science of the City of New York 1: Number 4, October, 1910.

9.4.   Rose Schneiderman Responds to the Triangle Shirtwaist Fire in 1911

In 1911 a fire broke out at the Triangle Shirtwaist Factory. Because the doors to the fire escapes were locked, more than 140 people, nearly all women, lost their lives, most by jumping out of upper-story windows. The fire was emotionally devastating for the Jewish women organizers who had put so much of their energy into building the ILGWU. Ignored by male unionists, mistrustful of the allies in the WTUL and the suffrage movement, Rose Schneiderman despaired of ever winning better conditions for women workers in her speech before the New York City Citizens Committee on Safety that same year.

"THESE POOR BURNED BODIES"

I would be a traitor to these poor burned bodies if I came here to talk good fellowship. We have tried you good people of the public and we have found you wanting. The old Inquisition had its rack and its thumbscrews and its instruments of torture with iron teeth. We know what these things are today: the iron teeth are our necessities, the thumbscrews the high-powered and swift machinery close to which we must work, and the rack is here in the "fire-proof" structures that will destroy us the minute they catch on fire. . . . Every year thousands of us are maimed. The life of men and women is so cheap and property is so sacred. There are so many of us for one job it matters little if 143 of us are burned to death.

We tried you, citizens; we are trying you now, and you have a couple of dollars for the sorrowing mothers and daughters and sisters by way of . . . charity. . . . But every time the workers come out in the only way they know to protest against conditions which are unbearable, the strong hand of the law is allowed to press down heavily upon us.

Public officials have only words of warning to us—warning that we must be intensely orderly and must be intensely peaceable, and they have the workhouse just back of all their warnings. The strong hand of the law beats us back when we rise into the conditions that make life bearable.

I can't talk fellowship to you who are gathered here. Too much blood has been spilled. I know from my experience it is up to the working people to save themselves. The only way they can save themselves is by a strong working-class movement.

Source: Rose Schneiderman and Lucy Goldthwaite, *All for One*. New York: Paul S. Erikson, 1967: 100–101.

9.5.   Struggling for Women's Interests in the ILGWU

Fannia Cohn was one of the few woman officials of the ILGWU, serving as a vice-president from 1916–1925. Believing that women garment workers, most of whom were young and unmarried, needed a different kind of union than older male workers, she established worker education programs in the ILGWU and summer school vacations for them. In 1917 she summarized her goals and her worries that women's voices were not being heard in a labor movement dominated by men at a convention of the WTUL.

INTERNATIONAL LADIES GARMENT WORKERS' REPORT

Madame Chairman and Fellow Delegates: We have within our organization about 50,000 women, and it may be interesting to you to know what is going on in that organization. We have carried on numerous strikes among workers of different trades that come under our jurisdiction. In the last eight months all the strikes we have called have been among women. We have had more than twenty organizers working among women only. . . .

One of our largest local unions, and the largest women's local union in the world, Local No. 25 of the Ladies' Waist Makers . . . have an educational department . . . and one of the achievements of that department is the Unity House. They have a winter Unity House and last summer a Unity House was maintained in the Catskill mountains. In such a summer Unity House each member can spend two weeks' vacation for $5 a week. The fellowship that Unity House develops we cannot over value.

We had the Board of Education turn over to this Unity House an entire school building, where the girls have their meetings, lectures, and classes; where they can buy suppers for 10 cents each, provided by the union. We hope in the near future the Ladies' Waist Makers' Union will be able to have their own building, something like clubrooms with a lunchroom attached. I think it is important to introduce education in our unions, managed by the girls, of course.

To many trade union women and men the organization is an economic proposition only. No doubt it is, but a union would be a very dry affair if we discussed nothing outside of our trade. I think that is wrong. I do not see how we can get girls to sacrifice themselves—and it takes sacrifice to build up a union—unless we discuss something besides trade matters. Many of us suffered for years because we were the pioneers in our trade unions. There must be something more than the economic question, there must be idealism. You will always get people to do greater things and bigger things if you emphasize the idealistic side rather than the materialistic side. . . .

To talk of democracy is not enough: democracy is judged by its actions and I wish we would talk less and practice democracy more within our unions. I do not think we are worse than other organizations, but I want that we should be better than other organizations, because this is a protest movement against industrial autocracy. . . . Let us open our doors to the newcomers; let us not concentrate power, it is dangerous. Keep everybody busy in the union, give everybody something to do, and then, and then only, will the union be effective; it will always move, it will always develop, it will never be stationary. . . .

I would invite our brother union men to come and learn something from these young girls. I challenge any of the men's organizations to say that their conventions are of greater interest or have a better spirit in them. That is the reason I am always in favor of a federation of women's unions where women are coming together to discuss the questions that interest them as women and workers, knowing their interests are not secondary but come first. I hope none of you will accuse me of trying to segregate the women workers from the men workers, on the contrary, I believe the women should go hand in hand with the men, and I believe this can be accomplished only when woman is man's equal on the industrial as well as the political field. And it is to bring about that glorious time we are assembled here to help build up the women's unions that will be equal to the men's unions.

Source: Sixth Biennial Convention Proceedings of the National Women's Trade Union League. Chicago: Glennon and Kern, 1917: 36–38.

9.6.   A Male Unionist Historian Describes the "Romantics"

> *In his 1944 history of the ILGWU Benjamin Stolberg belittled the role of the women in the great garment industry strikes. In contrast to the "philosophical" skilled cloakmakers, the "realistic" cutters, and the "proletarian" pressers, he claimed the waist workers were overly enthusiastic, unrealistic, and sidetracked by the kinds of activities Fannia Cohn thought so important. Stolberg's ideas were commonplace among male leaders of the ILGWU and were used to explain why so few women held positions of leadership in the union.*

"THE ROMANTICS"

[T]he dressmakers . . . appeared on the scene rather late, during the great shirtwaist makers' strike in 1909, which with characteristic romanticism they called the Uprising of the Twenty Thousand. Many of them were young Jewish women who had left Russia during the period of the first Russian Revolution in 1905—the dress rehearsal for the revolutions of 1917. Their radicalism was very different from that of the other garment workers, which stemmed from the theoretical and utopian socialisms of the eighties and nineties and which by this time had become Americanized into the industrial democracy of [Eugene] Debs and [Morris] Hillquit. Their leaders were definitely revolutionary in outlook, deeply class-conscious, idealistic firebrands. It is well to remember that the Russian Revolution of 1905, half forgotten today, created a great wave of sympathy and enthusiasm among American liberals and progressives. This helps explain the public support of the strike of 1909 which established the dressmakers' union.

Besides, in industrial struggles the Poor Working Girl, our favorite national Cinderella, always has had the edge on her brothers in the sympathies of the public. When a cop on the picket line begins shoving a girl around, especially if she is half-way good-looking, she becomes a martyr then and there. In the strike of 1909 the dressmakers had the help of the suffragettes, of broad-minded clergymen, of social workers, of honest or publicity-hungry liberals, of most of the newspapers. Great society ladies like Mrs. O.H.P. Belmont and Anne Morgan came to their aid and college girls discovered that the shirtwaist makers were sisters under the skin. Naturally this Joan of Arc appeal was wanting in the pressers or the cloakmakers, who had to fight the cops without co-operation from society matrons and Wellesley brigades.

This subtle art of fusing social exaltation with the technique of sound public relations . . . is still characteristic of the dressmakers. . . . But now that the International is powerful and prosperous, the revolutionary fervor of the dressmakers has become sublimated into a more generic idealism. They are always interested in progressive and humanitarian causes. They place a high value on educational activities, on culture with a capital C, and "the finer things in life." They have an exaggerated respect for intellectuals. They insist that the union must be more than a "mere" economic organization. They stress the need for sacrificial service to the union and exalt "the masses." And they demand from their leaders a demonstrative devotion to the ideals of labor to a degree that seems sentimental to the average man in the union.

All this does not mean that the dressmakers feel more deeply about their union than the cloakmakers or pressers or cutters. To the men the union is a marriage for life; to many of the girls it is only an affair of the heart. After all, they are less interested in the union than in marriage and a home, and the turnover among them is high. This is one of the reasons why they have developed few top leaders, though probably a more important reason is the general prejudice against women in high office, a prejudice just as strong among the feminine rank and file as among the male bureaucracy.

Source: Benjamin Stohlberg, *Tailor's Progress: The Story of a Famous Union and the Men Who Made It*. Garden City: Doubleday, Doran and Co., 1944: 18–20.

10

"Family Limitation": The Politics of Birth Control and Women's Rights

Women's attempts to limit their numbers of children through various practices, including home birth control remedies, abortion, and infanticide, have been documented across a wide variety of time periods and cultures. But women's bodies have never been perceived as belonging solely to themselves; they are also sites of political concern, religious moralizing, and state policy. The future of clans, ethnic groups, and nations seems to depend on women's cooperation with dominant ideologies of reproduction, and the perpetuation of lineage depends on controlling women's reproduction within carefully codified family relationships. The history of "family planning" in the United States has been characterized by the push and pull between women's attempts to obtain personal liberty over their bodies, moralists who seek to control sexual behavior, and public policymakers who seek to determine birth-rates. As birth control became legitimized at mid–twentieth century, moreover, the pharmaceutical industry played a growing role in the kinds of birth control available to women and men.

The birth rate in the United States fell by half between 1800 and 1900, even though there was no widely available contraception or birth control information. In a pattern similar to that of industrializing Europe, middle-class families in the United States sought to limit family size in the face of rising living costs in urban environments and the loss of children's productive labor. Some historians argue that the growing authority of women in the domestic sphere gave them more control over husbands' sexual behavior. Since self-restraint, abstinence, withdrawal, homemade douches, and patent medicines were the only available forms of birth control, historians agree that the remarkable drop in the birth rate over the course of the nineteenth century was largely due to abortion. As historian Michael Grossberg notes, this decline in the birth rate reveals "the coexistence of public opposition to family limitation along with a widespread resort to family planning," and a clear contradiction between "thought and practice."[1]

In the decades following the Civil War, social purists, licensed physicians, and anti-vice proponents formed coalitions to end sexual indecency and the advertisement of birth control and abortion medicines and services. Perhaps most important among them was Anthony Comstock, a business clerk in New York City who became a one-man vigilante force determined to wipe out sexual vices of all kinds. The smutty publications distributed by his fellow workers and the sensationalist accounts of abortionist crimes he read in the press repelled Comstock. Comstock conflated pornography and birth control, a conjunction that was to have long-lasting and sometimes tragic effects on sexual practice in the United States. He went to Washington, D.C., as a representative of the New York Society for the Suppression of Vice and successfully lobbied for a federal law to make the circulation of any obscene materials or devices illegal and subject to seizure by the U.S. Post Office. The 1873 law required federal marshals to seize birth control devices, abortion medicines, pornographic literature, and any printed information describing sex or reproduction. Foreign imports of any of these items were to be seized. Contraceptives, abortifacients, and information about human physiology were thus in the same category as pornography in the 1873 Act for the Suppression of . . . Circulation of Obscene Literature and Articles of Immoral Use, popularly known as the Comstock Law. Similar laws were soon passed by state governments, and Comstock returned to New York state to oversee the "suppression of vice" as postmaster of New York City.

Only a handful of free speech advocates mounted objections to the Comstock interpretation of obscenity. Nineteenth-century women's rights activists, who emphasized "voluntary motherhood," or women's control over the incidence of sex and the timing of pregnancies, condemned contraception (usually defined as abortion in their writings) as a practice forced upon women by depraved men.

Four historical developments "opened up" the issue of reproduction and contraception after 1900 and made birth control a legitimate topic of public discussion. A new sexual sensibility influenced by Freudian psychology divorced sex from reproduction and emphasized sexual pleasure for its own sake for both women and men, overthrowing some of the Victorian constraints of the past. The high incidence of venereal disease encouraged physicians to foster sex education and the distribution of condoms, which could be used for birth control as well as the prevention of disease. A modern *feminist* movement of bohemian and radical women sought birth control devices for themselves and for poor women on the grounds of women's rights. And finally, there was growing political concern in a new "eugenics" movement seeking to lower the birth rates of so-called "undesirables," ranging from the "mentally defective" to the criminally insane to poor people and recent immigrants.

Critical to the "opening up" of public debate on reproduction and contraception was the work and activism of Margaret Sanger. Sanger was a visiting nurse on the lower East Side of Manhattan who had witnessed poor women's desperate search for "the answer" to preventing pregnancy—and their illegal or self-induced abortions, abortions that sometimes cost them their lives. Sanger and her husband William belonged to the Industrial Workers of the World (IWW), a radical labor group that attempted to mobilize the least skilled and most exploited workers in massive strikes. Along with anarchists, socialists, and bohemians in New York City, the IWW subscribed to the theory that high rates of working-class reproduction provided a steady stream of workers for the capitalist class and kept lower-class families in abject poverty. Sanger and Emma Goldman, an anarchist and another visiting nurse, were among a small but militant group of radical sexual modernists who argued for women's right to control their bodies and to experience sexual pleasure without the repercussion of pregnancy. When Sanger published articles on what she was the first to call "birth control" in the *Woman Rebel* and distributed her 1914 pamphlet *Family Limitation* through the IWW, she ran headlong into a wall of censorship and the threat of arrest under the Comstock Act. In 1915 the Post Office confiscated her pamphlet, a warrant was issued for her arrest by the federal government on charges of "obscenity and incitement to murder and riot," and she fled to Europe to avoid imprisonment.

While Sanger was gone, feminists and socialist women in other cities challenged the anti-vice laws by distributing birth control information and opening clinics. New York activists formed the National Birth Control League in 1915, giving the birth control movement an institutional presence in American life. Ironically, Anthony Comstock died in the same year, although his laws lingered on for another fifty years. In 1916 the charges against Sanger were dropped and she returned to the United States. Influenced by her visits to birth control clinics in Holland, Sanger lectured on birth control on a national tour and opened a clinic for poor immigrant women in the Brownsville neighborhood of Brooklyn, New York, where she, her sister Ethel Byrne, and Fannie Mindell fitted women with diaphragms. The demand from poor Italian and Jewish mothers was overwhelming and continuous during the ten days that the clinic was open. But the New York state anti-vice agents soon closed down the clinic, seized the pessaries, and arrested Sanger, Byrne, and Mindell on the grounds that they had violated the penal code by distributing birth control information.

In 1918, the same year U.S. doughboys were sent off to France with packages of condoms supplied by the U.S. Army in their knapsacks, the New York State of Appeals upheld Sanger's conviction in the Brownsville clinic case. But Judge Frederick Crane also said that while it was inappropriate for lay people or nurses to distribute birth control devices for women, physicians might do so in a judicious way: "This exemption in behalf of physicians does not permit advertisements regarding such matters, nor promiscuous advice to patients irrespective of their condition, but it is broad enough to protect the physician who in good faith gives such help or advice to a married person to cure or prevent disease."[2] Pessimistic about the possibility of legalizing birth control through legislation or escaping its definition as obscene, Sanger modified her approach to lobby for birth control as a matter of professional medicine. She was politically perceptive in so doing, although feminist historians have often condemned her for it. In her defense, it is important to recall the conservatism and repression of the post–World War I Red Scare, the growing power of an anti–birth control Catholic Church in American life, and the reluctance of mainstream women's rights organizations to endorse any kind of birth control agitation.

Under the leadership of Mary Ware Dennett, the National Birth Control League pushed for a full repeal of the federal and state Comstock laws, but Sanger pursued the idea of securing "doctors-only" laws, laws that would enable physicians to prescribe diaphragms for women in clinics without directly challenging Comstock. She opened the first Birth Control Clinical Research Bureau (CRB) clinic in New York City on lower Fifth Avenue in 1923, staffed with female physicians and nurses willing to dispense diaphragms to "all married women who hoped to avoid pregnancy." Clinic fees were adjusted according to income, thousands of letters from around the country were answered with referrals to physicians and enclosures of *Family Limitation*, African-American women were not turned away, and records on the efficacy of varieties of pessaries, jellies, and spermicides were compiled. Women were interviewed about the results of birth control on their sex lives; many said that birth control enabled them to enjoy sex. Although an attempt at sustaining a clinic in Harlem failed in 1924, a second clinic served the African-American community between 1930 and 1935, but the effects of the Great Depression closed it down. By 1938 the Sanger clinics had seen 65,000 women and were serving engaged as well as married women; an "overdue" clinic provided some women with referrals to therapeutic abortions.

The medical profession as a whole was highly resistant to Sanger's attempts to draw them into the distribution of birth control in clinics. Fearing any hint of "socialized medicine" or non-fee-for-service relationships with clients, those physicians who were willing to prescribe birth control preferred to do so in private practice. Contraception was not taught in medical schools, and as late as 1935 the American Medical Association (AMA) condemned all methods of contraception as "unsafe" for women. In 1936 the case Sanger and Dr. Hannah Stone, a Sanger clinic physician, had been seeking to clarify birth control policy was finally in the courts. In *U.S. v. One Package of Japanese Pessaries*, a U.S. appeals court ruled that "medical prescription of contraception for the purpose of saving life or promoting the patient's well-being was not 'a condemned purpose' under . . . Comstock," and in 1937, the AMA endorsed birth control as medical practice. More doctors emerged from medical school with some knowledge of contraception.

The control of physicians over the distribution of birth control was, perhaps, a political compromise that had to be made, but it was a profound recasting of the original birth control movement's goal: to bring contraceptive knowledge and devices to poor and uneducated women. There is no doubt that the availability of birth control in the United States in the twentieth century has been structured along class and race lines. A survey by Helen Merrell Lynd and Robert Lynd of the community "Middletown" (Muncie, Indiana) in the 1920s found that class status and education played a critical role in whether or not women had access to physicians and used birth control. All the women of the "business class" who were interviewed had obtained birth control from their doctors, but in an era with no health insurance fewer than a third of the working-class families used either condoms or diaphragms. Resignation, sorrow, and lack of medical information characterized the sex lives of many working-class wives in Middletown. A woman who had five children in six years "knew of no way to prevent pregnancy and said that her husband would not find out for her. 'He doesn't care how many children I have.' "[3]

Rebuffed by most of the medical establishment, the birth control movement formed an uneasy alliance in the 1920s with the pseudo-scientific proponents of Darwinian "eugenics," or the breeding of human beings to weed out genetic defects and the "unfit." Most middle-class intellectuals and social reformers of the early twentieth century, including most birth control advocates, subscribed to some eugenic ideas. Some proponents of eugenics disapproved of birth control because they feared that native-born whites were being "outbred" by recent immigrants, African-Americans, and other "inferior races." Theodore Roosevelt publicly derided the role of birth control in what he feared would become the "suicide" of his own "race," northern European whites. Roosevelt was especially critical of women college graduates and their low marriage rates and claimed that suffragists and social reformers with higher education were undermining the future of the American nation with their refusal to bear children.

Sanger allied herself with the philosophical bent of the biological evolutionists, if not all their specific policies, when she claimed that the human race would only improve through the liberation of all women from the endless bearing of children. In her 1911 article, "Birth Control and Reproduction," she said that it was not the patriotic duty of each woman "to bear as many healthy children as possible." Rather "her duty to herself is her first duty to the state."[4] She also rejected the idea that poor people were more "fecund" than the better sorts. Higher infant and maternal mortality rates and poverty, in fact, kept working-class family survival rates abnormally low. Women's self-determination over the timing of their own pregnancies would enable immigrants and African Americans to assimilate into the dominant ethos of "family spacing" and adopt mainstream middle-class values.

The Sangerists did part company with the American Birth Control League in 1928, partly because the League's new leaders, largely male policymakers and physicians, sought to promote birth control "among the socially inadequate," thus reducing "the cost of relief babies to American taxpayers."[5] This "population control" view was more and more successful. In *Buck v. Bell* of 1927 the Supreme Court upheld sterilization as a proper medical practice, and by 1932, sterilization laws had been adopted by twenty-six states. Poor women, unmarried teenagers, Native-American women, and black women on relief were most likely to be sterilized. Between the 1930s and the 1970s, thousands of Puerto Rican women were sterilized under the auspices of the federal government. In the 1960s and 1970s, women on welfare in the United States were under heavy pressure, sometimes while in labor, to "consent" to sterilization. More recently the drug Norplant, a skin implant that dispenses birth control medication for two years and must be surgically removed, has been distributed on a widespread basis to women on welfare or whose childbearing is viewed by local agencies as undesirable.

Birth control technology, with the exception of male sterilization (vasectomy), continues to focus on women's bodies. In the 1950s benefactor Katherine McCormick worked with Sanger to fund research for a birth control pill; it was perfected by a Catholic doctor and first distributed in the 1960s. A decade later, the pill was widely used by American women and had been linked to growing rates of premarital sex among young women. The pill has revolutionized the reproductive lives of women, but it may cause unpleasant side effects and has been linked to some varieties of cancer.

Attempts to find new methods of birth control and to market them successfully included the IUD (intrauterine device). Put on the market in 1970 by the A.H. Robins Company, the Dalkon shield IUD had not been properly tested in clinical trials and by 1973 was declared harmful to health and taken off the market in the United States. (Many birth control medicines not deemed suitable for the United States continue to be sold or distributed in Africa, Latin America, and Asia.) The Dalkon shield was only 95 percent effective in preventing pregnancy, often caused pelvic inflammatory infection, and in some women, led to infertility, premature births, or death. Although widely tested and used in Europe and Great Britain, the drug RU486, which causes spontaneous abortion and is thus similar to the IUD, was banned in the United States during the Republican administrations of Ronald Reagan and George Bush, Sr., but was endorsed for sale by the Federal Drug Administration during Democrat William Clinton's presidency. The object of fierce opposition by modern-day social purists, the Catholic Church, and those opposed to the sexual freedom of teenagers and adult women outside the family, RU486's future remains unclear. As in the past, most physicians are reluctant to prescribe a new, politically controversial method of birth control, and many health insurance policies do not cover birth control medications of any kind.

Given the tug of war between women's individual rights to birth control, pharmaceutical companies and their profits, and birth control as coercive public policy, many African-American women and Latinas have been wary of the goals of the mainstream birth control movement. Poverty and poor health care foster higher rates of infertility in these groups than in the white middle class. The least likely to have access to good medical care or modern methods of birth control, they are also the most likely to seek abortions and the most likely to be sterilized, sometimes under coercion. Feminist health care activists maintain that women's access to birth control is only one aspect of sexual liberation. Assistance in escaping poverty and obtaining good medical insurance would give them the power—not only to prevent pregnancy but also to contemplate having as many children as they would like as well. And it is likely that the conflict between birth control as a woman's right, as a public policy of the state, and as a site of conflict between patients and physicians will continue to structure the practice of family limitation.

READING GUIDE

Allitt, Patrick, "Sex, Law and Nature," *Catholic Intellectuals and Conservative Politics in America, 1950–1985.* Ithaca: Cornell University Press, 1993: 163–203. Few Americans know that the basic science of the birth control pill was developed by John Rock, a Catholic physician, who argued that the pill was not in contradiction with church policy on sexual intercourse within marriage. Allitt explores the debate among American Catholics over birth control and shows that while the Vatican continued to link all birth control medicines and devices with abortion in the 1960s, many intellectuals and most of the lay church members in the United States began to do otherwise. The gulf between the dogma of the Catholic Church and the practice of its lay members continues.

Davis, Angela Y., "Racism, Birth Control and Reproductive Rights," *Women, Race and Class*. New York: Random House, 1981: 202–21. A militant civil rights scholar who in the 1970s played as important a role outside the classroom as she did inside, Davis was the first to popularize the historical links between the birth control movement, eugenics, and sterilization. Davis is clear on her own support for women's reproductive rights, but she also shows how a history of racism and attempts to control the fertility of poor women has penetrated every aspect of birth control thinking and policy in the United States. All of the topics that Davis raises have been more thoroughly researched in the last thirty years, but her eloquent writing and clear contrasts between what women (especially women of color) want and what they are likely to get from those in power remains persuasive.

Gordon, Linda, *Woman's Body, Woman's Right: A Social History of Birth Control in America*. New York: Penguin Books, 1977. A leader in the women's liberation movement and one of the first scholars of women's history, Linda Gordon's classic work is both a scholarly and political statement, the first real history of reproductive rights in the United States and a benchmark for all scholars of birth control. Demonstrating that birth control and abortion have always been practices of women everywhere, Gordon believes that birth control is "primarily an issue of politics, not of technology," and that the public claim for birth control was "largely produced by women's struggle for freedom" (xii).

Maschke, Karen J., ed., *Reproduction, Sexuality, and the Family*. New York: Garland Publishing, 1997. This collection of previously published essays explores reproduction and women's rights from the perspective of the law and public policy, many of them covering very recent developments. See, in particular, Charlotte Rutherford, "Reproductive Freedoms and African American Women," 113–49; Laurence C. Nolan, "The Unconstitutional Conditions Doctrine and Mandating Norplant for Women on Welfare Discourse," 227–50; and Darci Elaine Burrell, "The Norplant Solution: Norplant and the Control of African-American Motherhood," 277–320.

McCann, Carole R., *Birth Control Politics in the United States, 1916–1945*. Ithaca: Cornell University Press, 1994. McCann provides a wise and careful treatment of the birth control movement that re-evaluates Margaret Sanger in ways that make her neither a saint nor a villain. McCann is persuasive in arguing that Sanger, while caught up in the same romantic ideas about biological evolution as most social reformers of the first half of the twentieth century, tried to distance herself as much as she could from the "social engineering" aspects of the eugenics movement. One of McCann's most important contributions is to show that the mainstream women's movement, including the League of Women Voters, the Woman's Party, and the protectionists allied with the Children's Bureau and the Women's Bureau, was unwilling to adopt birth control as one of its planks, forcing Sanger to turn to physicians and eugenicists for support after the Red Scare destroyed her radical feminist base. Historians have often conflated the American Birth Control League and the Sanger clinics, which in fact, pursued very different policies with regard to women of color, poor women, and sexual liberation. Nonetheless, McCann shows that the Sangerists had limited success, despite their attempts to do so, in overcoming racist attitudes. As birth control became a more acceptable part of U.S. public policy in the 1930s, the humanism of the early feminist birth control activist was largely lost.

Mintz, Morton, *At Any Cost: Corporate Greed, Women, and the Dalkon Shield*. New York: Pantheon Books, 1985. This is an eye-opening exposé by a *Washington Post* reporter of the marketing of the Dalkon shield. Mintz's book is a good reminder that all birth control technologies need to be approached with caution and that there is still no easy solution to preventing pregnancy.

Tone, Andrea. *Devices and Desires: A History of Contraceptives in America*. New York: Hill and Wang, 2001. Tone examines the history of the birth control industry since 1873, arguing that Americans routinely sought birth control medicines from pharmacies, door-to-door salesmen, and in the mail. The poor success rate of both legal and black market remedies was only one factor in a steadily high rate of abortion that continues today. Tone agrees with many others that the medicalization of birth control has created effective birth control measures but that class and race often determine access to these medicines. Nonetheless, she reminds us that that "an astounding 80 percent of all American women born since 1945 have used oral contraceptives" (xv).

Tone, Andrea, ed. *Controlling Reproduction: An American History*. Wilmington, DE: Scholary Resources, 1997. This collection of scholarly essays and documents places birth control in the historical context of women's reproduction from the eighteenth century to the 1990s. It includes such classic pieces as Daniel Scott Smith, "Family Limitation, Sexual Control, and Domestic Feminism in Victorian America," 77–98; and Andrea Tone, "Contraceptive Consumers: Gender and the Political Economy of Birth Control in the 1930s," 211–32. It would be useful as a classroom text for college undergraduates.

NOTES

1. Michael Grossberg, *Governing the Hearth: Law and the Family in Nineteenth Century America* (Chapel Hill: University of North Carolina Press, 1958), 155.

2. As quoted by Carole R. McCann, *Birth Control Politics in the United States, 1916–1945* (Ithaca: Cornell University Press, 1994), 64.

3. Robert S. and Helen Merrell Lynd, *Middletown: A Study in American Culture* (New York: Harcourt Brace and World, 1956 [1929]), 125.

4. As quoted by McCann, *Birth Control Politics*, 111.

5. Ibid., 180.

DOCUMENTS

10.1.   Margaret Sanger Prints "Family Limitation"

In 1914 Margaret Sanger, a visiting nurse on the lower east side of Manhattan, published a pamphlet through the auspices of the Industrial Workers of the World (IWW) called Family Limitation. *The pamphlet included diagrams of a woman's reproductive system and of articles such as pessaries and douches that could be used to prevent pregnancy. Sanger also set forth the philosophy she shared with the IWW and the Socialists as to why the poor should not have so many children. The pamphlet represents the apogee of a radical approach to birth control, assuming that women themselves should possess knowledge about reproduction and the prevention of conception, including abortion, and that sexual satisfaction for women should be part of the sex act. Although seized and repressed in 1914 under the auspices of the Comstock law, the pamphlet was redrafted and distributed by the Sanger clinics in the 1920s and 1930s, but references to abortion as a legitimate method of birth control were omitted.*

"FAMILY LIMITATION"

There is no need for any one to explain to the working men and women in America what this pamphlet is written for or why it is necessary that they should have this information. They know better than I could tell them, so I shall not try.

I have tried to give the knowledge of the best French and Dutch physicians translated into the simplest English, that all may easily understand. . . .

I feel there is sufficient information given here, which, if followed, will prevent a woman from becoming pregnant unless she desires to do so. . . .

Of course, it is troublesome to get up to douche, it is also a nuisance to have to trouble about the date of the menstrual period. It seems inartistic and sordid to insert a pessary or a suppository in anticipation of the sexual act. But it is far more sordid to find yourself several years later burdened down with a half a dozen unwanted children, helpless, starved, shoddily clothed, dragging at your skirt, yourself a dragged out shadow of the woman you once were.

Don't be over sentimental in this important phase of hygiene. The inevitable fact is that unless you prevent the male sperm from entering the womb, you are going to become pregnant. Women of the working class, especially wage workers, should not have more than two children at most. The average working man can support no more and the average working woman can take care of no more in decent fashion. It has been my experience that more children are not really wanted, but that the women are compelled to have them either from lack of foresight or through ignorance of the hygiene of preventing conception.

It is only the workers who are ignorant of the knowledge of how to prevent bringing children in the world to fill jails and hospitals, factories and mills, insane asylums and premature graves, and who supply the millions of soldiers and sailors to fight battles for financiers and the ruling classes. The working class can use direct action by refusing to supply the market with children to be exploited, by refusing to populate the earth with slaves. It is also the one most direct method for you working women to help yourself *today*.

Pass on this information to your neighbor and comrade workers. Write out any of the following information which you are sure will help her, and pass it along where it is needed. Spread this important knowledge!

A Nurse's Advice To Women

Women of intelligence who refuse to have children until they are ready for them, keep definite track of the date of their menstrual periods. A calendar should be kept, on which can be marked the date of the last menstruation, as well as the date when the next period should occur. . . .

If a woman will give herself attention BEFORE the menstrual period arrives, she will almost never have any trouble, but if she neglects herself and waits to see if she "comes around," she is likely to have difficulty. . . . When once one has been convinced that an abortion is necessary, do not indulge in medicine of any kind. They only weaken the system, and require a much greater length of time to recuperate. Never allow a pregnancy to run over a month.

If you are going to have an abortion, make up your mind to it in the first stages, and have it done. Abortions will become unnecessary when means to prevent conception are better understood. It is for each woman to decide this for herself, but act at once, whichever way you decide.

There is current among people an idea that conception can take place only at certain times of the month. For instance: ten days after the menstrual period, and four or five days before the next period. This is not to be relied upon at all, for it has been proven again and again that a woman can conceive at any time in the month. . . . There is also the knowledge that nursing after childbirth prevents the return of the menstrual flow for several months and conception does not take place. It is well not to depend upon this too much, especially after the fifth or sixth month, for often a woman becomes pregnant again without having "seen anything" or without her realizing that she has become pregnant. She thus finds herself with one at the breast and another in the womb. Use some preventive. . . .

Perhaps the commonest preventive excepting the use of the condom is "coitus interrupts," or withdrawal of the penis from the vagina shortly before the ejaculation of the semen. No one can doubt that this is a perfectly safe method; and it is not considered so dangerous to the man as some authorities have formerly viewed it, but it requires a man of the strongest will-power to be certain that he has withdrawn before any of the semen has been deposited in the vagina. It is very difficult to determine exactly whether this has been done. The greatest objection to this is the evil effect upon the woman's nervous condition. She has not completed her desire, she is under a highly nervous tension, her whole being is perhaps on the verge of satisfaction. She is then left in this dissatisfied state, which is far from humane. This does her injury. A mutual and satisfied sexual act is of great benefit to the average woman, the magnetism of it is health giving, and acts as a beautifier and tonic. When it is not desired on the part of the woman and she has no response, it should not take place. This is an act of prostitution and is degrading to the woman's finer sensibility, all the marriage certificates on earth to the contrary notwithstanding. When a woman desires the sexual act, and is completely satisfied, her whole being is built up and beautified through it, her form developes [sic], her eyes become brighter, her health improves, color comes into her cheeks. All life is changed for her and would continue thus if it were not for the fact that she allows intercourse when she has no natural desire for it, and then allowing it, she is without means for prevention of conception, and is so throughout the act conscious and fearful of its consequences. Withdrawal on the part of the man should be substituted by some other means that does not injure the woman.

Douches and Their Importance—The Use of Condoms or "Cots"

The most important part which every woman should learn in the methods of preventing conception, is to cleanse herself thoroughly by means of the vaginal douche.

After the sexual act go as quickly as possible to the bath room and prepare a douche. Lie down upon the back in the bath tub. Hang the filled douche bag high over the tub, and let the water flow freely into the vagina, to wash out the male sperm which was deposited during the act.

Do not be afraid to assist the cleansing by introducing the first finger with the tube and washing out the semen from the folds of the membrane. One can soon learn to tell by the feeling when it is sufficiently clean. It is said, that the French women are the most thorough douchers in the world, which helps greatly in keeping the organs in a clean and healthy condition, as well as preventing the male sperm from reaching the womb to mate with the oveum. . . .

It is safer . . . to prevent the possibility of the contact of the semen and the ovum, by the interposition of a wall between them. One of the best is the condom or rubber "cot." These are made of soft tissues which envelope the male organ (penis) completely and serve to catch the semen at the time of the act. In this way the sperm does not enter the vagina.

The condoms are obtainable at all drug stores at various prices. From two dollars a dozen for the skin gut tissues to one fifty a dozen for the rubber tissues. These are seamless, thin and elastic and yet tough; if properly adjusted will not break. Fear of breaking is the main objection to their use. If space has not been allowed for expansion of the penis, at the time the semen is expelled, the tissue is likely to split and the sperm finds its way into the uterus. The woman becomes pregnant without being conscious of it. If on the other hand care is given to the adjustment of the condom, not fitting it too close, it will act as one of the best protectors against both conception and veneral [sic] disease. Care must be exercised in withdrawing the penis after the act, not to allow the condom to peel off, thereby allowing the semen to pass into the vagina. . . .

The condom is one of the most commonly known preventives in the United States. It has another value quite apart from prevention in decreasing the tendency in the male to arrive at the climax in the sexual act before the female.

There are few men and women so perfectly mated that the clamix [sic] of the act is reached together . . . with the consequence that he is further incapacitated to satisfy her desire for some time after. During this time the woman is in a highly nervous condition, and it is the opinion of the best medical authorities that a continuous condition of this unsatisfied state brings on or causes disease of her generative organs, besides giving her a perfect horror and repulsion for the sexual act.

Thousands of well meanig [sic] men ask the advise [sic] of physicians as to the cause of the sexual coldness and indifference of their wives. Nine times out of ten it is the fault of the man, who through ignorance and selfishness and inconsidearteness [sic], has satisfied his own desire and promptly gone off to sleep. The woman in self defense has learned to protect herself from the long hours of sleepless nights and nervous tension by refusing to become interested. . . .

The Pessary

In my estimation a well fitted pessary [diaphragm] is the surest method of absolutely preventing conception. I have known hundreds of women who have used it for years with the most satisfactory results. The trouble is women are afraid of their own bodies, and are of course ignorant of their physical construction. They are silly in thinking the pessary can go up too far, or that it could get lost, etc., etc., and therefore discard it. It can not get into the womb, neither can it get lost. The only thing it can do is to come out. And even that will give warning by the discomfort of the bulky feeling it causes, when it is out of place.

Follow the directions given with each box, and learn to adjust it correctly; one can soon feel that it is on right. After the pessary has been placed into the vagina deeply, it can be fitted well over the neck of the womb. One can feel it is fitted by pressing the finger around the soft part of the pessary, which should completely cover the mouth of the womb. If it is properly adjusted there will be no discomfort, the man will be unconscious that anything is used, and no germ or semen can enter the womb.

If the woman should fall asleep directly after no harm can happen, and it is not necessary to take a douche until the following morning. Take part or about a quart of an antiseptic douche BEFORE the pessary is removed; after removing it continue the douche and cleanse thoroughly.

Source: Margaret Sanger, *Family Limitation*. 1914.

10.2.   Theodore Roosevelt Condemns Birth Control as Race Suicide

---

> *One of the first public figures to raise the specter of "race suicide," ex-president Theodore Roosevelt commented on birth control and debated Margaret Sanger in print. Roosevelt believed that birth control would be used more by the well-off and the well-bred than by the poor, immigrants, or people of color and would put the United States in jeopardy in any struggle for world power. The high proportion of college graduates who never married or had very few children especially perturbed him, and like other eugenicists, he believed the fit should procreate at the expense of the unfit.*

"BIRTH REFORM FROM THE POSITIVE, NOT THE NEGATIVE, SIDE"

There has recently been published a "Study of the Birth Rate in Harvard and Yale Graduates." ... It should be circulated as a tract among all those most foolish of all foolish people, the half-baked educated people who advocate a profoundly immoral attitude toward life in the name of "reform" through "birth control." These people see that in the "submerged tenth" of society, and even among all the very poor, excessive child-bearing is a grave evil which crushes the woman, turning her into a broken-spirited, overworked, slatternly drudge; and which therefore crushes the family also, making it difficult for the children, on the average, to rise above a very low level. They do not see that it is the directly reverse danger against which we have to guard as soon as we rise above the class of the very poor. . . . As soon as we get above this lowest class the real danger in American families, whether of mechanics, farmers, railroad workers, railroad presidents, deep-sea fishermen, bankers, teachers or lawyers, is not lest they have too many children, but lest they have too few. Yet it is precisely these people who are really influenced by the "birth control" propaganda. What this nation vitally needs is not the negative preaching of birth control to the submerged tenth, and the tenth immediately adjoining, but the positive preaching of birth encouragement to the eight-tenths who make up the capable, self-respecting American stock which we wish to see perpetuate itself. . . .

The birth rate [figures] . . . for the two colleges in question by decades from 1850 to 1890. . . . prove conclusively that for over fifty years the men who have graduated from Harvard and Yale have left behind them a number of sons inferior to their own number . . . and that, therefore, this college stock, which in point of worthy achievement is certainly among the thoroughly good stocks of the country, is tending to die out; and they show that this tendency has hitherto been slightly accentuated with each decade. . . .

The most pitiable showing is made by the graduates of the women's colleges. So far, among the older classes of the older among these colleges, the average girl is represented in the next generation by only 0.86 of a child. This means, that for every five possible mothers there were two daughters. Do these colleges teach "domestic science," and if so, *what* is it that they teach? There is something radically wrong with the home training and the school training that produce such results. To say this, is not in the least to join with the ignorant and foolish man who denounces higher education for woman; he is usually himself a striking illustration of the need of wiser education for men. But it most certainly is a recognition of the fact, not that there should be any abandonment of, nor indeed any failure to enlarge, the scheme of higher education for women, but that for women as for men this higher education should keep a firm grip on the true perspective of life, and should refuse to sacrifice the great essentials of existence to even the easiest and pleasantest non-essentials. . . .

Under any circumstances an average of one or two children means rapid race suicide, and therefore profound moral delinquency in those willfully responsible for it. But this is not all! At present whoever has only three children must be understood to represent a slight drag on the forward movement of the nation, a slight falling below the average necessary standard in the performance of the indispensable duty without which there will in the end be no nation; the duty, failure to perform which means that all talk of eugenics and social reform and moral uplift and self-development represents mere empty threshing of the air, as pointless as similar talk by a suicide. . . .

Apparently some persons regard it as a satisfactory answer to point out that some worthless or hopelessly poverty-stricken family would benefit themselves and the country by having fewer children. I heartily agree to this, and will support any measures to make this agreement effective by limiting the production of the unfit, after we have first taken effective measures to promote the production of the fit. . . .

If our birth-rate continues to diminish we shall by the end of this century be impotent in the face of powers like Germany, Russia or Japan; we shall have been passed by the great states of South America. . . .

In a small group there may be good and sufficient explanations why the individual men and women have remained unmarried; and the fact that those who marry have no children, or only one or two children, may be cause only for sincere and respectful sympathy. But if, in a community of a thousand men and a thousand women, a large proportion of them remain unmarried, and if of the marriages so many are sterile, or with only one or two children, that the population is decreasing, then there is something radically wrong with the people of that community as a whole. The trouble may be partly physical, partly due to the strange troubles which accompany an over-strained intensity of life. But even in this case the root trouble is probably moral; and in all probability the whole trouble is moral, and is due to a complex tissue of causation in which coldness, love of ease, striving after social position, fear of pain, dislike of hard work and sheer inability to get life values in their proper perspective all play a part. . . .

Among human beings, as among all other living creatures, if the best specimens do not, and the poorer specimens do, propagate, the type will go down. If Americans of the old stock lead lives of celibate selfishness (whether profligate or merely frivolous or objectless, matters little), or if the married are afflicted by that base fear of living which, whether for the sake of themselves or of their children, forbids them to have more than one or two children, disaster awaits the nation. It is not well for a nation to import its art and its literature; but it is fatal for a nation to import its babies. And it is utterly futile to make believe that fussy activity for somebody else's babies atones for a failure of personal parenthood.

Source: Theodore Roosevelt, *The Foes of Our Own Household*. New York: George H. Doran, 1917: 250–64.

10.3.   Anthony Comstock Explains His Views

*In 1915 journalist and feminist Mary Alden Hopkins in-
terviewed Anthony Comstock for a popular weekly magazine.
Comstock believed that any materials that might be sexually stimulating to young men should be banned, that contraceptives
would encourage promiscuity, and that the key to limiting the
size of families was self control. Although Hopkins presents Comstock's views to the reader, she does so tongue-in-cheek, con-
veying her own modernist view that Comstock has been invested
with far too much power over the lives of those who would like
to obtain or distribute birth control.*

"BIRTH CONTROL AND PUBLIC MORALS: AN INTERVIEW WITH ANTHONY COMSTOCK"

Although the name Anthony Comstock is known all over the country
and over most of the civilized world, comparatively few people know
for exactly what Mr. Comstock stands and what he has accomplished.
. . . The Society for Suppression of Vice was formed to support Mr. Comstock . . . and . . . the tremendous accomplishments of the society in its
fight against vicious publications for the last forty years have been in
reality the accomplishments of Mr. Comstock.

Up to 1914, Mr. Comstock had caused to be arraigned in state and
federal courts 3,697 persons, of whom 2,740 were either convicted or
pleaded guilty. On these were imposed fines to the extent of $237,134.30
and imprisonments to the length of 565 years, 11 months, and 20 days.
To this remarkable record of activity can be added since that date 176
arrests and 141 convictions. . . .

"My attention was first drawn to the publication of vile books forty-
three years ago when I was a clerk here in New York City," said Mr.
Comstock.

"There was in existence at that time a kind of circulating library where
my fellow clerks went, made a deposit, and received the vilest of literature, and after reading it, received back the deposit or took other books.
I saw young men being debauched by this pernicious influence.

"On March 2nd, 1872, I brought about the arrest of seven persons
dealing in obscene books, pictures, and articles. I found that there were
169 books some of which had been in circulation since before I was born
and which were publicly advertised and sold in connection with articles

for producing abortion, prevention of conception, articles to aid seductions, and for indiscreet and immoral use. I had four publishers dealing in these arrested and the plates for 167 of these books destroyed. The other two books dropped out of sight. I have not seen a copy of one of them for forty years."

From this time on Mr. Comstock devoted his attention to this work, although it was, as he once said, like standing at the mouth of a sewer. Several times men whom he has arrested, have later tried to kill him.

There were no laws covering this ostracized business at that time. In March 1873, Mr. Comstock secured the passage of stringent federal laws closing the mails and the ports to this atrocious business. Two days afterwards, upon the request of certain Senators, Mr. Comstock was appointed Special Agent of the Post Office Department to enforce these laws. He now holds the position of Post Office Inspector.

Any one who has the patience to read through this carefully drawn law will see that it covers—well, everything. The detailed accuracy with which it is constructed partly explains Mr. Comstock's almost uniform success in securing convictions. One possible loophole suggested itself to me.

"Does it not," I asked, "allow the judge considerable leeway in deciding whether or not a book or a picture, is immoral?"

"No," replied Mr. Comstock, "the highest courts in Great Britain and the United States, have laid down the test in all such matters. What he has to decide is *whether or not it might arouse in young and inexperienced minds, lewd or libidinous thoughts."*

In these words lies the motive of Mr. Comstock's work—the protection of children under twenty-one. If at times his ban seems to some to be too sweepingly applied it is because his faith looks forward to a time when there shall be in all the world not one object to awaken sensuous thoughts in the minds of young people.

I was somewhat confused at first that Mr. Comstock should class contraceptives with pornographic objects which debauch children's fancies, for I knew that the European scientists who advocate their use have no desire to debauch children. When I asked Mr. Comstock about this, he replied—with scant patience of "theorizers" who do not know human nature:

"If you open the door to anything, the filth will all pour in and the degradation of youth will follow."

The federal law . . . covers only matter sent by post. This would leave large unguarded fields were it not for the state laws. The year following the passage of the federal law, Mr. Comstock obtained the passage of drastic laws in several states, and later in all states. . . .

"Do not these laws handicap physicians?" I asked, remembering that this criticism is sometimes made.

"They do not," replied Mr. Comstock emphatically. "No reputable physician has ever been prosecuted under these laws. Have you ever known of one?" I had not, and he continued, "Only infamous doctors who advertise or send their foul matter by mail. A reputable doctor may tell his patient in his office what is necessary, and a druggist may sell on a doctor's written prescription drugs which he would not be allowed to sell otherwise." . . .

"A doctor is allowed to bring on an abortion in cases where a woman's life is in danger. And is there anything in these laws that forbids a doctor's telling a woman that pregnancy must not occur for a certain length of time or at all? Can they not use self-control? Or must they sink to the level of the beasts?"

"But," I protested, repeating an argument often brought forward, although I felt as if my persistence was somewhat placing me in the ranks of those who desire evil rather than good, "If the parents lack that self-control, the punishment falls upon the child."

"It does not," replied Mr. Comstock. "The punishment falls upon the parents. When a man and woman marry they are responsible for their children. You can't reform a family in any of these superficial ways. You have to go deep down into their minds and souls. The prevention of conception would work the greatest demoralization. God has set certain natural barriers. If you turn loose the passions and break down the fear you bring worse disaster than the war. It would debase sacred things, break down the health of women and disseminate a greater curse than the plagues and diseases of Europe."

Source: Mary Alden Hopkins, *Harper's Weekly* 60 (May 22, 1915): 489–90.

10.4.   Margaret Sanger Describes the Importance of Voluntary Motherhood

---

After she and her sister Ethel Byrne were arrested for distributing diaphragms to women in Brownsville in 1916, Margaret Sanger wrote this brief leaflet while in jail. The term "voluntary motherhood" was important, because it had first been used in the nineteenth century by radical women's rights advocates, and it linked Sanger to a tradition that emphasized the liberation of women through their control over their own reproduction. Physicians figured as prominent villains in her account, and she advocated a kind of feminist view of Social Darwinism, namely,

*that the future of the human race required the uplifting of women
through birth control and attention to eugenics.*

"VOLUNTARY MOTHERHOOD"

Birth control when based on the theory of voluntary motherhood becomes the new moral standard and social principle which shall be the
foundation of a new glorified womanhood.

Long has woman been called the gentler and weaker half of human-
kind; long has she borne the brunt of unwilling motherhood; long has
she been the stepping stone of oligarchies, kingdoms and man-made
democracies; too long have they thrived on her enslavement. The time
has come at last when she demands her physical and spiritual freedom,—and her liberty.

When woman becomes conscious of her ego, her inner self, then shall
she become a pivot in the world's advanced thought, and shall hold
within her hands the reins of human destiny. Those who have opposed
her development and progress are simply those who refuse to accept this
new Moral Standard for her. They do not realize that Birth Control,
which shall place woman in possession of her own body, is an epoch-
making process in racial development. They do not realize that this new
social principle, born out of the hearts and desires of womankind, shall
be the *medium* to bring to the light of day the *sorrows* and *sufferings* that
have afflicted humanity; and shall point the way to their elimination. . . .

For centuries . . . [woman] has populated the earth in ignorance and
without restraint, in vast numbers and with staggering rapidity. She has
not become the mother of a nobler race but a mere breeding machine
grinding out a humanity which fills insane asylums, feeble-minded institutions, hospitals and penitentiaries, and provides cannon fodder that
despots and tyrants may rise in power on the sacrifice of her offspring. . . .

The Modern Woman answers: No! She denies the right of the State or
Kingdom to hereafter make her a victim of unwilling motherhood. . . .

It is the big battalions of undesired babies that have made of human
life *an endless burden of heavy work and misery.* The world is full of undesired babies and every undesired baby represents a terrible infringement of the *personal* rights of a mother. Women do not desire to spend
the whole of their adult lives in bringing children into the world. They
yield only because of ignorance of how to prevent it. They do not know
how reproduction can be avoided; when they do seek for medical advice
they are told that laws prevent their getting it.

For moral turpitude and human indifference it shall remain a dark
chapter in the annals of the American medical profession that physicians
have not availed themselves of knowledge to give relief to these poor

women that they may have saved from too frequent childbearing and saved from the horrors of frequent abortions. When we view it as an institution, I feel it has done more than any other single body to *prolong* the *misery* and *degradation* of womankind.

What has been the result? Owing to our obscenity laws and the stubborn silence of the medical profession we have the appalling spectacle of 250,000 abortions performed every year in this country, while it is said over 50,000 deaths result therefrom. No other country in the world has so large a number of abortions, nor so large a number of deaths resulting from abortions, as the United States. . . .

My constant thought was: How can I arouse the people and the women of this country especially to what I know so that these laws will be challenged and changed?

Source: Margaret Sanger, "Voluntary Motherhood." New York: National Birth Control League, 1916.

10.5.   Birth Control and the Eugenics Movement

> *William J. Robinson, an unusually liberal physician for his day, was an early supporter of birth control for women. In this Hartford, Connecticut, address in 1916, he begins with a reference to Theodore Roosevelt and accepts many of the elements of Roosevelt's argument regarding race suicide. Presenting himself as a scientist and medical expert, Robinson lays out the moral and medical reasons for distributing birth control on a widespread basis and characterized those who supported birth control as "people who have thrown off the shackles of tradition and medieval dogma."*

"BIRTH CONTROL: ITS INCALCULABLE BENEFITS TO THE INDIVIDUAL, THE FAMILY AND THE RACE, AND THE IMMORALITY OF ITS OPPONENTS"

Any person who is willing to *listen* to argument is not hopeless. I believe that in an intimate talk of an hour's duration I could convert even Theodore Roosevelt to our way of thinking; he could not help admitting the correctness of our principal propositions. . . .

Life is a serious matter, and I consider the Birth Control Movement a very serious phase of human progress. . . . It is in my opinion the most important *immediate* step in improving the race, in raising the level of our men, women and children, from every point of view: economic, moral, hygienic and eugenic. Such a movement deserves to be treated seriously and with a full sense of one's responsibility. . . .

Birth control means conscious, deliberate and desired instead of accidental, haphazard and undesired parenthood. It does not presume to prescribe the number of children. It does not say one, two, or three, it simply gives the parents the desired knowledge, believing that they are the best judges of how many children they will have and when they will have them. What is there terrible in this proposition?

It most emphatically does not mean abortion. . . . We recognise that abortion is occasionally justifiable, as in cases of rape, or in the unmarried. But as a general thing we consider abortion a great evil, an evil to be avoided and to be discouraged. And it is only the malicious and dishonest opponents of birth control who are trying to discredit the movement by making the people believe that we advocate abortion.

But, we are told, birth control means race suicide. We are accused of desiring to empty the cradles, of eventually leading the race to decay and destruction. Nothing is further from the truth. Birth control and race suicide are not synonymous terms, as our opponents would make you believe—they are, if anything, antonyms. . . .

The *lack* of contraceptive knowledge among the poor has a dysgenic effect. . . . And this is an important point . . . which must give every humanitarian cause for anxious thought. The middle classes, the rich, the professional classes, are in the possession of contraceptive knowledge and make use of it. Those who have not the knowledge can easily procure it. The people who are most in need of this knowledge, namely, the poor workingmen, do not possess this knowledge and have considerable difficulty in obtaining it. The result is disastrous, for if this keeps up, then the enormous preponderance of the lower and of the undesirable classes, will so overwhelm us that the general level of our racial stock must necessarily be lowered. . . . What is the remedy? To force the better classes to breed more? In some instances it would be a very desirable thing. But it cannot be done. You cannot force excessive maternity on those who have learned the secret of birth control. You cannot accomplish it by moral suasion, nor can you accomplish it by any law or any penalties in the world. Birth control is so easy to practise that no special appliances are needed, and no law in the world can forbid the sale of . . . mild antiseptics which have become common household articles. Nor would the most paternalistic government in the world go so far as to put a detective in the bedroom of every married couple in the land. So there is only one remedy left. And that is to spread the knowledge of birth control so energetically and so rapidly among the poor and the working classes that their fertility may go down to the same level that is now maintained by the rich, the well-to-do and the professional classes.

Source: William J. Robinson, ed., *Small or Large Families*. New York: The Critic and Guide Company, 1917: 97–150.

10.6.   The Supreme Court Authorizes Sterilization of the "Unfit"

In the wake of the eugenics movement in the years following World War I, a number of states passed sterilization laws to control the birth rates of the "unfit." In 1927 the Supreme Court upheld Virginia's 1924 law in Buck v. Bell. *The state of Virginia sought to sterilize Carrie Buck on the grounds that she, her mother, and her newborn child were "imbeciles." The medical proof was flimsy at best. The state's motive was more likely economic; Carrie Buck was a young unwed mother, and she and her mother were financial burdens on the state. After losing her case in the Supreme Court, Carrie Buck was sterilized and by 1932 more than two dozen states had passed similar laws. The Supreme Court ruling, written by Justice Oliver Wendell Holmes, implied that it was the duty of the state to supervise reproduction in the interests of the national good, and Holmes's final statement, "Three generations of imbeciles are enough," was widely repeated as an indisputable rationale for sterilization. In 1973, as some states were considering mandatory sterilization laws for women on welfare, the Supreme Court reversed itself when it declared that the sterilization of the teenaged Relf sisters in Alabama had been unconstitutional.*

BUCK V. BELL

The case comes here upon the contention that the statute authorizing the judgment is void under the Fourteenth Amendment as denying to the plaintiff . . . due process of law and the equal protection of the laws.

Carrie Buck is a feeble minded white woman who was committed to the State Colony . . . in due form. She is the daughter of a feeble minded mother in the same institution, and the mother of an illegitimate feeble minded child. . . . An Act of Virginia, approved March 20, 1924, recites that the health of the patient and the welfare of society may be promoted in certain cases by the sterilization of mental defectives under careful safeguard. . . .

We have seen more than once that the public welfare may call upon the best citizens for their lives. It would be strange if it could not call upon those who already sap the strength of the State for these lesser sacrifices, often not felt to be such by those concerned, in order to prevent our being swamped with incompetence. It is better for all the world, if instead of waiting to execute degenerate offspring for crime, or to let them starve for their imbecility, society can prevent those who are manifestly unfit from continuing their kind. The principle that sustains compulsory vaccination is broad enough to cover cutting the Fallopian tubes. . . . Three generations of imbeciles are enough.

Source: 174 U.S. 200, 1927.

11

"Votes for Women": The Passage of the Nineteenth Amendment

During the "Great Departure" of the 1870s a handful of militant women tried to vote under the rationale that the Fourteenth and Fifteenth Amendments had given men and women equal political rights. Suffragists were disappointed by a series of Supreme Court decisions that interpreted the amendments in the narrowest way possible; universal votes for American women seemed an unreachable goal for the foreseeable future. The split in the woman suffrage movement between the Lucy Stone and Henry Blackwell faction of Massachusetts and the Elizabeth Cady Stanton and Susan B. Anthony faction of New York remained a bitter one. Stone and Blackwell presented suffrage petitions and speeches before state legislatures and edited the widely read *Woman's Journal*. Stanton and Anthony explored radical feminism in their short-lived *Revolution* and argued for an amendment to the U.S. Constitution, a simple measure that was designed to enfranchise all Americans without reference to sex but one that was unacceptable to Congress and to most voters for decades.

The racist and ethnocentric tendencies of the suffrage movement became more pronounced in these "doldrums" years of the late nineteenth century, as middle-class white women saw men they considered to be their intellectual and moral inferiors go to the polls. The acerbic comments of Massachusetts activist Harriet Robinson were typical: "It was a sight to ... see the freed slave go by and vote, and the newly-naturalized fellow-citizen, and the blind, the paralytic, the boy of twenty-one with his newly-fledged vote, the drunken man who did not know

Hayes from Tilden, and the man who read his vote upside down. All these voted for the men they wanted to represent them, but the women, being neither colored, nor foreign, nor blind, nor paralytic, nor newly-fledged, nor drunk, nor ignorant, but only *women*, could not vote. . . ."[1]

As native-born white Americans pronounced "black Reconstruction" a failure and lamented the rise of immigrant voting blocs in the cities, talk of literacy and property requirements in suffrage circles intensified. Henry Blackwell of Massachusetts developed a strategy for solving the "negro problem" in the southern states as early as 1867. On the assumption that the Republican party would ensure black voting rights in perpetuity, Blackwell argued that southerners should develop good schools for all its citizens, require literacy for voting, and enfranchise women. Woman suffrage would guarantee white supremacy because whites outnumbered blacks in most southern counties and the electorate would become ever more enlightened. But the "solid South" moved, in the 1890s, not toward enfranchising women and supporting education but toward further disfranchisement of black men (and many poor whites) through various legal devices, including poll taxes and literacy tests, the latter two deemed constitutional by the Supreme Court well into the twentieth century. After a merger of the two suffrage factions into the National American Woman Suffrage Association (NAWSA) in 1890, northern suffragists made intense efforts to woo the south. Their acquiescence in the racism of the South peaked at the NAWSA convention in New Orleans in 1903. African-American women were asked not to attend the convention, and the president of NAWSA, Dr. Anna Howard Shaw, declared that Reconstruction had put "the ballot into the hands of your black men, thus making them the political superiors of your white women."[2] Talk of a national amendment, now referred to as the "Susan B. Anthony amendment," was suppressed to placate the South's position on states' rights and white supremacy.

What glimmers of hope there were for woman suffrage came first in the West and on a limited basis in some American towns and cities. The state of Wyoming granted women the vote in 1889, and by 1890 localities in sixteen states allowed women to vote in city or school board elections. Victories in Colorado in 1893 and in Utah and Idaho in 1896 seemed to indicate that woman suffrage might be on the horizon for more women sometime soon. But the western states that granted women suffrage did so for a variety of local reasons that did not necessarily apply east of the Rocky Mountains. The unbalanced ratio of men to women made women's voting power in the West a negligible factor. Local elites, such as the Latter Day Saints in Utah, welcomed women's votes as a way of re-enforcing their power; and many men saw women voters as a civilizing influence in places where miners, manual laborers, and cowboys abounded.

The Colorado campaign was the most portentous, because woman suffrage succeeded there through a coalition of several reformist third parties, including the People's and Prohibition parties. As thousands of women joined these two parties across the country in the 1890s and some of them became prominent speakers and advocates of women's rights, the major political parties began to pay more attention to women in politics. Women attended conventions and were incorporated into campaign rhetoric, even if no major party advocated woman suffrage. But the co-opting of the People's Party by the Democrats in 1896 and the election of Republican William McKinley to the White House dampened a surge toward votes for women and other political reforms that would not be given credence until after the Progressive movement addressed them between 1910 and 1920. Meanwhile, the task of convincing male politicians and male voters that a gender revolution should take place at the polling place was a monumental one. As scholar Susan Marilley says, "the story of how women won the vote reveals how a group that lacked direct political power generated a willingness among men to share this power."[3]

A number of factors built a momentum toward woman suffrage and made a victorious Nineteenth Amendment possible—but not inevitable—by 1920. Women's more active participation in the public sphere underlay a resurgence of the suffrage movement all over the United States. There was an explosion of college graduates and of ambitious women in the professions, of working women in factories and offices and social settlements. Black and white women joined women's clubs, unions, social reform movements, and the Woman's Christian Temperance Union (WCTU) by the tens of thousands. Often stressing the differences between men and women that necessitated a maternal presence in politics, the WCTU and the women's club movement was far more popular before 1910 with women than was the more radical NAWSA. WCTU president Frances Willard convinced many of her moderate followers to endorse a form of women's voting she called "home protection," or the enfranchisement of women at the local level for matters, especially drinking laws, that affected women's families. And women often went from the moderate WCTU to the suffrage movement. The National Association of Colored Women's Clubs continued to advocate an agenda that promoted suffrage along with race uplift, education, and anti-lynching campaigns.

By 1910 suffragists in New York City, Cleveland, Chicago, and Boston reached out to women workers, immigrant women, and Socialists across class and race lines in an attempt to expand the popularity of woman suffrage and make it more responsive to both urbanization and industrialization. Although suffrage workers continued to draft a variety of what scholar Aileen Kraditor has called "expedient" arguments to influence different sectors of the population, there was a critical turn in the suffrage movement away from restricting the franchise and toward expanding it instead. Suffrage leaders such as Carrie Chapman Catt, who played an important role in the woman suffrage campaign and spearheaded the final drive of the NAWSA with her "winning plan," began to drop the nativist and racist language they had used in previous decades. In a series of bruising confrontations with southern suffragists, NAWSA leaders refused to endorse the total exclusion of black voters from the polls, even though it temporarily cost them the support of most white women leaders in the South.

The changing context of American politics was fortuitous for woman suffrage. It was no accident that votes for women became more feasible as the United States left the conservatism and cynicism of the Gilded Age and moved into the larger optimism of the Progressive era. Women were at the forefront of any number of progressive reforms ranging from advocacy of maximum hours and minimum wages, to ending child labor, to bringing poor women birth control. Indeed, some scholars have suggested that the entire period was influenced by a feminized version of politics. Progressives espoused a new faith in American democracy and the possibility of changing the way human beings behaved. The Nineteenth Amendment was the last in a series of changes to the Constitution between 1913 and 1920 that included not only woman suffrage but a federal income tax, the direct election of senators, and Prohibition.

Woman suffrage also gained momentum because it appealed to a wide variety of constituencies for different reasons. Many suffragists believed that voting women would bring a new morality and social conscience to politics, ending war and political corruption, and "cleaning-up" the cities with their "civic housekeeping." Other suffragists were happy to make alliances with Progressive politicians, both native-born and immigrant, who sought to break the stranglehold that conservative elites had on state legislatures in the Northeast. After 1910 or so, although the formal leadership of the Socialist party remained suspicious of woman suffrage as a bourgeois reform, some women socialists, many of them Russian Jewish or German, were converted to suffrage and made important allies in the working class. Trade union women were recruited to speak for both labor and votes for women. As African-Americans moved to northern cities during the Great Migration of the teens, women were mobilized through the colored women's club movement to beef up the political power of black communities. Black women voters in Chicago played a critical role in electing reform candidates in that city in 1915, and leaders such as Ida Wells Barnett insisted on being more visible in national movements managed by white women. In the South, however, African-American suffragists were often more muted in their public endorsement for suffrage, fearful that any agitation might jeopardize black rights altogether, and often, because black male leaders, especially those clustered around Booker T. Washington, disapproved of woman suffrage.

New tactics developed between 1908 and 1918 brought wider visibility of woman suffrage to the general public through open-air speaking in immigrant neighborhoods, gigantic parades in New York City and Washington, D.C., and automobile touring through country towns. Astute at public relations, many younger suffragists understood, as did Florence Luscomb, a 1909 graduate of the Massachusetts Institute of Technology and an ardent campaigner for votes for women, that "Equal suffrage is not held back by opposition. That helps us. We are handicapped by indifference and its resulting ignorance. . . . We are required to prove our case in order to get in . . . [and] we have got to prove our case, not to a small body of lawmakers, but to a large body of the people . . . and to prove it to them, we must make them listen. How? They are not interested in Woman Suffrage, do not expect to appeal to them through the subject, but reach them by curiosity. . . . Make it picturesque. . . . Make it easy."[4]

Since support for woman suffrage crossed class lines, well-to-do women and men were able to infuse increasingly sophisticated campaigns with generous funding. Between 1906 and 1910, the NAWSA grew nearly ten-fold to a membership of 117,000; by 1920, two million people belonged to the NAWSA. Using the new political tactics that stressed open-air speaking, parades, and political lobbying, women gained the suffrage in Washington in 1910, California in 1911, and Kansas, Arizona and Oregon in 1912. In Illinois, the legislature granted women partial suffrage in 1913. (In some states partial suffrage could be passed by legislatures and did not have to be approved by all voters in referenda campaigns.) Although a number of state suffrage movements had been using the more militant tactics of the British Suffragette movement in the United States, Alice Paul's return to America from England in 1912 put new pressure on the NAWSA to revive the Susan B. Anthony amendment and to launch aggressive publicity measures. Carrie Chapman Catt, meanwhile, had developed the notion of a "woman's party" in New York state, using the tactics of the urban bosses to canvass precincts, get out the positive vote on election day, and target particular areas for heavy campaigning. Although state referenda failed in both New York and Massachusetts in 1915, a close victory in New York State in 1917 demonstrated that urban coalitions of trade unions, Socialists, and suffragists could convince men to vote for woman suffrage. Indiana, Michigan, Nebraska, and Rhode Island also gave women the suffrage that year.

Catt's "winning plan," announced to the NAWSA in 1912, involved a double-pronged strategy: winning partial or full suffrage in some of the states, pushing a federal amendment with the two major political parties in Congress, and, by 1918, working to defeat office-holders who opposed woman suffrage. Catt, after one more round of fractious arguments with southern suffragists, abandoned the states' rights faction, which had always opposed a federal amendment. Nonetheless, many younger and more progressive southern women did support the NAWSA, even though there was little hope of winning suffrage in even one southern state. The winning plan thus depended on squeaking by in both Congress and the states without the help of the deep South and much of New England, a daunting task when a two-thirds majority was required in Congress and three quarters of the states for ratification. A "front door lobby" was dispatched to Washington, D.C., to pressure senators and representatives into supporting woman suffrage, and in 1918, the NAWSA defeated two outspoken senatorial opponents of suffrage, a Republican in Massachusetts and a Democrat in Maryland.

Who opposed woman suffrage? Not surprisingly, those already in power who depended on a restricted franchise in order to wield money and influence in the political sphere were likely to organize anti-woman suffrage groups. The scholar Elna C. Green, for instance, has found that opposition to suffrage in the South was particularly intense among railroad magnates, urban political bosses, cotton factors, and plantation owners. Suffragists believed the "liquor lobby" feared a Prohibition amendment would be passed once women voted and suspected the liquor interests were behind most anti-suffrage financing; they also blamed an urban coalition of saloon keepers, immigrants, and political bosses for the defeat of woman suffrage referenda. But some urban politicians began to see advantages to, at least not blocking, and even, supporting woman suffrage. Suffragists tended to be Progressive, and with a new cohort of activist Irish-American women providing leadership in the local community, politicians found that they and the suffragists were often in support of the same reformist measures for working people and of an expanded democracy for liberalizing government. In Massachusetts the anti-suffrage movement was concentrated in the upper and upper middle class and in small towns. Rural folk and native-born rich people saw any expansion of the franchise as a threat to their hold over local governance and the state legislature. While Catholics were said to oppose woman suffrage, the Roman Catholic Church in the United States never took an official position on woman suffrage, and some priests spoke out for the enfranchisement of women. In Boston, Irish-American women made particularly dynamic and innovative suffrage leaders, even though Cardinal William O'Connell condemned any public roles for women. Conservative Protestant ministers were also likely to oppose woman suffrage, as did male and female traditionalists all over the United States. They viewed suffrage as a threat to femininity, to motherhood and separate spheres, and to the hegemony of native-born whites.

When the Russian Revolution erupted and the United States entered World War I in 1917, most everything had to be viewed in a new light, including woman suffrage. Socialists and pacifists who opposed the war were now considered detrimental to the suffrage cause. Anti-suffragists characterized suffragists as ultra-radicals whose disloyalty threatened the war effort. Catt, a pacifist herself, committed the NAWSA to "war work" and distanced the organization from the Socialists, who probably had provided the margin of victory in New York City in 1917. Alice Paul, impatient as ever, stationed her Congressional Union members in front of the White House, where they picketed President Woodrow Wilson, were arrested, and then force-fed in jail. On January 9, 1918, Wilson gave an address endorsing woman suffrage, and on January 10, the House of Representatives voted to approve the amendment without a single vote to spare. Entrenched opposition to woman suffrage lay in the Senate, where the ideology of states' rights and of hide-bound conservatism still reigned triumphant. In January 1919, the Senate defeated the amendment by one vote. Success in the Senate did not arrive until June, and it took fourteen months for enough states to ratify the amendment to make it law. The ultimate test came in a sweltering week in August, 1920, in the state capitol of Tennessee, where neither side could predict the outcome. Harry Burns, the youngest member of the Tennessee House, and whose mother was a suffragist, followed her advice to put the "rat" in ratification. Woman suffrage passed by a margin of two votes in Tennessee, and by a margin of one state in the United States.

To what extent did women take advantage of the right to vote? In the South, where African-American women leaders had been quietly struggling to convert white women to the cause of universal voting rights, a surprising number of black women attempted to exercise their voting rights. In Birmingham, Alabama, for instance, 4,500 attempted to register; mostly turned away by white registrars, only 225 actually voted in 1920. Native-born women in urban centers of the North were more likely to register to vote than immigrant women; with the Republican party firmly in control of Congress and the White House, many working-class women did not register to vote until the arrival of the New Deal. In the early 1920s the two major political parties courted the women's vote and feminists tried to rally the women's vote for progressive reforms. But it soon became clear that women were likely to vote in about the same ways as men and that ethnicity, race, class, and religion were more important determinants of voting than gender. But as more women headed households in the 1960s and issues of war and peace and of government funding for social welfare programs became matters of controversy in elections, a gender gap in voting did develop, with women more likely to vote for Democrats than men and to support moderates within the

Republican party. Since 1980, women voters have outnumbered men voters and the "women's vote" cannot be taken for granted.

READING GUIDE

DuBois, Ellen Carol, *Harriot Stanton Blatch and the Winning of Woman Suffrage*. New Haven: Yale University Press, 1997. This biography of Harriot Stanton Blatch, the daughter of Elizabeth Cady Stanton, brims with information about the new generation of woman suffragists, some of them college graduates, who created dramatic political tactics for the movement in the early years of the twentieth century. DuBois explores the innovative ways in which Blatch developed liaisons with trade union and working class women and shifted the mass base of suffrage activism out of polite parlors and lecture halls and into the streets and polling places of New York City. There is, however, little attempt to compare Blatch with other cross-class activists beyond New York City, which makes Blatch appear to be, perhaps, more exceptional than she actually was.

Edwards, Rebecca, *Angels in the Machinery: Gender in American Party Politics from the Civil War to the Progressive Era*. New York: Oxford University Press, 1997. This analysis of women's politics and women in politics before women could vote establishes definitively that the participation of women in American political life was well under way in the decades following the Civil War. Edwards's most innovative chapters detail the participation of women in third parties and the critical role of the People's Party in setting the stage for the Progressive era and its reformulation of women's political roles.

Flexner, Eleanor, *Century of Struggle: The Woman's Rights Movement in the United States*. Cambridge: Harvard University Press, 1959. This careful and exciting narrative was the first scholarly attempt to describe the political obstacles and triumphs that awaited the woman suffrage movement after the disappointments of the nineteenth century. Flexner interviewed several suffragists for her book, found materials that no one thought existed, and brought the political sensibilities of her mother's activism in the teens and her own political engagement in the 1940s to this astute analysis that still holds up today.

Gordon, Ann D., ed., with Bettye Collier Thomas, John H. Bracy, Arlen Voski Avakian, and Joyce Avrech Berkman, *African American Women and the Vote, 1837–1965*. Amherst: University of Massachusetts Press, 1997. This rich collection of chapters about black women's political activism ranges from the ante-bellum period to the 1960s, with critical essays by Rosalyn Terborg-Penn, Bettye Collier-Thomas, Elsa Barkley Brown, and Evelyn Brooks Higginbotham. The authors remind the reader that full suffrage was not granted to black women until the civil rights struggle of the 1960s.

Graham, Sara Hunter, *Woman Suffrage and the New Democracy*. New Haven: Yale University Press, 1996. Graham's account of the National American Woman Suffrage Association declares that "the largest democratic reform in American history has been ignored in most studies of political change and progressive reform" (xii). Emphasizing the political strategies of the last stages of the drive for woman suffrage, Graham contends that a combination of voluntarism and "power politics" enabled the movement to achieve success through a kind of "democratic centralization," despite the "outsider status" of women in the political sphere. While admiring of Carrie Chapman Catt's political skills, Graham is also careful to document her ruthlessness and willingness, like any good politician, to compromise principles for short-term political goals.

Green, Elna C., *Southern Women and the Woman Question*. Chapel Hill: University of North Carolina Press, 1997. Green focuses on the sociological characteristics of southern suffragists and on the political forces that both enabled and hobbled woman suffrage. The halting progress of the South toward suffrage was, as others have insisted, often a product of the region's obsession with white supremacy. But Green also shows that urbanization, modernization, and progressive movements in southern cities were undermining tradition and creating a movement that was similar to those in the North. As agitation for the Nineteenth Amendment grew, the increasingly marginalized states' rights faction of the suffrage movement became more anti-suffrage than not, allied as it was with the ruling white aristocratic class that saw any expansion of the suffrage as a threat to white supremacy. Once the vote was won, black and white women of the South attempted to register to vote.

Kraditor, Aileen S., *The Ideas of the Woman Suffrage Movement, 1890–1920*. New York: Columbia University Press, 1965. Kraditor was the first scholar after Eleanor Flexner to take votes for women seriously. In this sophisticated analysis of the leadership of the woman suffrage movement, she shows that a wide variety of arguments were used to promote suffrage and divides them into "justice" and "expediency" categories. Although Kraditor has often been criticized by subsequent scholars for expecting too much of women who were products of their times and had to make political compromises, her work has been seminal for all subsequent historians of women's politics. A second work by Kraditor, *Up From the Pedestal: Selected Writings in the History of American Feminism* (Chicago: Quadrangle Books, 1968) is a collection of primary source documents that shows the range of ideas among two centuries of women's rights activists.

Marilley, Suzanne M., *Woman Suffrage and the Origins of Liberal Feminism in the United States, 1820–1920*. Cambridge: Harvard University Press, 1996. Marilley concedes that while the leaders of the woman suffrage movement tended to come from elite sectors of American society, they were suggesting a radical change that had to be presented in liberal terms to achieve success. Marilley says that three major kinds of liberal arguments dominated feminist thinking: the feminism of equal rights, the feminism of fear, and the feminism of personal development. Her delineation of the feminism of fear has been particularly helpful, because she shows how feminists such as Frances Willard were determined to gain protection for women from male violence and dominance in the home through political participation. The feminism of fear often deteriorated into nativist and racist rhetoric, but a growing trend toward the feminism of equal rights in the early twentieth century made woman suffrage one of the great liberal reforms of American history.

Marshall, Susan E., *Splintered Sisterhood: Gender and Class in the Campaign of Woman Suffrage*. Madison: University of Wisconsin Press, 1997. This careful account of the anti-suffrage movement, based on statistical evidence, shows that anti-suffrage sentiment was often more the product of local and state political alignments than of a national movement. Marshall concludes that entrenched and powerful political interests often convinced "women of high social standing" to create anti-suffrage societies. These women, who were "close to the centers of power . . . perceived no need of the ballot themselves, and, like men of their class, regarded a mass electorate as a threat to their way of life" (5).

Wheeler, Marjorie Spruill, *New Women of the New South: The Leaders of the Woman Suffrage Movement in the Southern States*. New York: Oxford University Press, 1993. A definitive treatment of eleven women leaders of the southern suffrage movement based on extensive archival material. One of the virtues of Wheeler's book is her tracing of the relationships of these leaders with the national woman suffrage movement and the complicity of several generations of northern suffragists in an assault on Reconstruction and black voting rights.

NOTES

1. Elizabeth Cady Stanton, Susan B. Anthony, and Matilda Gage, eds., *History of Woman Suffrage, 1876–1885*, vol. III (Rochester: Susan B. Anthony, 1886), 282.

2. As quoted by Marjorie Spruill Wheeler, *New Women of the New South: The Leaders of the Woman Suffrage Movement in the Southern States* (New York: Oxford University Press, 1993), 118.

3. Suzanne M. Marilley, *Woman Suffrage and the Origins of Liberal Feminism in the United States, 1820–1920* (Cambridge: Harvard University Press, 1996), 1.

4. As quoted by Sharon Hartman Strom, *Political Woman: Florence Luscomb and the Legacy of Radical Reform* (Philadelphia: Temple University Press, 2001), 73.

DOCUMENTS

11.1.   A Protestant Minister Condemns Woman Suffrage

Reverend Lyman Abbott wrote this critique of woman suffrage in 1898, and it was widely reprinted by the anti-suffrage movement and distributed all over the Northeast. A classic conservative response, Abbott emphasized the different responsibilities of men and women in society, the protection afforded women by the cult of domesticity, and the "unnatural" aspects of women's assumption of public roles. To conservatives such as Abbott nothing less than the progress of modern civilization was at stake when women voted, and he had no qualms about speaking for what he assumed to be a silent majority.

Lyman Abbott, "WHY WOMEN DO NOT WISH THE SUFFRAGE"

Certainly few men or women will doubt that at the present time an overwhelming majority of women are either reluctant to accept the ballot or indifferent to it. . . . I believe it is because woman feels, if she does not clearly see, that the question of woman suffrage is more than political; that it concerns the nature and structure of society, the home, the church, the industrial organism, the state, the social fabric. And to a change that which involves a revolution in all of these she interposes an inflexible though generally a silent opposition. It is for these silent women—whose voices are not heard in conventions, who . . . deliver no lectures, and visit no legislative assemblies that I speak. . . .

The first and most patent fact in the family is the difference in the sexes. Out of this difference the family is created; in this difference the family finds its sweet and sacred bond. This difference is not merely physical and incidental. It is also psychical and essential. . . . It determines the relation between man and woman; it fixes their mutual service and their mutual obligations. . . . Because their functions are different, all talk of equality or non-equality is but idle words, without a meaning. Only things which have the same nature and fulfill the same function can be said to be superior to or equal with one another. . . . This distinction between the sexes . . . is universal and perpetual. . . .

It may be said that the work of battle in all its forms . . . belongs to man. Physcially and psychically his is the sterner and the stronger sex. . . . The war with Nature is not for her to wage. . . . This is not to say that her toil is less than man's; but it is different. It may be easier to be the man with the hoe than the woman with the needle . . . but these tasks are not the same. The ceaseless toil of the field requires exhaustless energy; the continuous toil of the household requires endless patience. . . . For like reason it is not woman's function to fight against human foes who threaten the home. She is not called to be a soldier. . . . It is not her function to protect the persons and property of the community against riot; it is man's function to protect her. Here at least the functional difference between the sexes is too plain to be denied, doubted, or ignored. . . .

This is the negative reason why woman does not wish the ballot; she does not wish to engage in that conflict of wills which is the essence of politics; she does not wish to assume the responsibility for protecting person and property which is the essence of government. The affirmative reason is that she has other, and in some sense, more important work to do. It is more important than the work of government because it is the work for the protection of which governments are organized among men. Woman does not wish to turn aside from this higher work, which is itself the end of life, to devote herself to government, which exists only that this higher work may be done. Nor does she wish to divide her energies between the two. . . .

In this work of direct ministry to the individual, this work of character-building, which is the ultimate end of life, woman takes the first place. The higher the civilization the more clearly is her right to it recognized. She builds the home, and she keeps the home. She makes the home sanitary; she inspires it with the spirit of order, neatness, and peace; she . . . teaches us to love by her loving. Her eye discerns beauty, her deft fingers create it, and to her the home is indebted for its artistic power to educate. . . . If she has no home in which she can and does minister, she instinctively seeks the school room as her field, and there substituting for the mother, imparts life, and endows with intelligence, and equips with culture the children intrusted to her charges. If necessity drives her or ambition entices her to other fields, her womanly instinct still asserts itself. If she enters the law, it is generally to be counselor rather than a combatant; if literature, her pen instinctively seeks the vital rather than the materialistic themes. . . .

If she were to go into politics, she would leave undone the work for which alone government exists, or she would distract her energies from that work, which she knows full well requires them all. . . . She has made her choice and made it wisely. . . . The great body of American women are true to themselves, to the nature God has given them, and to the service He has allotted to them, . . . and will neither be forced nor enticed from it by their restless, well-meaning, but mistaken sisters.

Source: Massachusetts Association Opposed to the Further Extension of Suffrage to Women, circa 1898, Sophia Smith Collection, Smith College.

11.2.   Suffragists Respond to Anti-Suffrage Rhetoric

Woman suffragists assembled a wide variety of responses to anti-woman suffrage rhetoric, including hard logic, irony, and parody. Alice Stone Blackwell, daughter of Lucy Stone and Henry Blackwell and editor of the Woman's Journal *after her parents died, encouraged all three. In these examples, Stone Blackwell pulled apart Lyman Abbott's argument about male military service, demonstrating that there were many men who could not exercise the police power but were still voters, and an anonymous suffragist compares pockets with votes in order to poke fun at the essentialist arguments of the antis.*

Alice Stone Blackwell, "VOTING AND FIGHTING"

It is said that, if women vote, they ought to fight and do police duty. If no men were allowed to vote except those who are able and willing to do military and police duty, women might consistently be debarred for that reason. But so long as the old, the infirm, the halt, the lame and the blind are freely admitted to the ballot box, some better reason must be found for excluding women than the fact that they do not fight.

By a comic fatality, this objection is almost always urged by some man who could not fight himself—some peaceful, venerable old clergyman, or some corpulent, elderly physician who would expire under a forced march of five miles. I have even heard it used by a man who had been stone blind ever since he was three years old.

It is said that we have to legislate for classes, not for individuals; and that men as a class can fight, while women cannot. But there are large classes of men who are regarded as disqualified to fight, and are exempt from military service, yet they vote. All men over 45 years of age are exempt. So are all who are not physically robust. Of the young men who volunteered for the Spanish war, more than half were rejected as unfit for military service. . . .

As for police duty, men are not drafted, but out of those who volunteer, and who come up to the prescribed conditions of strength, weight, etc., a sufficient number are hired, and they are paid out of tax money which is levied on the property of men and women alike. Women contribute to the policing of the country in just the same way that the majority of the men do—i.e., they help to pay for it.

Again, it must be remembered that it is women who furnish the sol-

diers. . . . Lucy Stone said: "Some woman risks her life whenever a soldier is born into the world. For years she does picket duty beside his
cradle. Later on she is his quartermaster, and gathers his rations. And
when that boy grows to be a man, shall he say to his mother, 'If you
want to vote, you must first go and kill somebody?' It is a coward's
argument!" Mrs. Humphrey Ward's sister tells us that every year, in
England alone, 3,000 women lose their lives in childbirth. This ought, in
all fairness, to be taken as an offset for the military service that women
do not render. . . .

Either the ability to fight is a necessary qualification for suffrage, or it
is not. If it is, the men who lack it ought to be excluded. If it is not, the
lack of it is no reason for excluding women. There is no escape from this
conclusion.

Source: National American Woman Suffrage Association, circa 1900, Sophia Smith
Collection, Smith College.

"WHY WE OPPOSE POCKETS FOR WOMEN"

1. Because pockets are not a natural right.
2. Because the great majority of women do not want pockets. If
   they did they would have them.
3. Because whenever women have had pockets they have not used
   them.
4. Because women are required to carry enough things as it is,
   without the additional burden of pockets.
5. Because it would make dissension between husband and wife as
   to whose pockets were to be filled.
6. Because it would destroy man's chivalry toward woman, if he
   did not have to carry all her things in his pockets.
7. Because men are men, and women are women. We must not fly
   in the face of nature.
8. Because pockets have been used by men to carry tobacco, pipes,
   whiskey flasks, chewing gum and compromising letters. We see
   no reason to suppose that women would use them more wisely.

Source: Alice Duer Miller, *Are Women People? A Book of Rhymes for Suffrage Times.*
New York: George H. Doran Company, 1915: 44.

11.3.   Southern Activists Make a Claim for Limited Suffrage

In 1903 the NAWSA held its national convention in New Orleans. African-American women were banned, and the NAWSA made clear overtures to white supremacists in the South. In her address to the convention, Belle Kearney of Mississippi adapted Henry Blackwell's 1867 pamphlet to her own advocacy of education for poor whites, woman suffrage, and literacy requirements for suffrage in order to preserve the hegemony of the "Anglo-Saxon" race and to win voting rights for educated white women.

Belle Kearney, "THE SOUTH AND WOMAN SUFFRAGE"

The world is scarcely beginning to realize the enormity of the situation that faces the South in its grapple with the race question which was thrust upon it at the close of the Civil War, when 4,500,000 ex-slaves, illiterate and semi-barbarous, were enfranchised. Such a situation has no parallel in history. In forging a path out of the darkness, there were no precedents to lead the way. All that has been and is being accomplished is pioneer statecraft. The South has struggled under its death-weight for nearly forty years, bravely and magnanimously.

The Southern States are making a desperate effort to maintain the political supremacy of Anglo-Saxonism by amendments to their constitutions limiting the right to vote by a property and educational qualification. If the United States government had been wise enough to enact such a law when the negro was first enfranchised, it would have saved years of bloodshed in the South, and such experiences of suffering and horror among the white people here as no other were ever subjected to in an enlightened nation.

The present suffrage laws in the different Southern States can be only temporary measures for protection. Those who are wise enough to look beneath the surface will be compelled to realize the fact that they act as a stimulus to the black man to acquire both education and property, but no incentive is given to the poor whites; for it is understood, in a general way, that any man whose skin is fair enough to let the blue veins show through, may be allowed the right of franchise.

The industrial education that the negro is receiving at Tuskegee and other schools is only fitting him for power, and when the black man becomes necessary to a community by reason of his skill and acquired wealth, and the poor white man, embittered by his poverty and humiliated by his inferiority, finds no place for himself or his children, then will come the grapple between the races.

To avoid this unspeakable culmination, the enfranchisement of women will have to be effected, and an educational and property qualification for the ballot be made to apply, without discrimination, to both sexes and to both races. It will spur the poor white to keep up with the march of progression [sic], and enable him to hold his own. The class that is not willing to measure its strength with that of an inferior is not fit to survive.

The enfranchisement of women would insure immediate and durable white supremacy, honestly attained; for, upon unquestionable authority, it is stated that "in every Southern State but one, there are more educated women than all the illiterate voters, white and black, native and foreign, combined." As you probably know, of all the women in the South who can read and write, ten out of every eleven are white. When it comes to the proportion of property between the races, that of the white outweighs that of the black immeasurably. The South is slow to grasp the great fact that the enfranchisement of women would settle the race question in politics.

The civilization of the North is threatened by the influx of foreigners with their imported customs; by the greed of monopolistic wealth, and the unrest among the working classes; by the strength of the liquor traffic, and by encroachments upon religious belief.

Some day the North will be compelled to look to the South for redemption from these evils, on account of the purity of its Anglo-Saxon blood, the simplicity of its social and economic structure, the great advance in prohibitory law, and the maintenance of the sanctity of its faith, which has been kept inviolate. Just as surely as the North will be forced to turn to the South for the nation's salvation, just so surely will the South be compelled to look to its Anglo-Saxon women as the medium through which to retain the supremacy of the white race over the African.

Source: Woman's Journal, April 4, 1903.

11.4.   African-American Women Say Why They Need the Vote

In 1913 The Crisis, *published by the National Association for the Advancement of Colored People, issued a special symposium by "leading thinkers of colored America" on the subject of "Votes for Women." The two women quoted here were respected and dynamic leaders in their communities, and each expands on a kind of "civic housekeeping" approach to voting, an approach echoed by many white women as well.*

"VOTES FOR WOMEN"

"Votes for Mothers" by Mrs. Coralie Franklin Cook, Member of the Board of Education, District of Columbia.

I wonder if anybody in all this great world ever thought to consider *man's* rights as an individual, by his status as a father? Yet you ask me to say something about "Votes for Mothers," as if mothers were a separate and peculiar people. After all, I think you are not so far wrong. Mothers *are* different, or ought to be different, from other folk. The woman who smilingly goes out, willing to meet the Death Angel, that a child may be born, comes back from that journey, not only the mother of her own adored babe, but a near-mother to all other children. As she serves that little one, there grows within her a passion to serve humanity; not race, not class, not sex, but God's creatures as he has sent them to earth. . . .

Woman should help both to make and to administer the laws under which she lives, should feel responsible for the conduct of educational systems, charitable and correctional institutions, public sanitation and municipal ordinances in general. Who should be more competent to control the presence of bar rooms and "red-light districts" than mothers whose sons they are meant to lure to degradation and death? Who knows better than the girl's mother at what age the girl may legally barter her own body? Surely not the men who have put upon our statute books, 16, 14, 12, aye, be it to their eternal shame, even 10 and 8 years, as "the age of consent!"

If men could choose their own mothers, would they choose free women or bond-women? Disfranchisement because of sex is curiously like disfranchisement because of color. It cripples the individual, it handicaps progress, it sets a limitation upon mental and spiritual development. I grow in breadth, in vision, in the power to do, just in proportion as I use the capacities with which Nature, the All-Mother, has endowed me. I transmit to the child who is bone of my bone, flesh of my flesh and *thought of my thought; somewhat* of my own power or weakness. Is not the voice which is crying out for "Votes for Mothers" the Spirit of the Age crying out for the Rights of Children?

"Votes for Children" by Mrs. Carrie W. Clifford, Honorary President of the Colored Women's Clubs of Ohio.

It is the ballot that opens the schoolhouse and closes the saloon; that keeps the food pure and the cost of living low; that causes a park to grow where a dump-pile grew before. It is the ballot that regulates capital and protects labor; that up-roots disease and plants health. In short, it is by the ballot we hope to develop the wonderful ideal state for which we are all so zealously working.

The family is the miniature State, and here the influence of the mother is felt in teaching, directing and executing, to a degree far greater than that of the father. At his mother's knee the child gets his first impressions of love, justice and mercy; and by obedience to the laws of the home he gets his earliest training in civics.

More and more is it beginning to be understood that the mother's zeal for the ballot is prompted by her solicitude for her family-circle.

That the child's food may be pure, that his environment shall be wholesome and his surrounding sanitary—these are the things which engage her thought. That his mind shall be properly developed and his education wisely directed; that his occupation shall be clean and his ideals high—all these are things of supreme importance to her, who began to plan for the little life before it was even dreamed of by the father.

Kindergartens, vacation-schools, playgrounds; the movement for the City Beautiful; societies for temperance and for the prevention of cruelty to children and animals—these and many other practical reforms she has brought to pass, *in spite of not having the ballot*. But as she wisely argues, why should she be forced to use indirect methods to accomplish a thing that could be done so much more quickly and satisfactorily by the direct method—by casting her own ballot?

The ballot! the sign of power, the means by which things are brought to pass, the talisman that makes our dreams come true! Her dream is of a State where war shall cease, where peace and unity be established and where love shall reign.

Yes, it is the great mother-heart reaching out to save her children from war, famine and pestilence; from death degradation and destruction, that induces her to demand "Votes for Women," knowing well that fundamentally, it is really a campaign for "Votes for Children."

Source: The Crisis, 10, August, 1915: 184–187.

11.5.   Defeating a Senator from Massachusetts in 1918

With the woman suffrage amendment stalled in Congress, the NAWSA reconsidered its long-standing policy of non-partisanship. Militant English suffragettes had focused on defeating politicians of the party in power with some success and inspired American women in the Congressional Union to picket the White House. Spurning the civil disobedience of the Woman's Party, the NAWSA leadership decided instead to try to defeat four anti-suffrage senators in the election of 1918 and managed to unseat two of them. One of them was Massachusetts Republican John W. Weeks, who with his co-senator Henry Cabot Lodge, had opposed not only woman suffrage but most progressive reforms. By 1918 liberal suffragists in Massachusetts had allied themselves with trade unions and progressives, many of whom were Irish Democrats, and in opposing Weeks, it was understood they would help to elect David I. Walsh, an Irish-American Progressive, for the Senate. In this campaign leaflet written by Irish-American activist and lawyer Teresa A. Crowley, they link woman suffrage with Progressive social reform in order to attract working-class and social reform voters in Massachusetts.

DEFEAT JOHN W. WEEKS

Your vote should help to
DEFEAT JOHN W. WEEKS
for United States Senator at the election November 5th

His record in Congress speaks for itself. He was—

AGAINST the popular election of United States Senators. If Mr. Weeks' opinion had prevailed, you would not now have the opportunity to vote for or against him.

AGAINST the right of the United States to tax incomes. This was at a time when taxation of large incomes only was contemplated; without this right now, it would be impossible to finance the war. The public demand was so great that the vote stood 318 in favor and 14 against. Mr. Weeks was one of fourteen.

AGAINST increasing taxation on war profits.

AGAINST the creation of the Federal Trade Commission, the body which is undermining the alleged monopoly of the Meat Packers, and which provides a prompt and inexpensive redress for victims, large and small, of unfair practices in interstate commerce. . . .

AGAINST the Clayton Act, an act to strengthen the Sherman Anti-trust Law in curbing the abuses of big business while shielding from unjust attack labor and farm organizations.

AGAINST extending government credit to farmers, Rural Credits Bill.

AGAINST the Equal Suffrage Amendment to the United States Constitution, in spite of the stand taken by the National Republican Committee and in spite of the President's personal appeal to the Senate to submit this measure to the Legislatures of the various States as a help in the war emergency.

AGAINST the extension of the Parcel Post, a measure to benefit the people and limit further the power of the Express Companies.

AGAINST the Prohibition Amendment to the United States Constitution.

He voted—

FOR the Shields Water Power Bill. This bill, if passed, would have turned over the public water power of the country to private interests.

FOR the reduction of benefits of the Soldiers' and Sailors' insurance to our boys who are fighting in France.

DO THESE VOTES REPRESENT *YOU*?

If not, vote AGAINST John W. Weeks.

It is your PATRIOTIC DUTY in these critical times to GO TO THE POLLS ON ELECTION DAY and help DEFEAT a man with a record like this.

Source: Boston, 1918, Maud Wood Park Papers, Library of Congress.

11.6. The Catholic Priesthood Considers Woman Suffrage

> *As more Catholics, particularly Irish-American women, became advocates of and organizers for the woman suffrage movement, the Roman Catholic clergy was called upon to take a political position on the matter. In these examples, William Cardinal O'Connell of Boston connects "feminism" (a perjorative substitute for the more neutral woman suffrage) to a decline in male authority and young women "running rampant." Paulist Father George M. Searle of San Francisco, California, where women had gained the vote in 1911, argues that exercising the right of suffrage is proper for women. However, with women in his state now eligible to run for public office, he advised married women to forego such unsuitable pursuits.*

" 'SINISTER FEMINISM' IS DUE TO THE ABDICATION OF MAN,
SAYS CARDINAL O'CONNELL"

Cardinal O'Connell made a vigorous protest against what he termed "sinister feminism" at the closing exercises of the mission for men in the Holy Cross Cathedral yesterday. He urged men to exert their rightful authority in the home against certain tendencies of the times, and also spoke of the prevailing unrest and warned against the tendency toward "perpetual strikes." . . .

"The one thing that will preserve proper order in your house is the Christian authority of the Christian father of a family," said the Cardinal. "There is no doubt that one of the main causes of this sinister feminism, of which we read so much and see quite enough, is what would appear to be a growing weakness on the part of the manhood of the Nation.

"The very fact that women are so often clamoring to take all power and authority into their hands is certainly no compliment to the manhood of the Nation. And really we must admit that there are signs of decadence or lack of proper authority and self-respect in fathers of families.

"After all, women, the wife and the children, expect a father to have and to exercise the rightful authority due to his position. But if he abdicates that position, if he has no love for his home, if he is away from it whenever he can be, if he takes no interest in the children except merely to give enough money to support them—well, no one can be surprised if, little by little, women learn to do without the authority of man and begin to usurp a great deal of it themselves.

"That leads to a false feminism which certainly, unless it is curbed in time, will have disastrous results for humanity, because it is unnatural. I am not talking now about the proper sphere of woman. I am talking of the lack of authority in the household and the Nation on the part of man which is giving an undue prominence to the feminine side.

"The women are becoming masculine, if you please, and the men are becoming effeminate. This is disorder. The remedy is the proper exercise of authority by man in his own place, and especially as the father of a family. Not domination, not tyranny, but rightful, legitimate, kindly authority.

"How can he look on and see his children, especially the girls, running rampant, without any consideration for the modesty, the beautiful womanly virtues, which they ought to inculcate in their manners, in their habits of life? You say they won't listen to you, but there must be something wrong in you if they do not listen to your authority.

"Now, my dear, good Catholic men, you have no right to abdicate the position you occupy by the grace of God as the Christian head of the house. You must be kind, of course, and considerate, but there must be order, and the man, by every natural and divine right, is the head of the family. That headship means that he ought to look after the morals of the whole family."

Source: New York *World*, March 9, 1920.

"MY DEAR MRS. RORKE"

It is quite true that I am, and have been all along, in favor of woman suffrage; that is to say, as far as the right to vote is concerned; which is, of course, the strict and proper meaning of the word. As to being voted for, and holding public office, the principal objection to that, with regard to married women, especially with families, seems to be their necessary occupation with other duties. The same objection, of course, also applies to the clergy, to priests especially, and in fact to doctors and business men generally. But the man's business can usually be given up or delegated to some one else, whereas that can hardly be said of mothers of families.

When it comes, however to voting for others for public office, or for measures submitted to popular vote, I regard the argument so commonly advanced about woman's "sphere" being the home as simply and obviously absurd. One might as well say that the doctor's sphere is his office or the hospital, or his patient's houses; or the priest's sphere the pulpit, the altar, or the confessional. The point is that no time need be taken from one's regular duties in order to vote. I have never found that more than an hour, at the very outside, needed to be taken from my usual employments, in the whole course of the year, in order to register and vote. It seems to be absurdly assumed that women, if they vote, must plunge into a whirlwind of political meetings, parades, and the like. There is no reason why they should, any more than there is why quiet and business-like men should do so. . . . Women may have to make some fuss in order to get the right to vote; but when they have got it, as they have in this State, they make less fuss than men do. That is our experience here. . . .

As to . . . whether the Church is opposed to woman suffrage, the answer is simply that it is not. Probably the majority of our prelates and priests have been so; but just as a matter of private opinion, due mainly to a conservative habit of mind, which Catholics, especially ecclesiastics, naturally get into. But no official action has been taken, and there is no probability whatever that any ever will be.

And it is quite plain that with regard to moral questions, the interests of morality would be advanced by woman suffrage, in the sense in which I have used it; that is of women voting, not of their being voted for, for public offices. They seem, in some cases, to have made a success at the latter; but, for married women, at any rate, common sense would probably, as a rule, deem it unadvisable, just as it would be to elect a priest as mayor of a city. He has his own business to attend to, and the two cannot be combined.

Source: Letters and Addresses on Woman Suffrage by Catholic Ecclesiastics, compiled by Margaret Hayden Rorke. National Woman Suffrage Publishing Co., 1914: 6–8.

11.7.   Woman Suffrage and the Red Scare

*Women in the anti-suffrage movement faced a political con-
tradiction; their male spokespersons had argued that women naturally retreated from the public sphere and were loath to engage
in political sparring. So how could the antis mobilize their
supporters? Inactive on a national level until the 1910s, anti-
suffragists did not have counterparts to the talented and dynamic
political strategists of the pro-suffrage campaign. This 1914 National Anti-Suffrage Association pamphlet links woman suffrage
with feminism, divorce, Socialism, and free love, but with none
of the finesse and clarity typical of the pro-suffrage argument. By
1917, when the Russian Revolution and the entry of the United
States into World War I created a backlash against radicalism,
the attempt to tar women's movements with guilt by association
was more resonant, and the NAWSA distanced itself from both
pacifists and Socialists. Although the Red Scare of 1919 did not
have much of an impact on the passage of the Nineteenth
Amendment, red-baiting would have a chilling effect on women's
social reform movements in the 1920s.*

"THE CASE AGAINST WOMAN SUFFRAGE"

All the facts bear out the statement that Woman Suffrage, Feminism
and Socialism are marching hand in hand toward "a complete social
revolution." "ONE MILLION SOCIALISTS WORK AND VOTE FOR
WOMAN SUFFRAGE!" was the slogan inscribed on the red banner carried by the socialist contingent in the big Suffrage parade in Washington,
D.C., in March, 1913. Every Socialist and every Feminist is an Ardent
worker in the cause of Votes For Women. . . .

Radical Socialists and Feminists . . . are engaged as speakers on Suffrage platforms and their most radical Feministic and Socialistic utterances are published, advertised and sent broadcast by the National
Woman Suffrage Association as arguments for Votes for Women. So
close is the partnership between Woman Suffrage, Feminism and Socialism that in order to dissolve it, this is what the Suffrage associations
would have to do: Drop all their Socialist and Feminist Officers, speakers
and writers, withdraw from circulation all the Feminist and Socialist literature published and sent broadcast by the National Woman Suffrage

Association in the effort to gain Suffrage converts, and pass resolutions repudiating the doctrines of Socialism and Feminism. Imagine the violent upheaval in the UPPER CIRCLES OF SUFFRAGISM that would inevitably follow a serious movement on the part of Suffragists to adopt such drastic measures of reform! Yet they must be adopted before the Woman Suffrage movement can come before the people free from the stains of Socialism and Feminism. . . .

Woman Suffrage, according to [a] . . . noted suffragist, is "an essential branch of the tree of Feminism." "Feminism," she says, . . . "is gradually supplying to women the things they most need." And among these things she mentions "EASY DIVORCE" and "ECONOMIC INDEPENDENCE." "Easy divorce," as Feminists explain it, is "DIVORCE AT WILL." It would permit a wife to cast off her husband and take another without consulting the courts! "Economic Independence" is the theory that wives must engage in gainful occupations outside the home in order to be independent. FOR A WIFE TO BE SUPPORTED BY HER HUSBAND, IS, ACCORDING TO FEMINISM, TO BE A "PARASITE."

Feminism, therefore, would compel wives to compete with husbands in business and industry! It would make marriage a farce and the home, as we know it, a thing of the past! Feminism is a revolt against nature and Christian morals. . . .

TO PROTECT THE HOME AND SOCIETY FROM THE FEMINIST MENACE, WE MUST FIGHT THE WOMAN SUFFRAGE MOVEMENT.

That Woman Suffrage is ESSENTIAL TO THE SUCCESS OF SOCIALISM is the claim of the most enlightened Socialists. One of the cardinal principles of Socialism is that the interests of husband and wife are different, that the INDIVIDUAL and NOT THE FAMILY should be the unit of the State, and the enfranchisement of woman . . . is necessary to put this principle in operation. . . . IT WOULD ABOLISH MARRIAGE, BREAK UP THE FAMILY AND GIVE THE CHILDREN OVER TO THE CARE OF THE STATE.

In all Woman Suffrage countries Socialism is rampant, and in this country it prevails out of all proportion in states where women vote. Socialists want Woman Suffrage in order to advance Socialism. They believe it is the only weapon with which they can break up the home. IF WE DO NOT WANT TO HELP SOCIALISM, WE MUST OPPOSE WOMAN SUFFRAGE.

Source: Boston, National Anti-Suffrage Association, circa 1914.

12

Title VII, Sexual Harassment, and *EEOC v. Sears and Roebuck*: Women's Rights in the Modern Workplace

Few young women in the United States know that restrictions based on gender permeated the law only forty years ago. Most states did not allow women who married to retain their surnames. Widowed or divorced women were often denied credit on the basis of their marital status. Separate job listings for men and women appeared in newspaper want ads, with all secretarial jobs for women and all construction jobs for men. It was not illegal for an employer to inquire about a woman job candidate's marriage or pregnancy plans, and married or pregnant women could be fired at will. What came to be defined as "sexual harassment"— a hostile workplace created by the display of pornography, unwanted touching and sexual remarks, or *quid pro quo* demands for sexual favors—was so ubiquitous, according to feminist lawyers, as to be invisible. Overall, women earned about 59 percent of what men did, with women working at the same or similar jobs as men often receiving blatantly unequal pay. Despite the steadily climbing rates of married women with children in the workforce between 1940 and 1960, women and children continued to dominate the ranks of the poor. At the same time, the rising divorce rate and the growing number of mothers in the workplace made many conservatives uneasy; were working women responsible for undermining men's employment and family stability?

In the 1960s challenges to discrimination against women came from several directions. A long-standing women's rights coalition in the Women's Bureau (an agency of the U.S. Department of Labor created in the Progressive era) and liberal elements of the Republican and Democratic parties criticized the ubiquity of unequal pay for women and occupational sex segregation. Working women challenged male hegemony in their unions and demanded promotions, higher salaries, and maternity leave from employers. The civil rights movement of the 1960s provided a model for bringing women's grievances to the attention of the public and trained many women in the art of political protest. A key piece of congressional legislation—Title VII of the Civil Rights Act of 1964—enabled women's rights activists to make parallels between racial and sexual discrimination and to encode them in legislation and federal policy. A vigorous and varied political movement, often referred to as the "second wave of feminism," organized to demand that the federal and state governments enforce equal protection of the law.

In 1960, at the urging of the Women's Bureau and women in the Democratic party, President John F. Kennedy created a Commission on the Status of Women and appointed the highly revered Eleanor Roosevelt as its chairperson. When the Commission issued its report in 1963, the results were more shocking than even women's rights advocates had feared. The report revealed that women were confined to a very small number of occupations, and their pay was abysmal. The numbers of women in law, medicine, and academia were miniscule, and clearly unreflective of the greater numbers of women attending college and graduate school. There was still no federal Equal Pay Act for women, although twenty-three states had such laws. The Commission urged the passage of a federal bill mandating equal pay not only for equal work but for *comparable* work. Asking the federal government to enforce equal pay for comparable work continues to be controversial. Proponents of comparable worth argued that the occupational job structure was so sex specific that few women would benefit from equal pay for equal work while opponents argued that comparable pay for comparable work would bankrupt the economy. Congress passed an Equal Pay Act in 1963 without a proviso for comparable work.

With the United States in the midst of the civil rights revolution of the 1960s, Congress deliberated legislation to end racial discrimination in employment, voting, and public accommodations. Title VII of the Civil Rights Act of 1964 would make it unlawful for an employer to discriminate against any individual on the basis of that person's race, color, religion, or national origin and create an Equal Employment Opportunity Commission (EEOC) to hear complaints of workers who believed they had been victims of discrimination in employment. Remnants of the old Woman's Party, a feminist organization launched in the 1910s to ratify the Nineteenth Amendment and to agitate for an Equal Rights Amendment (ERA), demanded that Title VII include the word "sex" as well, a cause taken up by Representative Martha Griffiths of Michigan. Representative Howard Smith of Virginia offered an amendment to Title

VII adding the word "sex." Some historians have argued that southerners such as Smith hoped to sink the Civil Rights Bill with his amendment. Indeed, it was considered ludicrous enough to be greeted with laughter on the floor of the House of Representatives. The debate over Title VII had some parallels with the discussion of the Fourteenth Amendment after the Civil War, when opponents of African-American voting rights for men tried, in vain, to defeat the Fourteenth by proposing voting rights for women as well. But Title VII passed with Smith's amendment and sexual equality was incorporated into the federal civil rights mandate.

As civil rights activists celebrated the 1964 act and President Lyndon Johnson signed an Affirmative Action executive order in 1965 to promote access to employment for racial minorities, there were a number of unresolved issues with regard to Title VII and sex discrimination in employment. Title VII included a "bona-fide occupational qualification" clause, that is, permission for employers to assign jobs on the basis of sex, religion, or ethnicity for "bona-fide" reasons. (There was no such clause for race.) Might BFOQs, as they came to be called, keep women from holding police or fire department jobs? Taking jobs requiring heavy labor? Might men become nurses or flight attendants? What would Title VII do to protective laws, such as those that prevented women from working at night, or lifting heavy objects? Would sex-segregated job advertisements be banned, as the law seemed to imply? Would affirmative action ever be applied to women?

Charged with issuing guidelines for the enforcement of Title VII, the EEOC stressed that BFOQs should be applied under narrow circumstances; women were entitled, for example, to consideration for jobs in the building trades, public safety, and the skilled labor jobs of the telephone industry. Some of the first attempts by employers to block lawsuits brought by women under Title VII cited protective legislation barring, for instance, women's night work or heavy lifting, as a rationale for unequal treatment. The courts usually rejected such claims, and began to strike down most protective legislation based on sex as unconstitutional as a result. However, the EEOC did little to promote actively the sex provision of Title VII and in 1965 found sex-segregated job advertisements within the parameters of the law. Most liberal men continued to assume that Title VII was primarily intended to end discrimination on the basis of race. A 1965 editorial in the *New Republic*, for example, asked why "a mischievous joke perpetrated on the floor of the House of Representatives" should "be treated by a responsible administration body with this kind of seriousness?"[1]

This kind of rhetoric alienated a growing number of women who thought that sex discrimination was equivalent to racial bias. Betty Friedan, a journalist who had written about equal pay and other women's issues for the United Electrical, Radio and Machine Workers (UE) in the late 1940s, published her best-selling book, *The Feminine Mystique*, in 1963. Friedan's analysis of the "problem that had no name" articulated for many women the psychological deprivation they felt when they gave up their jobs after marriage and were confined to childrearing and housework. In coalition with what she termed "a feminist underground" in Washington, Friedan sparked the founding of the National Organization for Women (NOW), whose first convention in October 1966, issued a widely read "Statement of Purpose" often compared to the Seneca Falls 1848 Declaration of Sentiments. Welcoming like-minded men, the founders of NOW placed women's rights in the mainstream of "the worldwide revolution of human rights now taking place within and beyond our national borders." Much of the focus of the NOW statement was on economic and legal barriers to women's equality, but it also described the personal arrangements in the family that kept women from full employment. NOW called for men to share housework and the rearing of children and for publicly funded daycare, and questioned the "traditional assumption that a woman has to choose between marriage and motherhood . . . and serious participation in industry or the professions." Although conservatives would later argue that NOW ridiculed the role of "homemaker," a close reading of the Statement shows otherwise: "We believe that proper recognition should be given to the economic and social value of homemaking and child-care." But NOW did say that men should no longer be expected to be the sole breadwinners of their families. Nor should women assume they were "automatically entitled to lifelong support by a man upon her marriage, or that marriage, home, and family are primarily woman's world and responsibility." Single mothers and most working-class families had never been able to share in this domestic ideal, but its denunciation seemed to question a way of life cherished by many traditionalists and that was seemingly the linchpin of economic security for middle-class women.

The agitation of liberal women in NOW and a growing liberation movement of more radical young women affected American politics in dramatic new ways, despite the ridicule often heaped upon feminists in popular culture and elite intellectual circles. Supposedly bra-burning, man hating, and out to destroy the American way of life, feminists of the 1960s and 1970s became pernicious symbols of vast social and economic changes that had been underway since World War II. But many Democrats and Republicans saw the logic of the liberal feminist position and the value of placating a vast constituency of female voters. In 1967 President Johnson extended affirmative action guidelines to women. In 1970 thousands of women staged a day-long "strike for equality" across the nation, and growing agitation for the Equal Rights Amendment (ERA) led to its passage by Congress in 1972. Many state legislatures immediately ratified the ERA and the deadline of 1979 seemed, in the heady days of the early 1970s, easy enough to meet. In 1972 Congress passed the Educational Amendments to the Civil Rights Act mandating sex equality in education (Title IX), the Equal Employment Opportunity Act, and explicitly extended Title VII to women in professional, administrative, and executive positions. The AFL-CIO abandoned its long-time opposition to the ERA in 1973. Congress passed an Equal Credit Opportunity Act in 1974 and a Pregnancy Discrimination Act in 1978. The EEOC won major class action agreements for women employees from AT&T in 1973 and Ford Motor Company in 1980.

The ERA was a simple statement declaring that "equality of rights under the law shall not be denied or abridged by the United States or any state on account of sex." Exactly what the ERA might have changed that was not already underway in the courts and in upcoming legislation is not clear. Many legal authorities believe the equal protection clause of the Fourteenth Amendment gives women full equal rights under the Constitution and that the ERA would simply have been a symbolic affirmation of its umbrella for all citizens. Others, such as Supreme Court Justice Ruth Bader Ginsburg, believe women need a specific declaration of their equality in the Constitution. Conservatives immediately claimed that what appeared to be a simple declaration of sexual equality under the law would lead to, even mandate, the more radical demands of the feminist movement. In 1971 President Richard Nixon vetoed a Comprehensive Child Development Bill that would have provided federal dollars for daycare.

The following year Phyllis Schlafly of the Eagle Forum organized a STOP ERA movement. Schlafly, a lawyer and conservative activist in the Republican party, declared that full equal rights could only hurt women. She accused feminists of eradicating traditional protections for women in both cultural practice and in the law. If the ERA were passed, she argued, women would no longer be entitled to alimony or custody of their children in cases of divorce. Women would be drafted, serve in combat, and forced to use unisex bathrooms. ERA would end a woman's right "to be a full-time wife and mother, in her own home, taking care of her own babies."[2]

Right-leaning Republicans introduced a Family Protection bill in Congress in 1981 that was squarely pointed at the agenda of feminists. Its provisions included the repeal of federal laws supporting equal education, federal endorsement of the teaching of marriage and motherhood as the most important career for girls, and the banning of federal legal aid to women seeking divorce. It included tax incentives large enough to encourage middle-class women to stay at home as full-time homemakers, but not munificent enough to enable working-class women to do so.

These measures were unlikely to be passed as a package, but the election of Ronald Reagan in 1980 emboldened conservatives in government, who slashed programs linked to the feminist agenda. The EEOC was one among the agencies most severely cut, and in 1986, an understaffed and conservative led EEOC lost a critical class action suit against Sears, Roebuck, & Company. Sears had an equal employment and affirmative action policy in place, but men dominated the high commission selling of automobile parts, appliances, and furniture. Some women employees of Sears claimed they had not been able to move up to male-dominated departments with high-paying salaries. Sears claimed that most women did not want positions in these departments. A Reagan-appointed federal circuit court judge ruled in favor of Sears, arguing that Sears had proved that women's lack of competitiveness, aversion to overtime and stressful work, and preferences for "soft-selling" meant they had less ambition than men, and were therefore uninterested in higher paying and more responsible positions. The EEOC relied on statistical evidence that seemed to show that discrimination was apparent. But Sears was successful in dismissing "hard evidence" by suggesting psychological factors could explain what seemed to be discrimination against women. As of this writing, the EEOC has not joined a similar suit filed by female employees of Wal-Mart stores that seeks redress for about 700,000 employees throughout the United States.

One aspect of women's employment that did receive close attention from the federal government in the 1980s was "sexual harassment," a term coined by feminist legal scholars in 1974. Once identified and named, sexual harassment was easily recognized by many working women; estimates are that seven out of every ten women have experienced what they believe to be sexual harassment on the job. Catharine MacKinnon, a feminist lawyer who represented women clients in the workplace in the mid-1970s, heard endless stories from those clients about demands for sexual favors or sexual intercourse from bosses, unwanted groping and grabbing of private body parts, and a hostile climate created in the workplace by dirty "jokes," pornographic calendars, and sexual insults. The first few cases charging that sexual harassment at work was a form of sex discrimination in employment were unsuccessful. But in 1980 the EEOC adopted regulations defining and prohibiting sexual harassment, and in 1986 the Supreme Court ruled in *Meritor Savings Banks, FSB v. Vinson* that the prevention of both *quid pro quo* harassment and a hostile sexual environment were the responsibility of employers, drawing much of the ruling from MacKinnon's brief for the defendant. Mitsubishi Motor Manufacturing Company settled a multimillion dollar lawsuit with the EEOC in 1999 to compensate for the sexual harassment of women factory workers. Similar cases have been settled at other automobile companies, although women workers in automobile factories contend the problem is far from solved.

Despite the number of complaints that continue to come forward in union grievances and in lawsuits by women—and, increasingly, men— feminist lawyers believe that only a small fraction of those who experience sexual harassment ever complain. The entire country witnessed an example of this when Anita Hill, a lawyer who had worked under the supervision of Clarence Thomas at the EEOC in the 1980s, was subpoenaed by the Senate Judiciary Committee in 1991 during confirmation hearings for Thomas's appointment to the Supreme Court. She testified, reluctantly, that she had been a victim of sexual harassment committed by Thomas, a charge he denied vehemently, characterizing the hearings as a "public lynching." Many women in the military have had similar difficulties in having their cases heard with any sympathy.

Young women entering the workforce have more legal safeguards than they did forty years ago. But only a small number of women have the financial and emotional resources to risk recouping their losses through the courts. Many of the problems of female economic inequality remain intractable. Most women do not have any alternative to working while they raise children at the same time. The feminization of poverty has reached shocking proportions because so many women are raising families on their own, are stuck in low-paying and low-end jobs, or have no other recourse than welfare payments, which have been cut severely in the wake of "welfare reform." Although women made 75 percent as much as men by 1998, the narrowing of the wage gap in the 1990s was largely due to a decline in men's wages, not relative increases in women's pay. Surveys continue to indicate that women are still likely to work a double shift at home and at work because women still do more of the housework and childcare, on average, than their husbands do. While some daycare costs are federally financed, working families in the United States have far fewer benefits than working parents in most European countries and the standard American workday of eight hours is often simply incompatible with the household schedules of working parents with small children. Although women (and men) need to be aware of any legal protection they may have on the job, the rhetoric of condemning sexual harassment is in some ways a sexualized distraction from the material reality of most women's lives.

READING GUIDE

Chrisman, Robert and Robert L. Allen, eds, *Court of Appeal: The Black Community Speaks Out on the Racial and Sexual Politics of Clarence Thomas vs. Anita Hill*. New York: Ballantine Books, 1992. This book of essays commissioned by the journal *Black Scholar* contains the testimony of Hill and Thomas before the Senate

Judiciary Committee in 1991. Many commentators wondered, and rightly so, why the most widely publicized case of sexual harassment in recent memory ended up highlighting a black man and a black woman in ways that re-enforced racial stereotypes. The voyeurism of the all-white male Senate committee and of most of the press seemed to have no limits, and made the public humiliation of these two individuals complete. Nonetheless, the case highlights the difficulties of women who claim sexual harassment, particularly when powerful men are involved. In the end, although public opinion polls showed that many people believed Hill, her testimony did not persuade a majority of senators, who voted to confirm the appointment of Thomas to the Supreme Court.

Faludi, Susan, *Backlash: The Undeclared War Against American Women*. New York: Doubleday, 1991. Faludi examines the many fronts of anti-feminism in the 1990s in a highly readable and witty account. She concludes that not only conservatives, but psychologists, biologists, toy manufacturers, and creators and purveyors of popular culture dismissed women and girls who did not correspond to traditional feminine stereotypes as unnatural and socially deviant. Women and their changing roles were blamed for nearly every social problem conceivable, including declines in fertility and the birthrate, rising welfare costs, the alleged demasculinization of men and boys, and the undermining of men's place in the workforce.

Gabin, Nancy, *Feminism in the Labor Movement: Women and the United Auto Workers, 1935–1975*. Ithaca: Cornell University Press, 1984. This fine account of women in the automobile industry and participation in the United Auto Workers recounts the struggle to put women's issues into union politics and onto the bargaining table. Gabin shows that UAW women were instrumental in raising questions about maternity leave, child care, and the discriminating effects of so-called protective legislation. Unions had historically opposed the ERA, but women in the UAW argued for its passage and convinced the AFL-CIO to do likewise, a critical element in ERA's chances for ratification.

Horowitz, Daniel, "Betty Friedan and the Origins of Feminism in Cold War America," *American Quarterly* 48 (1998): 1–42. Horowitz, a biographer of Friedan, went back to her past in the UE in the late 1940s to find much of what inspired her assault on society's treatment of women in *The Feminine Mystique*. A leftist union that included members of the Communist Party, UE pioneered in addressing issues of sexual inequality in the workplace, issues that Friedan wrote about for the union's newspaper. As a consequence of the anti-Communist crusade of the 1950s, activists such as Friedan often buried their past associations, giving the mistaken impression that the left had little to do with the historical development of women's rights in the post–World War II period.

Kaminer, Wendy, *A Fearful Freedom: Women's Flight from Equality*. Reading, MA: Addison-Wesley Publishing, 1990. Kaminer, a lawyer and highly regarded journalist, examines the equality and difference debate as it emerged in the 1980s. Protectionism developed historically from the idea that women were vulnerable to exploitation on the basis of their biological characteristics, and Kaminer argues that many women and men find it difficult to ignore difference and its implications for protectionism. She discusses Title VII, Title IX, pregnancy and child care policies, reproductive rights, and "theories of rights," or "how we view law."

Lemoncheck, Linda, and James P. Sterba, *Sexual Harassment: Issues and Answers*. New York: Oxford University Press, 2001. This anthology of popular and scholarly pieces explores the history of sexual harassment policy, the evolving law, and the debate over how sexual harassment should be defined. The authors also emphasize multicultural and international aspects of the issue.

MacKinnon, Catharine A., *Sexual Harassment of Working Women: A Case of Sex Discrimination*. New Haven: Yale University Press, 1979. MacKinnon developed the legal rationale for defining sexual harassment as sex discrimination, based on what she defines as uneven gender power relationships in the workplace and the sexual objectification of women that is prevalent in American culture. A clear writer and straightforward thinker, MacKinnon had a significant impact on the development of sexual harassment theory as it has been used in the courts.

Meyerowitz, Joanne, ed., *Not June Cleaver: Women and Gender in Postwar America, 1945–1960*. Philadelphia: Temple University Press, 1994. This reader includes several essays that demonstrate significant connections between the older women's rights movement and the second wave of women's liberation. Together, the authors show that feminism was nurtured in unions, Washington agencies, ethnic and civic organizations, the peace and civil rights movements, and that the reversion to domesticity after World War II, or what Betty Friedan described as the "feminine mystique," was not as pervasive as Friedan claimed.

Schlafly, Phyllis, *The Power of the Positive Woman*. New Rochelle, NY: Arlington House, 1977. A working mother, lawyer, vigorous politician, and leading opponent of the ERA whose own life seemed to belie her emphasis on stay-at-home mothers and the importance for social policy of the biological differences between men and women, Schlafly urges women to find fulfillment in their lives as women and condemns the feminist agenda entirely. She contends it is but another liberal attempt to expand the power of the federal government over people's lives and to destroy traditional protections for women in culture and the law.

Stetson, Dorothy McBride, *Women's Rights in the U.S.A.: Policy Debates and Gender Roles*, 2nd edition. New York: Garland Publishing, 1997. This helpful account of the history of public policy with regard to women's rights provides historical background, up-to-date changes in the law, and concise discussions of major philosophical issues, including the equality-difference debate. Topics include education, work and pay, women in the military and in sports, and reproductive rights. Useful as a classroom textbook for women's studies or sociology classes.

NOTES

1. *New Republic* 153 (September 4, 1965): 3.
2. Phyllis Schlafly, *The Power of the Positive Woman* (New Rochelle, NY: Arlington House, 1977), 72.

DOCUMENTS

12.1. The Founding of a National Organization for Women

In response to the 1963 report of the Commission on the Status of Women, women in a variety of unions, government agencies, and civil rights organizations joined state commissions on the status of women and contemplated a "civil rights organization for women." By 1965 working women were filing grievances with the EEOC, but the agency continued to monitor race discrimination alone. Members of the state commissions assembled in June 1966, in Washington, D.C., for a national convention. Criticism of EEOC was the dominant refrain. A group of fifteen women met in Betty Friedan's hotel room to discuss their grievances. The next day they founded the National Organization for Women. This Statement of Purpose was issued at NOW's first national convention the following October.

"STATEMENT OF PURPOSE OF THE NATIONAL ORGANIZATION FOR WOMEN"

We, men and women who hereby constitute ourselves as the National Organization for Women, believe that the time has come for a new movement toward true equality for all women in America, and toward a fully equal partnership of the sexes, as part of the world-wide revolution of human rights now taking place within and beyond our national borders. . . .

NOW is dedicated to the proposition that women, first and foremost, are human beings, who, like all other people in our society, must have the chance to develop their fullest human potential. We believe that women can achieve such equality only by accepting to the full the challenges and responsibilities they share with all other people in our society, as part of the decision-making mainstream of American political, economic, and social life. . . .

Enormous changes taking place in our society make it both possible and urgently necessary to advance the unfinished revolution of women toward true equality, now. With life span lengthened to nearly seventy-five years it is no longer either necessary or possible for women to devote the greater part of their lives to child-rearing; yet childbearing and rearing—which continues to be a most important part of most women's lives—still is used to justify barring women from equal professional and economic participation and advance.

Today's technology has reduced most of the productive chores which women once performed in the home and in mass-production industries based upon routine unskilled labor. This same technology has virtually eliminated the quality of muscular strength as a criterion for filling most jobs, while intensifying American industry's need for creative intelligence. In view of this new industrial revolution created by automation in the mid-twentieth century, women can and must participate in old and new fields of society in full equality—or become permanent outsiders. . . .

Discrimination in employment on the basis of sex is now prohibited by federal law, in Title VII of the Civil Rights Act of 1964. But although nearly one-third of the cases brought before the Equal Employment Opportunity Commission during the first year dealt with sex discrimination and the proportion is increasing dramatically, the Commission has not made clear its intention to enforce the law with the same seriousness on behalf of women as of other victims of discrimination. Many of these cases were Negro women, who are the victims of the double discrimination of race and sex. Until now, too few women's organizations and official spokesmen have been willing to speak out against these dangers facing women. Too many women have been restrained by the fear of being called "feminist."

There is no civil rights movement to speak for women, as there has been for Negroes and other victims of discrimination. The National Organization for Women must therefore begin to speak.

WE BELIEVE that the power of American law, and the protection guaranteed by the U.S. Constitution to the civil rights of all individuals, must be effectively applied and enforced to isolate and remove patterns of sex discrimination, to ensure equality of opportunity in employment and education, and equality of civil and political rights and responsibilities on behalf of women, as well as for Negroes and other deprived groups. . . .

WE BELIEVE that this nation has a capacity at least as great as other nations, to innovate new social institutions which will enable women to enjoy true equality of opportunity and responsibility in society, without conflict with their responsibilities as mothers and homemakers. In such innovations, America does not lead the Western world, but lags by decades behind many European countries. We do not accept the traditional assumption that a woman has to choose between marriage and motherhood, on the one hand, and serious participation in industry or the professions on the other. We question the present expectation that all normal women will retire from job or profession for ten or fifteen years, to devote their full time to raising children, only to reenter the job market at a relatively minor level. This, in itself, is a deterrent to the aspirations of women, to their acceptance into management or professional training courses, and to the very possibility of equality of opportunity or real choice, for all but a few women. Above all, we reject the assumption that these problems are the unique responsibility of each individual woman, rather than a basic social dilemma which society must solve. True equality of opportunity and freedom of choice for women requires such practical and possible innovations as a nationwide network of child-care centers, which will make it unnecessary for women to retire completely from society until their children are grown, and national programs to provide retraining for women who have chosen to care for their own children full-time. . . .

WE REJECT the current assumptions that a man must carry the sole burden of supporting himself, his wife, and family, and that a woman is automatically entitled to lifelong support by a man upon her marriage, or that marriage, home, and family are primarily woman's world and responsibility—hers, to dominate, his to support. We believe that a true partnership between the sexes demands a different concept of marriage, an equitable sharing of the responsibilities of home and children and of the economic burdens of their support. We believe that proper recognition should be given to the economic and social value of homemaking and child-care. To these ends, we will seek to open a reexamination of laws and mores governing marriage and divorce, for we believe that the current state of "half-equality" between the sexes discriminates against both men and women, and is the cause of much unnecessary hostility between the sexes. . . .

WE BELIEVE THAT women will do most to create a new image of women by acting now, and by speaking out in behalf of their own equality, freedom, and human dignity—not in pleas for special privilege, nor in enmity toward men, who are also victims of the half-equality between the sexes—but in an active, self-respecting partnership with men. By so doing, women will develop confidence in their own ability to determine actively, in partnership with men, the conditions of their life, their choices, their future, and their society.

Source: New York: National Organization for Women, October 29, 1966.

12.2.   Conservatives Attack the Equal Rights Amendment

Many political conservatives opposed the ERA, and none was more effective than Phyllis Schlafly, founder of the Eagle Forum. A talented public debater and spokeswoman, Schlafly launched STOP ERA in 1972. She argued that the ERA would weaken the family and wives' traditional protections under the common law and that working women could not be absorbed into the economy without undermining male salaries. In her 1977 book The Power of the Positive Woman, *she indicted the feminist movement for what she perceived to be its attacks on homemakers.*

"A WIFE'S RIGHT TO SUPPORT"

Americans have the immense good fortune to live in a civilization that respects the family as the basic unit of society. This respect is not merely a matter of social custom. We have a great fabric of federal and state laws designed to protect the institution of the family. These laws are not for the purpose of giving one sex a preference over the other. They were not born of oppression or discrimination, but of vision and enlightened judgment. They are designed to keep the family together and to assure the child a home in which to grow up.

The results of these laws are highly beneficial to the wife. Based on the fundamental fact of life that women have babies and men don't—which no legislation or agitation can erase—these laws make it the obligation of the husband to support his wife financially and provide her with a home. Since God ordained that women have babies, our laws properly and realistically establish that men must provide financial support for their wives and children. The women's liberation movement has positioned itself in total opposition to the entire concept of "roles," but in so doing, they are opposing Mother Nature herself....

This network of laws gives the wife her legal right to be a full-time wife and mother, in her own home, taking care of her own babies....

The Equal Rights Amendment would invalidate all the state laws that require the husband to support his wife and family and provide them with a home, because the Constitution would then prohibit any law that imposes an obligation on one sex that it does not impose equally on the other. Thus, if ERA ever becomes part of the United States Constitution, all laws that say the *husband* must support his *wife* would immediately become unconstitutional. In the liberationist jargon, such laws are "sexist." ERA would impose a constitutionally mandated legal equality in all matters, including family support. This would be grossly unfair to a woman because it would impose on her the double burden of financial obligation plus motherhood and homemaking. The law cannot address itself to who has the baby, changes the diapers, or washes the dishes....

No one can predict for sure which kind of "equality" will be enforced by the courts and by legislatures if ERA is ever ratified.... Most ERA proponents concede in debate that *if* the wife takes a paying job, she would then be *obligated* to provide half the financial support of the family.

Some pro-ERA lawyers try to argue that under the sex-neutral language required by ERA the courts will hold that the *principal wage-earning spouse* must support the spouse who stays in the home. This would reduce the wife's rights even further. Taking the pro-ERA argument, this means that, if the husband is lazy and wants to spend his time drinking and watching television, and the wife is a conscientious woman who takes a job to feed her hungry children, then she, as the "principal wage-earning spouse," would acquire the obligation to support her lazy husband, subject to criminal penalties if she failed to support him and pay all his debts.

Whichever of these alternative versions of equality might ultimately become the rule under ERA, it would bring a drastic reduction in the rights of the wife and a radical loosening of the legal bonds that tend to keep the family together.

Some ERA proponents argue that husbands support their wives only because of love, not because of the law. But a relationship that is based exclusively on love, or on sex compatibility, is not apt to survive all those years "for better or worse, for richer or poorer, in sickness and in health, till death we do part." Love is a concept that may embrace many relationships with many different persons. Duty is essential to marriage. The moral, social, and legal evil of ERA is that it proclaims as a constitutional mandate that the husband no longer has the primary duty to support his wife and children.

Far more probable than the prospect of husbands immediately taking advantage of their new liberation from duty is the likelihood that wives will voluntarily leave the home and join the labor force because they see the handwriting on the wall. If ERA deprives wives of their economic security in the home, their natural instinct for survival will impel them to seek economic security in employment seniority.

There are today some 40 million wives who are supported by their husbands. If even half these wives enter the labor market, the most relevant question is, where are the jobs? America today has a very high unemployment rate. If 10 or 20 or 30 million homemakers enter the labor market seeking to protect their own financial future (because ERA has relieved their husbands of that duty), this will be a jolt to our economy worse than any we have ever experienced.

Furthermore, the high divorce rate proves that many husbands have stopped loving their wives. In 1975 American divorces passed the one-million mark. Should a husband have the legal right to stop supporting his faithful wife of twenty or thirty years by the simple expedient of saying, "I don't love her anymore; I love a younger woman"? Even though love may go out the window, the obligation should remain. ERA would eliminate that obligation.

Source: Phyllis Schlafly, *The Power of the Positive Woman*. New Rochelle, NY: Arlington House, 1977: 70–73, 75–76.

12.3.   Working Women and Homemakers Demand Recognition

On Labor Day, 1980, the Coalition of Labor Union Women, the Displaced Homemakers Network, Wider Opportunities for Women, and the National Commission on Working Women issued a political platform that sought to improve the rights of the 52 percent of all women who worked outside the home and to recognize the economic contributions of wives and mothers as well. The platform was directed to the presidential candidates of 1980 and was designed to "focus public attention on the concerns of working women." It was a good reminder that very few women could afford to define themselves as "homemakers" in the way that Phyllis Schafly had used the term, particularly if they were women of color, and that the unpaid labor of homemaking was critical to the economy of the United States.

"WORKING WOMEN'S PLATFORM OF 1980"

1. RECOGNITION: Recognize, understand and value the strong tradition and increasing importance of women as workers in all aspects of social, political, and economic life in America.
2. MINORITY WOMEN: Recognize the special needs, concerns and problems of minority women workers who face both sexism and racism.
3. JOB OPTIONS: Eliminate job segregation by sex.
4. WAGES: Eliminate wage discrimination by sex.
5. EDUCATION AND TRAINING: Eliminate sex-stereotyping and other barries [*sic*] to equity in all publicly funded educational, employment and training programs, and promote equal access to these programs.
6. EMPLOYMENT PROGRAMS: Expand and create special programs to improve employment opportunities for all women (including young women, women on welfare, ex-offenders, displaced homemakers, handicapped, older and minority women), providing them with career development, skills training (including nontraditional work), supportive services, and access to upwardly mobile jobs.

7. ENFORCEMENT: Enforce laws and regulations mandating equal employment opportunities for women.

8. HEALTH AND SAFETY: Promote healthy and safe working conditions.

9. SEXUAL HARASSMENT: Maintain work environments free of sexual harassment and intimidation.

10. DEPENDENT CARE: Provide accessible, quality care for children and other dependents.

11. ORGANIZING: Support the organization of the millions of unorganized women workers, and strengthen the role and participation of women in labor unions.

12. HOMEMAKING: Recognize homemakers as an important segment of the country's labor force, and recognize unpaid labor in the home as a significant contribution to the national economy.

13. BENEFITS: Promote equitable benefits for women, including pensions, social security, paid maternity leave, health care and health insurance.

14. WORK SCHEDULES: Promote alternative work schedules (including flex-time, part-time, compressed work week, and job sharing) with appropriate benefits.

15. PUBLIC POLICY: Promote the participation of women in the formulation and evaluation of public policy affecting employment.

Source: Labor Today, October, 1980: 7.

12.4.   The Supreme Court Incorporates Sexual Harassment into the Law

---

In 1978 Mechelle Vinson filed a lawsuit seeking damages from Meritor Savings Bank on the grounds that her immediate supervisor had subjected her to continuous sexual harassment at her job. A U.S. District Court ruled that if there had been sexual intimacy, it had been voluntary and that Meritor was, therefore, not liable for damages. The Court of Appeals reversed the decision, and Meritor appealed to the Supreme Court. The Supreme Court upheld the Court of Appeals and ruled in favor of Vinson in a vote of 9 to 0. Chief Justice William Rehnquist wrote the opinion,

affirming that a hostile environment created by sexual harassment
fell under the aegis of Title VII.

MERITOR SAVINGS BANK V. MECHELLE VINSON

In 1974, respondent Mechelle Vinson met Sidney Taylor, a vice president of what is now petitioner Meritor Savings Bank (the bank) and
manager of one of its branch offices. . . . With Taylor as her supervisor,
respondent started as a teller-trainee, and thereafter was promoted to
teller, head teller, and assistant branch manager. She worked at the same
branch for four years, and it is undisputed that her advancement there
was based on merit alone. In September 1978, respondent notified Taylor
that she was taking sick leave for an indefinite period. On November 1,
1978, the bank discharged her for excessive use of that leave.

Respondent brought this action against Taylor and the bank, claiming
that during her four years at the bank she had "constantly been subjected
to sexual harassment" by Taylor in violation of Title VII. She sought
injunctive relief, compensatory and punitive damages against Taylor and
the bank, and attorney's fees.

At the 11-day bench trial, the parties presented conflicting testimony
about Taylor's behavior during respondent's employment. Respondent
testified that during her probationary period as a teller-trainee, Taylor
treated her in a fatherly way and made no sexual advances. Shortly
thereafter, however, he invited her out to dinner and, during the course
of the meal, suggested that they go to a motel to have sexual relations.
At first she refused, but out of what she described as fear of losing her
job she eventually agreed. According to respondent, Taylor thereafter
made repeated demands upon her for sexual favors, usually at the
branch, both during and after business hours; she estimated that over
the next several years she had intercourse with him some 40 or 50 times.
In addition, respondent testified that Taylor fondled her in front of other
employees, followed her into the women's restroom when she went there
alone, exposed himself to her, and even forcibly raped her on several
occasions. These activities ceased after 1977, respondent stated, when she
started going with a steady boyfriend. . . .

Finally, respondent testified that because she was afraid of Taylor she
never reported his harassment to any of his supervisors and never attempted to use the bank's complaint procedure. . . .

The District Court. . . . ultimately found that respondent "was not the
victim of sexual harassment and was not the victim of sexual discrimination" while employed at the bank. . . .

The Court of Appeals for the District of Columbia Circuit reversed. . . .
[T]he court stated that a violation of Title VII may be predicated on either
of two types of sexual harassment: harassment that involves the condi-

tioning of concrete employment benefits on sexual favors, and harassment that, while not affecting economic benefits, creates a hostile or offensive working environment. The court drew additional support for this position from the Equal Employment Opportunity Commission's Guidelines on Discrimination Because of Sex, . . . which set out these two types of sexual harassment claims. . . . The Court of Appeals held that if the evidence otherwise showed that "Taylor made Vinson's toleration of sexual harassment a condition of her employment," her voluntariness "had no materiality whatsoever." . . .

As to the bank's liability, the Court of Appeals held that an employer is absolutely liable for sexual harassment practiced by supervisory personnel, whether or not the employer knew or should have known about the misconduct. The court relied chiefly on Title VII's definition of "employer" to include "any agent of such a person." . . .

Title VII of the Civil Rights Act of 1964 makes it "an unlawful employment practice for an employer . . . to discriminate against any individual with respect to his compensation, terms, conditions, or privileges of employment, because of such individual's race, color, religion, sex, or national origin."

Petitioner apparently does not challenge this proposition. It contends instead that in prohibiting discrimination with respect to "compensation, terms, conditions, or privileges" of employment, Congress was concerned with what petitioner describes as "tangible loss" of "an economic character," not "purely psychological aspects of the workplace environment." . . .

We reject petitioner's view. First, the language of Title VII is not limited to "economic" or "tangible" discrimination. The phrase "terms, conditions, or privileges of employment" evinces a congressional intent "to strike at the entire spectrum of disparate treatment of men and women" in employment. . . .

For sexual harassment to be actionable, it must be sufficiently severe or pervasive "to alter the conditions of [the victim's] employment and create an abusive working environment." . . . Respondent's allegations in this case—which include not only pervasive harassment but also criminal conduct of the most serious nature—are plainly sufficient to state a claim for "hostile environment" sexual harassment. . . .

Finally, we reject petitioner's view that the mere existence of a grievance procedure and a policy against discrimination, coupled with respondent's failure to invoke that procedure, must insulate petitioner from liability. While those facts are plainly relevant, the situation before us demonstrates why they are not necessarily dispositive. Petitioner's general nondiscrimination policy did not address sexual harassment in particular, and thus did not alert employees to their employer's interest in correcting that form of discrimination. Moreover, the bank's grievance procedure apparently required an employee to complain first to her supervisor, in this case Taylor. Since Taylor was the alleged perpetrator, it is not altogether surprising that respondent failed to invoke the procedure and report her grievance to him.

Source: U.S.L.W. 4703, 1986.

12.6.   The Sears Case

In 1979 the EEOC filed a sex discrimination class action suit against Sears, Roebuck & Company. Although Sears had an equal employment policy in writing, some women who worked there claimed that actual practice prevented them from moving into commission sales and more responsible positions. In similar kinds of cases the courts had accepted statistical evidence as evidence of discrimination in employment, and the EEOC was able to show that women were underrepresented as a class in the better-paying jobs at Sears. In its defense, Sears sought to show that it had an affirmative action policy in place and that the psychological attitudes of women, not sex discrimination, explained women's employment patterns at the company. District Court Judge John A. Nordberg, a President Ronald Reagan appointee, wrote this opinion denying EEOC's suit and his ruling was upheld in the Court of Appeals.

EEOC v. SEARS, ROEBUCK & CO.

The . . . allegations EEOC sought to prove at trial were that Sears engaged in a nationwide pattern or practice of sex discrimination: by failing to hire female applicants for commission selling on the same basis as male applicants, and by failing to promote female noncommission salespersons into commission sales on the same basis as it promoted male noncommission salespersons into commission sales (commission sales claim) . . . beginning March 3, 1973 and ending December 31, 1980. . . . The court concludes that the EEOC has failed to prove its case on either claim of discrimination and finds that Sears has not discriminated against women in hiring, promotion, or pay, as claimed. . . .

Virtually all the proof offered by the EEOC in this case is statistical in nature, or related to the statistical evidence. Statistics are an accepted form of circumstantial evidence of discrimination. In some cases, where "gross disparities" are shown, statistics alone may constitute a prima facie case. . . . Statistical evidence, like other evidence, must not be accepted uncritically. . . . Without a sound theoretical basis, which is carefully reasoned and closely tailored to the factual circumstances of the case, the statistical results can be meaningless. Close attention will therefore be paid in this case to the assumptions made by the experts and their relation to reality. . . .

During 1973–1980, Sears retail stores were divided into approximately 55 retail divisions. Salespersons in these divisions were paid either on a commission or noncommission basis. Merchandise sold on commission was usually much more expensive and complex than merchandise not sold on commission. Commission selling usually involved "big ticket" items, meaning high cost merchandise, such as major appliances, furnaces, air conditioners, roofing, tires, sewing machines, etc. Noncommission selling normally involved lower priced "small ticket" items, such as apparel, linens, toys, paint and cosmetics. . . .

No written document at Sears specifically identifies the qualifications for commission sales positions. Sears' Retail Testing Manual . . . contains the only written description of a desirable commission sales candidate. The commission salesperson is described as a "special breed of cat," with a sharper intellect and more powerful personality than most other retail personnel. According to the manual, a good commission salesperson possesses a lot of drive and physical vigor, is socially dominant, and has an outgoing personality and the ability to approach easily persons they do not know. A good commission salesperson needs the ability to react quickly to a customer's verbal suggestions and modify the approach accordingly. Thus, according to the Retail Testing Manual, a higher level of "salemanship" is required of the commission salesperson than is required of the general salesperson. . . .

However, most of the essential qualities for commission selling could be determined only from an interview, not from a written application. . . . During the interview, managers looked for a number of important qualities, including aggressiveness or assertiveness, competitiveness, the ability to communicate effectively, persuasiveness, an outgoing, social or extraverted personality, self-confidence, personal dominance, a strong desire to earn a substantial income, resilience and the ability to deal with rejection, a high level of motivation and enthusiasm for the job, maturity, and a good personal appearance. The extent that each of these characteristics was required depended on the particular job opening. . . . However, as with all hiring decisions at Sears, the qualifications sought in commission sales applicants were often modified or relaxed to comply with Sears' Affirmative Action Plan. . . .

Sears has for many years had a far ranging and effectively enforced affirmative action program. Sears was the first major retail employer in the nation to institute an affirmative action program. Sears' program became a model plan followed by other corporations in the retail industry and in other industries as well. . . . In 1969, Sears set a long-term goal of 38 percent women in all jobs at Sears. This figure was derived from the government's estimates of women in the labor force. Because the female percentage of Sears employees substantially exceeded 38 percent, Sears concentrated on promoting women into non-traditional areas. . . . Each store's compliance was monitored at the group and territorial level. Regularly scheduled personnel meetings always included discussions of affirmative action. . . . The sincere dedication and commitment of Sears management at all levels to affirmative action was evident from the testimony of the Sears' officials and employees, whom the court found to be highly credible witnesses. Sears' program exceeded the requirements of Title VII or any other governmental regulation. . . .

Despite the comprehensive, nationwide scope of its lawsuit, EEOC did not produce any victims of discrimination by Sears, or any persons who claimed they witnessed discrimination against women by Sears. EEOC points, instead, to two aspects of Sears' selection process to support its statistical analyses: the subjective nature of Sears' selection process, and its testing practices. First, EEOC asserts that the absence of objective criteria for selection provides a ready mechanism for discrimination. . . . EEOC also relies on Sears' Retail Testing Manual, discussed above, which apparently contains the only written descriptions of the desirable characteristics of a commission salesperson. . . .

EEOC has relied almost exclusively on its statistical analyses to meet its burden of persuasion on its commission sales claim. There is so much imprecision in all of the underlying data being used that the mathematical presentation connoting precision is highly misleading. EEOC's statistical evidence is so flawed that it is not sufficient to meet its burden of persuasion. . . .

Sears has proven, with many forms of evidence, that men and women tend to have different interests and aspirations regarding work, and that these differences explain in large part the lower percentage of women in commission sales jobs in general at Sears, especially in the particular divisions with the lowest proportion of women selling on commission. . . .

Female applicants who indicated an interest in sales most often were interested in selling soft lines of merchandise, such as clothing, jewelry, and cosmetics, items generally not sold on commission at Sears. Male applicants were more likely to be interested in hard lines, such as hardware, automotive, sporting goods and the more technical goods, which are more likely to be sold on commission at Sears. These interests generally paralleled the interest of customers in these product lines. Men, for example, were usually not interested in fashions, cosmetics, linens, women's or children's clothing, and other household small ticket items. Women usually lacked interest in selling automotives and building supplies, men's clothing, furnaces, fencing and roofing. Women also were not as interested as men in outside sales in general, and did not wish to invest the time and effort necessary to learn to sell in the home improvements divisions. Women often disliked Division 45 (men's clothing) because it sometimes involved taking personal measurements of men. . . . As is evident from the above discussion, interests of men and women often diverged along patterns of traditional male and female interest.

This lack of interest of women in commission sales was confirmed by the number of women who rejected commission sales positions. . . . Women at Sears who were not interested in commission sales expressed a variety of reasons for their lack of interest. Some feared or disliked the perceived "dog-eat-dog" competition. Others were uncomfortable or unfamiliar with the products sold on commission. There was fear of being unable to compete, being unsuccessful, and of losing their jobs. Many expressed a preference for noncommission selling because it was more enjoyable and friendly. They believed that the increased earnings potential of commission sales was not worth the increased pressure, tension, and risk. . . .

The most egregious flaw is EEOC's failure to take into account the interests of applicants in commission sales and products sold on commission at Sears. EEOC turned a blind eye to reality in constructing its artificial, overinclusive "sales" pool, and assuming away important differences in interests and qualifications. . . .

Moreover, evidence presented by Sears provided a more reasonable basis for evaluating Sears, and showed that Sears met all reasonable estimates of the proportion of qualified and interested women. Its evidence demonstrated that, when interest and qualifications are taken into account, EEOC's alleged disparities are virtually eliminated.

Source: 628 F. Supp. 1264, North District Illinois, 1986.

13 _____

The Right to Privacy, Abortion, and the Debate over *Roe v. Wade*

Perhaps no aspect of women's rights in modern American history has been as divisive and produced as much emotion as the right to obtain an abortion in the first two trimesters of pregnancy. Widely practiced as a form of birth control in the nineteenth century, mainly by married women, abortion was a difficult practice to regulate, let alone outlaw entirely. Historians estimate that as many as one in five to one in eight pregnancies ended in abortion before the legalization of abortion, and although slightly on the decline at the end of the twentieth century, and despite better birth control methods, the abortion rate remains about the same. The demand for abortion rights and the revulsion of those who oppose abortion on religious or philosophical grounds remains an unbridgeable divide; unlike most questions in American politics and law, this confrontation over principle cannot be simply solved through compromise, or so its most ardent debaters believe. Although part of the struggle over abortion has to do with "when life begins" versus "a woman's right to choose," it is also profoundly rooted in differing conceptions of women's duties as mothers, or what Kristen Luker has aptly characterized as "the politics of motherhood."

A "century of silence" surrounded the secret practice of abortion and its elision from public discussion from the mid-nineteenth century to the mid-twentieth. Before the late 1960s, each woman who had an abortion saw it as a private, individual act, rarely calling into question the illegality of abortion or its supervision by the medical profession. But all this changed dramatically as abortion suddenly became a matter of intense public debate, especially after the Supreme Court handed down its *Roe v. Wade* decision in 1973. *Roe v. Wade* took both feminists and religious conservatives by surprise and proved to be as controversial as the Court's desegregation order in *Brown v. Board of Education* in 1954. *Roe* was a relatively new interpretation of the Constitution that found a "right to privacy" implicit in the First, Fifth, Ninth, and Fourteenth Amendments.

In the early nineteenth century, most women and their physicians used "quickening," or the moment when the mother feels the fetus move within her womb, as a benchmark for the propriety of terminating pregnancy. "Restoring menstruation" or "removing blockage" were agreed-upon euphemisms for abortions provided by physicians, midwives, or women themselves. Abortion was regulated by the states, and most states permitted abortion at the discretion of physicians, often recognizing "quickening" as a legal turning point in pregnancy beyond which abortion should be considered a criminal act. Women who secured abortions or aborted themselves were rarely arrested and almost never found guilty by juries, and before 1900, unless maternal death was the result, practitioners of abortion were not likely to be prosecuted. Most women who sought abortions were married, and historian James Mohr contends that abortion was a decision usually made by husband and wife together. If performed in the first trimester by a skilled practitioner under antiseptic conditions, abortion was, as it remains still, not a very dangerous procedure. Maternal death rates have always been higher for women who carry pregnancies to term.

Stricter laws with regard to abortion were drafted by the states between 1860 and 1880. The American Medical Association adopted an anti-abortion stance in its code of ethics in 1859, and licensed physicians pushed for legislation in the states to make abortions illegal, unless the abortion was performed by a physician for the health of the mother. They did so for a variety of reasons. Physicians now had a better understanding of fetal development, and some were uncomfortable with the folklore dividing line of quickening. Doctors also sought to drive "irregular" medical practitioners, particularly midwives, out of business and to underscore their own moral legitimacy with the general public. It was in the interest of physicians to create a higher birth rate among paying patients in the middle class; obstetrics and family medicine continued to be their chief source of revenue. Others agreed with the view, as did many moral critics, that women's desire to control their own bodies was subversive of male dominance in the family. Publicizing their opposition to abortion as a profession was a way to accomplish all of the goals.

After the Civil War, both social purists and the Catholic Church joined the crusade against abortion. In 1869 Pope Pius IX issued a papal encyclical making the performance of an abortion at any stage of pregnancy grounds for the excommunication of Catholics. Social purists succeeded in passing the Comstock Law in 1873, which made it a federal offense to circulate obscene literature and articles, including information on contraceptive devices and abortions, through the mails. Individual states passed similar laws in an attempt to drive abortionists and makers of patent medicines to induce abortion out of business. But exemptions in most states' abortion laws continued to give individual physicians the option of performing abortions, mostly in the privacy of their offices or their patients' homes. Whatever the law, abortion continued to be widely practiced in the nineteenth century.

Before 1900, women's rights advocates viewed abortion as an odious practice forced upon women by callous lovers or tyrannical husbands who could not control their sexual feelings and condemned its practice by women. In their advocacy of what they called "voluntary motherhood," women's rights leaders stressed securing better cooperation from men in preventing pregnancy through abstinence. With the arrival of more liberal views about female sexuality at the turn of the twentieth century, feminists urged the use of birth control devices so that women could achieve both sexual satisfaction and the prevention of pregnancy. In her dramatic tale of the death of Sadie Sachs, a young Jewish mother who died from a botched abortion on the lower East Side of New York before World War I, Margaret Sanger presented abortion as a horrible but inevitable alternative for women who could not obtain birth control information from uncaring physicians. In her first version of *Family Limitation* in 1915, Sanger endorsed women's "right to destroy" in the range of birth control options, but she soon retreated to the more politically acceptable view that good birth control would ultimately end abortion. In 1920 she asked, "Shall normal, safe, effective contraceptives be employed, or shall we continue to force women to the abnormal, often dangerous surgical operation?"[1]

The dream of safe, reliable, and easy-to-use birth control, however, has yet to be realized. By the 1930s diaphragms and vaginal douches remained the most viable choices in birth control for women, and diaphragms were only available from physicians, at a cost, and to—for the most part—married women. As premarital sex increased during the 1940s and exploded in the 1950s and 1960s, moreover, the rate of unplanned pregnancies skyrocketed. Estimates are that as many as one in three women was pregnant when she married in the 1950s, a premarital pregnancy rate that had not been as high at any time since the end of the eighteenth century. There was growing concern among social policy makers and moral leaders about teenage "unwed mothers." While middle-class white teenagers were usually sent away to maternity homes and gave their children up for adoption, African-American working-class teenagers were much more likely to keep their babies with the consent and support of their families, making black "unwed mothers" far more visible. But all unwed mothers were considered to be socially deviant; white women were characterized as psychologically disturbed and black women as promiscuous and a drain on the taxpayers. There was, as there is now, a far greater demand for white babies in the adoption market, making white unwed mothers part of an underground economy of reproduction. In the 1960s, some young women had better access to birth control, including the newly invented pill, but teenagers usually faced early sexual experiences without sex education or birth control. The demand for abortions was higher than ever, particularly among young, unmarried women.

Ironically, this demand peaked at a time when legal abortions were more difficult to obtain than ever. By the 1960s the medical profession had largely succeeded in pressuring licensed physicians to "regularize" abortion, putting hospital boards in charge of weighing evidence for a particular woman's need for a so-called "therapeutic abortion." Therapeutic abortions were difficult to obtain and did not begin to meet requests submitted to hospitals by women. Physicians no longer had the discretion to perform abortions they once had. With the rise of better prenatal care, antibiotics, and medical procedures for risky pregnancies, "saving the life of the mother" could rarely be used as a rationale for abortion; moreover, nearly all gynecological surgeries were now performed in hospitals. While some hospital boards were willing to grant a limited number of abortions to preserve the mental health of the mother, many did not, and Catholic hospitals refused to perform abortions at all. The result was a tangle of policies that appeared to be random and to have little merit as far as women seeking abortions were concerned: "Some hospitals turned their therapeutic abortion boards into quota systems. . . . A case could be turned down simply because the month's quota had already been exceeded. At the same time, these boards also tended to become market systems, in which women with wealth, information, and medical advocates were far more likely to be granted abortions than their poorer, less well-informed, and less well-connected peers."[2] As a result, physicians saw victims of botched abortions come into hospitals on a routine basis and were the first to know how large was the gap between the law and practice; some of these victims died from perforated uteruses, hemorrhaging, and raging infections. In states such as New York and California, physicians were among the first to propose the liberalization of nineteenth-century abortion laws, and in 1967 the American Medical Association passed a cautious resolution endorsing some abortion law reform.

Changes in women's lives also made many women more aggressive in demanding better birth control and abortion services. The rate of married women working outside the home increased dramatically and continuously after World War II, as did the proportions of women attending college and graduate school, entering the professions, and raising children as single parents. Many of these women were sexually active but sought to control their fertility and saw the power to do so as a fundamental right. The social movements of the 1960s included women as well as men, and inspired rebellion against authority, a rebellion that was accompanied by a sexual revolution. Grass-roots organizations formed abortion referral networks that tried to match up reliable abortion practitioners with women seeking abortions and provide supplemental funding to women who could not afford the fee, typically $500 an operation. One such network was "Jane" in Chicago, which both lobbied for repeal of abortion laws and provided women with referrals. When the referrals proved to be incompetent or too costly, members of Jane performed abortions themselves. A shift in the consciousness of many women over a variety of health issues, including abortion, was clear when the Boston Women's Health Collective published a health handbook for women in 1970 entitled *Our Bodies, Ourselves*. Like Sanger's pamphlet on "family limitation," it contained explicit information on abortion and challenged the notion that women must learn everything to do with their own bodies through the filtered advice of physicians.

Meanwhile, important changes in constitutional law were laying the groundwork for overturning restrictions of abortion. In 1965 the Supreme Court ruled in *Griswold v. Connecticut* that married couples had "a right to privacy" that could be extrapolated from the due process clauses of the Fifth or Fourteenth Amendments. In 1972 that same right to privacy was extended to unmarried persons in *Eisenstadt v. Baird*, and a similar ruling in 1977 in *Carey v. Population Services International* extended the right to minors under the age sixteen. While these cases all involved the distribution of birth control information and devices prohibited by old obscenity statutes in the states, their potential for abortion rights was clear.

Moreover, a variety of fledgling feminist organizations began to demand the repeal of abortion laws, not their reform. In 1967 the National Organization for Women endorsed reproductive rights at its national convention. That same year the Women's Liberation Workshop of the Students for a Democratic Society called for "the dissemination of birth control information and devices to all women regardless of age and marital status, and . . . the availability of a competent medical abortion for all women who so desire."[3] Abortion rights advocates staged speakouts by those who had experienced abortion or knew someone who had died from an abortion gone wrong, and in so doing, began to end the secrecy surrounding abortion and to make it a public question. Nonetheless, the rapid developments in the law and the depth of "pro-choice" sentiment took many "pro-life" citizens by surprise. California liberalized its law in 1967, and a year later, the number of legal abortions in the state had increased three-fold. In 1970 Hawaii and then New York created new abortion laws. The New York law was especially important, because it did not restrict abortion to state residents and was not shot through with medical restrictions; feminists had demonstrated their version of an ideal law by holding up a blank piece of paper. There were only four women in the New York State Assembly at that time, but Constance Cook, a liberal Republican from Ithaca, co-sponsored the bill. The vote on the floor of the Assembly was too close to call, and with a tie of 74 to 74, Assemblyman George M. Michaels rose to change his vote from "nay" to "aye." Michaels was from a heavily Catholic district, and he knew that if he voted yes his political career would be over. But he explained that two of his sons had condemned his no vote: "Dad, for God's sake, don't let your vote be the vote that defeats this bill." As he cast the deciding vote, Michaels heard both epithets and kudos. In the words of one reporter, "to one side it was an epochal breakthrough for women's rights. To the other, it felt like the end of civilization."[4]

When *Roe v. Wade* was decided by the Supreme Court in 1973, building on the right to privacy arguments in the *Griswold* and *Eisenstadt* cases, the same sense of miracle and catastrophe echoed through the nation. The sudden shift in national policy regarding abortion, which appeared to transfer regulation from the states to Washington, D.C., angered many conservatives. In her 1984 study of California pro-life and pro-choice activists, sociologist Kristin Luker found that most pro-life leaders believed that abortion had not been widely practiced when it was illegal, and that common decency would prevent any national legalization of what they viewed as a heinous crime. Not surprisingly, conservative and religious mobilization against *Roe* began almost immediately.

What did *Roe* say? First, the Supreme Court noted that existing abortion law in the states was not of "ancient or even of common-law origin." The chief validation for the current laws lay in the late nineteenth-century desire to protect the health of women from botched abortions and medical quackery. Modern medical procedures were now safe and regulated enough to make abortion a matter of private consultation between a woman and her physician in the first trimester of pregnancy without interference from the government. However, the states might fully supervise the termination of pregnancies beyond the end of the first trimester "in ways that are reasonably related to maternal health." As for fetal rights, the majority rejected the idea that the Supreme Court should determine "when life begins." It deemed this matter a religious question and not a constitutional one. Instead, the Court fixed fetal viability, or the point at which a fetus can survive outside the womb and is therefore considered by the law to be a person, as the point beyond which abortions were unacceptable, except in those cases where it was "necessary for the preservation of the life or health of the mother." A carefully argued and detailed decision, written by Justice Harry Blackmun, *Roe* offered historical, philosophical, and legal precedent analysis as a justification for overturning state restrictions on abortion, but left the door open, at the same time, for challenges to such subjective concepts as the right to privacy, fetal viability, fetal rights, and maternal health, and under which circumstances the states might regulate abortion practice.

The momentous changes in the law between 1965 and 1973 mobilized a number of constituencies who opposed one or more aspects of modern sexuality, the women's liberation movement, and the freer distribution of birth control. In 1966 the Catholic magazine *Triumph* was launched to oppose the liberal tenets of Vatican II, the use of birth control by Catholics, and any legalization of abortion. *Triumph* editor William Bozell formed a "Sons of Thunder" group to initiate civil disobedience demonstrations at birth control clinics. In 1971, "pro-life" Catholics founded Americans United for Life and invited members of other religious groups to join. In 1972, 10,000 people, most of them women, marched in New York City to demand the repeal of New York's abortion rights law. The National Right to Life Committee was formed in 1973, and in 1975 Dr. Mildred Jefferson became its president. Jefferson, an African-American physician in Boston, viewed abortion as another means of regulating the birth rates of the poor and people of color, a view also held by the acerbic black comedian, Dick Gregory. The National Council of (Catholic) Bishops deemed abortion murder in 1973 and drafted a "Pastoral Plan for Pro-life Activity," intended to mobilize Catholic parishes for demonstrations, political lobbying, and selection of political candidates based on their abortion views.

Fundamentalist Protestants did not join the movement in large numbers until the late 1970s, but when they did they organized pro-life citizens for the political agenda of the New Right and helped to elect Ronald Reagan as president in 1980. In the 1980s Operation Rescue was able to mobilize hundreds of demonstrators of a variety of faiths to picket and block birth control clinics, where most abortions were and are performed. Clinic workers and doctors have been killed and clinics bombed by individuals who carry the goals of the anti-abortion movement to violent extremes.

Anti-abortion forces have thus far been unable to bring a "human life amendment" before the U.S. Congress that would declare the fetus a human being at the point of conception. But they have succeeded in chipping away at *Roe* in a series of closely decided Supreme Court decisions that allow states to regulate abortion more strictly. The most important of these are restrictions on funding to public hospitals and parental consent laws for minors who seek abortions. Between 1976 and

1980 Representative Henry Hyde of Illinois attached amendments to appropriations bills in the Congress that denied government funding for abortions for women on Medicaid, and in 1980 the Supreme Court declared the so-called Hyde amendment constitutional. Similar exclusions are applied to women in the military. President George Bush, Jr.'s executive policies regarding reproductive rights have not only made gaining abortions more difficult but severely limited birth control funding for public agencies. Many global health experts believe women's health in not only the United States but in poor countries around the world will be severely jeopardized as a result.

Even without Medicaid funding, evidence suggests that despite Hyde, poor urban women in the United States are likely to seek abortion. Poor women in rural areas, however, are at a distinct disadvantage in finding abortion services close to home. In some places—on military bases, or in states such as Louisiana or North Dakota—legal abortions are not available at all. By 1988 there were no abortion services in 83 percent of all U.S. counties; one scholar concludes that the "maldistribution of abortion services . . . worsens each year."[5] The nation's physicians are increasingly leaving medical school with no abortion training; the mergers of many Catholic and non-Catholic hospitals have decreased the settings where abortions can be learned or performed and put pressure on physicians to conform to anti-abortion standards. The *New York Times* found that "the percentage of OB-GYN's willing to perform abortions dropped from 42 percent in 1983 to 33 percent in 1995," and that "59 percent of all abortion doctors are at least 65 years old."[6] There are constant attempts by anti-abortion state legislators to limit the practice of abortion in birth control clinics. The term "partial birth abortion" has been used recently in Congress to blur the stages of pregnancy and to throw abortion at any point—not just before fetal viability—into the realm of infanticide.

Abortion remains a political flash point for a number of reasons. Many people oppose abortion on the basis of religious principle and see it as the taking of human life. Feminists perceive control over their bodies to be an essential condition of human freedom. But the social and economic conditions that have produced the demand for abortion rights—and opposition to it—are not likely to disappear in the United States. Unwanted pregnancy will continue to remain a problem. As historian Rosalind Pollack Petchesky argues, " 'perfect' contraception—that defies human error, unforeseen circumstances, or medical risk—is an illusion."[7] The history of abortion in the United States tells us that women will seek abortion no matter how difficult, costly, or dangerous. And a popular American culture that endorses liberal sexuality without universal sex education and reliable birth control for teenagers will continue to make the demand for abortion particularly widespread among young women.

READING GUIDE

Daniels, Cynthia, *At Women's Expense: State Power and the Politics of Fetal Rights*. Cambridge: Harvard University Press, 1993. Focusing on the newly evolving concept of fetal rights in the law, Daniels looks at what she describes as "a deep crisis in reproductive relations in the United States" (2). In the 1990s, more criminal charges were being brought against pregnant women who, in the perception of prosecutors, had endangered their unborn children by using drugs, drinking alcohol, or refusing blood transfusions. Women were barred from employment in certain kinds of workplaces unless they produced evidence of sterilization. Is this simply a matter of protecting the unborn, asks Daniels, or is it a thinly disguised effort to supervise pregnancy and reproduction by the state?

Eisenstein, Zillah R., *The Female Body and the Law*. Berkeley: University of California Press, 1988. Eisenstein examines the ways in which liberal political thought constructs equality in bodies that are implicitly male. When the female body, and in particular the pregnant female body, is introduced into this discourse, it is assumed to be abnormal and disruptive, to introduce difference, and to reduce the likelihood of equality for women. Conservative political theorists and politicians develop difference, particularly as it is located in the pregnant (or potentially pregnant) woman in a way that conflates women and pregnancy, thus posing women as biological vessels in need of protection or supervision. Eisenstein explores the evolution of these ideas in the years of Reagan administration and their influence on abortion, divorce and custody law, welfare, birth control, and protective legislation, which she sees as connected in a conservative paradigm of womanhood.

Faux, Marian, Roe v. Wade: *The Untold Story of the Landmark Decision That Made Abortion Legal*. New York: Macmillan Publishing Co., 1988. Linda Coffee and Sarah Weddington, two young women lawyers just out of law school, agreed to represent Norma McCorvey, a pregnant woman who could not find a legal abortion in Texas in 1969, thus launching the case that led to the *Roe v. Wade* decision in 1973. This is a highly readable account of the personalities involved in the *Roe* case and the drama of the Supreme Court hearings that changed abortion law in the United States. Faux is convinced that outlawing abortion will never end abortion, and sees those who dared to bring *Roe* to a conclusion as feminist heroes. Norma McCorvey (*"Roe"*) later regretted her participation in the case and has spoken before religious conservatives about that regret.

Luker, Kristin, *Abortion and the Politics of Motherhood*. Berkeley: University of California Press, 1984. In perhaps one of the most compassionate books available on the divide in American consciousness evoked by *Roe v. Wade*, Luker examines the nineteenth-century history of birth control and then presents her findings in a study of both pro-life and pro-choice activists in California. She finds that physicians were among the first to advocate limited abortion law reform but soon found that out-and-out repeal was to be the order of the day. Luker sees the abortion controversy as a clash over the "politics of motherhood." While men dominated the upper levels of the pro-life movement that arose in California, women were the foot soldiers. They were motivated by a profound sense that motherhood is no longer valued in modern society and that the "weak"—in particular stay-at-home wives, infants, and children with birth defects—are vulnerable to economic expediency. The more educated women are, the more they work outside the home and expect the right to plan their families, the more likely they are to support abortion rights and to see "motherhood" as something they should control and not just assume as the predominant aspect of their lives.

Merton, Andrew H., *Enemies of Choice: The Right-to-Life Movement and Its Threat to Abortion*. Boston: Beacon Press, 1981. This was the first attempt to describe the rise of the Right to Life Movement and the major personalities who created a vast movement against abortion rights. Merton provides a useful chronology and the variety of places in which opposition to abortion rights rose in the 1960s and 1970s. He is clearly pro-choice, but does a credible job of introducing the major activists and presenting their views in their own words. While Catholics dominated the early years of the movement, evangelical Protestants became more active after 1980 and began to be major players in the Republican party.

Mohr, James C., *Abortion in America: The Origins and Evolution of National Policy, 1800–1900*. New York: Oxford University Press, 1978. One of the first accounts of the history of abortion in the nineteenth century, Mohr's book outlines the widespread practice of abortion by married women and the role of the medical establishment in making the campaign against abortion a major factor in its growing respectability in American life. Mohr also provides a careful history of abortion laws in the states and the growing consensus for regulation on the national level that resulted in the Comstock Law of 1873.

Petchesky, Rosalind Pollack, *Abortion and Woman's Choice: The State, Sexuality, and Reproductive Freedom*. Boston: Northeastern University Press, 1985. Although overly long and frequently digressive, Petchesky's work remains one of the most important works on abortion ever written. The heart of the book deals with the tug of war between actual sexual practice, changing abortion law, and the conservative and religious backlash against women's reproductive rights in the 1970s and 1980s. Laced with theoretical discussions of women in the family and the ongoing struggle for/resistance to women's independence outside the family, Petchesky helps to explain why abortion is such a fault line between so-called "pro-family" forces and the women's liberation movement. She reminds us that abortion rights are in constant jeopardy, that the delivery of health, birth control and abortion services to women is highly structured by age, race, and class, and that many women still have no safe, dependable, and affordable method of birth control.

Solinger, Rickie, *Wake Up Little Susie*. New York: Routledge, 2000 [1992]. This comparative study of black and white women's unmarried pregnancy before *Roe v. Wade* shows how racial constructions created differing views of teenage mothers after World War II. Young white women were usually made to feel as though they had shamed their families, sent to "rescue" maternity homes, pressured to give their babies up for adoption, and characterized as psychologically disturbed. Young black women usually kept their children and were absorbed into their extended families. The legacy of this racial and class difference in the treatment of pregnancy has been to demonize African-American teenage pregnancy and to repress the memory of white women's sexuality before *Roe*. Whatever the racial distinctions made by social agencies and political commentators, the growing demand of young women of all classes and races for birth control and abortion services was a definite factor in the explosion of the abortion issue in the 1970s.

NOTES

1. Margaret Sanger, *Woman and the New Race* (New York: Blue Ribbon Books, 1920), 121–22.

2. Kristin Luker, *Abortion and the Politics of Motherhood* (Berkeley: University of California Press, 1984), 57.

3. *New Left Notes* (July 10, 1967), 4.

4. Richard Perez-Pena, " '70 Abortion Law: New York Said Yes, Stunning the Nation," *New York Times*, April 9, 2000: 27, 1.

5. Susan Gluck Mezeh, Raymond Tatalovich, and Michael Walsh, "Keeping Abortion Clinics Open: The Importance of *Ragsdale v. Turnock* in the Post-*Casey* Era," *Policy Studies Review* 13 (1994): 111.

6. Jack Hitt, "Who Will Do Abortions Here?" *New York Times Magazine*, January 18, 1998: 22.

7. Rosalind Pollack Petchesky, *Abortion and Woman's Choice: The State, Sexuality, and Reproductive Freedom* (Boston: Northeastern University Press, 1985), 197.

DOCUMENTS

13.1.   Seeking Abortion in the Late 1960s

> *Margaret Cerullo, who recounts her 1968 abortion experience here, did not have access to medically prescribed birth control and became pregnant. Abortion was illegal in Pennsylvania, and, determined to end her pregnancy, she contacted an underground network that referred women to abortionists. This account was presented at Hampshire College in a "speakout" in 1989, at a point when many feminists feared that abortion rights were in grave danger from Congress and the Supreme Court.*

"HIDDEN HISTORY: AN ILLEGAL ABORTION IN 1968"

My story is not unusual. Like many women of my generation . . . my commitment to abortion rights drew its initial passion from my own illegal abortion, 21 years ago. I have come to think of my story most recently as part of the hidden history of 1968–1969, as an emblem for a period of profound social upheaval in this country, indeed throughout the world. . . . In 1968 I was 20 years old and . . . a junior in college at the University of Pennsylvania. In 1968 I was a revolutionary and, in 1968, against my will, and much to my dismay, I was pregnant, a fact I discovered the Saturday before my final exams were going to begin. Not only was abortion illegal in 1968, so was birth control. In Philadelphia where I lived (not a backwater) you could only get the pill (the only form of birth control I thought of) if you were married, had your parents' permission, or were 21 years of age. I was too young, I wasn't married, and my parents were practicing Catholics. Women students at Penn had just discovered a doctor in Philadelphia . . . who would accept a letter of permission not only from your parents, but also from your aunt. So, we sat around the dorms granting our "nieces" permission to use birth control. I participated in these letter-writing sessions, knowing that by the time I got the pill it might already be "too late."

I was nine or ten weeks pregnant by the time I figured out where I could get a pregnancy test, had one, and waited for the results. I really had very little idea how I was going to go about getting an abortion, but I was absolutely clear that I did not want to have a child. Like so many young women who get pregnant, I had not been sexually active for long.

I felt I was only beginning to know the possibilities of my body, as I was only beginning to dream the possibilities of my life.

I really cannot remember exactly how I found the phone numbers, but I suppose I got them through the various means of the underground student/political/counter-cultural scene. I began making phone calls all over the East Coast. . . . "Hello, this is Mary; I'm calling because I just saw John; well, actually, I saw John about nine and a half weeks ago." You coded the relevant information about what you wanted and how serious the situation was. I made three or four of these calls from pay phones in between taking exams, and the person on the other end of each one of them hung up abruptly after I blurted out the critical information. Eventually, I found out there was a major crackdown in process, just a chance regular kind of repressive crackdown on illegal abortionists on the East Coast. The weeks were ticking away and I was starting for the first time to feel nervous. I knew after twelve weeks I would really be in trouble and I had to go home to see my family after exams were over. I was worried about how I would disguise nausea and morning sickness.

Finally I got the number of the "Clergymen's Council on Problem Pregnancies" and I went to visit a clergyman in the Philadelphia suburbs. The Council tried to match you with clergymen of your own faith, but there were none of my faith participating. It was explained to me that there was one place they thought it would be possible to have an illegal abortion very quickly, a place called Towson, Maryland, outside of Baltimore. I would have to appear with $600 in small bills.

It seemed an enormous amount of money then (I was living on $5 a week spending money) and not simple to find. . . . The money was what made me decide to tell the guy I had gotten pregnant with. He agreed to dress up in a suit and go to the bank and apply for a loan. He got it and that's how I came up with $600 in small bills. I was to appear in Towson at 2:00 in the afternoon outside the movie theater and wait until a man carrying a bag of groceries appeared at the theater and follow him. The clergyman with whom I spoke suggested that I think about the experience I was going to have as an act of civil disobedience against an unjust law. To call up righteous anger at a moment of terror was a great help to me.

I was a philosophy student then, and another student had recently suggested that I read a book by John Barth in which the lead character was a philosophy professor. The book was called *The End of the Road* and I can't remember much about the philosophy professor. What I do remember is the story of a woman who had an illegal abortion in Towson, Maryland. The procedure was botched and she died: that was the "end of the road." So I went to Towson with that vivid image fresh in my mind. I encountered the man carrying a bag of groceries. He gestured and I went off with him to his car. There was another woman already there, another college student. She told me later she got pregnant the first time she slept with her boyfriend. We stopped by the mall and picked up a third woman, then drove for about 45 minutes. The third woman, who was from near Towson, said that we had taken an amazingly circuitous route to arrive at a little cottage in the woods where the grocery bag man lived with his wife. On an end table in the living room was a gold-leaf-framed picture of their son in his military uniform, a formal portrait taken before he left for Vietnam. In his absence, his bedroom had been turned into an "operating room."

The "doctor" eventually came, carrying a black bag (the sign that he was a doctor) and wearing a mask that made me think of the Lone Ranger. We tossed coins to determine who would go first and proceeded to have our abortions in turn. Mine was a straightforward procedure, an old-fashioned "D&C" with no complications, and not more pain than I expected or was stoically prepared to endure. One of the other women, however, the other student, bled for a very long time, so instead of turning up back at the movie theater in Towson at 6:00 P.M. as I had been told, we didn't return until about 10:00 P.M. At about 7:00, I was allowed to call my friends in Baltimore to say I would be late, so those waiting in Towson had only about an hour and a half of anxiety that something had gone wrong or, almost unspeakable, that I would not return.

As I rode in the back seat of the car through Maryland countryside on my way to have an illegal abortion that day in May 1968, I came to a shocking realization. For the first time in my life, I understood that I was a woman, not a "human being," but a woman. For the first time, I understood something about what it meant to be a woman in this society— that the lives of women were not of value. And I realized, in an inchoate rage that is with me today as I recall this story, that in this society, *because I had sex, someone thought I deserved to die.*

Source: Marlene Gerber Fried, ed., *From Abortion to Reproductive Freedom: Transforming a Movement.* Boston: South End Press, 1990: 87–90.

13.2.   The Supreme Court Overturns State Laws Restricting Abortion

---

In 1973 the cases of "Jane Roe" from Texas and "Mary Doe" from Georgia reached the Supreme Court after both plaintiffs prevailed in federal district courts. The Supreme Court upheld the lower courts' decisions in both cases and legalized abortion throughout the United States. Justice Harry Blackmun delivered the majority opinion for seven justices. A future Supreme Court Chief Justice, William Rehnquist, wrote a dissent for the minority, finding no protection for a "right to privacy" in the Fourteenth Amendment, and holding the cases moot because Roe and Doe were no longer pregnant and could not serve as representatives of an entire class.

ROE V. WADE

We forthwith acknowledge our awareness of the sensitive and emotional nature of the abortion controversy, of the vigorous opposing views, even among physicians, and of the deep and seemingly absolute convictions that the subject inspires. . . . In addition, population growth, pollution, poverty, and racial overtones tend to complicate and not to simplify the problem.

It perhaps is not generally appreciated that the restrictive criminal abortion laws in effect in a majority of States today are of relatively recent vintage. Those laws, generally proscribing abortion or its attempt at any time during pregnancy except when necessary to preserve that pregnant woman's life, are not of ancient or even of common-law origin. Instead, they derive from statutory changes effected, for the most part, in the latter half of the nineteenth century. . . .

At the time of the adoption of our Constitution, and throughout the major portion of the nineteenth century, abortion was viewed with less disfavor than under most American statutes currently in effect. Phrasing it another way, a woman enjoyed a substantially broader right to terminate a pregnancy than she does in most States today. At least with respect to the early stage of pregnancy, and very possibly without such a limitation, the opportunity to make this choice was present in this country well into the nineteenth century. Even later, the law continued for some time to treat less punitively an abortion procured in early pregnancy.

Three reasons have been advanced to explain historically the enactment of criminal abortion laws in the nineteenth century and to justify their continued existence.

It has been argued occasionally that these laws were the product of a Victorian social concern to discourage illicit sexual conduct. Texas, however, does not advance this justification in the present case, and it appears that no court or commentator has taken the argument seriously. . . .

A second reason is concerned with abortion as a medical procedure. When most criminal abortion laws were first enacted, the procedure was a hazardous one for the woman. This was particularly true prior to the development of antisepsis. Antiseptic techniques . . . were not generally accepted and employed until about the turn of the century. Abortion mortality was high. Even after 1900, and perhaps until as late as the development of antibiotics in the 1940s, standard modern techniques such as dilation and curettage were not nearly so safe as they are today. Thus, it has been argued that a State's real concern in enacting a criminal abortion law was to protect the pregnant woman, that is, to restrain her from submitting to a procedure that placed her life in serious jeopardy.

Modern medical techniques have altered this situation. . . . Abortion in early pregnancy, that is, prior to the end of the first trimester, although not without its risk, is now relatively safe. Mortality rates for women undergoing early abortions, where the procedure is legal, appear to be as low or lower than the rates for normal childbirth. Consequently, any interest of the State in protecting the woman from an inherently hazardous procedure, except when it would be equally dangerous for her to forgo it, has largely disappeared. Of course, important state interests in the areas of health and medical standards do remain. The State has a legitimate interest in seeing to it that abortion, like any other medical procedure, is performed under circumstances that insure maximum safety for the patient. . . .

The third reason is the State's interest—some phrase it in terms of duty—in protecting prenatal life. Some of the argument for this justification rests on the theory that a new human life is present from the moment of conception. The State's interest and general obligation to protect life then extends, it is argued, to prenatal life. Only when the life of the pregnant mother herself is at stake, balanced against the life she carries within her, should the interest of the embryo or fetus not prevail. . . .

Parties challenging state abortion laws have sharply disputed in some courts the contention that a purpose of these laws, when enacted, was to protect prenatal life . . . [and] they claim that most state laws were designed solely to protect the woman. . . . The few state courts called upon to interpret their laws in the late nineteenth and early twentieth centuries did focus on the State's interest in protecting the woman's health rather than in preserving the embryo and fetus. . . .

The Constitution does not explicitly mention any right of privacy. In a line of decisions, however, . . . the Court has recognized that a right of personal privacy, or a guarantee of certain areas or zones of privacy, does exist under the Constitution. . . . These decisions made it clear that only personal rights that can be deemed "fundamental" or "implicit in the concept of ordered liberty," . . . are included in this guarantee of personal privacy. They also make it clear that the right has some extension to activities relating to marriage . . . family relationships . . . and child rearing and education. . . .

This right of privacy, whether it be founded in the Fourteenth Amendment's concept of personal liberty and restrictions upon state action, as we feel it is, or, as the District Court determined, in the Ninth Amendment's reservation of rights to the people, is broad enough to encompass a woman's decision whether or not to terminate her pregnancy. . . .

On the basis of elements such as these, appellant and some *amici* argue that the woman's right is absolute and that she is entitled to terminate her pregnancy at whatever time, in whatever way, and for whatever reason she alone chooses. . . . With this we do not agree. . . . The Court's decisions recognizing a right of privacy also acknowledge that some regulation in areas protected by that right is appropriate. . . . [A] State may properly assert important interests in safeguarding health, in maintaining medical standards, and in protecting potential life. At some point in pregnancy, these respective interests become sufficiently compelling to sustain regulation of the factors that govern the abortion decision. . . .

We need not resolve the difficult question of when life begins. When those trained in the respective disciplines of medicine, philosophy, and theology are unable to arrive at any consensus, the judiciary, at this point in the development of man's knowledge, is not in a position to speculate as to the answer. . . .

In view of all this, we do not agree that, by adopting one theory of life, Texas may override the rights of the pregnant woman that are at stake. We repeat, however, that the State does have an important and legitimate interest in preserving and protecting the health of the pregnant woman . . . and that it has still *another* important and legitimate interest in protecting the potentiality of human life. These interests are separate and distinct. Each grows in substantiality as the woman approaches term and, at a point during pregnancy, each becomes "compelling."

With respect to the State's important and legitimate interest in the health of the mother, the "compelling" point, in the light of present medical knowledge, is at approximately the end of the first trimester. This is so because of the now-established medical fact, referred to above, that until the end of the first trimester mortality in abortion may be less than mortality in normal childbirth. It follows that, from and after this point, a State may regulate the abortion procedure to the extent that the regulation reasonably relates to the preservation and protection of maternal health. . . .

This means, on the other hand, that, for the period of pregnancy prior to this "compelling" point, the attending physicians, in consultation with his patient, is free to determine, without regulation by the State, that, in his medical judgment, the patient's pregnancy should be terminated. If that decision is reached, the judgment may be effectuated by an abortion free of interference by the State.

With respect to the State's important and legitimate interest in potential life, the "compelling" point is at viability. This is so because the fetus then presumably has the capability of meaningful life outside the mother's womb. State regulation protective of fetal life after viability thus has both logical and biological justifications. If the State is interested in protecting fetal life after viability, it may go so far as to proscribe abortion during that period, except when it is necessary to preserve the life or health of the mother.

Measured against these standards, Article 1196 of the Texas Penal Code, in restricting legal abortions to those "procured or attempted by medical advice for the purpose of saving the life of the mother," sweeps too broadly. The statute made no distinction between abortions performed early in pregnancy and those performed later, and it limits to a single reason, "saving" the mother's life, the legal justification for the procedure. The statute, therefore, cannot survive the constitutional attack made upon it here.

Source: 410 U.S. 113, 1973.

13.3.   Responding to *Roe v. Wade*

> As people around the country picked up their newspapers the day after the Roe decision some responded with dismay. Those whose religious principles did not allow for abortion were the most deeply offended. Scholar Kristin Luker interviewed pro-life activists in California in the 1980s and uncovered a profound sense of loss as a result of Roe. A woman who joined the pro-life movement described her determination to oppose abortion as a moral obligation when she learned of the Court's decision.

"THE BOLT FROM THE BLUE"

[It was my oldest son's] third birthday and I was making his cake . . . and we were at this table, this same table, and I was decorating, it was right over here, and there was a bunch of junk piled, like normal, on this table, this same table. This time it was toys—birthday toys. My husband came in with a newspaper. It said there would be peace in Vietnam, and of course that overshadowed the Supreme Court decision. So he was going through the paper and he saw this [article] about legalizing abortion. After I'd felt so good about those states voting it down in the referendums . . . the people voting it down. I wasn't in any organizations or anything, and I had only written one letter several years before. I had read [newspaper] articles because the issue had struck me as something I felt from the heart. . . . And so, all of a sudden he walked into the kitchen and he showed me, he said, "Hey, did you see this, Maria?" I says . . . you know I was too busy doing the cake but he says, "lookit here," he says, "read this." And I read that and it very much upset me. I've got that paper to this day. It wasn't saved because of the peace in Vietnam. It was saved because inside in the pages is that article. . . . It had a photograph of the justices, and it mentions how abortion was to be legal and all of that. And it was Jamie's birthday. And I sat down, I was very upset. . . . I wanted to cry in a way. . . . All of these things in my personal life—things that were no concern of mine, so to speak, you say "that's somebody else's business"—all came together in one. And being Jamie's birthday, my very first son . . . that kind of made it a personal thing . . . almost like seeing Providence. God was saying, "Lookit, sister, you better see what's going on there." Because . . . I'm religious even though my background isn't.

Source: Kristin Luker, *Abortion and the Politics of Motherhood*. Berkeley: University of California Press, 1984: 137.

13.4.   Defending the "Right to Choose"

Mary Frances Berry, already active in civil rights and community work, testified before the Judiciary Committee of the U.S. Senate in 1974. She was particularly eloquent in making the case for the abortion rights of African-American women.

"EVERY WOMAN SHOULD HAVE THE RIGHT"

As a black woman, I support the abortion campaign for reasons inherent in being a member of the black minority in racist America. I want to talk about rights and choices. Every woman should have the right to control her body and its usage, as she so chooses. Every woman should have the right to conceive, when she so chooses. Every woman should have the right to sexual fulfillment without fear of conception, if she so chooses. Women must secure these rights by liberating the minds of those legislators opposed to the personal freedoms of any of America's second-class citizens; women, being 53 percent of the population, are America's largest number of second-class citizens.

The legislators of this country are overwhelmingly male and overwhelmingly white. While rejecting legalized abortion, these very men sit in hypocritical splendor and refuse to provide an adequate guaranteed annual income for those children born to women without financial and social access to safe abortion. While rejecting legalized abortion, these very men refuse to fund quality, inexpensive prenatal and postnatal care to women without access to abortion. While rejecting legalized abortion, these very men refuse to fund quality education and training for the children of the women without access to abortion.

These men have never been faced with a knitting needle or coat-hanger in the greasy backroom of an urban garage, nor have they swallowed masses of quinine tablets or turpentine only to permanently endanger physical well-being. Yet their wives, mistresses, and girlfriends have ready access to (and have always had ready access to) psychiatrists and therapeutic abortions. . . .

Black women have been economically and socially denied access to legal abortion or therapeutic abortion. Black women do not have more babies than white women; they have simply had fewer abortions. Very few black women have had $500 or more for illegal abortions. Very few black women have had access to the white psychiatric community granting therapeutic abortions.

At this point, a few members of my community will tell me that legalized abortion is simply another white man's trick to foster racial genocide. They will say that we need to reproduce as many black children as possible, which only adds numbers. The fight for black self-determination needs expertise, not numbers. There is no magic in a home where someone has reproduced five or more black babies and can manage neither economically, educationally, spiritually, nor socially to see that these five black babies become five highly trained black minds. . . .

Black women particularly need this personal freedom to be able to fulfill themselves sexually without fear of conception. The outside pressures of this society wreak enough havoc within the black home and the black unit. It is unspeakable that legislated, racist pressures should accompany the black woman to her bedroom and creep insidiously into the center of her bed. I will stay out of the legislature, if the legislature will stay out of my bed. Nor can black people afford to have their personal freedoms imposed upon by religious tenets or rhetoric. Let no church dare to define womb life to me when every day I see black life defiled, maimed, and killed both physically and psychologically. . . .

Finally, a word to men: this society has encouraged men to view fatherhood as proof of their masculinity. Some men, in turn, have put this trip on women to conceive, to the benefit of no one concerned. Tremendous value is placed on the male heir and the continuance of the family name. We as black people have no time for these misconceptions and perversions of values. We cannot get caught up in the misconception that fatherhood proves masculinity and motherhood reinforces femininity.

Source: Senate Committee on the Judiciary, Hearings on Constitutional Amendments, 93rd Congress, 1st Session, March 4, 1974, Part 4: 683–85.

13.5.   An Argument Against Abortion

John T. Noonan, a Roman Catholic intellectual and jurist, presented a forceful set of arguments for overturning Roe. In his view, abortion rights were unconstitutional, disruptive of family life, undermining of fathers' rights, nationally divisive, and destructive of human life. He does not, however, feminists would say, acknowledge women's rights over their own bodies or the decision to continue pregnancies, and purports to speak for "what American women believe and want." By Noonan's thinking, once women are pregnant, their bodies must become subject to a higher law.

"WHY THE LIBERTY MUST BE LIMITED AND SURPASSED"

First. The liberty established by *The Abortion Cases* had no foundation in the Constitution of the United States. It was established by an act of raw judicial power. Its establishment was illegitimate and unprincipled, the imposition of the personal beliefs of seven justices on the women and men of fifty states. The continuation of the liberty is a continuing affront to constitutional government in this country. . . . If it becomes settled that it is the Supreme Court's will that confers personhood and existence, no one is safe.

Second. The Abortion Cases rest on serious errors. They invoke history but mistakenly assert that the historical purpose of American abortion laws was the protection of the health of the *gravida*. They invoke medical standards but mistakenly treat abortion as a procedure medically acceptable after the fifth month. . . . They invoke the freedom of women but ignore what American women believe and want. They claim not to decide when human life begins and in fact decide that human life begins at birth. Their multiple errors of history, medicine, constitutional law, political psychology, and biology require their erasure.

Third. The liberty established by *The Abortion Cases* is destructive of the structure of the family. It sets up the carrier as autonomous and isolated. It separates her from her partner in procreation. It separates her when she is a minor from her parents. It is destructive of the responsibility of parents for their daughters. It is destructive of a father's responsibility for his offspring. Its exercise is the reverse of a mother's care for her offspring. Its exercise is a betrayal of the most paradigmatic of trusts, that which entrusts to a mother the life of her helpless child.

Fourth. The liberty is oppressive to the poor. Its existence has led to depriving the pregnant poor of assistance for their dependent unborn children. Its existence has intensified the pressure on the poor to destroy their unborn children. The obligation of the government is to aid the disadvantaged by social assistance and economic improvement; the liberty transforms this responsibility to the poor into a responsibility to reduce poverty by reducing the children of the poor.

Fifth. The liberty violates the ethic of Western medicine from Hippocrates to the present. It narrows the service of the obstetrician from caring for two patients, mother and child, to caring for one. The doctor's duty to preserve every human life he touches is converted into a duty to take human lives. He is turned from a healer in all seasons to a bringer of death on occasion.

Sixth. The liberty divides the country. . . . It is the abortion liberty which has fanned religious animosity by setting Protestants against Catholics, secularists against believers. It is the abortion liberty which has assaulted the structure of the family, setting daughter against mother and father, wife against husband, mother against unborn child. It is advocates of abortion who have made the liberty of abortion part of the ideology of the emancipation of women. It is expounders of the liberty who say men and women are not partners in procreation and make a woman a solo entity and the sole judge of whether jointly conceived offspring shall live or die.

Seventh. The liberty encourages the coercion of conscience. Already it has led college administrators to force students to pay for acts the students believe to be the killing of human beings. Already it has led judges to order communities to pay for actions the communities believe are evil. Already it has permitted governors to disregard the consciences of their citizens and force them to finance abortions repugnant to their consciences. . . . The dynamism of the liberty does not allow for neutrality. He or she who does not conform must be made to cooperate.

Eighth. Implementation of the liberty has subverted other parts of the Constitution in addition to the Ninth and Fourteenth Amendments, which were specifically distorted by *The Abortion Cases.* The organic distribution of powers made by Article I has been violated. A federal court has ordered the federal government to pay money not appropriated by Congress. . . . The Treasury has complied, paying out large sums for elective abortions for which no congressional appropriation existed.

Ninth. The liberty has fostered a sinister and Orwellian reshaping of our language in which "child" no longer means child in the womb; the unborn dead have become fetal wastage; a dying infant has become a fetus *ex utero*; pregnancy has come to mean abortion; and new human life within a mother has been officially declared to be not alive.

Tenth. The liberty has led to the use of the unborn child and the dying infant for experiments. . . . In disregard of the great codes of medical ethics . . . they have been treated as disposable; and the liberty has permitted their classification and use as things.

Eleventh. The liberty has diminished the care due a child capable of life outside the womb if the child is marked for abortion. . . . Whether such child had been born alive has been made a matter of cursory examination. . . . Lawyers and judges have assaulted the laws protecting the infant outside the womb.

Twelfth. The liberty of abortion has caused a very high loss of human life. The liberty of abortion is acting as its proponents expected it to act: It is reducing the birthrate by increasing the number of abortion deaths. The loss of human life now annually attributable to the liberty in the United States is in the hundreds of thousands. More than one million have died through the exercise of the liberty. No plague, no war has so devastated the land.

There must be a limit to a liberty so mistaken in its foundations, so far-reaching in its malignant consequences, and so deadly in its exercise. There must be a surpassing of such liberty by love.

Source: John T. Noonan, Jr., *A Private Choice: Abortion in America in the Seventies.* New York: Free Press, 1979: 189–92.

13.6.   The Future of Abortion Rights

The federal guarantee of abortion rights still rests primarily in Roe v. Wade. *Since 1980 the Court has made a series of five-to-four decisions that allow further abortion restrictions by the states but still reaffirm the fundamental principle of* Roe. *Justice Sandra Day O'Connor has played a critical role in these cases, sometimes voting with centrist justices and at other times with conservatives. Modifications to Pennsylvania's abortion law in 1988 and 1989 required a twenty-four-hour waiting period, the distribution of information about "fetal life," and the notification of husbands of wives' intent to abort. O'Connor wrote the majority opinion for the Court in* Planned Parenthood of Southeastern Pennsylvania v. Casey *in 1992. She did not find the waiting period or the distribution of information an "undue burden" on women, but did object to the notification of husbands. In a ringing reaffirmation of the right to abortion, O'Connor suggested that coverture is a relic of the past, and that a woman's independent liberty outside the family includes the right to choose abortion without the consent of her husband. By placing abortion rights under the equal protection clause of the Fourteenth Amendment, O'Connor sanctioned choice as a personal liberty, perhaps a more defendable constitutional rationale for abortion than the "right to privacy."*

PLANNED PARENTHOOD OF SOUTHEASTERN PENNSYLVANIA V. CASEY

Liberty finds no refuge in a jurisprudence of doubt. Yet 19 years after our holding that the Constitution protects a woman's right to terminate her pregnancy in its early stages . . . that definition of liberty is still questioned. . . . After considering the fundamental constitutional questions resolved by *Roe* . . . we are led to conclude this: the essential holding of *Roe v. Wade* should be retained and once again reaffirmed. . . . Constitutional protection of the woman's decision to terminate her pregnancy derives from the Due Process Clause of the Fourteenth Amendment. It declares that no State shall "deprive any person of life, liberty, or property, without due process of law." . . . It is a premise of the Constitution that there is a realm of personal liberty which the government may not enter. . . .

Men and women of good conscience can disagree, and we suppose some always shall disagree, about the profound moral and spiritual implications of terminating a pregnancy, even in its earliest stage. Some of us as individuals find abortion offensive to our most basic principles of morality, but that cannot control our decision. Our obligation is to define the liberty of all, not to mandate our own moral code. . . .

Our law affords constitutional protection to personal decisions relating to marriage, procreation, contraception, family relationships, child rearing, and education. . . . These matters, involving the most intimate and personal choices a person may make in a lifetime, choices central to personal dignity and autonomy, are central to the liberty protected by the Fourteenth Amendment. At the heart of liberty is the right to define one's own concept of existence, of meaning, of the universe, and of the mystery of human life. Beliefs about these matters could not define the attributes of personhood were they formed under compulsion of the State. The woman's right to terminate her pregnancy before viability is the most central principle of *Roe v. Wade*. It is a rule of law and a component of liberty we cannot renounce.

On the other side of the equation is the interest of the State in the protection of potential life. The *Roe* Court recognized the State's "important and legitimate interest in protecting the potentiality of human life." . . . That portion of the decision in *Roe* has been given too little acknowledgment and implementation by the Court in its subsequent cases. . . . Though the woman has a right to choose to terminate or continue her pregnancy before viability, it does not at all follow that the State is prohibited from taking steps to ensure that this choice is thoughtful and informed. Even in the earliest stages of pregnancy, the State may enact rules and regulations designed to encourage her to know that there are philosophic and social arguments of great weight that can be brought to bear in favor of continuing the pregnancy to full term. . . . We reject the trimester framework, which we do not consider to be part of the essential holding of *Roe*. . . . Measures aimed at ensuring that a woman's choice contemplates the consequences for the fetus do not necessarily interfere with the right recognized in *Roe* . . . not every law which makes a right more difficult to exercise is, ipso facto, an infringement of that right. . . .

We . . . see no reason why the State may not require doctors to inform a woman seeking an abortion of the availability of materials relating to the consequences to the fetus. . . . Whether the mandatory 24-hour waiting period is . . . invalid because in practice it is a substantial obstacle to a woman's choice to terminate her pregnancy is a closer question. [We do not agree with the District Court] that the waiting period constitutes an undue burden. . . . We have already established the precedent, and we reaffirm today, that a State may require a minor seeking an abortion to obtain the consent of a parent or guardian, provided that there is an adequate judicial bypass procedure. . . .

Pennsylvania's abortion law provides, except in cases of medical emergency, that no physician shall perform an abortion on a married woman without receiving a signed statement from the woman that she has notified her spouse that she is about to undergo an abortion. . . . In well-functioning marriages, spouses discuss important intimate decisions such as whether to bear a child. But there are millions of women in this country who are the victims of regular physical and psychological abuse at the hands of their husbands. . . .

[A]s a general matter . . . the father's interest in the welfare of the child and the mother's interest are equal. Before birth, however, the issue takes on a very different cast. It is an inescapable biological fact that state regulation with respect to the child a woman is carrying will have a far greater impact on the mother's liberty than on the father's. . . .

There was a time, not so long ago, when a different understanding of the family and of the Constitution prevailed. In *Bradwell v. Illinois* . . . , three Members of this Court reaffirmed the common-law principle that "a woman had no legal existence separate from her husband." . . . Only one generation has passed since this Court observed that "woman is still regarded as the center of home and family life," with attendant "special responsibilities" that precluded full and independent legal status under the Constitution (*Hoyt v. Florida* . . .). These views, of course, are no longer consistent with our understanding of the family, the individual, or the Constitution. . . . Women do not lose their constitutionally protected liberty when they marry.

Source: 112 U.S. 2791, 1992.

14

"The Personal Is Political" and Its Aftermath: Addressing Sexual Liberation and Sexual Violence

Sex was a topic of unending conversation in the fledgling women's liberation movement of the 1960s and early 1970s. Many women recalled that sex was so privatized in the 1950s that they rarely talked about it explicitly with each other, much less in public settings. Young women who participated in the social and cultural movements of the 1960s, however, began to question the sexual revolution that accompanied those movements and that had so alarmed traditionalists and religious conservatives. Many young women had experienced one version or another of the idea that the only position for women in a social movement was "prone," as Stokely Carmichael of the Student Non-Violent Coordinating Committee (SNCC) is alleged to have said. Karen Lindsey, an activist in Students for a Democratic Society (SDS), recalled "that the sexual revolution . . . was based on myth. Part of the myth was that male sexuality, unlike female romanticism, was based on real, honest, animal lust, and women would have to learn to be as free as men and everything would be fine. But what I had seen in men was . . . the necessity for conquest."[1] As new left women broke away from groups such as SDS in 1968 and 1969 to claim space for a movement of "women's liberation," they began to analyze what they described in "consciousness raising" sessions as the "chauvinism" of their male companions. Was casual sex beneficial for women? What constituted pleasurable sex for women? Might women be better off making love to each other?

The expansion of rights before 1970 had dealt with the public sphere and liberal notions of political equality. Liberalism has historically focused on rights in the public sphere and assumed the state should not intervene in the private sphere of the family or the personal lives of individuals. Women's liberationists questioned the separation between public and private in order to get at what was most worrisome to them in their lives. They were going to college and to graduate school, finding better jobs, creating political organizations, and exercising their rights as full-fledged citizens. But they believed they were responsible for preventing pregnancy, caring for children, and doing most of the housework. They were often subjected to sexual exploitation and violence.

Sexual violence directed at women remains one of the great imbalances between the sexes. Although boys and men can be victims of rape, women and girls are much more likely to be, most often by men and boys they know. The National Violence Against Women survey of 1998 found that about 18 percent of all women have been the victims of rape or attempted rape, and of these victims, more than half were under seventeen. Most rapes or attempted rapes are never reported to the police. As the discussion of everything sexual became more public in the 1970s, feminists argued that rape—whether of children, men, or women—is an act of violence, acted out in the context of uneven power relationships. Feminists also agreed that rape was only one aspect of sexual violence toward women. Wife battering, father-daughter incest, and the murder of women by husbands and boyfriends are part of the same continuum.

When Carol Hanisch, a former civil rights worker in the South and a pioneer in the women's liberation movement in New York City, coined the phrase, "the personal is political," feminists had a ringing slogan for their cause. In 1968 Hanisch's group, the New York Radical Women, staged a demonstration at the Miss America pageant in Atlantic City, New Jersey, protesting the display of women's bodies in bathing suits and high heels as a kind of "meat market" for men's consumption. The media cast the event as a "bra-burning," although cosmetics, aprons, and uncomfortable shoes were the items actually torched in trashcans on the boardwalk. A year later the group Redstockings made an explicit connection between the sexual and economic oppression of women: "We are exploited as sex objects, breeders, domestic servants, and cheap labor. We are considered inferior beings, whose only purpose is to enhance men's lives. Our humanity is denied. Our prescribed behavior is enforced by the threat of physical violence."[2]

In making the personal political, women's liberationists asked why rape and other kinds of personalized male violence against women were so prevalent. Some believed the entire culture was permeated with images and language that turned women into objects, legitimized sadism, and justified their rape, even their murder. Subjects that formerly had been taboo were now researched and fit into an overall pattern of patriarchal control. "Between 1965 and 1980," says historian Ruth Rosen, "thousands of women participated in an enormous archaeological dig, excavating crimes and secrets that used to be called, with a shrug, 'life.' "[3]

Drawing on ideas articulated in the French philosopher Simone de Beauvoir's 1948 work, *The Second Sex*, literary critic Kate Millet used the term "sexual politics" in 1970 to explore and criticize what had long been viewed as normative sexual relationships. Millet exposed the sadism and violence that were common to male novelists of the twentieth century including D.H. Lawrence, Henry Miller, and Norman Mailer. In her widely read book, *Men, Women and Rape*, published in 1975, Susan Brownmiller characterized rape as a critical aspect of patriarchal control, a patriarchy that seemed to be timeless, inevitable, and violent: "From prehistoric times to the present, I believe, rape has played a critical function. It is nothing more or less than a conscious process of intimidation by which *all* men keep *all* women in a state of fear."[4] It was now possible to think of women as a class, and like the working class described in Marxist texts, a class exploited by those in power. Just as workers were exploited in order to produce goods for the capitalist system, women were exploited for their sex characteristics by patriarchy. As feminists struggled for reproductive rights, they also mobilized to fight rape, prostitution, pornography, and wife battering. They sought to call attention to the connections among these in the degrading representations of women in smut, not only in underground-made videos and printed materials, but in such seemingly legitimate magazines as *Penthouse*, *Hustler*, and *Playboy*, and in Hollywood films such as *Deep Throat*.

There was, in fact, an explosion of explicit sexual images in the 1970s, and the line between illicit and licit pornography had been blurred. In 1970 a presidential commission found no harmful effects of pornography and urged a loosening of obscenity laws, and in 1973 the Supreme Court liberalized obscenity standards in *Miller v. California*. Red-light districts in most American cities offered prostitution, pornographic movie houses and bookstores, and sex clubs with near naked female dancers. By 1977 feminists were staging demonstrations and protests in the streets and in publishing offices against pornographic images of women; they were also researching the possible connections between pornography and rape. Robin Morgan asserted that "pornography is the theory, and rape is the practice."[5] Marital rape, described and documented by Diana Russell and Laura X, became the subject of attempts to change existing state laws, which rarely defined coercive sex of women by their husbands as a criminal offense. In 1978 the first national feminist anti-pornography conference was held in San Francisco, culminating in a "Take Back the Night" candlelight procession through the city's porn district. Take Back the Night processions became annual events in many places. They proclaimed that pornography and rape were not only demeaning to women, but also robbed women of the freedom to move around in public places, especially at night. They countered the popular rule of thumb that women who wished to avoid rape should stay home; if they went out at night or to the "wrong places," or wore the wrong clothing, they were often said to "deserve" whatever they got.

Feminists and sympathetic policy makers experimented with what could be done to end the sexual degradation of women. Women's liberationists in cities around the country created rape crisis centers and battered women's shelters, pressuring the police, hospitals, and local governments to take crimes against women more seriously. Within a decade there was a consensus that rape should become a more widely prosecuted crime and that the police, the legal profession, and the courtroom should be less hostile to victims of rape. Battered wives gained enormous sympathy; in many communities public services were created to assist them in leaving dangerous marriages with some degree of safety. Child molestation of both girls and boys became a much more widely recognized crime, although proving cases in court to the satisfaction of juries can be difficult. Sexual harassment on the job was eventually defined as work-related sex discrimination and a violation of women's civil rights. But what to do about pornography triggered an explosive debate. Did pornography cause rape? Even if it did, how might the censorship of pornography be squared with First Amendment rights protecting free speech? Would the regulation of pornography result in a modern-day version of the Comstock Law of 1877, a federal law that had been used to prevent the distribution of birth control information and devices and, in general, to rob women of knowledge about their own bodies? Modern-day women had often struggled for the freedom to explore their own sexuality and sexual pleasure; might new restrictions on sexual expression limit that exploration?

Feminists faced opposition to their analysis of pornography and rape from a variety of different sources. Those who sold sexual images for a living were among the most vociferous critics of women against pornography and characterized anti-pornography feminists as women with no sense of humor and the new "social purists." First Amendment rights activists in the American Civil Liberties Union declared there was no way to censor pornography that would be constitutional. Sex workers in the prostitution, pornography, and film industry protested that they were not victims in need of rescue but legitimate workers in a profitable industry.

The pornography debates quickly revealed there was no philosophical consensus on women's sexuality in the feminist movement. While many women were rethinking their relationships with men, others abandoned heterosexuality altogether, arguing that a kind of "compulsory heterosexuality" permeated society and prevented women from finding solace—and sexual satisfaction—with each other. The Stonewall incident of 1969, in which New York City police raided gay bars and provoked a riot, brought lesbians and gays out into the open fighting for their rights. Lesbians who had kept quiet about their sexual preference before 1969 proudly identified themselves as part of the "lavender menace," a term originally attributed to Betty Friedan of the National Organization for Women (NOW). Friedan was said to have worried that the distraction of lesbianism would divert feminists from what she perceived as the more important issue of legal equality. After an internal debate over whether lesbians should openly participate, NOW incorporated lesbian rights as part of its political agenda in 1973.

While heterosexual sex had a long tradition of prescribed behaviors for women, including what Anne Koedt termed "the myth of the vaginal orgasm," lesbian sex was uncharted territory for many of the women who experimented with same-sex love in the 1970s and 1980s. How might gay women find their way toward a sexuality that was not merely a copy of male/female sex? Was lesbian sex inherently more loving and less damaging than heterosexual sex? Some gay women were part of the anti-pornography movement, but others protested that, just at the historical moment when lesbianism was emerging with a legitimate life of its own, the last thing needed was a crackdown on sex. Censorship, whether administered by the law or by the women's movement, would squash experimentation with new manifestations of female sensuality. Some women, both lesbian and straight, were willing to admit that they enjoyed pornography and the frequently depicted trope of sado-masochism in pornographic materials. Power and domination might be played at in the bedroom not only by men but also by women; fantasy and desire should not be confused with real life. Conflict between anti-pornography activists and radical lesbian feminists exploded at a special conference on sexuality held at Barnard College in 1992.

In a series of theoretical essays, liberal and socialist feminists also questioned the theoretical analysis of the anti-pornographers. They suggested that sexual practice was socially constructed, not a timeless given of male behavior. However upsetting some pornographic images were, there were many other ways in which women, particularly poor women and women of color, were abused by patriarchy: in the welfare system, health care, and employment. An obsession with the demeaning of women in pornography stressed women's victimization, not their ability to fight back, and recalled the "feminization of fear" that had characterized the prohibition and sexual purity movements of the nineteenth century. Wendy Kaminer argued that "calling pornography a practice of abuse instead of the propaganda of abusers was an ominous shift for feminists. Calling an image an act . . . reflects women's acceptance of their own powerlessness."[6]

Moreover, some feminists argued that turning the regulation of sex over to the state through censorship would not be in the interests of women, especially in light of the election in 1980 of Ronald Reagan, a candidate of the Republican right. Some conservatives hoped to criminalize abortion once again, to bar sex education and birth control from the public schools, and to use the law to discourage premarital sex and homosexuality. Reagan appointed a new Commission on Pornography in 1986, which recommended a crackdown on pornography because it encouraged sexual violence against women. But what would be defined as obscenity under the auspices of a conservative state? Critics of the Commission believed that gay and lesbian sex images and texts would be among the first items to be banned; open discussion of birth control and abortion, particularly for teenagers, would almost certainly be next.

Two anti-porn feminists made the regulation of pornography one of their major political goals in the 1980s. Andrea Dworkin and Catharine MacKinnon worked together on the rationale for anti-pornographic legislation and helped to draft the first versions of them. Dworkin, a powerful speaker and writer, argued in her book *Woman Hating* that the sexual degradation of women is a critical element of male power and the rule of women by fear. In her testimony before the 1986 Pornography (Meese) Commission, she declared that "pornography creates bigotry and hostility and aggression toward all women, targets all women, without exception."[7] MacKinnon, a brilliant legal theorist, continues to argue that freedom of speech cannot be said to exist in a world where men hold political power and women are forced to submit to manifestations of that power in employment, family relationships, and sex.

Dworkin and MacKinnon drafted a municipal anti-pornography statute for Minneapolis and Indianapolis in the mid-1980s. The statutes characterized pornography as a form of sexual discrimination, enabling its victims to sue producers and sellers of porn for civil damages on the basis of personal harm. But a mutually agreed upon definition of pornography and its harmful effects remained difficult to formulate. The list of unacceptable images in the statutes was a long one, and for many feminists and civil libertarians, a list too subjective to be used effectively. In what appeared to liberals to be an ominous development, conservative activists such as Phyllis Schlafly defended the ordinance. The mayor of Minneapolis vetoed that city's ordinance, and the Indianapolis version was immediately challenged in court. The Feminist Anti-Censorship Taskforce filed a brief for the plantiffs that convinced the Supreme Court, which invalidated the Indianapolis law in *American Booksellers Association, Inc. v Hudnut* in 1985.

Whatever the outcome of anti-pornography campaigns, public awareness of violence toward women was far greater at the turn of the twenty-first century than it was in 1970. Most colleges and universities educate men and women students on the dangers of date rape. Rape crisis centers and battered women shelters are commonplace, many of them supported in part by public funds. Marital rape is now a crime in all fifty states. The U.S. Congress enacted a federal Violence Against Women Act in 1994, strengthening federal penalties for sex crimes. On May 15, 2000, however, the Supreme Court invalidated a key provision of the act, one that enabled victims of crimes "motivated by gender" to sue for damages in federal court. The conservative cast of the current-day Supreme Court, which has not been in favor of expanding federal powers over local jurisdictions, will continue to be problematic for victims of sexual violence, who, for the foreseeable future, must continue to seek redress in local criminal courts. Many feminists agree that "fair trials" for victims of sexual violence are often nullified by the force of local public opinion and male power.

In some ways, very little progress has been made in stemming sexual violence against women. More American women report rape, but there is still less than a two-percent chance that attackers will be arrested, convicted and go to jail. Male lovers or ex-lovers, spouses or ex-spouses are still responsible for 60 to 70 percent of all the murders of women. Sexually explicit or sexually evocative images are routinely incorporated into advertising, popular music, and displays of fashion, many of them sexually degrading of women. Astonishing reports of sexual violence against women—and men—during the recent wars in the former Yugoslavia verified Susan Brownmiller's claim that brutal sexual degradation is routinely used by victors to conquer and break the will of defeated peoples. The global traffic of women and children for prostitution and sexual slavery has reached new depths of human cruelty. In many ways the struggle of sexual violence against women has become an international struggle for human rights, one addressed by the United Nations and its non-governmental organization (NGO) conferences in Nairobi in 1985 and in Bejing in 1995.

READING GUIDE

Brownmiller, Susan, *Against Our Will: Men, Women and Rape*. New York: Simon and Schuster, 1975. Polemical and highly readable, Brownmiller's popular work was among the first attempts to theorize rape. Brownmiller demonstrated that rape is violence, that it is an inevitable byproduct of war, slavery, and class subjugation, and that sexual violence belongs in the realm of politics rather than in the privacy of personal relationships.

Burstyn, Vanda, ed., *Women Against Censorship*. Vancouver, Canada: Douglas and McIntyre, 1985. Largely a response to the Indianapolis pornography ordinance drafted by Dworkin and MacKinnon in 1984, this collection of original essays by Canadian and U.S. feminists raises critical questions about the regulation of sexuality by the state. Agreeing that violence against women is a widespread problem, the authors contend that censorship will not contribute to the solution of the problem. Once censorship is installed, what is considered "obscene" will be defined by those in power and will inevitably be directed at gays and lesbians, sex education, abortion rights, and sexual expression outside the mainstream.

Crow, Barbara A., ed., *Radical Feminism: A Documentary Reader*. New York: New York University Press, 2000. Crow has assembled a wonderful collection of manifestos, policy statements, and essays drafted by radical feminists between 1967 and 1975. Altogether, the selections explore the various ways in which early women's liberationists made the personal political. Crow includes helpful lists of feminist journals of the period and of scholarly archives holding primary sources.

DuPlessis, Rachel Blau and Ann Snitow, *The Feminist Memoir Project: Voices from Women's Liberation*. New York: Three Rivers Press, 1998. This collection of oral histories and reflective essays by participants in the women's liberation movement between 1968 and 1980 provide many examples of the struggle to articulate "the personal is political" as a strategy. Authors include Barbara Smith, Kate Millett, Naomi Weisstein, Michele Wallace, Rosalyn Fraad Baxandall, Carol Hanisch, and Meredith Tax.

Dworkin, Andrea, *Letters from a War Zone: Writings, 1976–1989*. New York: E.P. Dutton, 1988. Many of Dworkin's most important speeches and essays on pornography and violence against women are collected here. Dworkin remains an unrelenting advocate of constructing pornography as a civil rights issue, and she is an eloquent spokesperson for that cause.

Lederer, Laura, ed., *Take Back the Night: Women on Pornography*. New York: William Morrow, 1980. A book that had an enormous impact on thinking about sexual violence, this collection of original essays and reprinted selections is an indispensable source for feminists' early thinking about pornography. Among the well-known contributors are Susan Brownmiller, Diana Russell, Alice Walker, Charlotte Bunch, Robin Morgan, Susan Griffin, Andrea Dworkin, and Audre Lorde.

MacKinnon, Catharine A., *Feminism Unmodified: Discourses on Life and Law*. Cambridge: Harvard University Press, 1987. This collection of MacKinnon's lectures is a must-read for those who are interested in an influential feminist's reconstruction of legal theory. MacKinnon has been tireless in pointing up the ways in which the Constitution and the Bill of Rights do not protect women in the family, or in employment, and have allowed for sexual violence and sexual harassment under the guise of personal liberty.

Morgan, Robin, ed., *Sisterhood Is Powerful: An Anthology of Writings from the Women's Liberation Movement*. New York: Random House, 1970. Those of us who were teaching courses in women's history and politics in the early 1970s found this to be an exhilarating read for our students and ourselves. It still is. A compendium of essays on sex, family roles, conditions in employment, and political ideas for change, many of the most important early women's liberation texts are in this volume. See, in particular, (no author) "No More Miss America! Ten Points of Protest"; Pat Mainardi, "The Politics of Housework"; Mary Daly, "Women and the Catholic Church"; Marge Piercy, "The Grand Coulee Dam"; and Florynce Kennedy, "Institutionalized Oppression *vs.* the Female."

Rich, Adrienne, "Compulsory Heterosexuality and Lesbian Existence," *Signs*, 5 (1980): 631–60. One of the most distinguished U.S. poets of the twentieth century, Rich suggested in this seminal and accessible essay that rather than being a natural, predetermined biological function, heterosexuality is culturally and politically constructed. Rich rejects the Freudian notion that women's primary psychic energy is attraction to their fathers; rather, their relationship with their mothers is more salient, and whether they become lesbians or not, all women have sexual feelings for other women that exist on a continuum of sexual identities. The essay had a profound an effect on legitimizing women's sexual feelings for other women and has been widely reprinted.

Rosen, Ruth, *The World Split Open: How the Modern Women's Movement Changed America*. New York: Penguin Books, 2000. Written by a participant in the women's liberation movement, this comprehensive and witty account of the second wave of feminism is also a fine work of scholarship. Rosen contends that the women's movement, although often derided in popular culture and the object of political backlash in the 1980s, made fundamental changes in American life. Still a work in progress, women's liberation now belongs to the next generation of women, whose relationship to the "founders" is, inevitably, fraught with ambivalence.

Schneir, Miriam, *Feminism in Our Time: The Essential Writings, World War II to the Present*. New York: Vintage Books, 1994. This inexpensive and wide-ranging collection of primary sources is useful for classroom teaching and finding the pivotal manifestos, essays, and government documents associated with the feminist movement.

Strossen, Nadine, *Free Speech, Sex, and the Fight for Women's Rights*. New York: Scribner's, 1995. Strossen, an activist with the American Civil Liberties Union, deplores censorship of pornography as a violation of First Amendment rights, and argues that women, like all citizens, will have more freedom through the support of free speech.

NOTES

1. As quoted by Ruth Rosen, *The World Split Open: How the Modern Women's Movement Changed America* (New York: Penguin Books, 2000), 146.

2. "Redstockings Manifesto," *Notes from the Second Year: Women's Liberation— Major Writings of the Radical Feminists*, April, 1970: 112.

3. Rosen, *The World Split Open*, 144.

4. Susan Brownmiller, *Against Our Will: Men, Women and Rape* (New York: Simon and Schuster, 1975), 15.

5. Robin Morgan, *Going Too Far: The Personal Chronicle of a Feminist* (New York: Random House, 1977), 163.

6. Wendy Kaminer, *A Fearful Freedom: Women's Flight from Equality* (Reading, MA: Addison-Wesley Publishing, 1990), 201.

7. Adele Stan, ed., *Debating Sexual Correctness: Pornography, Sexual Harassment, Date Rape and the Politics of Sexual Equality* (New York: Delta, 1995), 34.

DOCUMENTS

14.1.   Women in the Civil Rights Movement Explore the "Personal"

In 1965 two young white women drafted "a kind of memo" in which they analyzed their roles in SNCC (Student Non-Violent Coordinating Committee). They saw parallels between racism and sexism and could see how to use black liberation as a model for a women's movement. It would be another few years before these thoughts exploded in radical student movements of the 1960s, when "the personal is political" became the watchword of the second wave of feminism.

Casey Hayden and Mary King, "SEX AND CASTE: A KIND OF MEMO," November 18, 1965

We've talked a lot, to each other and to some of you, about our own and other women's problems in trying to live in our personal lives and in our work as independent and creative people. In these conversations we've found what seems to be recurrent ideas or themes. Maybe we can look at these things many of us perceive, often as a result of insights learned from the movement:

- Sex and caste: There seem to be many parallels that can be drawn between treatment of Negroes and treatment of women in our society as a whole. But in particular, women we've talked to who work in the movement seem to be caught up in a common-law caste system that operates, sometimes subtly, forcing them to work around or outside hierarchical structures of power which may exclude them. Women seem to be placed in the same position of assumed subordination in personal situations too. It is a caste system which, at its worst, uses and exploits women.

  This is complicated by several facts, among them: 1) The caste system is not institutionalized by law (women have the right to vote, to sue for divorce, etc.); 2) Women can't withdraw from the situation (*à la* nationalism) or overthrow it; 3) There are biological differences. . . . Many people who are very hip to the implications of the racial caste system, even people in the movement, don't seem to be able to see the sexual caste system, and if the question is raised they respond with: "That's the way it's supposed to be.

There are biological differences." Or with other statements which recall a white segregationist confronted with integration.

- Women and problems of work: The caste-system perspective dictates the roles assigned to women in the movement, and certainly even more to women outside the movement. Within the movement, questions arise in situations ranging from relationships of women organizers to men in the community, to who cleans the freedom house, to who holds leadership positions, to who does secretarial work, and who acts as a spokesman for groups. Other problems arise between women with varying degrees of awareness of themselves as being as capable as men but held back from full participation, or between women who see themselves as needing more control of their work than other women demand. And there are problems with relationships between white women and black women.

- Women and personal relations with men: Having learned from the movement to think radically about the personal worth and abilities of people whose role in society had gone unchallenged before, a lot of women in the movement have begun trying to apply those lessons to their own relations with men. Each of us probably has her own story of the various results, and of the internal struggle occasioned by trying to break out of very deeply learned fears, needs, and self-perceptions, and of what happens when we try to replace them with concepts of people and freedom learned from the movement and organizing. . . .

- Men's reactions to the questions raised here: A very few men seem to feel, when they hear conversations involving these problems, that they have a right to be present and participate in them, since they are so deeply involved. At the same time, very few men can respond nondefensively, since the whole idea is either beyond their comprehension or threatens and exposes them. The usual response is laughter. That inability to see the whole issue as serious, as the strait-jacketing of both sexes, and as societally determined often shapes our own response so that we learn to think in their terms about ourselves and to feel silly rather than trust our inner feelings. The problems we're listing here, and what others have said about them, are therefore largely drawn from conversations among women only—and that difficulty in establishing dialogue with men is a recurring theme among people we've talked to.

- Lack of community for discussion: Nobody is writing, or organizing or talking publicly about women, in any way that reflects the problems that various women in the movement come across and which we've tried to touch above. . . .

The reason we want to try to open up dialogue is mostly subjective. Working in the movement often intensifies personal problems, especially if we start trying to apply things we're learning there to our personal lives. Perhaps we can start to talk with each other more openly than in the past and create a community of support for each other so we can deal with ourselves and others with integrity and can therefore keep working.

Objectively, the chances seem nil that we could start a movement based on anything as distant to general American thought as a sex-caste system. Therefore, most of us will probably want to work full-time on problems such as war, poverty, race. . . .

Source: Liberation 11, April, 1966: 35–36.

14.2.   Women Take Back the Night

> On August 18, 1979, the Boston organizers of Take Back the Night discussed a recent string of rapes in their community and their efforts to combat violent crimes against women with 5,000 marchers in Blackstone Park. The organizers did not want to cast themselves as pitiful victims, nor did they subscribe to a "feminism of fear," that is, the profiling of certain racial or social groups as the source of danger to women. Their statement was printed in the September, 1979 issue of Sojourner, a Boston feminist newspaper.

"5,000 WOMEN MARCH TO TAKE BACK THE NIGHT"

We should be energized by our gains and victories. However, 1979 has been a year of brutal violence against women in Boston. The losses cannot be forgotten; they should be held in memory to motivate each of us to continue our struggle against violence against women. . . . You do not need to be reminded of the slaying of twelve Black women and two white women . . . since January or of the series of eight rapes reported . . . between December and February. . . . Yet how many of us know that between November 1978 and April 1979 Boston police received 317 reports of sexual assault. And the unreported, unpublicized rapes and murders continue in every city and institution throughout the country.

In the United States, one out of three women will be raped; one-half of all married women are victims of battering; a woman is raped every three seconds; a woman is beaten every eighteen seconds; one out of every four women experiences sexual abuse before she turns eighteen; and nine out of ten women have received unwanted sexual advances and harassment at their jobs. Women of color have been particularly subjected to acts of violence because of their color. Those of us who are lesbians are targets of male violence not only because we are women but because of our sexual choice. There is *no* safe place for a woman!

The legal system, which we have been taught to rely on for our safety and for justice, betrays us constantly. The racist actions by the police force in framing and arresting Black men . . . does not insure women's safety. Safety does *not* mean arresting a Black man on very flimsy charges. That only perpetuates the rampant racism of this society. We will not be appeased with unjust arrests. We will not have our demand for safety pitted against a community that has little power in this society. We want to be safe—and safety means preventing murders and beatings, preventing harassment. It means creating a society in which those actions are not condoned.

Clearly, the state cannot be relied upon to provide women's safety. We must do that ourselves. Our efforts of the past year have shown that by unifying our energy, women can build strength, take power, and accomplish victories across race and class lines.

Since last year's march, community organizing among women has given birth to programs and networks within which we are creating and controlling our *own* safety systems. The Greenlight programs . . . and the Safehouse program . . . provide women a network of safe places to go when in danger. . . . Three new groups for battered women have come into existence. . . . The Massachusetts Coalition of Battered Women's Service Groups . . . is now a network of seventeen shelters across the state. . . .

Perhaps the strongest victory this past year has been the birth of the coalition for women's safety, comprised of white and Third World women. . . . The formation and continuation of these groups shows that women are joining together and recognizing that violence against women affects women of all races, women of all classes, and women in all communities. . . .

It is not enough for women to resist and organize against violence. Violence against women will not be stopped by women's efforts alone. If that were true we would have stopped it already. It is time for men to take responsibility. They must change their own attitudes, and they must interrupt and challenge acts of violence, threats of violence, and exploitative attitudes of men against women. They must stop the violence! . . .

Let us each take away from this march inspiration, a sense of power and unity, and the reality that for this one night we have experienced what it might be like to live in a society free of violence against women. Let us take that experience and build a movement that will make it a reality.

We will take back the night. We will take back the day. We will take back our lives and live them as free women!

Source: Karen Kahn, ed., *Front Line Feminism, 1975–1995: Essays from* Sojourner's *First Twenty Years*. San Francisco: Aunt Lute Books, 1995: 379–81.

**14.3.   A Conservative Explains the Cause of Sexual Violence
            Against Women**

---

*George Gilder, a liberal political activist in the 1960s, was con-
verted to conservatism in the 1970s and became a staunch critic
of feminism and the changing roles of women. He blamed
women's new roles for many of the ills of modern society, including pornography and a growing rate of sexual assault. His
argument that men needed safe outlets for aggression became
popular in "men's movements" of the 1990s.*

"MEN AND WORK"

What is happening in the United States today—to explain most of our social strains and disruptions—is the steady erosion of the key conditions of male socialization. From the hospital, where the baby is abruptly taken from its mother; to early childhood, when he may be consigned to public care; to the home, where the father is frequently absent or ineffectual; to the school, where the boy is managed by female teachers and excelled by girls; possibly to college, where once again his training is scarcely differentiated by sex; to a job that, particularly at vital entry level positions, is often sexually indistinct and that may not even be better paid than comparable female employment—through all these stages of development the boy's innately amorphous and insecure sexuality may be further subverted and confused.

In the end his opportunity to qualify for a family—to validate in society his love and sex through becoming a husband and provider—may be jeopardized. The man discovers that manhood affords few distinctive roles except in the decreasingly respected military. The society prohibits, constricts, or feminizes his purely male activities. It is increasingly difficult for him to hunt or fight or otherwise assert himself in an aggressive, male way. Most jobs reward obedience, regularity, and carefulness more than physical strength or individual initiative. If he attempts to create rituals and institutions like the ones used by similarly beleaguered men in primitive societies, he finds them opened to women. If he fights, he is sent to jail. If he is aggressive at his job, he may be fired. Thus the man finds few compensatory affirmations of masculinity to make possible his expected submission to female sexual and social rhythms; and without a confident manhood he feels a compulsive need to prove it sexually. . . .

The American woman, meanwhile becomes increasingly self-sufficient. While he is almost completely dependent on women for a civilized role in the society and for biological and sexual meaning, women are capable of living successful—though often discontented—lives without men. The culture no longer much disapproves of unmarried mothers. The state gives them welfare and, increasingly, day care and maternity leave. In any case, birth control and abortion give women complete control of procreation; and sexual liberation—not to mention masturbation and lesbianism—opens sexual enjoyment to them with only the most tenuous commitment to males. Well-paid female employment further obviates dependency. . . .

Although the man may find sexual partners more easily than before—though less easily than is generally believed—the meaning of his sexuality is diminished, and he can derive less assurance from it. His only sex act is devalued and the world of important sexuality—the womb and its procreative mysteries—is more remote than ever. Just proving himself a man becomes a full-time job.

As he has in every such historic extremity, he turns away from the family. He frequents all-male bars and behaves loudly and abusively enough to keep them that way. He watches televised football and other male sports for hours on end and argues about them incessantly; or he bombards himself with the music of male sexuality—the aggressive phallic rock now dominating youth culture. Otherwise he is obsessed with women. He tries as much as possible to reduce them to their sexual parts and to reduce their sexuality to his own limited terms—to meaningless but insistent copulation. Exiled from the world of women, he tries to destroy consciousness of its superiority by reducing it to his own level. He insists—against all his unconscious and ulterior knowledge—that women are as sexually contemptible as his society tells him he is.

He turns to pornography, with fantasies of sex and violence. His magazines—*Male* and *Crime* and *Saga* and *True Detective*, even refined male publications like *Playboy*—are preoccupied with barren copulation, or with war, perversion, and crime. And usually he drinks—as recent studies show, chiefly for the illusion of a potency that the society refuses him. He is an exile: an outlaw under the sexual constitution. Often he becomes a legal outlaw as well.

Such single males—and married ones whose socialization fails—constitute our major social problem. They are the murderers, the rapists, the burglars, the suicides, the assailants, the psychopaths. What they are not is powerful oppressors, with hypertrophied masculinity. They are impotent figures. . . . The women's movement seems determined to create more and more such exiled "chauvinist" males, all the while citing their pathetic offenses as a rationale for feminism.

Source: George Gilder, *Sexual Suicide*. New York: Quadrangle Books, 1973: 103–6.

14.4.   A Lesbian Activist Distinguishes Between Erotica and Pornography

---

> *In a speech given at an anti-pornography rally in November of 1979, Charlotte Bunch observed that pornography manufactured for men had often used choreographed lesbian sex scenes to stimulate male desire, but that most Americans considered authentic lesbian sex obscene. She faced a common problem among critics of pornography then and now; how can one distinguish between erotica and pornography? She insists that feminists will recognize the difference, but the subjectivity of regulating obscenity has been a steady problem for the law. Bunch later became an activist for women's rights as human rights on the international scene, a cause she anticipates here.*

Charlotte Bunch, "LESBIANISM AND EROTICA IN
PORNOGRAPHIC AMERICA"

Lesbians are tired of having our love labeled "pornographic," while the real pornographers go free and make money off all women's bodies and oppression. Lesbians know what love, sex, and eroticism of the female body is. . . . And we know that it has nothing to do with pornography, which is based on woman-hatred, not woman-love. Indeed, it is only in woman-hating pornography in which men exploit lesbianism for their own ends, that the portrayal of lesbianism becomes okay to patriarchy. Lesbian love is for ourselves, for women. It is abused precisely because it is outside of male control; the label "pornographic" is used against lesbianism just as the term "dyke" was used against feminism— to frighten women and to give men greater control over their lives. . . .

Lesbians are tired of having our love, our culture, and our publications threatened by these labels of "perversion," and we will continue fighting for our right to proclaim and portray our love and our sexuality openly. . . .

Some people ask: Where do you draw the line? But every woman that I know, lesbian and heterosexual, can draw the line. We can tell the difference between eroticism and anti-female pornography. We don't all like or respond to the same things sexually, but we do all know the distinction between eroticism, which celebrates our sexuality, and pornography, which degrades us. . . .

Pornography is not just symbolic violence against women. It is part of an international slave traffic in women that operates as a multinational corporation, where our bodies are the product, often procured unwillingly and always abused. Our fight against the violence in pornography in its widest implications is therefore a global fight. It extends from local street actions to the United Nations, where reports on the slave trade in women have been covered up for decades.

Source: Laura Lederer, ed., *Take Back the Night: Women on Pornography*. New York: William Morrow and Co., 1980: 91–94.

14.5.   A Feminist Writer Questions the Anti-Pornography Movement

---

In 1979 Ellen Willis, a popular feminist columnist for the Village Voice, *was among the first to question the premises of the anti-pornography movement. A long-time advocate of more liberal sexual attitudes and freer sexual expression, the* Voice *was often a target of anti-obscenity critics.*

"FEMINISM, MORALISM AND PORNOGRAPHY"

When I first heard there was a group called Women Against Pornography, I twitched. Could I define myself as Against Pornography? Not really. In itself, pornography—which, my dictionary and I agree, means any image or description intended or used to arouse sexual desire—does not strike me as the proper object of a political crusade. As the most cursory observation suggests, there are many varieties of porn, some pernicious, some more or less benign. About the only generalization one can make is that pornography is the return of the repressed, of feelings and fantasies driven underground by a culture that atomizes sexuality, defining love as a noble affair of the heart and mind, lust as a base animal urge centered in unmentionable organs. Prurience—the state of mind I associate with pornography—implies a sense of sex as forbidden, secretive pleasure, isolated from any emotional or social context. I imagine that in utopia, porn would wither away along with the state, heroin, and Coca-Cola. At present, however, the sexual impulses that pornography appeals to are part of virtually everyone's psychology. For obvious political and cultural reasons nearly all porn is sexist in that it is the product of a male imagination and aimed at a male market; women are less likely to be consciously interested in pornography, or to indulge that interest, or to find porn that turns them on. But anyone who thinks that women are simply indifferent to pornography has never watched a bunch of adolescent girls pass around a trashy novel. Over the years I've enjoyed various pieces of pornography—some of them of the sleazy Forty-second Street paperback sort—and so have most women I know. Fantasy, after all, is more flexible than reality, and women have learned, as a matter of survival, to be adept at shaping male fantasies to their own purposes. If feminists define pornography, per se, as the enemy, the result will be to make a lot of women ashamed of their sexual feelings and afraid to be honest about them. And the last thing women need is more sexual shame, guilt, and hypocrisy—this time served up as feminism.

So why ignore qualitative distinctions and in effect condemn all pornography as equally bad? WAP organizers answer—or finesse—the question by redefining pornography. They maintain that pornography is not really about sex but about violence against women. Or, in a more colorful formulation, "Pornography is the theory, rape is the practice." Part of the argument is that pornography causes violence; much is made of the fact that Charles Manson and David Berkowitz had porn collections. This is the sort of inverted logic that presumes marijuana to be dangerous because most heroin addicts started with it. It is men's hostility toward women—combined with their power to express that hostility and for the most part get away with it—that causes sexual violence. Pornography that gives sadistic fantasies concrete shape—and, in today's atmosphere, social legitimacy—may well encourage suggestible men to act them out. But if *Hustler* were to vanish from the shelves tomorrow, I doubt that rape or wife-beating statistics would decline. . . .

To lump pornography with rape is dangerously simplistic. Rape is a violent physical assault. Pornography can be a psychic assault, both in its content and in its public intrusions on our attention, but for women as for men it can also be a source of erotic pleasure. A woman who is raped is a victim; a woman who enjoys pornography (even if that means enjoying a rape fantasy) is in a sense a rebel, insisting on an aspect of her sexuality that has been defined as a male preserve. Insofar as pornography glorifies male supremacy and sexual alienation, it is deeply reactionary. But in rejecting sexual repression and hypocrisy—which have inflicted even more damage on women than on men—it expresses a radical impulse.

So far, the issue that has dominated public debate on the anti-porn campaign is its potential threat to free speech. Here too the movement's arguments have been full of contradictions. WAP organizers claim not to advocate censorship and dismiss the civil liberties issue as a red herring dragged in by men who don't want to face the fact that pornography oppresses women. Yet at the same time, WAP endorses the Supreme Court's contention that obscenity is not protected speech, a doctrine I— and most civil libertarians—regard as a clear infringement of First Amendment rights. . . .

WAP's fantasies about influencing the definition of obscenity are appallingly naïve. The basic purpose of obscenity laws is and always has been to reinforce cultural taboos on sexuality and suppress feminism, homosexuality, and other forms of sexual dissidence. No pornographer has ever been punished for being a woman-hater, but not too long ago information about female sexuality, contraception, and abortion was assumed to be obscene. In a male supremacist society the only obscenity law that will not be used against women is no law at all. . . .

In contrast to the abortion rights movement, which is struggling against a tidal wave of energy from the other direction, the anti-porn campaign is respectable. It gets approving press and cooperation from the New York City government, which has its own stake (promoting tourism, making the Clinton area safe for gentrification) in cleaning up Times Square. It has begun to attract women whose perspective on other matters is in no way feminist ("I'm anti-abortion," a participant in WAP's march on Times Square told a reporter, "but this is something I can get into"). Despite the insistence of WAP organizers that they support sexual freedom, their line appeals to the anti-sexual emotions that feed the backlash. Whether they know it or not, they are doing the good cops' dirty work.

Source: Ellen Willis, *Village Voice*, October and November, 1979.

14.6.   Indianapolis Restricts Pornography

In 1984 the cities of Minneapolis and Indianapolis passed ordinances defining pornography and making distributors of pornography liable for damages on the basis of sex discrimination. The city of Los Angeles also considered such an ordinance. The mayor of Minneapolis vetoed the ordinance, and the Indianapolis ordinance was subject to a lawsuit on the grounds of free speech. Pornography was defined in the Indianapolis statute in the following way.

INDIANAPOLIS ORDINANCE

1. Women are presented as sexual objects who enjoy pain or humiliation; or

2. Women are presented as sexual objects who experience sexual pleasure in being raped; or

3. Women are presented as sexual objects tied up or cut up or mutilated or bruised or physically hurt, or as dismembered or truncated or fragmented or severed into body parts; or

4. Women are presented as being penetrated by objects or animals; or

5. Women are presented in scenarios of degradation, injury, abasement, torture, shown as filthy or inferior, bleeding, bruised, or hurt in a context that makes these conditions sexual; or

6. Women are presented as sexual objects for domination, conquest, violation, exploitation, possession, or use, or through postures or positions of servility or submission or display.

Source: Indianapolis Code 16–3, 1984.

14.7.   The Federal Courts Reject the Indianapolis Statute

In 1985 a group of feminists opposed to the pornography ordinance in Indianapolis formed FACT (Feminist Anti-Censorship Task Force). FACT participated in the preparation of the brief used by the plaintiffs to overturn the ordinance, and Circuit Judge Frank H. Easterbrook used many of FACT's premises in his decision.

AMERICAN BOOKSELLERS ASS'N, INC. V. HUDNUT

Under the First Amendment the government must leave to the people the evaluation of ideas. Bald or subtle, an idea is as powerful as the audience allows it to be. A belief may be pernicious—the beliefs of the Nazis led to the death of millions, those of the Klan to the repression of millions. A pernicious belief may prevail. Totalitarian governments today rule much of the planet, practicing suppression of billions and spreading dogma that may enslave others. One of the things that separates our society from theirs is our absolute right to propagate opinions that the government finds wrong or even hateful. . . .

Under the ordinance graphic sexually explicit speech is "pornography" or not depending on the perspective the author adopts. Speech that "subordinates" women and also, for example, presents women as enjoying pain, humiliation, or rape, or even simply presents women in "positions of servility or submission or display" is forbidden, no matter how great the literary or political value of the work taken as a whole. Speech that portrays women in positions of equality is lawful, not matter how graphic the sexual content. This is thought control. It establishes an "approved" view of women, of how they may react to sexual encounters, of how the sexes may relate to each other. Those who espouse the approved view may use sexual images; those who do not, may not.

Indianapolis justifies the ordinance on the ground that pornography affects thoughts. Men who see women depicted as subordinate are more likely to treat them so. Pornography is an aspect of dominance. It does not persuade people so much as change them. It works by socializing, by establishing the expected and the permissible. In this view pornography is not an idea; pornography is the injury....

We accept the premises of this legislation. Depictions of subordination tend to perpetuate subordination. The subordinate status of women in turn leads to affront and lower pay at work, insult and injury at home, battery and rape on the streets. In the language of the legislature, "[p]ornography is central in creating and maintaining sex as a basis of discrimination. Pornography is a systematic practice of exploitation and subordination based on sex which differentially harms women. The bigotry and contempt it produces, with the acts of aggression it fosters, harm women's opportunities for equality and rights [of all kinds]."...

Yet this simply demonstrates the power of pornography as speech. All of these unhappy effects depend on mental intermediation. Pornography affects how people see the world, their fellows, and social relations. If pornography is what pornography does, so is other speech. Hitler's orations affected how some Germans saw Jews. Communism is a world view, not simply a *Manifesto* by Marx and Engels or a set of speeches. Efforts to suppress communist speech in the United States were based on the belief that the public acceptability of such ideas would increase the likelihood of totalitarian government....

Racial bigotry, anti-semitism, violence on television, reporters' biases— these and many more influence the culture and shape our socialization. None is directly answerable by more speech unless that speech too finds its place in the popular culture. Yet all is protected as speech, however insidious. Any other answer leaves the government in control of all the institutions of culture, the great censor and director of which thoughts are good for us....

A power to limit speech on the ground that truth has not yet prevailed and is not likely to prevail implies the power to declare truth. At some point the government must be able to say (as Indianapolis has said): "We know what the truth is, yet a free exchange of speech has not driven out falsity, so that we must now prohibit falsity." If the government may declare the truth, why wait for the failure of speech? Under the First Amendment, however, there is no such thing as a false idea. . . .

Free speech has been on balance an ally of those seeking change. Governments that want stasis start by restricting speech. Culture is a powerful force of continuity; Indianapolis paints pornography as part of the culture of power. Change in any complex system ultimately depends on the ability of outsiders to challenge accepted views and the reigning institutions. Without a strong guarantee of freedom of speech, there is no effective right to challenge what is.

Source: 771 F.2d 323, 7th Circuit Court, 1985.

15

Title IX and Women in Sport

Organized sports in the United States developed at the turn of the twentieth century in a variety of settings. While upper-class men and women played in colleges and private clubs, working-class men and women played in industrial leagues and community facilities, sometimes using them as vehicles for launching professional careers. Sports were strictly segregated by race, with parallel but unequal sports facilities and funding for African Americans and Native Americans. While the color bar in professional baseball and basketball began to lift after World War II, most high school and college sports were not racially integrated until well into the 1960s or even the 1970s. Except for golf and tennis, there were few professional sports for women, and very few people of color played these elite sports either. The Olympics began in 1900 with clear strictures against the participation of women in most team sports, especially those with body contact. These strictures took decades to reverse. For example, swimming, fencing, and ice skating for women were added in 1924, track and field in 1928, skiing in 1936, volleyball in 1964, basketball in 1976, and soccer and softball in 1996. Women's sports, whatever their setting, were characterized by inadequate facilities and meager funding. In 1972 Congress passed Title IX of the Educational Amendments Act, supposedly mandating equality for women in educational facilities receiving federal funding, including sports, but nearly thirty years later there is still heavy resistance to equal funding for women's athletics.

American sport was indelibly marked by the ethos of "muscular Christianity," a social movement for male athletes that began in England in the late nineteenth century. Advocates of muscular Christianity feared that industrialization and urbanization were undermining manliness, moral character, and military preparedness. The decline of self-employment and physical work required a new arena for teamwork and the channeling of aggression in a positive way. Muscular Christianity hoped to create a homosocial world of competitive sport by recreating the Olympics and introducing team sports, particularly football, into schools and colleges. Pierre du Coubertin, a French advocate of muscular Christianity, organized the modern Olympics in 1900. He believed that sports played by boys in elite boarding schools laid the groundwork for England's success as a world power and should be emulated by all Europeans. Women had to be excluded from the Olympics—except in the audience—or "the solemn and periodic exaltation of male athleticism" might be undermined.[1]

Although more men played baseball and basketball than football, football was the quintessential manly sport, one that defined both male character and collective "school spirit." Injuries and the metaphor of the playing field as battleground characterized early football. The first attempts to regulate the game were initiated by President Theodore Roosevelt, himself an advocate of sport as "the moral equivalent of war," leading to the creation of the Inter-Mural Athletic Association in 1905, precursor of the 1910 National Collegiate Athletic Association (NCAA).

Excluded from football and the Olympics, women were, nonetheless, playing a wide variety of sports as a more dynamic and athletic paradigm of womanhood emerged at the turn of the twentieth century. Educators created exercise and sport programs for women students in the most elite private women's schools. Although the major goal of these programs was to improve women's health, educators were also feeling their way toward what might constitute female athleticism. Many physicians still believed that excessive studying and physical exercise were damaging to women's reproductive organs, and as late as the 1920s urged women not to exercise during menstruation. Already fearful of charges that women's schools were hotbeds of lesbian relationships and that women college students were overly "mannish," female educators set out to police women's sports with fervor, insisting that women athletes be "feminine" as well as agile. Tennis, golf, archery, swimming, and field hockey—a team sport designed for women and imported from upper-class England—were all respectable enough for college women. The Committee on Women's Athletics (CWA) created different rules for women players in track and field, tennis, golf, and basketball to protect women from physical injury and to create clear differences from men's games. Co-ed sports were largely taboo. Early women's physical education teachers adopted a credo that deplored inter-collegiate competition, physical contact between players, and any semblance of female aggression. In their view sports for women should emphasize participation for all, improving skills, and downplaying commercialism, an ethos still held by the Association for Intercollegiate Athletics for Women (AIAW) on the eve of the passage of Title IX.

By the 1920s, however, most women who engaged in team sports were uninterested in the physical education ethos. They were playing basketball in high school, industrial leagues, and settlement houses, and often played by the same rules as men, sometimes before wildly appreciative audiences in openly competitive events. The 1930s saw a rise in both men's and women's softball, played by the same rules, and given a boost by a rash of public park building during the Great Depression. Women's softball and basketball teams like the Raybestos Brakettes, the Jax Brewers, and the Tribune Girls (an African-American team) provided hard-up Americans with rousing entertainment in troubled times. The most famous woman athlete of the twentieth century, Mildred "Babe" Didrikson, began her career as a basketball player for the Employers Casualty Insurance Company of Dallas, Texas. Her promoter, Colonel M.J. Mc-Combs, trained Didrikson for the 1932 Olympic trials in track and field, where she won two gold and one silver medals. Tuskegee College and Tennessee State University, both African-American institutions, pioneered in training women for track and field, a sport not very popular among white middle-class women or in the women's colleges. When the Olympic Games were resumed after World War II in 1948, nine of eleven women on the U.S. Track and Field team were African-American and in 1960 Wilma Rudolph of Tennessee State won three gold medals in Rome. Two professional women's baseball leagues of all white players entertained audiences during World War II, and one of them, the American Girls Baseball League (AGBL), lasted until 1954. But Chicago Cubs owner Phil Wrigley, who had organized the AGBL, insisted the athletes wear skirts, attend Charm School, and be chaperoned at all times.

The decade of the 1950s is considered by many to be a low point in women's sport. The formal organization of "Little League" teams came along with the total exclusion of girls from "hardball." Women athletes who did not meet subjective standards of feminine appearance and physical build were often characterized as freaks of nature. African-American track and field athletes were assumed to be good at what they did because of innate racial differences, not because of their first-rate training and hard work. Strong, physically developed women athletes were often assumed to be lesbians at worst, or, unwomanly at best. Babe Didrikson, who had been characterized by one sportswriter as a "muscle moll," was unable to continue her career in track and field or baseball, married a professional wrestler, and settled on golf as an acceptable sport for a lady. *Life* magazine approved with a headline: "Babe Is a Lady Now:

The World's Most Amazing Athlete Has Learned to Wear Nylons and Cook for Her Huge Husband."[2]

The next two decades would bring dramatic changes to sports for women. In 1957 Althea Gibson became the first African-American woman tennis player to win at Wimbledon and Forest Hills. Katharine Switzer, registered as K. Switzer and wearing a baseball cap, ran the Boston Marathon in 1967, despite the efforts of an angry official to pull her out of the race. In 1966 the Commission on Intercollegiate Athletics for Women (CIAW) liberalized its long-standing ban on female varsity competition, and in 1971 full-court, five-player basketball rules were adopted for women. Title IX was passed in 1972, and the first academic scholarships for college women athletes were awarded the following year. The resurgence of a second wave of feminism emboldened many women athletes to demand more than they would have dreamed of a decade earlier. Although her openness about her sexual orientation cost her many product endorsements, prominent tennis star Martina Navratilova broke the silence for gay women in sport and encouraged others to do the same.

One of the most daring female athletes of these years was pro tennis player Billie Jean King. In 1970 King was the first woman player to earn more than $100,000, but Rod Laver, who played in one third as many tournaments as King, earned three times as much. That same year Jack Kramer, a self-styled tennis "czar," organized a Pacific Southwest Championship offering men prize money of $12,500 and women $1,500. When King and others threatened to boycott the event, Kramer refused to modify his plans, and Gladys Heldman, founder of *World Tennis* magazine, organized an alternative tournament for women, recruiting Philip Morris, manufacturer of Virginia Slims cigarettes, as a bank-rolling sponsor. "You've come a long way baby" would soon become both an advertising slogan and a reaffirmation that vast changes in women's lives, including the world of sport, were under way in the early days of the women's liberation movement. The United States Lawn Tennis Association absorbed the Virginia Slims tournament in 1973, and was forced by public opinion and the defiance of women players to treat women more equitably.

Greater notoriety, bigger rewards, and greater respect soon came the way of women tennis players. In the early 1970s Bobby Riggs, an aging pro, challenged Margaret Smith Court, who had beaten Billie Jean King, to a match with a large prize for the winner. King urged Court not to demean women's tennis by playing Riggs, but when Riggs beat Court handily, King agreed to play Riggs in 1973 for a purse of $100,000. Men and women all over the United States debated whether a woman at the top of her form could possibly defeat a male has-been. Billed by the media as "the Battle of the Sexes," more than 30,000 people viewed the event at the Houston Astrodome and as many as fifty million watched on television. King beat Riggs in three straight sets and used her earnings to found a Women's Sports Foundation and *WomenSports* magazine. Women's tennis is now one of the most exciting sports in America, and in 2000–2001 women's matches at Grand Slam tournaments drew larger television ratings than the men's competition.

When Title IX of the Educational Amendments Act was passed in 1972, it was aimed at a broad spectrum of gender inequities in education, leaving the particulars of guidelines to the U.S. Department of Health, Education and Welfare. The NCAA immediately lobbied HEW for the exemption of athletic departments from Title IX and received the support of Senator John Tower in legislation introduced in 1974. The Tower amendment was defeated, but Title IX supporters were dismayed in 1984 when the Supreme Court ruled in *Grove City College v. Bell* that individual programs that did not receive federal money could be exempted from Title IX. Three years later the U.S. Congress passed the Civil Rights Restoration Act, over Ronald Reagan's veto, to make Title IX applicable to all programs in all schools receiving federal funding. Title IX has since been invoked, for example, to award punitive damages to victims of sexual harassment in the public schools and to expand vocational education opportunities to high school girls. Conservatives view Title IX and the Supreme Court rulings' affirmation of Title IX as but another example of extremist feminism and the federal government's interference in local matters.

Much of the impact of Title IX was on sports. There is no question that vast changes have taken place: in 1970, one in twenty-seven girls played a sport in high school; by 2000 that figure was one in three and at the college level 37 percent of all college athletes were women. However, there is still a vast difference in spending on female and male athletics. On average men's sports receive five times as much for recruiting, three times as many operating funds, and twice as much scholarship money, with the most lop-sided allocations in Division I schools. Many of these disparities are a result of spending on football. In 1998, 53 percent of all the money spent on sports in Division I-A schools went to football. Although most Division I schools run a deficit in sports spending, schools with nationally ranked football teams consider them to be critical to donations by alumni, recruitment of future students, and relationships between colleges and their surrounding communities. Many schools responded to Title IX by cutting sports for both men and women in order to protect football and men's basketball. Between 1980 and 1992, 75 percent of all college wrestling and gymnastic teams were eliminated. Male critics blamed women and Title IX: "It is a devastating betrayal for these young men when they learned that their faith has been misplaced. It is worse when they are informed that the reason for the elimination of their program is Title IX or gender equity."[3] In 1991 Brown University cut men's golf and water polo, and women's gymnastics and volleyball, for a loss in program funds of $16,000 for men and of $62,000 for women. A group of Brown women athletes sued, and in 1995, the Supreme Court ruled in *Cohen v. Brown* that these disparities were inequitable and that Brown was not in compliance with Title IX. Title IX guidelines are still evolving, and only a handful of institutions are in full compliance.

Some schools have discovered that high-powered women's sports create school spirit, revenue, and valuable publicity. While they welcome the excitement of watching women play at the top of their game, some critics fear that women's sport will be infused with the same win-at-all costs ideology that has long been typical of most male sports. Others welcome that shift. As one mother of a player on a nationally ranked high school women's soccer says, "Our kids will give back. They're intimidated by nobody. When they step on the field, any friendship stops. . . . The beauty of it is, it teaches them professionalism."[4]

Some effects of Title IX have been deleterious for women. The NCAA began to sponsor intercollegiate varsity sport for women athletes in 1980, and as a result the CIAW collapsed, leaving no female women's sports organization involved in the management of intercollegiate play. Men who dominate the NCAA have been less than welcoming to women at the higher levels of the organization. Many schools and colleges merged their male and female athletic departments, and scores of women administrators and coaches lost their jobs. Before Title IX 90 percent of all women's teams were coached by women; today more than 50 percent of the coaches of women's teams are men. Charges of sexual harassment of female athletes by male coaches have increased.

U.S. sports, however, have been transformed for the foreseeable future. American women softball players at the Olympics, soccer players at the World Cup, and basketball players in NCAA tournaments have become national heroines in recent years, many of them combining sheer athleticism and the ethos of women's sport that had so inspired early leaders in physical education: teamwork, sportsmanship, and grace. Millions of girls all over the United States play soccer, tennis, and basketball with Mia Hamm, Serena Williams, and basketball players from the University of Connecticut and University of Tennessee in mind, and some have even braved attempts to play Little League baseball. Conflict over how women athletes should persist in sport will continue, but women athletes have done much to change the public's perception of what women are and what they can do.

READING GUIDE

Cahn, Susan K., *Coming on Strong: Gender and Sexuality in Twentieth-Century Women's Sport*. Cambridge: Harvard University Press, 1994. This excellent overview of women's sports history begins with the new female athleticism at the turn of the twentieth century and ends with changes in women's sports in the 1980s. There are chapters on the shaping of women's basketball, the women's baseball leagues of the World War II era, and the origins of women's track. Cahn shows how persistent concepts of how women should look and behave in American sport have been, with race playing a large role. The pejorative image of the lesbian or mannish athlete is still employed by coaches, the media, and athletes, male and female, as a way of intimidating the independent, outspoken, and physically fit female athlete.

Cohen, Greta L., ed., *Women in Sport: Issues and Controversies*, 2nd edition. Oxon Hill, MD: American Alliance for Health, Physical Education, Recreation and Dance, 2001. This collected volume of essays discusses gender issues in sport, including government policy, physiological and psychological perspectives, the economics of sport, women in the Olympic Games, and representations of women athletes in the media. Athletic directors and coaches in high schools and colleges will find the latest information on women's participation in sport here, as well as health recommendations and the status of Title IX. The chapters by Lynn Couturier and Stevie Chepko on the history of women in sport are especially valuable (57–110).

Festle, Mary Jo, *Playing Nice: Politics and Apologies in Women's Sports*. New York: Columbia University Press, 1996. This well-researched account looks at women's sports from the 1950s through the 1990s, with particularly good information about Title IX. Festle's title refers to the long-time tension in women's sports between college sports and professional sports, and the pressure on women athletes to be feminine as well as athletic, to "play nice" as well as to compete.

Griffin, Pat, *Strong Women, Deep Closets*. Champaign, IL: Human Kinetics, 1998. This book takes on the common assumption that "all women athletes are lesbians" by saying, yes, some are, and that not only lesbians but all women have been damaged by lesbian-baiting in athletics. One chapter, "Unplayable Lies," includes interviews with lesbian athletes and coaches that many young women may find inspiring.

Hastings, Penny, *Sports for Her: A Reference Guide for Teenage Girls*. Westport, CT: Greenwood Press, 1999. This helpful source for girls and their parents summarizes information on rules, equipment, and training for the eight sports high school girls are most likely to play, and gives advice for creating girls' teams or joining boys' teams in non-traditional women's sports. Hastings also includes sections on gender bias, overtraining, drugs, and overly enthused parents.

Ladd, Tony, and James A. Mathisen, *Muscular Christianity: Evangelical Protestants and the Development of American Sport*. Grand Rapids, MI: Baker Books, 1999. A fascinating account of the origins of muscular Christianity in the nineteenth century, its influence on sports in the early twentieth, and its new importance in a resurgent Protestant fundamentalism after World War II. Particularly in the Midwest, attempts to promote prayer and revivalism with team sports for men, have re-enforced conservative gender values, the exclusion of women, and an emphasis on manliness.

Messner, Michael A. and Donald F. Sabo, eds., *Sport, Men, and the Gender Order: Critical Feminist Perspectives*. Champaign, IL: Human Kinetics, 1990. Messner and Sabo have been tireless critics of what they see as a conjunction of power, violence, and winning in male athletics, and were among the first male scholars to assume that feminist theory offers analysts of male sport some valuable tools. They and other authors in this collection also address the influence of ideologies of manliness on the development of female and male sport. See, in particular, the introductory essay, "Toward a Critical Feminist Reappraisal of Sport, Men, and the Gender Order," 1–16.

Nelson, Mariah Burton, *Are We Winning Yet? How Women Are Changing Sports and Sports Are Changing Women.* New York: Random House, 1991. This highly readable assessment of women in sport summarizes interviews with a runner, a race car driver, a weight lifter, a rower, a disabled tennis player, a gay golfer, and several women coaches. Burton concludes that, "dismayed by the 'winning is the only thing' ethic that presides over . . . sport, women are once again questioning the dualism and danger inherent" in the "military model" of male sport (9). The "partnership model" restores many of the values of the early female sports educators: cooperation, coaching of women by women, and a focus on safety and developing skills.

NOTES

1. As quoted by Andrew Zimbalist, *Unpaid Professionals: Commercialism and Conflict in Big-Time College Sports* (Princeton: Princeton University Press, 1999), 54.

2. *Life* magazine (June 23, 1947), 90.

3. As quoted by Ellen J. Staurowsky, "Critiquing the Language of the Gender Equity Debate," *Journal of Sport and Social Issues* 22 (February, 1998): 11.

4. As quoted by T. Trent Gegax and Evan Thomas, "The Sound of the Fury," *Newsweek* (August 13, 2001): 50.

DOCUMENTS

15.1.   A Woman Athlete Tries Out for Baseball

Until the rise of formalized sports for both girls and boys after World War II, many young women grew up playing games along-side boys. Wilma Briggs was a Rhode Island farm girl who grew up with a big family of brothers and defied gender norms in dress, behavior, and sport. Here she describes how she was recruited for the All-American Girls' Professional Baseball League and how much she enjoyed playing ball.

"A FARM GIRL PLAYS PROFESSIONAL BASEBALL"

I was born in 1930 and grew up on a farm in East Greenwich. There were 11 living children in my family. We had a 60 acre dairy farm, and a lot of work to do. Not a lot of money, but a lot of food. We had our own garden, grew our own food, and played a lot of baseball. . . .

We would get up at 6:30 and go to the barn before breakfast. We had probably 35 milking cows, and we milked by hand. It was only my father, my two older brothers, and myself. We all milked, or the boys would milk and my father and I would feed, which meant I swept out in front so that it was clean for the grain to be put down. When we got home from school, we'd have to clean the barn. Homework was a problem. When I got home I had farm work to do, which meant if I didn't get homework done in school, it didn't get done. But we fit everything around baseball as much as we could because that was our hobby. We had baseball equipment because my father had a team. All the neighborhood kids came to our house to play which was convenient for us because sometimes they helped us finish up the work so we could play earlier. . . .

I wore dungarees, even to school. I wore them every day because we didn't have a lot of money. My mother and father had to buy dungarees for the boys and I'd say, "Well, get me some too." I was wearing them in the barn. And we wore the same style clothes working as we did to school. By the time I got to high school and started playing basketball, and was on the gym team—I needed slacks anyway, so I wore slacks or dungarees to school, and I got away with it. I was the only girl that did, but then I was the only girl who played on the boys' basketball team, too.

Had it not been for the war, I never would have played professional baseball. . . . Phil Wrigley of the Chicago Cubs was certain that all the men would be drafted, and the major league ballparks would be empty. That's the reason he started that league, the All-American Girls' Professional Baseball League.

So, because of the war, I got that chance. That league started in 1943, and I joined it after high school in 1948. Had it not been for the war, that part of my life would never have come to pass. And I think because I went out there and played ball—I met a lot of people from all over the United States, Canada, and Cuba, which I never would have done. I traveled, lived in the best hotels, ate in restaurants, lived in private homes—that's an experience. I think it gave me the courage years later to say, "I think I'll go to college." The league ended finally in '54. All those things that people couldn't do during the war years they could now do. They had money in their gas tanks, and television came out. I think that's what broke the back of the league.

Source: What Did You Do in the War, Grandma? Providence, Rhode Island: South Kingstown High School and Rhode Island Historical Society, 1989: 10–11.

15.2.   Billie Jean King's Coming of Age in Tennis

One of the most determined sports figures of the twentieth century, Billie Jean Moffitt King later founded the Women's Sports Foundation. King's father was a fireman and her mother a housewife; her brother Randy became a professional baseball player. In this excerpt from her autobiography she describes how her self-determination and the support of her parents enabled her to challenge the gender rules of organized tennis at an early age.

"THIS IS NEVER GOING TO HAPPEN TO ME AGAIN"

No matter how talented I might have been, how could I have improved if my mother hadn't driven me all over Southern California so I could play the best players?

The single occasion where finances really hurt me was the summer of 1957, when I was fourteen and being recognized as a real prospect. . . . Perry Jones, who ran the Southern California Tennis Association, decreed that I could go to the national championships. . . . It wasn't going to cost him a nickel, either, because the Long Beach Tennis Patrons and the Long Beach Century Club staked me to $350. . . . But then . . . Mr. Jones declared that I was too young, and, as a girl, would require a chaperon [*sic*]. This was absolute discrimination. The players stayed with families, and I certainly was old enough to be put on a plane and met at the other end. But Mr. Jones would not listen.

So finally we decided that if my mother and I traveled by railroad, the two of us could manage. . . . When we got there, it was the first time I had ever played on clay, and I was beaten in the quarterfinals. . . . But I really wasn't discouraged. . . . I had seen the competition from all over the country and I was not at all intimidated.

And then . . . it was time for Mom and me to get back on the train. . . . Many of the other girls were getting in cars to go to the airport . . . to fly . . . to Philadelphia, where the next tournament was being held. That broke my heart. A lot of the ones going back East weren't nearly as good as I was.

I can remember so vividly standing on the corner with my mother and just fighting back the tears as I said good-by to the other players. . . . I turned to Mom and I said, "This is never going to happen to me again."

Source: Billie Jean King with Frank Deford, *Billie Jean*. New York: Viking Press, 1982, 35–38, 43–45.

15.3.   Title IX of the Education Amendments Act of 1972

Representative Edith Green of Oregon first proposed using the civil rights language of Titles VI and VII of the Civil Rights Act to equivalent legislation covering education. Although everything ranging from faculty hiring to student admissions was covered by the Education Amendments Act, its most controversial aspect was its potential impact on college sports programs. The enforcement of Title IX was handed to the U.S. Department of Health, Education, and Welfare.

TITLE IX, EDUCATION AMENDMENTS ACT

No person in the United States shall, on the basis of sex, be excluded from participation in, be denied the benefits of, or be subjected to discrimination under any education program or activity receiving Federal Financial assistance. . . .

Each Federal department and agency which is empowered to extend Federal financial assistance to any education program or activity, by way of grant, loan, or contract . . . is authorized and directed to effectuate the provisions of . . . this title with respect to such program or activity by issuing rules, regulations, or orders of general applicability which shall be consistent with achievement of the objectives of the statute.

Source: Public Law 92–318, 1972.

15.4.   Congress Debates Title IX

In May 1995, a special U.S. congressional subcommittee held hearings on Title IX in Washington, D.C. Critics of the federal guidelines for implementing Title IX believed they had gone too far and that many men's sports had been eliminated because of so-called "gender quotas." These critics were also convinced that football should be exempted from Title IX. Supporters of Title IX believed that the guidelines had not gone far enough, had rarely been implemented, and had left the sacred cow of college football untouched. Although there are no quotas in the HEW guidelines, athletic programs around the country have had difficulty envisioning their implementation in any other way than "proportionality."

HEARING ON TITLE IX OF THE EDUCATION AMENDMENTS
OF 1972

J. Dennis Hastert, Representative of Illinois:

I started coaching in high school in 1965 when women didn't have an opportunity to go out for organized athletics. All there was at that time was a . . . Girls Athletic Association, and they didn't really have traveling teams. . . . So I appreciate what Title IX has done for women and girls in this country. I think it has been a wonderful opportunity for women to be able to participate and become involved in athletics and to have the same experience that men have had previous to 1972.

My interest in this issue . . . has been fostered in many ways. . . . I coached both wrestling and football for 16 years. . . . I married a women's athletic coach who is still teaching elementary P.E. after 29 years. I love seeing young men and young women involved in athletics because I know what they get out of it. . . .

Secondly, in the last year I have received hundreds of letters from youngsters around this Nation who are no longer able to participate in sports because their sport is being eliminated at the various universities that they attend. I have heard from kids from . . . California all the way to Pennsylvania. They don't understand how schools can promise them an opportunity to compete and later drop those programs in the middle of their eligibility. . . . Coaches representing a wide variety of sports—including wrestling, gymnastics, track and field, rowing, baseball, swimming, soccer, water sports, volleyball, and fencing—have created a coalition to halt this alarming trend. . . .

When sports are eliminated, the universities cite their need to comply with Title IX and the proportionality rules as part or all of their reason. While I want all schools to comply with Title IX, I strongly believe that the elimination of opportunities for anyone was not the intent of Title IX. These lost opportunities are what I call the "unintended consequences" of Title IX.

So why should a university cut sports to comply with Title IX? Title IX was supposed to be a statute to increase opportunities.

Let me explain briefly. One way a university tries to comply with Title IX is by meeting the "opportunities test," that is, effectively accommodating the interests and abilities of both genders. There are numerous tests, 13 approximately, that a school must meet in order to comply with Title IX and ensure that discrimination does not exist in their athletic programs. These range from money spent on scholarships to coaches' salaries to athletic facilities. However, it is the "opportunities test" that forces schools to drop certain sports. The "opportunities test" has three prongs: first, the proportionality rule, which says participation numbers for male and female students must be substantially proportionate to the respective enrollment numbers; second, the history and continuing practice of program expansion for the underrepresented sex; and third, fully and effectively accommodating interests and abilities of the underrepresented sex. According to the Office of Civil Rights at the Department of Education, . . . meeting any *one* of these three prongs signals compliance.

However, that is not what I have been hearing from the field, and the courts have *de facto* made proportionality the only applicable standard . . .

This *de facto* reliance on proportionality alone leads me to these questions. Are we as a Nation saying that numbers alone indicate discrimination? Has this, in fact, become a quota system that we have imposed on athletic systems in this country? More importantly, have we created a quota system that does not help the underrepresented sex as much as it should because universities can simply cut the overrepresented sex as a means of meeting the test? It does not help create opportunities for women when a school simply cuts a sport such as soccer, swimming, wrestling, or baseball to comply. And we should not support such tactics. This only hurts young women and men across the Nation who are denied the opportunities that should be afforded them. . . .

It really disturbs me to hear people claim that it is fine to cut opportunities for men to eradicate discrimination. Well, Mr. Chairmen, that is *not* fine. That view represents everything that is wrong about Title IX.

When a law ceases to work for positive improvements and simply be-comes a way to get back at the system that perpetrated discrimination, we have lost our focus on what it means to work toward gender equality. It doesn't help anyone just to keep tearing the future of these kids out from under them.

Cardiss Collins, Representative from Illinois:

I certainly appreciate this opportunity to testify on Title IX and its impact upon sports. For the past four years, when I chaired the Subcom-mittee on Commerce, Consumer Protection, and Competitiveness, I took a particular interest in this subject. . . .

During that period, I learned that many concepts taken as fact simply are not. Frankly, I have learned that there is only one overriding fact and it is simply this: The number of girls and young women interested in participating in sports has been increasing by leaps and bounds over the past two decades. That is a very simple truth, but it is at the heart of the debate over Title IX and cannot be ignored. Too often those with very little contact with what is going on in our schools, or perhaps those without daughters or nieces or granddaughters, fail to understand that the sports scene is radically different from the way it was a generation ago. Vast numbers of girls and young women are now playing sports with the same enthusiasm that generations of boys and young men have shown. They play all kinds of sports, and they play them very well.

Whether Title IX has been responsible for generating this enthusiasm, or whether Title IX has been a force for making schools react to this interest, is irrelevant. What is relevant is that Title IX guarantees women the same opportunities as men.

I am sure that during the course of your hearings you will hear the same old tired arguments that Title IX is taking opportunities away from men and that Title IX establishes quotas. Most of these arguments come from school administrators or football coaches who fear that increasing opportunities for women will come out of their hides or, better still, out of their school's pocketbooks.

The reality is the exact opposite. Athletic directors and coaches are the ones who establish the quotas, if you will, at the schools. They decide, often arbitrarily, how many men and how many women get to play sports. Schools, not the Department of Education, are responsible for quotas assuring that men receive over two-thirds of all opportunities and 75 cents of every dollar spent on sports. The purpose of Title IX is to eliminate these artificial quotas and ensure that opportunities are based on student interest, without gender bias.

Title IX simply says that no person shall, on the basis of sex, be ex-cluded from participation in, denied the benefits of, or be subjected to discrimination under any education program or activity receiving Fed-eral financial assistance.

The law does not require fixed quotas. The law has been interpreted to mean that if schools have participation rates equal to enrollment rates, the school is automatically considered in compliance. However, even if the numbers are not the same, the regulations recognize a school as being in compliance either by showing a history of expanding opportunities in women's programs or by showing that the interests of women have been accommodated. . . .

Observers of college sports can recount dozens of examples of patterns of sexual discrimination over decades. Women often have far inferior training facilities, practice times, and game times. On road trips there may be three or four women in a room while men have single rooms.

In the case of Colgate, where the women's teams wanted to increase their budget from $6,000 to $12,000, but were denied, the school increased the men's [hockey] team's stick budget to the same $12,000. The men's team had a budget of $300,000, while the women's team received a meager $4,000.

At the start of my testimony, I mentioned that the biggest problem in the debate over Title IX is the assumption of "facts" that are fully myths. Therefore, let me leave you with just a few of these myths, and the actual facts as I see them:

Myth #1: The increased participation of women in sports has come at the expense of men. The Facts: According to the NCAA itself, over the past 15 years, participation in women's sports increased by 16,230 while the participation in men's sports increased by 12,320. For every new dollar spent on women, two dollars was spent on men.

Myth #2: Football actually pays the cost of women's sports, so football should be excluded from Title IX considerations. The fact: Again, according to the NCAA, an analysis of 1989 budgets found that 45 percent of Division I-A schools reported a deficit in football, while 94 percent of Division I-AA reported a deficit; and that 98 percent of Divisions II and III schools operated at a deficit. Of the 45 percent of Division I-A schools reporting a deficit in 1989 in football, the average deficit was $638,000, which was up from $251,000 in 1981.

Myth #3: The Department of Education is imposing quotas on schools for Title IX compliance. The fact: The Department of Education and the Office of Civil Rights have been spectacularly unsuccessful in forcing schools to do anything. . . . In fact, victims of sex discrimination testified at our hearings that OCR was the last place they would go to seek relief. They had to turn to the courts.

Myth #4: Women's sports have no popularity with the public and, therefore, can generate no revenue. The fact: While it is true that schools that fail to provide any promotion for women's sports and schedule teams at odd hours find the results self-fulfilling, interest in women's sports is on the rise. At Stanford, for example, average attendance for women's basketball was 5,284 compared to 5,386 for the men. The 17,000 seats for the women's Final Four games were sold out last September. The women's final game on Sunday afternoon had higher ratings than the NBA game opposite it and higher ratings than a men's semifinal the day before.

In summary, when you get to know the facts, you find out that the issue is simply how schools accommodate the growing interest in women's sports. If schools stick to quotas to ensure artificial advantage for men, the courts will strike them down. However, if schools take steps to accommodate that interest, everyone's child will benefit. It is time for the schools to share their resources fairly and eliminate their self-imposed quotas.

Tom Osborne, Head Football Coach, University of Nebraska:

My name is Tom Osborne, and I have been head football coach at the University of Nebraska for the past 22 years. . . .

The University of Nebraska has long been a leader in the enhancement of opportunities for women in college athletics. Last year Nebraska added women's soccer, at a cost of roughly $350,000, bringing the total of women's sports to eleven, exactly the same as men. All women's programs are funded to the scholarship limits permitted by NCAA legislation. All women's programs have exactly the same access to academic assistance, training table meals, equipment, travel, and coaching as do the men's teams.

It is important to know that excepting the numbers and the expenses of the Nebraska football program, more funds are committed to the women's program than to the men's. More women than men receive athletic scholarships, when football—[which] allows 85 scholarships under NCAA rules—is eliminated from the equation. There is no women's sport that approaches the numbers required to field a competitive football team.

Currently there are those who are urging that football scholarships and expenditures be reduced and/or men's sports be eliminated so that funds can be transferred to enhance funding of women's athletics. I am sure this was never the intent of Congress when Title IX was passed to bring about equal opportunity for women.

Ignored in the effort to diminish football, is that fact that at the University of Nebraska, for example, and at most major college institutions, it has been the football program that has funded most women's programs and insured the growth of women's athletics. Women's sports generally do much better at schools with major football programs because of a larger revenue base. . . .

Our football program has made a contribution to the University as a whole as well as to women's and men's non-revenue sports. Since 1982, the Nebraska football program has generated $105,000 for the general scholarship fund at the University—money which is awarded to men and women in the student body who are not athletes. Funds generated by the Nebraska football program, which operates without state or federal tax support or student fees, have enabled the University of Nebraska to build a campus recreation and physical education facility at a cost of $16,000,000 generated primarily from football gate receipts. . . .

Reducing college football to a "bare-bones" activity in an effort to enhance women's athletics is not the answer.

Source: Subcommittee on Postsecondary Education, Training and Life-Long Learning of the Committee on Economic and Education Opportunities of the House of Representatives. Washington, D.C.: Government Printing Office, 1995: 9–13, 18–21, 385–86.

15.5.   The Women's Sports Foundation Answers the Critics of Title IX Policies

---

Established and funded by Billie Jean King, the Women's Sports Foundation has been a tireless advocate of women athletes and critic of the allocation of resources at colleges and universities. In this editorial, Dr. Donna Lopiano, the 2001 director of WSF, criticizes the assumptions behind Division I collegiate football and basketball articulated above by Tom Osborne.

"THE REAL CULPRIT IN THE CUTTING OF MEN'S OLYMPIC SPORTS"

Division II and III schools, the poorest colleges and universities, are not dropping men's sports. It's the richest Division I athletic programs that are cutting men's swimming, gymnastics and wrestling programs (Olympic sports). Whenever a men's sport is eliminated, these educational institutions blame Title IX and women's sports. They say they can't afford to add new women's sports programs as required by federal gender equity laws and keep men's Olympic sports. What's wrong with this contention is the fact that there are plenty of new dollars going into Division I college Athletic programs that could fund both women's sports and men's Olympic sports. What the public doesn't know is that these new moneys are being used to fuel the arms races being fought in men's football and basketball. NCAA research shows that for every three new dollars going into college athletic programs over the last five years, two are going to men's sports and only one to women's sports. The $1 to women's sports is not closing the significant expenditure gap and the majority of the new money allocated to men's sports is pumping up the already bloated budgets of men's football and basketball.

The problem is not Title IX. The problem is college presidents not putting a stop to the embarrassing waste of money occurring in men's football and basketball. Alumni of private colleges and state legislators of public institutions should be calling for investigations of misuse of funds. Just because the football or basketball team brings in money at the gate, doesn't mean they have a right to spend it however they wish. All revenues generated by institutional activities are institutional funds and it is the fiduciary responsibility of the Boards of Regents and Boards of Trustees to insure the public that these non-profit educational institutions are fiscally responsible. . . .

Schools should be expected to retain all men's sports programs while they bring women's sports into compliance with Title IX. Remedying discrimination does not mean bringing formerly advantaged men's sports down to where women's sports were—with no opportunities to play. Affording current men's sports programs and new women's sports programs requires belt-tightening in Division I. However, colleges should be willing to do whatever it takes to make sure that male athletes in Olympic sports have programs. If necessary the NCAA must legislate across the board expenditure limits and insist on a cessation of the arms race to make this happen. Neither the NCAA nor its member institutions currently show any signs of doing either.

If our institutions of higher education are going to act irresponsibly; continuing to discriminate against women's sports, dropping Olympic sports and operating select teams like professional franchises with million dollar coaches and excessive expenditures, then the IRS should remove their non-profit status and treat them like commercial sports enterprises. Maybe this is the kind of legislative pressure that must be brought to bear in order to force educational institutions to control their expenses. It's about time the media did some good investigative reporting to reveal the real extent of financial waste and put pressure on college presidents to clean up their acts before the government does so.

Title IX is a good law. We need to keep steady on the course of ensuring that our sons and daughters are treated equally in all educational programs and activities, including sports. We also have to protect sports participation opportunities for our sons by making it clear to high school principals, superintendents and college presidents that excessive expenditures on one or two priority men's sports and failure to control spending in all sports is unacceptable for educational institutions accorded non-profit tax status.

Source: Donna Lopiano, *Issues and Action*. East Meadow, NY: Women's Sports Foundation, 2001.

Selected Bibliography

BOOKS

Altbach, Edith, ed. *From Feminism to Liberation*. Cambridge, MA: Schenkman Publishing Co., 1980.

Anderson, Kristi. *After Suffrage*. Chicago: University of Chicago Press, 1996.

Becker, Susan. *The Origins of the Equal Rights Amendment*. Westport, CT: Greenwood Press, 1985.

Beeton, Beverly. *Women Vote in the West: The Woman Suffrage Movement, 1869–1896*. New York: Garland Publishing, 1986.

Berkeley, Kathleen C. *The Women's Liberation Movement in America*. Westport, CT: Greenwood Press, 1999.

Berry, Mary Francis. *The Politics of Parenthood: Child Care, Women's Rights and the Myth of the Good Mother*. New York: Viking, 1993.

———. *Why the ERA Failed: Politics, Women's Rights, and the Amending Process of the Constitution*. Bloomington: Indiana University Press, 1986.

Boles, Janet K. *The Politics of the Equal Rights Amendment: Conflict and the Decision Process*. New York: Longman, 1979.

Brodie, Janet Farrell. *Contraception and Abortion in Nineteenth-Century America*. Ithaca: Cornell University Press, 1997.

Buechler, Steven M. *Women's Movements in the United States: Woman Suffrage, Equal Rights, and Beyond*. New Brunswick. NJ: Rutgers University Press, 1990.

Buhle, Mari Jo. *Women and American Socialism, 1870–1920*. Urbana: University of Illinois Press, 1983.

Buhle, Mari Jo and Paul Buhle, eds. *A Concise History of Woman Suffrage: Selections from the Classic Work of Stanton, Anthony, Gage and Harper*. Urbana: University of Illinois Press, 1989.

Burrell, Barbara C. *A Woman's Place Is in the House: Campaigning for Congress in the Feminist Era.* Ann Arbor: University of Michigan Press, 1995.

Christiansen, Karen, Allen Guttman, and Gertrude Pfister, eds. *International Encyclopedia of Women and Sports.* New York: Macmillan, 1999.

Collins, Patricia Hill. *Black Feminist Thought: Knowledge, Consciousness, and the Politics of Empowerment.* New York: Routledge, 1990.

Cornell, Drucilla, ed. *Feminism and Pornography.* New York: Oxford University Press, 2000.

Cott, Nancy F. *The Grounding of Modern Feminism.* New Haven: Yale University Press, 1987.

———. *Public Vows: A History of Marriage and the Nation.* Cambridge: Harvard University Press, 2000.

Echols, Alice. *Daring to Be Bad: Radical Feminism in America, 1965–1975.* Minneapolis: University of Minnesota Press, 1989.

Eisenstein, Zillah R. *Feminism and Sexual Equality: Crisis in Liberal America.* New York: Monthly Review Press, 1984.

Evans, Sara. *Personal Politics: The Women's Liberation Movement and the New Left.* New York: Oxford University Press, 1979.

Feree, Myra Marx and Beth Hess. *Controversy and Coalition: The New Feminist Movement.* Boston: Twayne Publishers, 1985.

Foner, Philip S. *Women and the American Labor Movement: From the First Trade Unions to the Present.* New York: Free Press, 1979.

Francke, Linda Bird. *Ground Zero: The Gender Wars in the Military.* New York: The Free Press, 1997.

Frankfort, Ellen. *Vaginal Politics.* New York: Quadrangle Books, 1972.

Friedan, Betty. *The Feminine Mystique.* New York: Dell Publishers, 1963.

Garcia, Alma M., ed. *Chicana Feminist Thought: The Basic Historical Writings.* New York: Routledge, 1997.

Gilmore, Glenda Elizabeth. *Gender and Jim Crow: Women and the Politics of White Supremacy in North Carolina, 1896–1920.* Chapel Hill: University of North Carolina Press, 1996.

Ginsburg, Faye D. *Contested Lives: The Abortion Debate in an American Community.* Berkeley: University of California Press, 1989.

Gluck, Sherna, ed. *From Parlor to Prison: Five American Suffragists Talk About Their Lives.* New York: Vintage Books, 1976.

Goldstein, Leslie Friedman. *Contemporary Cases in Women's Rights.* Madison: University of Wisconsin Press, 1994.

Griffin, Susan. *Pornography and Silence: Culture's Revenge Against Nature.* New York: Harper and Row, 1981.

Harrison, Cynthia. *On Account of Sex: The Politics of Women's Issues, 1945–1968.* Berkeley: University of California Press, 1988.

Hartmann, Susan M. *From Margin to Mainstream: American Women and Politics Since 1960.* New York: Alfred A. Knopf, 1989.

Hewitt, Nancy A. *Southern Discomfort: Women's Activism in Tampa, Florida, 1880s–1920s.* Champaign: University of Illinois Press, 2001.

———. *Women's Activism and Social Change: Rochester, New York, 1822–1872.* Ithaca: Cornell University Press, 1984.

Hine, Darlene Clark. *Black Women and the Reconstruction of American History*. Bloomington: Indiana University Press, 1997.

Hole, Judith and Ellen Levine. *The Rebirth of Feminism*. New York: Quadrangle Books, 1971.

hooks, bell. *Ain't I a Woman: Black Women and Feminism*. Boston: South End Press, 1981.

Jaffe, Frederick S., Barbara L. Lindheim, and Philip R. Lee. *Abortion Politics, Private Morality and Public Policy*. New York: McGraw-Hill, 1981.

Jeansonne, Glen. *Women of the Far Right: The Mother's Movement and World War II*. Chicago: University of Chicago Press, 1990.

Joseph, Gloria and Jill Lewis. *Common Differences: Conflicts in Black and White Feminist Perspectives*. Garden City, NY: Doubleday, 1981.

Kahn, Karen, ed. *Frontline Feminism, 1975–1995: Essays from* Sojourner's *First Twenty Years*. San Francisco: Aunt Lute Books, 1995.

Kaplan, Laura. *The Story of Jane: The Legendary Underground Feminist Abortion Service*. Chicago: University of Chicago Press, 1995.

Klatch, Rebecca. *Women of the New Right*. Philadelphia: Temple University Press, 1988.

Lemons, J. Stanley. *The Woman Citizen: Social Feminism in the 1920s*. Urbana: University of Illinois Press, 1975.

Luker, Kristin. *Dubious Connections: The Politics of Teenage Pregnancy*. Cambridge: Harvard University Press, 1996.

Lynn, Susan. *Progressive Women in Conservative Times: Racial Justice, Peace, and Feminism, 1945 to the 1960s*. New Brunswick, NJ: Rutgers University Press, 1992.

Mansbridge, Jane J. *Why We Lost the ERA*. Chicago: University of Chicago Press, 1986.

Mathews, Donald G. and Jane Sherron De Hart. *Sex, Gender and the Politics of the ERA: A State and the Nation*. New York: Oxford University Press, 1990.

Matthews, Glenna. *The Rise of Public Woman: Woman's Power and Woman's Place in the United States, 1630–1970*. New York: Oxford University Press, 1992.

Melich, Tanya. *The Republican War Against Women: An Insider's Report from Behind the Lines*. New York: Bantam Books, 1996.

Milkman, Ruth. *Gender at Work: The Dynamics of Job Segregation by Sex during WWII*. Urbana: University of Illinois Press, 1997.

Newman, Louise Michele. *White Women's Rights: The Racial Origins of Feminism in the United States*. New York: Oxford University Press, 1999.

Park, Maud Wood with Edna Lamprey Stantial. *"Front Door Lobby."* Boston: Beacon Press, 1960.

Reagan, Leslie J. *When Abortion Was a Crime: Women, Medicine, and the Law, 1867–1973*. Berkeley: University of California Press, 1997.

Rupp, Leila J., and Verta Taylor. *Survival in the Doldrums: The American Women's Rights Movement, 1945 to the 1960s*. New York: Oxford University Press, 1987.

Ryan, Barbara. *Feminism and the Women's Movement: Dynamics of Change in Social Movement, Ideology and Activism*. New York: Routledge, 1992.

Ryan, Mary. *Women in Public: Between Banners and Bullets, 1825–1880*. Baltimore: Johns Hopkins University Press, 1990.

Smith, J. Clay, Jr., ed. *Rebels in Law: Voices in History of Black Women Lawyers.* Ann Arbor: University of Michigan Press, 1998.

Smith, Susan L. *Sick and Tired of Being Sick and Tired: Black Women's Health Activism in America, 1890–1950.* Philadelphia: Temple University Press, 1995.

Spitzer, Robert J. *The Right to Life Movement and Third Party Politics.* Westport, CT: Greenwood Press, 1987.

Swerdlow, Amy. *Women Strike for Peace: Traditional Motherhood and Radical Politics in the 1960s.* Urbana: University of Illinois Press, 1993.

Tax, Meredith. *The Rising of the Women: Feminist Solidarity and Class Conflict, 1880–1917.* Champaign: Illinois University Press, 2000.

Terborg-Penn, Rosalyn. *African-American Women and the Vote, 1850–1920.* Bloomington: Indiana University Press, 1998.

Tilly, Louise and Patricia Gurin, eds. *Women, Politics, and Change.* New York: Russell Sage Foundation, 1990.

VanBurkleo, Sandra F. *"Belonging to the World": Women's Rights and American Constitutional Culture.* New York: Oxford University Press, 2001.

Walsh, Mary Roth. *Doctors Wanted: No Women Need Apply: Sexual Barriers in the Medical Profession, 1825–1975.* New Haven: Yale University Press, 1977.

WEB SITES

"Documents from the Women's Liberation Movement," Duke University, http:// scriptorium.lib.duke.edu/wlm.

"The Emma Goldman Papers," University of California at Berkeley, http:// sunsite.berkeley.edu/Goldman.

"Margaret Sanger and The Woman Rebel," Margaret Sanger Papers, http:// mep.cla.sc.edu/ms/ms-table.html.

"Temperance and Prohibition," Ohio State University, http://prohibition history.ohio-state.edu.

"Uses of Liberty Rhetoric Among Lowell Mill Girls," Catharine Lavender, College of State Island, http://www.library.csi.cuny.edu/dept/americanstudies/ lavender/start.html.

"Votes for Women," Huntington Library, San Marino, California, http:// www.huntington.org/vfw.

"Women and Social Movements in the U.S., 1775–1940," Center for the Study of Women and Gender, State University of New York at Binghamton, http:// Binghamton.edu.

MEDIA PRODUCTIONS

Daughters of Free Men (1987, 30 mins., American Social History Project). Examines the economic and cultural factors that sent New England women to the Lowell mills and the turnouts that followed.

Heaven Will Protect the Working Girl (1993, 28 mins., American Social History Project). Using two fictional characters, "Ida" and "Angelina," this portrayal of the the Shirtwaist Strike of 1909 in New York City looks at sweatshops, ethnic tensions and solidarity, and the help of middle class allies.

Ida B. Wells: A Passion for Justice (1990, 53 min., William Greaves Productions). A superb account of Wells, set in the context of African-American history from Reconstruction through World War I.

La Operación (1982, 39 mins., The Cinema Guild). An historical account of the widespread sterilization of Puerto Rican women.

Not for Ourselves Alone: The Story of Elizabeth Cady Stanton and Susan B. Anthony (1999, 3 hrs., PBS Video). A highly acclaimed TV series by Ken Burns and Paul Barnes about the long-time friendship of Stanton and Anthony and their devotion to women's rights.

One Woman, One Vote (1995, 1 hr., 46 min., PBS Video). A stirring account of the suffrage movement from the 1840s through final passage of the Nineteenth Amendment in 1920.

Playing (Un)Fair: The Media Image of the Female Athlete (2001, 30 mins., Media Education Foundation). An analysis of the post–Title IX treatment of women athletes in the media that finds both homophobia and stereotyping in the coverage of female sports.

Standing Tall: Women Unionize (2000, 50 min., Donald Blank, Filmmakers Library). The struggle of Delta Pride Catfish workers, mostly African-American women, to unionize in Mississippi.

When Abortion Was Illegal: Untold Stories (1999, 28 mins., Bullfrog Films). Uses oral history to document the search for abortion services before *Roe v. Wade*.

The Women of Hull House (1992, 18 min., Hull House Museum, University of Illinois at Chicago). An account of many of the social reformers who lived at Hull House and promoted the Women's Bureau and protective legislation.

The Women of Summer (1986, 55 min., Suzanne Bauman and Rita Heller, Filmmakers Library). The story of the Bryn Mawr Summer School for Women, which gave hundreds of blue-collar workers an opportunity in the 1920s and 1930s to expand their horizon beyond the factory.

Index

About the Author

SHARON HARTMAN STROM teaches in the History department at the University of Rhode Island. Her books include *Political Woman: Florence Luscomb and the Legacy of Radical Reform; Beyond the Typewriter: Gender, Class and the Origins of Modern American Office Work, 1900–1930;* and a co-edited book, *Moving the Mountain: Women Working for Social Change.*